THE
POPE'S
BODY

THE
POPE'S
BODY

Agostino Paravicini-Bagliani

Translated by David S. Peterson

THE UNIVERSITY OF CHICAGO PRESS

CHICAGO AND LONDON

Originally published as *Il corpo del Papa*
© 1994 Giulio Einaudi editore s.p.a., Torino

AGOSTINO PARAVICINI-BAGLIANI is a professor of medieval history
at the University of Lausanne, Switzerland.

The University of Chicago Press, Chicago 60637
The University of Chicago Press, Ltd., London
© 2000 by The University of Chicago
All rights reserved. Published 2000
Printed in the United States of America

ISBN 0-226-03437-2

09 08 07 06 05 04 03 02 01 00   1 2 3 4 5

Library of Congress Cataloging-in-Publication Data

Paravicini Bagliani, Agostino.
[Corpo del Papa. English]
The pope's body / Agostino Paravicini Bagliani : translated by
David S. Peterson
p.   cm.
Includes bibliographical references and index.
ISBN 0-226-03437-2 (hardcover: alk. paper)
1. Papacy—History.   2. Body, Human—Religious aspects—
Catholic Church—History of doctrines—Middle Ages, 600–1500.
3. Catholic Church—Doctrines—History.   I. Title.
BX1069.5.P3713 2000
262'.13—dc21   99-36181
                                                           CIP

♾ The paper used in this publication meets the minimum
requirements of the American National Standard for Information
Sciences—Permanence of Paper for Printed Library Materials,
ANSI Z39.48-1992.

To Martine, Lorenzo, and Clelia,
and to the memory of
Anneliese Maier and Gerhart B. Ladner

CONTENTS

ILLUSTRATIONS

Following page 74

INTRODUCTION

1277. Witelo, the greatest student of optics in the Middle Ages, was residing at Viterbo, a city rich in thermal baths and the temporary seat of the Roman curia. He had come as the ambassador of Ottocar, king of Bohemia and pretender to the imperial crown. In a passage of his *Perspectiva (Optics)*, the Polish scholar recalls going down a number of times around sunset to a waterfall situated near Bagno dello Scoppio, not far from Viterbo, to observe the refraction of sunlight in the water "that rushed down tempestuously."

Witelo does not identify the curialists who accompanied him in his efforts to grasp the physical laws of the rainbow, but we know that four other students of vision were then living in Viterbo. The pope, John XXI (Peter of Spain), was a renowned doctor who had written a noted treatise on ophthalmology. The English Franciscan John Peckham, a reader in theology at the papal school *(Studium curiae)*, had authored the *Perspectiva Communis (General Optics)*, so called because it was adopted in the universities. The papal chaplain, Campano of Novara, had written a commentary on Euclid's *Elements* that provided a useful mathematical introduction to optical studies. The Dominican friar and papal penitentiary, William of Moerbeke, had translated Aristotle and various Greek scientific works, and Witelo admiringly referred to his studies in the philosophy of light in the dedication of his *Perspectiva*.

Roger Bacon, too, had touched frequently on optics in the great works he had sent Pope Clement IV a decade earlier. He even devoted a treatise to the subject, his *On Rays (De radiis)*. Thus, in a single decade, 1267–77, the most important medieval works on optics, destined to be studied well beyond the

Renaissance, were either produced or first put into circulation at the papal court at Viterbo.

ℰ

The existence of such a distinctive circle of scientists raised new and unexpected historical problems. My surprise increased when I realized that Bacon continually recurs to a problem that at first glance seems odd: that of how a man might rejuvenate himself, and delay old age, in order to prolong his life. In Bacon's view, optics and biology were intimately connected. Only the experimental sciences—optics, applied astronomy, and alchemy—were capable of restoring youth and retarding aging. Bacon's writings suggested that for the *prolongatio vitae* ("prolongation of life"), just as for the study of optics, mediation by the cultural elites at the papal court had been a decisive stimulus.

But what could be the meaning of this striking interest shown by popes and cardinals in studies of nature and the body, which had only recently entered Europe thanks to the influx of Arabic science (Avicenna, Alhazen)? Were they driven purely by intellectual curiosity? Altogether, the scientific ferment of the thirteenth-century Roman curia raised new problems concerning the history of the body.[1]

ℰ

The testaments of thirteenth-century curial officials provide an illuminating vantage point for observing another aspect of the history of the body: the postmortem disposition of the corpse itself.[2]

Some cardinals, especially those from France, willed that their corpses be dismembered and eviscerated to facilitate rapid transport to their prescribed places of burial. Others, instead, notably the Italians, preferred to forgo the possibility of being entombed in prestigious settings, such as Saint Peter's Basilica at the Vatican, rather than risk having their corpses subjected to the dismemberment necessary for immediate shipping to places that might be far from where they had actually died.

Papal documents from the same period point to yet another aspect of great contemporary concern regarding the history of the body. In the last decades of the thirteenth century, the debate over bodily integrity and dismemberment became furious, and reached a conclusion of sorts when Boniface VIII issued his decretal *Detestande feritatis* ("Of Loathsome Savageness," 1299–1300), forbidding the procedures of boiling and cutting up corpses.

Boniface's solemn and impassioned pronouncement in favor of maintaining corporal integrity was a highly personal statement that agreed remarkably with anthropological premises that Bacon had made central to his theory on the equilibrium of bodily elements essential to the *prolongatio vitae*. And because Bacon's theses had first been disseminated at the papal court itself, it was natural to wonder whether it was not here, too, that the future Pope Boniface VIII had become aware of them.[3] Boniface's famous bull thus raised questions touching the history of corporeity that implicated the very person of the pope himself.[4]

℘

The cardinals' testaments and Boniface's bull reveal private sensibilities and attitudes in the face of death. A study by the German historian Reinhard Elze, on the other hand, framed the problem of the pope's death in its institutional dimensions. His observations proved to be of fundamental importance, not least because they pointed to a new contradiction.[5]

Elze had taken a cue from Jacques de Vitry's account of the stripping and abandonment of the corpse of Pope Innocent III. When he arrived at Perugia—then the provisional seat of the Roman curia—Jacques found Innocent dead but not yet buried. During the night of July 16–17, 1216, certain persons had surreptitiously stripped the pope of the precious vestments in which he should have been entombed and had abandoned his body—nearly naked and decomposing—in the church. Upon entering, Jacques recounts that he beheld with his own eyes how fleeting and vain is the illusory splendor of this world.

Expanding his studies to encompass the entire period of the Middle Ages and the Renaissance, Elze drew together other accounts of analogous episodes to formulate a sort of maxim. What had happened to Innocent's corpse should be taken literally: "The pope did not have two bodies or substances, like a sovereign, but only a natural body that is born and dies. What remained were Christ, the Roman church, and the Apostolic See; but not the pope."[6]

℮

Elze's reflections extended themes dear to Ernst H. Kantorowicz, author of the now famous study of *The King's Two Bodies*.[7] The king has two bodies, one physical, which is destined to perish, the other institutional, which is perpetuated in the kingdom. Kantorowicz also took account of the problems relating to the pope, but only marginally, more than anything else to illustrate the comments of fourteenth-century jurists, who had discussed the physical natures of pope and emperor to underscore their differences from those of kings. Kings perpetuated themselves in the institutions they embodied: pope and emperor did not.

By calling attention to a theme—the pope's death—that modern historiography had ignored, Elze's observations suggested a fruitful line of investigation on the pope's body itself. But even with regard to the literature on the *prolongatio vitae* from which I had begun, the Perugia episode raised new difficulties. How is it possible to understand historically the contradiction between the rhetoric of mortality employed by Jacques de Vitry, and individual popes' interest in the possibility of rejuvenation? Is it purely coincidental that the papal documents concerning two such apparently contradictory characteristics—mortality and longevity—appeared for the first time, and in such abundance, in the space of only a few decades?

℮

Further questions were raised by Julian Gardner's and Ingo Herklotz's studies of thirteenth-century Roman funeral monuments, a subject that among other things reveals—thanks to the conference *Rome in the Year 1300 (Roma anno 1300)* organized by Angiola Maria Romanini—how in the last decades of the century Rome became an artistic magnet of the first importance throughout Europe.[8]

Could the history of the pope's death really be reduced to the simple contradiction between mortality and longevity? If "even the pope dies" and cannot be perpetuated within the church, does the pope's body truly lose all signs of its former majesty *(maiestas)*?

And further: if the pope loses his power *(potestas)* at death, in what manner, and with what degree of institutional awareness, did the Roman church attempt to fill ritualistically the power vacuum that a pope's death would inevitably create? On this point, should we not reexamine the role of the cardinals who, from 1059 onwards, exercised the exclusive right of electing popes?

℮

Such questions drew me back anew to the issues raised by Kantorowicz, who indeed had discerned the roots of the heightened concern for dynastic continuity within late medieval and Renaissance kingdoms precisely in the comments of eleventh- and twelfth-century canonists on the theme that "the dignity does not die" *(dignitas non moritur),* but who did not go on to investigate the ecclesiological and ritualistic consequences that such a concern would have had within the Roman church itself. Kantorowicz did not do so because his purpose lay elsewhere. But the field he had thus opened up nevertheless turned out to be immense. Within the framework of a systematic study of the pope's body, a subject that was assuming ever greater complexity, the problem of how the papacy might have attempted to ritualize the transfer of the pope's power *(potestas papae)* emerged as a key issue, one that had to be examined from the ground up, *ab initio,* not only because specialized studies of the subject were lacking, but for chronological reasons as well. The first bits of evidence I gathered here and there indicated, in fact, that the theories born within the Roman church to resolve the problems surrounding a pope's death preceded—often by a good deal—the chronological lines that had emerged from the studies of Kantorowicz and Giesey.

℮

Any history of the body of a sovereign must pay constant attention to the nature of his power. Now, the pope was a sovereign different from a king or even the emperor, because papal power in the Middle Ages was not only, nor even primarily, temporal and political, but rather spiritual and churchly.

Seen from this standpoint, the essential question is the following: beyond the contradiction between the pope's physical transience and the church's institutional continuity, how did the Roman church articulate the relationship between the pope's mortal human condition and the ongoing exercise of his office? By what rhetorical and ritual means did the church attempt to remedy the potential conflict between the pope's physicality and his lofty office?

Here, too, lay difficulties that could not be ignored without running the risk of truncating the history of the pope's body of one of its essential features. The problem was how to proceed. To my good fortune, the historical studies of two outstanding scholars of the medieval papacy, Michele Maccarrone and Gerhart B. Ladner, were a great help. They enabled me to reconstruct on solid foundations the history of the metaphors and images that Roman ecclesiological theories had attached to the person of the supreme pontiff between the eleventh and the thirteenth centuries.[9]

ℭ

The complexities of the thirteenth century alone suggest a variety of possible approaches. But to investigate the relationships between individuals and institutions, transience and perpetuity, glory and the ephemeral nature of power, humility and the exaltation of office, the *cura corporis* ("care of the body") and symbolic purification, as well, obviously, as the relationship between mortality and longevity, I found it necessary to extend my research to other historical periods. For nearly all the aspects of this history of the pope—transience, symbolic purification, death—the chronological framework ended up encompassing the eleventh to the sixteenth centuries.

But the thirteenth century remained my point of reference. This was prompted by the need to verify the accuracy of my initial intuition, that it was precisely then that the problem of the pope's body emerged for the first time in all its complexity. To avoid diluting over a broader stretch of time that heightened interest in the body from which I began, I have focused on the history of the *cura corporis* and of the *prolongatio vitae* in the period from the pontificate of Innocent III to that of Boniface VIII (1198–1303). To the latter I have devoted special attention, because it seems to constitute a sort of epilogue.

This by no means implies that the situation in the thirteenth century can simply be projected mechanically onto other historical periods. Nor should we imagine that the problems that erupted then did not make themselves felt in other epochs as well. One of the most famous specialists in the problems of "aging and rejuvenation" was twice summoned to Rome to treat Pope Pius XII.[10] The first time was in December 1954; the second on October 8, 1958, the eve of the pope's death.[11]

℮

The sources that give access to the many aspects of the treatment of the pope's body in the later centuries of the Middle Ages are widely dispersed and varied. Of primary importance, I gradually realized, are the ceremonial books of the Roman church for the eleventh to the fifteenth centuries, which we can now examine systematically thanks to Bernhard Schimmelpfennig's essential studies of the textual traditions and symbolic significance of medieval papal ceremonials, and to the corpus of texts edited by the late Father Marc Dykmans.[12]

Here it should be noted that reading the *ordines* (the term by which medieval ceremonial books are generally designated) entails a series of difficulties, the first of which is that medieval ceremonials rarely corresponded to actual practice.[13] But for my purposes, the ritual travails of the Roman church in these centuries had to be studied nevertheless, not so much to determine whether ceremonial prescriptions were actually observed, but rather as evidence of a line of thought that by its very nature was born and grew within the institution of the papacy itself.

From the outset, it appeared clear to me as well that a historical analysis of such a lengthy span of time would require special attention to moments of heightened intensity, as well as to occasional silences. Only by respecting chronology would it be possible to recover a sense of the historical and institutional, ecclesiological and cultural contingencies that might have influenced the history of the relationship between the physicality of the pope, understood in his human dimension, and the papal office.

Only by taking such critical precautions could I hope to avoid the perils of an exaggerated ceremonialism.

℮

The starting point for this history of the pope's body had been suggested by the extraordinary interest shown at the thirteenth-century papal court in medicine and the natural sciences, which I came upon by chance in reading the intellectual biographies of such figures as Witelo, Campano of Novara, William of Moerbeke, Simon of Genoa, and many others. By themselves, the aims of popes and cardinals regarding the *cura corporis* and the *prolongatio vitae* alone might have warranted an entire study. But the historiographical stimuli described above, and my desire to locate these attitudes toward the body in a context that also considered the characteristics—including institutional factors—of the social world of which they were an expression, led me down quite different paths, including those of ritual and metaphor.

In the end, therefore, my attention came to center less on the problem of physical corporeity narrowly defined—the "body of doctors and anatomists"—than on the subtler interplay underlying the relationship between the person of the pope, understood in his human dimension, and the sacred office he was called upon to fill. The term *body* therefore involves not only the pope's physical body, but the themes of mortality and the purity of life as well. Thus conceived, this study moves beyond the boundaries of a history of medicine and of the *cura corporis,* and attempts to understand whether, and in what way, these various levels of corporeity—physical and metaphorical—became interwoven and reciprocally conditioning in the period at hand, until they eventually opposed each other.

These, in short, were the questions that my research brought ever more sharply into focus. In the figure of the pope, is corporeity—understood in its fullest sense—not always in some way tied to the nature of his office? Is the pope's body not an essential element for a more complete history of the Roman papacy in the last centuries of the Middle Ages?

Acknowledgments

To complete a study like this requires being able to draw on the advice of other scholars who know how to mix friendship with critical analysis. Carlo Ginzburg played such a role over the entire course of this book's conceptual development and writing. It could even be said that it was his friendly intellectual challenge to me at the University of California, Los Angeles, during my visiting professorship in the History Department there, that persuaded me to go ahead with it.

At UCLA, and in all the years since, I was able to discuss these problems with Gerhart B. Ladner, an expert on the medieval papacy in its intellectual and ideological dimensions. These were conversations that extended an old friendship, begun in the reading rooms of the Vatican Library, that was always precious to me.

At the Vatican Library Anneliese Maier, a superb scholar of medieval scientific thought, set me on the path of studying the natural sciences in the course of unforgettable and nearly daily conversations in the last two years of her life. Through his work on Innocent III, which it was my good fortune to be able to follow partly within his own exacting study, Michele Maccarrone taught me how patiently the intricate ideological twists and turns of the medieval papacy must be reconstructed.

A period of study at Oxford, where All Souls College hosted me as a visiting fellow, enabled me to refine still further the aim and substance of this study. The seminars that I had the opportunity to conduct in Paris at the École Pratique des Hautes Études en Sciences Sociales by invitation of Jacques Le Goff, Jean-Claude Schmitt, and Alain Boureau, and the Seminar in Religious History led by André Vauchez, were important occasions for discussion and reflection. In numerous seminars held at the Ettore Majorana Center for Scientific Culture, Erice, such as the International Workshop on Medieval Societies and the International Seminar on Frederick II, I was able to discuss issues relating to my work and received numerous helpful suggestions. The same was true of the Lezioni Comparettiane held at the Scuola Normale Superiore at Pisa.

Georges Duby's lively interest in my studies was always a

great help. Claudio Leonardi was kind enough to read the manuscript. Francesco Santi has accompanied me with stimulating friendship through the various phases of this labor. His suggestions lie hidden in numerous pages of this book.

My friends Gilmo Arnaldi, Jacques Chiffoleau, the late Jean Coste, Chiara Crisciani, Julian Gardner, Christiane Klapisch-Zuber, Michel Pastoureau, Michela Pereira, and Pierre Toubert, as well as my colleagues at the University of Lausanne, Bernard Andenmatten, Jean-Daniel Morerod, Véronique Pasche, and Ansgar Wildermann, have all advised and aided me, sometimes without even knowing it. To all of them, and in a special way to Louis Duval Arnould, Scriptor of the Vatican Library, goes my most sincere gratitude.

Martine, Lorenzo, and Clelia know that without their understanding patience this book would never have been written.

THE
POPE'S
BODY

PART I

❦

The Carnal Metaphor

1 Mortality and Transience

The Short-Lived Popes

June 1064. Peter Damian (1007–72), one of the leading lights of the eleventh-century movement for church reform, sent Pope Alexander II (1061–73) a small treatise in the form of a letter, *De brevitate (On Brevity),* raising a problem that at first sight seems peculiar: "Why," he inquired, "does the head of the Apostolic See never live very long, but always dies within a short time?" [1]

The question was unusual and audacious. No one until then had really reflected on the brevity of the popes' lives in office. Moreover, Damian was addressing a pope who himself had reigned but a few years. The Synod of Mantua had only recognized Alexander II as the legitimate pope in June 1064, thereby ending a schism precipitated two years earlier by the election of the antipope Honorius II (Cadalus of Parma). [2]

According to Damian, it was Alexander himself who had asked him to reflect on this strange coincidence: none of his predecessors had lived more than four or five years in office. [3] In seeking the reasons for this alarming phenomenon, Damian cast his view broadly over the history of the papacy, and consulted the collection of papal biographies in the *Liber pontificalis (Book of the Popes).* There he discovered an even more remarkable chronological fact: no pontificate had ever lasted longer than that of Saint Peter, which a venerable tradition, running back to the beginnings of Christianity, set at twenty-five years. [4] The chronologies of the *Liber pontificalis* were clear: no pope had ever reached, let alone exceeded, "Peter's years." [5] The discovery must have made an impression, not least because the first millennium from the death of the apostle Peter (1067) was only three years away. [6]

℃

Fortified by his friendship with the pope and by his own un-
questioned authority, Damian promptly drew a first conclusion:
short life was a distinguishing characteristic of the popes; a like
"requirement of a brief life occurs in no other church in the
world," he observed. Nor did it affect any king: the "Savior of
the world was born of the Virgin during the lengthy reign of
Caesar Augustus (fifty-six years), and King David, from whose
line he deigned to descend, ruled for forty years."[7] The two most
important reigns in history, Damian seems to suggest, had both
been considerably longer than that of any pope; not even the
"minuscule" reigns of lesser princes were as short as those of the
popes.[8]

℃

For Damian, therefore, brevity was a basic characteristic of a
pope's life, one that in fact distinguished him from a bishop or a
king. His short life meant that the pope was different from any
other sovereign. It was a unique phenomenon willed by God.
The brevity of the popes' lives was indeed "a mystery ordained
by Providence to instill in the human race a fear of death flowing
from its very summit, so that the glory of temporal life may be
despised." The pope, "'first among men' [praecipuus hominum], is
called on to die within a brief space of time; and the terror of
this event impels every other man to note well the presage of his
own death: the tree of the human race, seeing its top brought
down so easily, trembles in all its branches under the violent
winds of fear."[9] The terror induced by the death of a pope was
unique and unmistakable, because it carried the weight of a universal message: at the pope's death, everyone "feels their viscera
grip with fear of their own end."[10] The pope's death was a warning to all men, reminding them of the vanity of worldly glory
and inciting them to prepare for their own deaths.

The death of a king impacted only the administration of his
kingdom; when the pope died, the whole world lost its common
father. Damian advanced further proofs: what did Africa know
of the kings of Asia, or Ethiopia of the princes of Hesperia?
They ignored each other completely, whether living or dead,
because each was entirely separate from the others. Because

earthly princes were confined within the borders of their own kingdoms, notice of their deaths never reached the other parts of the world. But the news of the pope's death spread to every kingdom, for he was the one *episcopus universalis* ("universal bishop") of all the churches.[11] And again: kings' deaths inspired little fear because secular princes regularly died by the sword and were exposed to "various deathly fates." But the pope's life ended in accordance with natural law. News of his death could not but be the cause of widespread fear.[12]

Damian went on in his treatise to offer a lengthy disquisition, demonstrating that all of creation—sky, land, air, and seas—and everything within it had been rendered harmonious in accordance with wisdom and goodness for the happiness and exclusive use of man. Water and land combined to provide man plants and trees for his sustenance. Grasses were consumed by animals fattening themselves to become savory food. All the beasts of the sky, the land, and the oceans were at the service of man, and subject to his dominion. The elements of nature, air, heat, water, and earth conspired among themselves to provide man with a marvelous variety of goods.[13]

This hymn to the harmony of the universe, which takes up more than half of Damian's letter to Alexander II, amounts almost to a treatise in itself. Not surprisingly, in eight manuscripts of *De brevitate* the title contains a double question: "Why does the pope not live longer, and why does all creation serve the needs of men?"[14] But the digression is nonetheless only apparent. Indeed, it is at this point that Damian's discussion of humility becomes subtler and more precise. He begins by casting his eye over the condition of humanity in general. Man may have dominion of the created world, but he is only truly man so far as he recognizes "the creator of men," God. Disobeying His precepts, man can no longer define himself as such. Ignoring God, he will himself be ignored. As the Book of Job says (25: 5), even "the stars are not clean in his sight," much less man, who is a maggot.[15] In the end, Damian's strictures on humility implicitly encompassed the pope himself. Even Abraham, when he was raised to the height of "full colloquium with God, and was made worthy of his good graces," was mindful of his (original) humility, and proclaimed: "Behold, I have taken upon myself to speak to the Lord, I who am but dust and ashes" (Gen. 18: 27).[16]

Damian immediately proceeded to tell the pope about the rituals of humility used in Byzantine imperial coronations:

> among the Greeks [i.e., at Byzantium] is recorded the custom that as soon as the emperor, or rather he who has been elevated to the imperial dignity, has been invested with the imperial insignia, at precisely the moment at which he is to be graced with the glory of crown and scepter, and while he is surrounded by the obsequies of the nobles, and embraced by the melodies of the choir, a person approaches him bearing in one hand a vase full of the bones and ashes of the dead, and in the other some fine-combed linen flax with its threads hanging gently behind. And this is immediately set on fire, so that in the blink of an eye it is devoured by the flames. Thus, on the one hand the emperor must consider what he is, while in the other he can see what he has. For in the ashes the emperor recognizes that he is himself but ashes; while in the burning flax he beholds the speed with which the world will be incinerated at the moment of judgment. Considering the vanity of his life and all that he possesses, he will not be made prideful by the summit of imperial glory to which he has been raised. For since it is beyond doubt that both the possessor and all he possesses are subject to a common fate, he who has been elevated to the highest honors will not be puffed up with pride.[17]

At the conclusion of the treatise, man is again invited to admire the wondrous order of creation and to credit it not to himself but to God. For while the whole of creation serves man and is subject to him, he receives it as a gift, rather than by right or merit. For the same reason, man should disdain earthly glory, consider that the "vigor of the flesh is like dust already grown arid," and tremble in expectation of the Last Judgment. What applied to one man applied to all, especially to those who had been raised to the apex of glory: to the Byzantine emperor, to whom Damian appealed as a model and example for the first time in the Latin West, and who submitted to a ritual of self-humbling at his own coronation ceremony; but above all to the Roman pontiff, to whom Damian dedicated his entire treatise. His final sentence carries an unmistakable ring of warning: "He who appears illustrious among the creatures of this world will be truly sublime in the celestial glory as well if he submits to the laws of his creator." [18]

℮

As we have seen, in responding to Alexander II's query Peter Damian was led to reflect on three essential themes: the brevity of the popes' lives, the supremacy of the pontifical dignity to all created things, and the mortality of the Roman pope.

1. If it was indeed Alexander II who raised the issue—and we have no reason to doubt it—his question is understandable: to a newly elected pope, the brevity of his predecessors' reigns must have seemed a sort of death sentence. Might his question not have concealed his own fear of dying? Paradoxically, although Damian's response is saturated with the theme of life's brevity, it is also in certain respects consolatory. Though no pope had lived longer than Saint Peter, some had come close to the twenty-five years of his pontificate. And though the brevity of life was a given, Alexander II might nevertheless hope to live longer than his immediate predecessors. After all, twenty-five years was a long time in those days, practically a generation.

2. But the real novelty of Damian's discussion lay in his discovery that no pope had exceeded "Peter's years." It was this that enabled him to undertake a real analysis of the popes' "brevity of life," which he took to be a unique phenomenon distinguishing them from all other sovereigns. Precisely because it was millennarian—let us not forget that he wrote his treatise just three years before the anniversary of the first millennium from Saint Peter's death in Rome—this extraordinary rule of historical chronology could not but be taken as a sign of the divine will, one that only enhanced the value of humility.

3. At this point it must be noted that *De brevitate* is the treatise in which Damian applied to the figure of the pope his most recent and audacious formulas on the theme of papal supremacy. The terms he used to define the pope were powerfully charged: the pope was "the first among men" *(principuus hominum)*, "the height and summit of the human race" *(cacumen et vertex humani generis);* he was the "sole ruler of the entire world" *(unus omni*

mundo praesidens), because he was the "king of kings and prince of emperors" *(rex regum et princeps imperatorum)* as well as their "common father" *(communis pater).*

Some of these definitions demonstrate "that no one was more conscious of Roman prerogatives than Peter Damian"; the titles *rex regum, princeps imperatorum,* and *universalis episcopus* used by Damian in his treatise attest to a "renewed consciousness of papal authority, so seriously obscured in the preceding period." [19]

Is this not important? Damian reflected on the brevity of the popes' lives in the very treatise in which he used the new terminology of exclusive dominion to define papal power. Was the pope not like Abraham? Worthy of "full colloquium" with God, had it not behooved him above all others to remember that he was merely dust? Of all Christians, was it not to the pope that the language and rituals of humility most fully applied? Here was why, in Damian's view, the pope was the sole ruler upon whom a "brief" pontificate had been imposed: he was in fact the "first among men," superior "in honor and dignity [to] everyone living in the flesh." It was therefore also to exalt the papal office that Damian emphasized the popes' physical mortality. Fully aware of this tradition, the German poet Henry of Würtzburg (c. 1265) used exquisitely Damianian language to contrast the transience and universality of the papal office: "Pope is a brief word *[papa brevis vox est],* but the virtue of his name traverses all the longitudes [of the globe], and rules them all." [20]

4. But caution: Damian affirmed that the pope "is superior in honor and dignity to all those who live in the flesh," because "omnipotent God wills that the life of the pope should edify all men"; for the same reason, God "decreed that even his [the pope's] death should be an offering for the salvation of all peoples." [21] More than any other death, therefore, that of the pope served as an instrument of salvation. Even this was an argument that might assuage the anxiety of the letter's recipient, Pope Alexander II. For Damian, a pope's life and death were laden with significance that made him an example for all Christians. His life was the shortest because it was the most intense. [22] The singularity of a pope's life and death amounted to superiority respective of any other bishop or king, but also imposed on him a mode of living that radically underscored his humanity:

"while he should regard himself as the father of the universe, he ought never rest idly from instilling his example into so many sons."[23]

5. For Damian, the nature of the pope's death set him entirely apart from other leaders. It excelled that of any king because it inspired greater terror. Damian emphasized order in the pope's death, speaking of a transit that was peaceful and orderly rather than violent. To the "natural" deaths of popes he contrasted those of kings, who "often die by the sword"—that is, frequently meet violent ends.

The violent deaths of kings "underline the basic discontinuity of power," and "the dramatic atmosphere of a magical regality based on ruptures and difficult renewals."[24] The "natural" deaths of popes instead inscribed themselves in a predictable historical line, based on order. It was an order whose purpose was to control the "terror" inspired by the death of a pope, so much the greater insofar as it concerned all of Christendom. By emphasizing the universal significance of the pope's death, Damian set it apart from common mortality. The pope's death concerned not only Rome, like that of a bishop his diocese or of a king his kingdom, but affected all of Christianity, or rather, the church universal.

6. Not content to illustrate his extraordinary chronological discovery of "Peter's years," Damian busied himself gathering information on the rites of humility reserved to the Byzantine emperor and brought them to the attention of Alexander II. He clearly intended to encourage papal humility by ritual means as well as with the rhetoric of brevity and of "Peter's years."

"You'll Not See Peter's Years"

Less than half a century later, the theme of the brevity of the popes' lives reappears in the *Liber pontificalis*. The occasion was the exceptionally long pontificate of Paschal II, who ruled fully nineteen years (1099–1118). The problem seemed important enough to induce his biographer to dwell on a vision centering on the duration of his pontificate.

During a religious ceremony, a certain person had shown Bishop Alberto of Alatri a card with the words *Quater quaterni ternique* written on it, which signified nineteen (four times four plus three). Alberto hurried to Rome, approached the newly elected pope as he sat on his throne *(intronizatum),* and exclaimed: "That which you see, I see by the grace of God; and you too will see it, so long as you live." Alberto then called out at the top of his voice the words of the vision—*quater quaterni ternique*—which, according to the *Liber pontficalis,* represented not days, weeks, or months already elapsed, but the years of the pope's life "to which we can look forward by the grace of God."

The meaning of a prophecy based on an event, *ab eventu,* can scarcely elude us: only the divine will could grant a pontificate so long and perilously close to the prophetic term of "Peter's twenty-five years."[25]

The *Vita* (Life) of Calixtus II (1119–24) introduces the account of the pope's death with a rhetorical allusion to the brevity of life: "No power lasts long."[26] Here, the evocation of the brevity theme was politically motivated. Calixtus reigned only five years, but his pontificate was a stunning political success. By negotiating the Concordat of Worms (1122) with Emperor Henry V, Calixtus brought the papacy victoriously out of the protracted investiture conflict. The glory of his pontificate found a necessary counterweight in its transience.

č̃

Writing two decades later, Bernard of Clairvaux touched regularly on the theme of the mortality of the pope's physical person. Though he never cites Damian directly, the memory of his reflections is evident. In his very first letter to the first Cistercian pope in history, Eugenius III (1145–53), Bernard warned him never to forget that he was but a man, and "never to cease fearing Him who bears away the souls of princes." He invited Eugenius to reflect on the brevity of the popes' lives, and added a new twist: "How many popes have you seen die in just a short time with your own eyes?" he asked. "Your very predecessors are warning you: the end of your office is not just certain but near. The brief terms of their pontificates announce the shortness of your own days. Never forget, among the daily pleasures of your glory, to meditate on your death: for it is certain that you will follow to the grave those whom you have succeeded to the throne." [27]

Thus, Bernard also deployed the "brevity" topos to contrast mortality with the prestige of the papal office, but with some new accents: brevity was now a theme aimed directly at the ruling pope, who was no longer exempt from the duty of continual humility that applied to the series of his deceased predecessors as well. A generation after the Concordat of Worms, the unchallenged preeminence of the papacy indeed induced Bernard to radicalize the rhetoric of humility. The incisiveness of his discussion, based on the strict monastic tradition of "contempt of the world" *(contemptus mundi)*, signaled moreover the differences and potential conflict between the refined style of life at the papal court and the austere simplicity of Cistercian monasticism:

> Behold then two salutary ideas: consider that you are the pope, and consider that you are—not that you "were"—a miserable speck of dust. . . . If you do not wish to deprive yourself of the benefit and efficacy of this thought, you must meditate not only on the fact that you are a man, but also on the circumstances in which you were born. . . . Perhaps you sprang from the womb with the tiara already on your head? Were you sparkling with gems, decked out in silk robes and feather garlands, or covered with gold jewelry? If you shake off these vanities like a daydream that quickly passes and dissolves, and drive them from your mind, you will behold yourself a man naked, poor, miserable, and wretched; a man who suffers from being a man, who is ashamed of his nudity, who weeps at having been born, who bemoans his very existence; a man born for toil, not honors; born of a woman, and therefore in sin; who lives but a little while, and therefore in fear; with endless miseries, and thus in tears. [28]

Bernard's warning would not be forgotten. Just a decade later the first English pope, Adrian IV (1154–59), spoke of the burdens of the papacy with images and turns of phrase worth recalling here. We know the pope's words thanks to the testimony of John of Salisbury. [29] Taking as his point of departure the title "Servant of the servants of God" *(Servus servorum Dei)*, which was already then traditionally applied to the Roman pontiff, John expressed himself in the following manner:

Who can doubt that the pope is the servant of servants? I call as a witness our Lord Adrian (may it please God that his years be happy ones!). He used to say that no one is more wretched than the Roman pontiff, no condition more unhappy than his. Even had he no other problems, the weight of his duties alone would overwhelm him. He confided to me that he had found so many cares in the cathedral of Peter that by comparison all his earlier troubles seemed like joyful moments and happy times. He used to declare, moreover, that the see of Rome is a prickly seat; that the papal mantle is covered everywhere with thorns and is heavy enough to crush, wear down, and break even the strongest shoulders; and lastly, that if the crown and the tiara seem to shine, it is because they burn like fire. And he added that were it not for fear of opposing the decision of God, he would have preferred never to have left his native England, where he might have lived forever hidden in the cloister of the Blessed Rufus, rather than face so many anxieties. While he was still living I questioned him directly, and someone with personal experience can be believed. He repeated to me many times that his rise from being a simple cloistered cleric through so many offices to the papal throne had added nothing to the happiness and serenity of his earlier life. But because whenever I was with him his grace wished that nothing should be hidden from my eyes, I will use his own words: "The Lord has always beat me between the anvil and the hammer. But now, if it please Him, may He raise up with His right hand the burden that He has imposed upon my infirmity, since for me it has become unbearable." [30]

These declarations, perhaps the oldest expression of such explicit humility on the part of a pope, would be repeated by Petrarch in one of his *Letters on Familiar Matters (Epistolae familiares):*

Less well known is the saying of Adrian IV, which I recall having read in a collection of philosophical anecdotes. He used to say that "no one is more unfortunate than the Roman pontiff, that no condition is more wretched than his and that, even if nothing injure him directly, he will inevitably be quickly reduced to less by the sheer burden of what he has undertaken." . . . He indeed described the throne of the Roman pontiff as being full of needles, and his mantle quilted by the sharpest thorns and heavy enough to wear down, oppress, and weaken the strongest shoulders. And he said that the crown and tiara seem to shine because they are made of fire, adding often as well that in his long rise through all the offices from the cloister to the supreme pontificate he had in fact gained nothing like the serenity and calm repose of his earlier life.[31]

The next long pontificate after Paschal II's was that of Alexander III (1159–81). Robert of Torigny, a French chronicler alert to numerical signs, alluded specifically to Damian's brevity topos in noting that of the 174 successors of Peter, only 3 had come close to the twenty-five years of his pontificate: Popes Sylvester I (314–35) and Adrian I (772–95) had ruled twenty-three years apiece, Alexander III twenty-two. The unusual length of Alexander's pontificate required an explanation that Robert found, as had the biographer of Paschal II, in the "special grace of Providence."[32]

After a long silence of more than two centuries,[33] the pontificate of Benedict XIII (1394–1423) of Avignon again inspired talk of "Peter's years."[34] Having reigned for twenty-nine years, Pedro de Luna had died at Peñiscola on March 23, 1423, without ever acknowledging his deposition by the Council of Constance on July 26, 1417. It would seem that he had broken Damian's rule, and with it one of the principal supports of the necessity of papal humility. But Benedict XIII was not recognized as a legitimate pope by fifteenth-century church historians. On the contrary, the fact that his pontificate had exceeded "Peter's years" served as additional grounds for his condemnation and the damning of his memory (damnatio memoriae). For Antoninus of Florence (1389–1459), "Benedict the Apostate[,] . . . persevering in his obstinacy, exceeded Peter's years to his own damnation; nor should this be marveled at, since not only did he not die in the See of Peter but, as he was dying, he tried to force the election of his own successor."[35]

℃

With the elimination of Benedict XIII from the series of legitimate popes, the axiom of "Peter's years" was saved. Its message of necessary papal humility could continue to apply. But for the first time, the validity of the thesis had been cast into serious doubt. Perhaps for this reason, the Spanish theologian Rodriguez Sanchez de Arévalo (d. 1470) subjected Damian's entire theory to a critical analysis. His *Mirror of Human Life*

(Speculum vitae humanae) is itself devoted to the life of a pope, Paul II (1464–71).[36]

The wished to investigate "the causes and reasons for this brevity of life, which distinguishes the supreme pontiffs from other monarchs and princes."[37] "Brevity" is described as "a serious misfortune": "Scarcely have they assumed office than the supreme pontiffs are in fact struck down and die, so that from the time of the apostle Peter, who ruled the church for twenty-five years, none of his successors has achieved such a long pontificate."[38] Arévalo repeated Peter Damian's historical analysis almost verbatim, even when he added that "right down to our own times, those who ascend to the summit of the Roman see barely rule for half of a few years."[39]

Arévalo's originality certainly lies not in the arguments he adduced to demonstrate that Providence shortened the lives of the popes for good reasons: by their short lives the popes followed the example of Christ, who had been "taken from this world at the midpoint of his years"; "life belongs to immortal God, who like a most just judge apportions it among his ministers and faithful in such a way that none of them will be made proud by the gifts he has received, nor others envious of his happiness"; Divine Providence "withholds long life from the vicar (of Christ), lest such happiness should make him prideful."[40] The interest of his thought lies in the continual attacks he leveled at Damian's central notion of the uniformity assured by "the brevity of life of the Roman pontiffs," which could not be considered a "prerogative of the see." Such brevity, in fact, ran counter to the unity of the church, because the popes' frequent deaths could be a cause for schism: premature death could not be a "characteristic of the see" because the church was "everlasting," and it would therefore be absurd that "he who sits [on the throne of Peter] must necessarily live too briefly."

The criticism of Damian had a specific aim, that of warning the popes that they would enjoy "long and untroubled days" only if they ruled the church in a manner that enhanced its honor: "if the pope rules [the church] with rectitude and piety, he in effect lives a long time even if [in fact] he lasts but a few years after his ascent to the pontificate, for he will have merited all the years of his pontificate," which would have been for him truly a "time alive." Whenever, instead, "the Roman pope has not lived righteously and piously, even should his pontificate last a hundred years he will not have governed the church but 'for a very brief period,' because the whole course of his pontificate will have amounted only to dead time. . . . If, in his pontificate, he comports himself in a vain and reprehensible manner, the pope lives but a little while." In contrast, "the Roman pontiff who rules the church with piety is continuously in meditation and the expectation of death, indeed longing for it: for truly he lives but a little who little values life." [41]

With Sanchez de Arévalo, the brevity topos thus became an argument and a motive for personal reform. The pope faced a dilemma: he must either spiritualize his earthly comportment to the utmost, or the *tempus pontificatus* ("time of his pontificate") would amount to nothing, passing from a state of life to one of death. Moral considerations outweighed ritual and rhetorical concerns. What counted was not the body but the spirit. The church had no need of such an exterior sign (the brevity of the popes' lives), because it was the pope's moral, ethical, and political comportment that mattered. Nor did it have any use for that other mechanism proposed by Damian, the automatic terror provoked by the frequency of the popes' deaths: "at most," declared Arévalo, "we are more saddened by the premature deaths of youths in their first flower than by the natural death of one old man." [42] The pope must sacrifice his (brief) life for the church; only in this way would he live fully, renouncing a long (physical) life in favor of intensity of action. The popes' lives were brief, and could only be prolonged spiritually. It was the quality (intensity) of action that transformed brevity into durability. This is why Arévalo, though addressing his treatise to Pope Paul II, never hesitated to denounce those "Roman pontiffs who fear death and complain, desiring to live . . . not in order to escape life, but because they are alienated from it. They complain of having lived little because they never want to die. Would that the popes not let themselves be deceived by the desire to prolong their own lives!" [43]

૮

In the sixteenth and seventeenth centuries, the topos of "Peter's years" suffered new setbacks. In an oration dedicated to Pope Paul III (1534–49), Pietro Aretino offered him his best wishes for a pontificate exceeding "Peter's years": "Now for his greater glory and further reward / Nature puts a check on time and turns it back / so that he may exceed by far the years of Peter."[44] At more or less the same time an Italian doctor, Tommaso Rangoni of Ravenna, dedicated to Popes Julius III (1550–55), Paul IV (1555–59), and Pius IV (1559–65) a singular work on the possibility of prolonging the popes' lives beyond 120 years. With each new papal election, Rangoni republished his treatise in its entirety, updating only the frontispiece. In an appendix, he explained that the popes might "see Peter's years and more," thanks to an elixir and other paramedical devices.[45]

With Urban VIII (1623–44) a new reading appears: it is recorded that when he was near death a cleric whispered to the pope that "you'll not see Peter's years" *(non videbis dies Petri);* to which the pope, having heard, immediately replied: "It is not an article of faith" *(Non est de fide).*[46] But the topos was not forgotten: in 1726 Guillaume de Bury, a Belgian oratorian and the author of a well-known chronological history of the popes, noted that Leo X, having assumed the papacy "at the age of thirty years," died "immediately afterward, at the age of forty," and commented on the fact in verses that recapitulate Damian's warning: "Even if they are elected young to the pontificate, no pope ever lives to see Peter's years."[47]

℃

At the turn of the eighteenth and nineteenth centuries, two successive pontificates again nearly reached "Peter's years." The last pontificate of the eighteenth century—Pius VI's (1775–99)—lasted almost as long as Peter's: twenty-four years, six months, and fourteen days. The fact was greeted even then as a "divine" decision, an excellent sign for the church: "Sylvester I, Adrian I, Leo III, Alexander III, and Pius VI lived longer than the others because they were able to meet the church's greatest needs."[48] And when his immediate successor, Pius VII (1800–23), appeared likely to reach the prophetic term of "Peter's twenty-five years," couplets were circulated offering him enthusiastic best wishes.[49] At more or less the same time, however, the twenty-five-year span of Peter's pontificate was itself called into doubt. In various encyclopedic works, not always indeed directly concerned with the history of the papacy, the duration of Peter's

Roman pontificate was no longer set at twenty-five but at thirty-two years—one less than the life of Christ.[50]

"Peter's years" were reached for the first time by Pius IX (1846–78). The pope of the First Vatican Council was able to celebrate the twenty-fifth jubilee of his coronation in 1871. Only a few years had gone by since the 1867 festivities of the eighteenth centenary of the death of the apostle Peter—and a good eight centuries since Peter Damian had first revealed to the reigning pope the fateful fact of historical chronology in 1064. The event did not pass unnoticed. To commemorate the fact that Pius IX had been the first to reach "Peter's years," epigraphs were placed in the principal Roman basilicas (Saint John Lateran, Saint Peter's at the Vatican, Santa Maria Maggiore) and other churches of the ancient city (Santa Maria in Via Lata, S. Teodoro).[51] To justify the by now complete abandonment of the brevity topos, the phrase Urban VIII was reputed to have uttered on his deathbed was transformed into a prophesy *ab eventu:* Pius IX was said to have declared from the very outset of this pontificate that the "rule" of "Peter's years" "is not an article of faith." [52]

Leo XIII (1878–1903) also celebrated the twenty-five years of his pontificate on March 4, 1903. But this time Damian's topos had definitively lost its humbling purpose.

A Warning Tomb and Rumbling Bones

After this wide-angle survey of nine centuries of papal history, we must turn back and focus on the first decades of the twelfth century.

To confirm his theory on the brevity of the popes' lives, Peter Damian had turned to arguments drawn from papal history and Byzantine imperial ritual. Several decades later, the theme of transience and mortality resurfaced in a new field, that of legend, and took on concrete form in the tomb of a famous pope, situated moreover in the cathedral church of the bishop of Rome, the Lateran Basilica. The theme of the pope's death (and therefore of his inevitably "brief life") was no longer enclosed, as it had been in Damian's work, within a moral discourse, but emerged now as an object of popular belief.

Around the middle of the twelfth century, in several versions of the famous legend of Gerbert (Pope Sylvester II, 999–1003), an element appears that cannot go unremarked: his tomb began to emit moisture announcing the imminent death of each reigning pope.[53]

William Godell, the author of a chronicle (Chronicon) written between 1135 and 1175, recounts that when the death of a pope drew near, Sylvester's tomb in the basilica of Saint John Lateran gave off so much moisture that everything around it turned to mud. If, instead, it was the death of a cardinal or some other ranking member of "the circle of clerics surrounding the supreme [Apostolic] See" that was approaching, so much water flowed from the tomb that it was completely flooded. Godell seems to have been uncertain whether to accept this feature of the legend or to leave his readers free to draw their own conclusions.[54] The legend's hierarchical aspect was also underlined by another English writer, Walter Map (1135–1200). According to his On the Trivialities of Courtiers (De nugis curialium), when the death (migracio) of a pope drew near, a stream of water flowed from the tomb right into the ground; in the case of other potentates (magnates), the burial urn sweated three, four, or five times less.[55] The amount of liquid flowing from Sylvester's sepulcher was therefore directly proportional to the dignity of the prelate whose imminent death it announced.

In Rome itself, the only one to talk about the moisture emitted by Sylvester's tomb was John the Deacon. In the version of his Descriptio Lateranensis Ecclesiae (Description of the Lateran Basilica) that he composed for Alexander III, John notes that the emissions were a source of amazement. He was surprised himself and seems to have believed that they had some supernatural cause. The dampness could not be explained simply by the tomb's location: "In this same portico (of the Lateran) lies the body of Archbishop Gerbert of Rheims, who was called Sylvester when he became pope. Often his sepulcher, even when the air is very pure, and although it is not situated in a damp place, gives off drops of water, a phenomenon that stirs up curiosity among the people."[56] The legend was thus already well established. Of the tomb's warning function, however, John says not a word. Why not? Whether his silence was due to ignorance or reticence is hard to say. What is certain is that John was writing for a pope,

Alexander III, and to glorify the Lateran Basilica, whose prestige had recently begun to be challenged by the canons of Saint
Peter's in the Vatican.

ɾ̃

Why was Gerbert's tomb entrusted with the task of announcing
the imminent deaths of popes and cardinals?

One explanation is provided by the history of the Lateran
Basilica itself, where the pope's sepulcher had been placed in the
year 1000. By the first decades of the twelfth century, in fact, it
had become a virtual papal necropolis. From 496 to 824 all but
three of the popes had been interred in Saint Peter's in the Vatican. In the tenth century this tradition was interrupted: John X
(914–28), Agapitus II (946–55), Sylvester II (999–1003), as well
as his two immediate successors, John XVII (1003) and Sergius
IV (1009–12), all found their final abode in Saint John Lateran.[57]
With Paschal II (1099–1118) a new series of papal tombs was
begun there.[58] Of the twelve popes who died in Rome in the
twelfth century, ten were buried in the Lateran. From Paschal II
to Celestine III (1191–98) "the role of papal necropolis belonged
to the church of the bishop of Rome."[59]

Innocent II (1130–43) and Anastasius IV (1153–54) even
chose porphyry sepulchers, in what amounted to a genuine re-
discovery in the Latin West of the "imperial" stone par excellence.[60] The first had the former sarcophagus of the emperor
Hadrian brought from Castel Sant'Angelo to the Lateran.[61]
The second had the sarcophagus of the emperor Constantine's
mother, Helen (decorated on all sides with triumphal reliefs),[62]
transferred to the Lateran from Via Labicana. Anastasius justified
this remarkable initiative with the excuse that the holy empress's
mausoleum had been despoiled and no longer contained her
mortal remains.[63]

Does the warning role of Sylvester's sepulcher not provide a
contrast, therefore, to the development of papal funeral customs
that clearly imitated imperial rites?[64] With its premonitions of
impending death, did the legend of the "magus pope" not counterbalance perfectly the innovations of popes who now wished
to die and be buried like emperors in the Lateran Basilica that
had been founded by Constantine? After all, Sylvester II had
been one of the most important counselors of Emperor Otto III

(d. 1002), and the architect of the "renewal of the empire" *(re-novatio imperii)* of the year 1000.[65]

℮

The legend's evolution took a new turn in the late thirteenth century. The Dominican Martin of Troppau (d. 1278) inserted the story of Sylvester's tomb into his *Chronicle of the Emperors and Popes.* But to the sepulcher's sweating, the papal penitentiary now added the rumbling of bones: Sylvester II lay "buried in the Lateran Basilica; as a sign of [God's] mercy his tomb serves as a presage of the pope's [imminent] death, both by the rumbling of his bones and by the sepulcher's sweating; thus it is written on the tomb's inscription." [66]

Why did Martin demote the sepulcher's emissions to secondary importance? The fact is that in the thirteenth century most popes died outside of Rome; the Lateran was no longer a papal necropolis. Moreover, since the first years of the century the Vatican Hill had become a secondary residence for the curial administration as well. The Vatican Palace built by Innocent III (1198–1216) was enlarged by Innocent IV (1243–54) and transformed by Nicholas III around 1280.[67] Martin imperceptibly "delocalized" the legend: the tomb's warning no longer came from the sweating of Sylvester's (Lateran) sepulcher, but from the rumbling of his bones. At the same time, the legend's message was reinforced. Even before the sepulcher's sweating, it was now the trembling body of a pope that announced the imminent death of the reigning pontiff, the specific object of the warning. In Martin's version, every other hierarchical aspect of the legend (including the cardinals) dropped out.

Papyrus Pillows

The first decades of the twelfth century, to which the legend of Pope Sylvester has brought us, appear to have been especially important in the development of the ritual of humility reserved for the Roman pontiff. This is suggested by the fact that the *Ordo XI* by the canon Benedict of Saint Peter's, the first ceremonial book of the post-Gregorian Roman church, composed between 1140 and 1143, contains a series of rites that are of particular interest to us, and which we should therefore analyze with the greatest care.

Benedict describes, among other things, a curious ceremony performed every year on Ash Wednesday. On that day, the pope walked barefoot in a procession to the church of Santa Sabina on the Aventine Hill. At the end of the mass, a priest took a piece of papyrus and dipped it in candle wax; having carefully cleaned it, he then carried it to the Lateran Palace before the pope's arrival there.[68] Here he intoned the words: "May it please my lord to give the blessing" (*Jube, domne, benedicere*). After the pope had given the benediction, the cleric announced: "Today the stational service has been celebrated in Santa Sabina, which greets you"; to which the pope responded "Thanks be to God" (*Deo gratias*). The acolyte then handed him the papyrus. After kissing it with pious devotion, the pope turned it over to a chamberlain who was to "carefully store it away" for conservation until the pope's death. From all of these papyruses was to be made a pillow, which would be placed in the tomb under the head of the deceased pope.[69]

Despite the technical problems of dating this portion of Benedict's *Ordo XI* exactly, it should be observed that the funeral rite he suggested here, centered so exclusively on the person of the pope, nevertheless presents a striking analogy to a tradition of imperial Rome.[70] Pompeus Festus, in fact, relates that straws and bands of verbena were used to make pillows "for the heads of the gods," to wit, of the (deceased) emperors.[71] In the papal rite, numerous elements seem deliberately to recall the *imitatio imperii* ("imitation of empire"): the papyrus was to be presented to the pope before the Lateran Palace constructed by Constantine, and there the papyri were to be stored until the pope's death. Innocent II, for whom Benedict composed the *Ordo XI,* was the first in a series of popes who chose to be entombed at the Lateran in a porphyry sarcophagus.

Nor does this exhaust the rite's symbolism. The pope's role was passive when the acolyte presented him with the papyrus dipped in candle wax, active when he devoutly kissed this symbol of his life as a pope. Repeated every year, the ceremony became a commemorative purification of the entire *tempus pontificatus.* Only the memory of a life entirely blessed could accompany the pope beyond death. But on just this point there were notable deviations from the Roman imperial rite. While the *imitatio imperii* was a powerful element in the papal rite, so also was the desire to underscore the pope's difference from any other ruler. He was distinguished from other sovereigns because his power was not merely temporal but also eminently spiritual, and his life as a pope had to be worthy of that power. These are points that had already appeared in Peter Damian's letter on the brevity of the popes' lives, but which here found expression in a ritualization of extraordinary refinement.

The history of this ritual is nevertheless difficult to reconstruct, because the only ceremonial book that talks about it is Benedict's *Ordo XI*. Could the silence of the other twelfth- and thirteenth-century Roman ceremonials be due to a subsequent abandonment of the rite because of its pagan origin? Was the symbolic significance of papal humbling suddenly considered to be too weak or difficult to grasp?

Here it should be noted that two other ceremonies figure in Benedict's book, centered on flames and ashes as symbols of mortality and the transience of power: the rites of the flax and of the ashes. We may therefore wonder whether it was not the celebration of the ashes that eliminated the rite of the papyrus pillow. Ashes, too, are celebrated on Ash Wednesday!

The abandonment of the rite of the wax-dipped papyrus would then be attributable to the papal ceremonialists' desire to emphasize more clearly the theme of the pope's physical mortality with the aid of a more reliable symbolism drawn clearly from Christian sources. It is true that in this sober and elegant rite, the sense of mortality was not reinforced by symbols or metaphors directly recalling the "base" side of life (ashes, bones of the dead, excrement). But the pillow on which the head of the deceased pope would repose did, on the other hand, contain ritual and symbolic elements suggesting odor, pallor, and dampness.

Ashes

Peter Damian had twice recurred to the humbling symbolism of the ashes: to remind Pope Alexander II that when Abraham was raised to the summit of "full colloquium with God," he was obliged to recall that he was himself but "dust and ashes" (Gen. 18: 27); and to inform the pope that on the day of the emperor's coronation in Byzantium an acolyte presented him with bones and ashes of the dead, in order that he should recognize himself "to be ashes" as well.

In Damian's time there were no rites that called for the presentation or immolation of the pope with ashes. The reason is simple: placing ashes on the heads of the faithful, clergy as well as laity, was first proposed as a Christian rite only by Pope Urban II (1088–99) in 1091.[72] It is thus quite reasonable that a description of the papal ash ceremony should first appear in Benedict's *Ordo XI* in his treatment of Ash Wednesday.

It should quickly be noted that the pope's role was entirely active. Benedict's ceremonial tells us that the pope conferred the ashes, but not whether he also received them: "[In the Roman church of] Saint Anastasius, to which he comes with all his curia, the pope, after the collection of the offering, and having been dressed in the proper vestments, ascends to the altar to present the ashes."[73] Even the twelfth-century Roman pontifical indicates only that the pope distributed the ashes. These were blessed by the youngest of the cardinals, who pronounced the biblical verse: "Remember, man, that just as you were made from dust, so also you will return to dust" (Job 34: 15).[74]

In later ceremonial books, the *ordines* of Albinus (1189) and Cencius (1192), the cardinals' participation is complete, and involves all three of their orders (bishops, priests, deacons). Around the third hour of Ash Wednesday, they rode with the pope on horseback to Saint Anastasius and accompanied him right up to his throne. While the pope and cardinals donned their liturgical vestments, the youngest cardinal priest blessed the ashes (as, already, in the Roman pontifical of the twelfth century). The pope received them seated on his throne from the first of the cardinal bishops, who recited to him out loud the words of the rite meant to remind him of the inevitability of death and the dust of the tomb. Afterward, the pope placed ashes on the cardinals of each order. When the ceremony was over, he walked barefoot to Santa Sabina. This procession was led by the youngest of the cardinal deacons. Once he had celebrated the mass there, the pope returned to the Lateran on horseback.[75]

℃

The Ordinal of Pope Innocent III (1198–1216) presents new variations.[76] The liturgical station now took place in Saint Anastasius only "if the pope [was] in Rome." The annotation reflects the frequent and regular mobility of the papal curia, already evident from the first years of Innocent's pontificate.[77] As before, the ashes were blessed by the youngest cardinal priest and placed on the pope by the first of the cardinal bishops.[78] For the procession to Santa Sabina, the pope removed his sandals and put on a black chasuble.[79] The Ordinal does not say whether the ritual words of warning were recited to the pope, but explicitly mentions the black color of the chasuble.

An anonymous papal ceremonialist describes in the following manner the ash ritual celebrated on February 20, 1303, the ninth year of Boniface VIII's pontificate: before sprinkling ashes over the cardinals dressed in cloaks, the pope received their bows of reverence. Afterward, the first of the order of cardinal bishops—who, as we have seen, had the duty of giving the ashes to the pope—presented him (now only) water for the ablution of his hands.[80] The ceremonialist specifies that Boniface made an analogous change of ritual for Candlemas (February 2) earlier that year.[81] The innovation was twofold: no earlier ceremonial refers to the ablution of hands or to the cardinals' bows.

℃

These two gestures show up again in the so-called *Long Ceremonial* of Avignon, drawn up under John XXII (1316–34) and Clement VI (1342–52). The pope went in procession to the rite of ashes dressed in a red mantle and wearing a white miter without pearls. Seated on a throne adorned with a violet cloth, he received the bows of the cardinals and prelates of the curia. On his left and right he was assisted by two of the elder cardinal deacons of rank. Once the pope's miter was removed, the first of the cardinal bishops sprinkled ashes on his head "in the form of a cross," but "[said] nothing." This last feature confirms the significance of the earlier ceremonials' silence on the words of the rite.[82] Immediately after placing the ashes on the pope, the first of the cardinal bishops had to put his head between the pope's knees in a gesture of full and complete submission. The first of the cardinal priests had the task of pouring water over the pope's hands, which he had to do also on the day of the Purification of Mary and on Palm Sunday.[83] The other cardinals (in hierarchical order), after receiving the ashes from the pope, had to kiss his knees. At the end of the ceremony, the pope received each of them according to his order for the kiss on the mouth and the breast.[84]

The element of submission by the first of the cardinal bishops appears distinctly attenuated in an explanatory note added to a ceremonial book composed in May 1377.[85] No longer did the first cardinal bishop place his head between the pope's knees; rather, he now kissed the pope's right knee. Two decades later (Feb. 24, 1395), instead, Boniface IX decided that henceforth the ashes must be sprinkled on the pope's head by one of the celebrants, whomever he might be.[86] This eliminated the cardinals from active participation in the ritual but reinforced its original purpose of humbling the pope.

In the modern Roman ceremonial produced after the Council of Trent, the person authorized to place ashes on the pope's head is again a cardinal, but his status—that of the senior cardinal penitentiary—only accentuates the penitential nature of the ceremony. The balance between mortality and office, moreover, is reinforced: "The Auditor of the Rota places himself kneeling to the pontiff's right, and the Cardinal Penitentiary, who always sings mass on this day, without gloves, without ring, without miter, standing over the pontifical stool, having made a deep bow, barefooted and in silence, places the ashes in the form of a cross upon the head of the pope, who is seated."[87] "Even while receiving the ashes, the Roman pontiff remains the high priest of the Church of God." The pope must receive the ashes in such a way that "it may be clear to all that, although he has been raised to a dignity thanks to which he greatly surpasses the condition of other men, he is nonetheless still a man: fragile, infirm by nature, and subject to death."[88]

Why did a rite that by its nature applied to all Christians end up focusing exclusively, in the pontifical liturgy, on the person of the pope? Why does the canon Benedict not tell us whether the pope received the ashes and submitted to the monitory words of

the ceremony? Why did the development of this ritual not un-
fold in a straightforward fashion, rather than wind through such
a long train of variations that ran well beyond the Middle Ages
and down to modern times?

The answer to the first question is obvious: more than any
other Christian, as Peter Damian saw it, the pope must follow
the example of Abraham and, in the words of Bernard of Clairvaux, remember that he is but "a miserable speck of dust." The
involvement of the pope in a liturgy of penance and humility
whose basic message applied to all Christians without exception
simply underscores the importance that the Roman church assigned to the popes' physical mortality from the mid–eleventh
century onward.

This involvement, however, seems to have been gradual, and
this explains the long silence on the pope's passive role in the
ritual. The fact is that the whole history of the ashes shows how
difficult it was to establish a ritual balance between emphasis on
the pope's physical mortality and the exaltation of his office. If,
in the *ordines* of Albinus (1189) and Cencius (1192), the pope
received the ashes and had to submit to the warning words of the
rite, the situation was already quite different by the time of Avignon: the ashes were placed on the pope while he presided on
his throne, and no one addressed the *memento homo* warning him
of his mortality. Moreover, the cardinal who placed the ashes on
his head was required to perform a gesture of complete submission. Several centuries later, the penitential significance of the
rite was further reinforced at the expense of its hierarchical element: in the ceremony born of the Counter-Reformation, it was
no longer the highest-ranking cardinal who put the ashes on the
pope's head, but the cardinal penitentiary.

The quest for a balance between highlighting the pope's
mortality and underscoring respect for his office was long and
difficult precisely because of the role reserved for the cardinals,
who here represented the continuity of the church. The insistence on the mortality of the pope's physical person could not be
permitted to diminish the papal office in any way: nor could the
cardinals' active participation be allowed to offer an interpreta-
tive opening for a trespass on the pope's *plenitudo potestatis* ("fullness of power").[89]

Bands of Flax

Besides ashes, Peter Damian had also talked about flax. Indeed, he was the first Western author to report that at Byzantium an acolyte presented the newly elected emperor with some linen flax that, when set afire, was instantly consumed by flames. Its rapid consumption was meant to induce the emperor "to see what he has."

Flax, used as a symbol of transience, recurs in various passages of the Bible (Sir. 21: 10–11; Isa. I: 31).[90] Its symbolism is powerful; basic in its simplicity, profound in its significance: "like nothing else, it symbolizes human . . . transience" viewed in relationship to the exercise of power *(gloria).*[91]

We do not know whether the rite of burning flax was then part of the papal ceremonial. But the fact that Damian talks about it as though it were unfamiliar to the recipient of his treatise, and the precise and detailed manner in which he describes it, suggests that he wished to propose its adoption.[92]

ℭ

Before turning our attention to Rome, we should note that a completely analogous rite appears in the liturgy of the cathedral of Besançon that was reorganized by Archbishop Hugh I (1031–66). The archdeacon presented the archbishop with some linen flax that had been set afire and addressed him with the words: "Reverend father, so passes the world and your vitality."[93] The calendrical cycle was intense: the ceremony was meant to be repeated four times a year, at Christmas, Saint Stephen's Day, Easter, and Pentecost.[94] As in the Byzantine ceremony, the archbishop of Besançon played only a passive role.

This fact is of interest, because Damian stayed in Besançon at the end of August 1063, while returning to Italy from a legation in France. Archbishop Hugh had shown him his "tomb, prepared with great care, as though it should receive you today," and had explained to him that "as a reward for the grave diggers, five *soldi* are tied to each of the four corners of the funeral drape. Thus those who have to perform the burial will see during the funeral that they will not go unrewarded for their charitable act." In a letter to Hugh, Damian complimented him—"illustrious

among the priests of the West, and of renowned fame"—for
having had the tomb built: he could thus contemplate "how the
vigor of this life vanishes before your eyes like that of weeds,"
and "if by chance your mind should allow itself to be seduced by
the splendor of some high office, turning your eyes to the tomb
will remind you that you are but dust and ashes." Damian's discussion then opened out into an exhortation to combat the luxu-
ries of the flesh "with the thought of the worms that will one
day be crawling out of that same body."[95] In their emphasis on
mortality and humility, Damian's observations are remarkably
similar to those he addressed to Pope Alexander II. The coincidence is chronological as well: his letter to the archbishop of Besançon bears the same date, 1064, as his *De brevitate*. It is thus
Damian's encounter with the archbishop of Besançon that explains this more ancient manifestation of the rite of burning flax
in a Western ceremonial. The use of the flax was unquestionably
a ritual innovation for the diffusion of which Damian was a leading proponent in the West.   𝑒̃

In Rome, the first to discuss flax was the canon Benedict of Saint
Peter's (1140–43). Bands of flax were lit at Christmas and Easter.
On Christmas morning the pope celebrated mass at Saint Anastasius, then went in procession to Saint Peter's. The route wound
through the antiquities of imperial Rome, between the Temple
of Jove and the Circus Flaminius, passed under the arch of the
emperors Gratian, Theodosius, and Valentinus, then opened out
finally across the Bridge of Hadrian, "before his temple, near the
Obelisk of Nero, and in front of the Memorial to Romulus."
When the procession reached the Vatican, the pope ascended to
the basilica and sang mass with the palace priests. Before beginning the procession that would take him back to the Lateran, a
crown (tiara) was placed on his head. On the return route, "because of the shortness of the day and the difficulty of the way,"
the liturgical station was held at Santa Maria Maggiore, during
which the rite of lighting the flax was celebrated.[96] When the
pope entered the presbytery, the sacristan presented him with a
rod tipped with a lighted candle. The pope used it to light the
flax that had been hung from the capitals of the columns at the
entrance of the basilica. The ceremony was repeated on Easter at
the threshold of the presbytery of Santa Maria Maggiore.[97]

There were fundamental differences between these rites and those held in Byzantium. Certainly, the Roman rite of igniting the flax did not lack elements that underlined the pope's temporal power and thus, implicitly, his transience. The procession route to Saint Peter's recalled imperial triumphs (the pope passing under the arch of the emperors Gratian, Theodosius, and Valentinus), but it ended in front of Hadrian's Mausoleum and the Memorial to Romulus.[98] The procession from Saint Peter's to the Lateran was called the "festival of the crown" *(festum coronae)*. But the ceremony also appears to have taken place in a strictly liturgical setting;[99] moreover, at Christmas and Easter, the pope played only an active role. It was he who set fire to the flax with the candle that was offered to him. For this reason, the rite's symbolic significance was broadly eschatological: the burning flax signified the end of a world destined to be destroyed by fire.

By Benedict's time the flax rite, as it was celebrated at imperial Byzantine coronations, had instead been fully incorporated into the Western imperial ceremonial. The description offered by the *Book of Ceremonies of the Imperial Court (Libellus de cerimoniis aule imperialis,* c. 1145), inserted into the *Golden Writings of the City of Rome (Graphia Aureae Urbis Romae),* follows Damian's text closely. The emperor *(monocrator),* "crowned with a garland of lilies" was presented with "the dust and bones of the dead, and the flax was set afire before him in prefiguration of the Last Judgment."[100] Like the Byzantine emperor, the Western emperor who was to be crowned played a passive role—submitting, that is, to the lighting of the bands of flax.

ẽ

Honorius Augustodunensis (c. early twelfth century) mentions the pontifical flax rite only in reference to Easter: "while the Apostolic One *(Apostolicus)* advances in the Easter procession, the band of flax is presented to him by being draped above him, and the burning flax is allowed to fall on him . . . in order that he may realize that he too will be reduced to ashes, and that the glory of his raiment will fade to mere glitter" (Ezek. 15: 4).[101] The same account is given by the Basel codex, which summarizes and updates Benedict's *Ordo XI.*[102] Should we conclude that the importance of the rite had been diminished? It

is hard to say. Certainly, compared to Besançon, where the
ceremony was meant to be held four times a year, the Roman
liturgy seems to have opted from the outset for a less frequent
calendrical cycle. Perhaps the explanation lies in the fact that, if
we take Honorius's text literally, the pope no longer played an
active role but a passive one. To the diminished frequency of the
rite would then have corresponded a deepening of its humbling
features.

For Lothar of Segni, the future Pope Innocent III, the fire of
the burning flax was a reminder of the Last Judgment and of the
end of time *(saeculum),* but concerned also the person of the celebrant: the pope lit the flax so that "he who advances gloriously
shall not delight in temporal glory," because "all creatures of the
flesh are but straw, and all their glories like the flowering of
straw." For Lothar, the celebrant's role was active. But the passage in which he describes the rite does not seem to concern the
Roman pontiff alone: Lothar in fact speaks of a rite that was celebrated "in some basilicas near the middle of the choir."[103] And
the images he uses are those he first deployed in his *De miseria
conditionis humanae (On the Misery of the Human Condition)* to stig-
matize the vanity of the prelates' "cosmetic ornamentation," and
to highlight the contrast between the "proud man" who "sits on
the throne" and the manner "in which he lies prostrate in the
tomb."[104]

Toward the middle of the thirteenth century we encounter a new
development. The Dominican Stephen of Bourbon, author of
one of the most important medieval collections of cases *(exempla,*
1250–61), describes the rite of burning the flax in a chapter
dedicated to the "remembrance of death" *(memoria mortis)* and
filled with examples of humility. The chapter contains a quo-
tation from Plato on the necessity of meditating regularly on
death, references to biblical texts concerning ashes, and a parable
on the value of humility that Aristotle was said to have recounted
at the end of his life.[105] In it, an old man gave Aristotle a precious
stone, capable of attaining any weight—provided it gathered no
dust. The stone represented his pupil, Alexander the Great: living (and thus not gathering dust), his weight was greater than that
of all other men; dead (and now covered with dust), he was of

no weight whatsoever.[106] Stephen went on to relate a story from the *Vita* of John the Almoner, Patriarch of Alexandria, according to which on the first day of his coronation a stoneworker set before the new (Byzantine) emperor three or four pieces of different-colored marble and asked him with which type he wished to build his funeral monument. "Man is mortal and must be ever mindful of death, in order to be humble." It was for this reason that the patriarch "wished to build himself an unfinished tomb, and ordered that during the most important solemnities, when he was seated in the place of honor, someone should approach urging him to finish the tomb: 'Lord, arrange to have your unfinished tomb completed, for you never know the hour of the thief's arrival.'" The last phrase is that which most concerns us: "It is therefore said that when the pope is being consecrated and raised to the highest honor the flax is lit before his eyes and he is told: 'Thus passes the glory of the world *[Sic transit gloria mundi]*, and so likewise should you think of yourself as ashes and mortal.'"[107] This is the first instance in the papal context in which the rite of burning flax is described as being like that of Byzantium: the flax was in fact ignited in the course of the ceremony of the pope's consecration (or coronation).[108] Moreover, the pope played a passive role in the ceremony and submitted to the rite's warning words.

The testimony of Stephen of Bourbon is important for another reason as well. His text is in fact the first instance in which the warning of transience, *Sic transit gloria mundi,* a phrase still used in common speech, was clearly applied to the pope.[109] The model is biblical, and identical to that which inspired the rite of burning the flax.[110]

☙

Around 1285 another curialist, the German Alexander of Roes, used the same words in a verse of his *Peacock (Pavo),* a parody in which the peacock represents the pope. Though the verse refers to no particular ceremony, it is beyond doubt that Alexander, then chaplain to the Roman Cardinal Giacomo Colonna, had in mind the words prescribed by the flax ceremony.[111]

But why must we wait until the middle decades of the thirteenth century before finding sources that present the papal flax rite in the same manner that Peter Damian first described it back in 1064? Is the long silence due simply to the loss of documents? Or is it possible to suggest that the pope may have waited until then to adopt the "new" rite of burning the flax?

It should be noted right away that Stephen of Bourbon's account comes prior to the ceremonial book of Gregory X, in which for the first time the sequence of the ritual of the papal coronation is presented in a manner different from the traditional one. The pope was now to be crowned at Saint Peter's before going to the Lateran to take possession of the papal cathedral (and, thus, of the papal see).[112] According to earlier *ordines*, the newly elected pope was to be crowned the Sunday after he had taken possession of the Lateran and before making the cavalcade from Saint Peter's to the Lateran.[113] The innovation was crucial: in Gregory X's ceremonial book, the coronation itself became a solemn and autonomous constituting element in the creation of a new pope.

Gregory X's biography emphasizes as well his intention to assign maximum importance to the act of coronation. Recalling the Donation of Constantine, Gregory justified his decision to the cardinals to have himself crowned in Rome:

> As you know, dearest brothers, the emperor Constantine, monarch of the world, took his crown from the imperial head and in his munificence gave it to Blessed Sylvester, then the Roman pontiff, in sign of royal dignity and temporal dominion. And since it is said that this was done in Rome itself, it is reasonable, equitable, and honest that, though I be unworthy, I should be conferred that same diadem in that same church.[114]

The last pope to be elected and consecrated in Rome had been Gregory IX (1227–41), and it was therefore more than a coincidence that Tedaldo Visconti chose Gregory X as his pontifical name. The point should be emphasized, especially because the *Vita* of Gregory IX describes the cavalcade from Saint Peter's to the Lateran in such emphatically regal language that the question naturally arises of whether it did not directly inspire Gregory X. On March 21, 1227, the pope was first of all "magnificently enthroned" at the Lateran Basilica, a rite that allowed the church to "cast aside its lugubrious garments, while the crumbling walls of the city recovered in part their ancient splendor."

The following Sunday, March 28, the pope received the pallium in Saint Peter's Basilica. On Easter (April 11), after the solemn mass in Santa Maria Maggiore, Gregory IX "returned amid jubilant crowds wearing the crown on his head." On the next day, Monday of Easter Week (April 12), "transformed into a Cherubim," and "father of the city and the world" *(pater Urbis et Orbis)*, the pope crossed Rome "crowned with the double diadem" (that is, with the tiara), riding a horse bedecked in "precious drapes" and accompanied by the cardinals adorned "in purple." The senator and prefect of the city of Rome followed him on foot, holding his horse's bridle *(lora)*.[115] The custom of celebrating the first "festival of the crown" *(festum coronae)* in such a solemn manner on the Monday of Easter Week was a feature of the *imitatio imperii.* In Byzantium, too, on Easter Monday the crowned Basileus went in procession from the church to the palace. Again in Byzantium, the nobles held the bridle *(lora)*, a symbol "of the splendor of the resurrection of Christ."[116]

The interest of the author of Gregory IX's *Vita* in the papal crown is also evident in his polemics against Emperor Frederick II, whom he accused of wanting the pope "to receive some ashes instead of the crown" *(cinerem pro corona suscipiat)*.[117] The period in which he wrote his life of Gregory IX was virtually the same as that in which Stephen of Bourbon drew up his *exempla,* providing a further indication of the exceptional interest in the papal crown shown in curial circles in the aftermath of the emperor's death.[118] Can it come as any surprise that the sources reveal the pope being called upon to submit to the Byzantine rite of burning the flax at precisely the moment when the coronation was assuming increasing importance, indeed, becoming a constituting and autonomous ritual element?

But the accounts by Stephen of Bourbon and Alexander of Roes, though important, remain isolated.[119] Not even Gregory X's ceremonial book speaks of the flax ritual in the context of the pope's coronation. But the lighting of the flax continued to be described in liturgical writings, and the pope's role in it remained active.[120] The liturgist William Durant produced in 1284 a kind of synthesis, in which different liturgical traditions drawn from Innocent III and Honorius Augustodunensis come together.[121] At Avignon, the Spanish theologian and curialist

Alvarus Pelagius recalled in his *Mirror of the King* (*Speculum Regum*, 1341–45) seeing a ceremony held in the cathedral in which, "while the pope proceeded in procession, flax, hung from a column in the center of the choir, was set afire with a suspended maniple, so that he who advanced in glory should not become enamored of temporal glory." Here, Alvarus copied word for word the text of Innocent III. It is therefore difficult to say whether he was referring to a coronation ceremony or to an Easter mass, particularly since he is unclear about the role played by the pope. Was it active (as in Lothar of Segni's text), or passive? [122]

℮

Was the flax-burning ritual celebrated at Avignon as part of the papal coronation ceremony? The only way of knowing is provided by an *ordo* that seems to contain instructions for Urban V's coronation (Nov. 6, 1362).[123] The procession route would have conformed to the plan of the Avignon palace complex completed by Clement VI (1342–52). The pope first left his chambers and entered the great chapel *(capella magna)*, where he donned his liturgical robes. Here, other ritual acts took place, including the lighting of the flax. After submitting to this humbling rite, the pope crossed the chapel with his head covered in a drape of gold cloth, symbolizing his newly acquired majesty *(maiestas)*. When he reached the choir, he received three cardinals as a sign of peace, who had to kiss his breast in a sign of reverence.[124]

A passage from the *ordo* indicates that the best way of celebrating the rite was much discussed within curial circles: "some maintain that on account of the presence of the people, it would be better to hold [the ceremony of igniting the flax] on a wooden platform *[cadestillum]*, in a place of greater glory." Thus, the need for the rite to be more visible made itself felt at precisely the moment in which the curia now had available, in the form of the new papal palace, a "place of greater glory" for the papal coronation. The discussion may have aimed at recreating conditions analogous to those of Rome, where the rite was held on the great exterior staircase leading up to Saint Peter's Basilica.[125]

℮

In the very first years of the fifteenth century, an eyewitness described for the first time a performance of the ceremony of igniting the flax. The English chronicler Adam of Usk was able to observe Pope Innocent VII's coronation in Saint Peter's:

> On the feast of St. Martin (Nov. 11, 1404) the new pope, for the solemnities of his coronation, descended from his palace into the basilica of St. Peter where, at the altar of St. George, he put on vestments for the mass that had been brought to him by the auditors of the curia. And at the exit of the chapel of St. George a cleric, bearing in hand a long cane covered with flax at one end, lit the flax with a candle and declared out loud: "Holy Father, thus passes the glory of this world" *[Pater sancte, sic transit gloria mundi]*; and twice again in the center of the chapel in an even louder voice he proclaimed: "Holy Father, Holy Father"; and still a third time, at the entrance to the altar of St. Peter's, he issued a triple exclamation in an even louder voice: "Holy Father, Holy Father, Holy Father!" And each time, immediately afterwards, the flax was extinguished.

The scene contains all the elements mentioned by Stephen of Bourbon and the Avignon *ordo:* the pope's passive role and the triple recitation of the monitory words of the rite. Adam of Usk himself felt obliged to explain that "in the same manner, at the coronation of the emperor, at the moment of his highest glory, stoneworkers would present him with pieces of marble of every sort and color, worked in every style, shouting at him: 'Most excellent Prince, from which marble do you want us to make your tomb?'" [126]

We know, moreover, that this rite was performed at Gregory XII's coronation (December 19, 1406), which was also celebrated at Saint Peter's in Rome. Jacopo Angeli talks about it in a letter to Manuel Chrysolaras of Constantinople.[127] As in the "Avignonese" ceremonial, the presentation of the flax to the newly elected pope was inserted into a ritual program in which gestures of papal humility alternated with the staging of regality that imitated imperial ceremonies. After putting his golden slippers (reputedly introduced by Diocletian) back on, the pope submitted to the ablution of the hands: after receiving the papal ring, he approached the highest *(sublimius)* altar. The setting was "divine": the pope even wore a white veil and a golden cross on his breast "on account of his holiness, not for pleasure." Jacopo's description of the flax ceremony follows a long digression on the "kingly ornaments" *(regum ornamenta)* given to the pope by the emperor Constantine; immediately after the lighting of the flax, the pope proceeded wearing a "veil of gold on his head."[128]

Two popes elected by the church councils were also subjected to the ritual burning of the flax: Alexander V at Pisa (June 26, 1409),[129] and Martin V at Constance (November 1417). For the latter, the sources are the "Avignonese" *ordo* adapted for the circumstances[130] and Ulrich of Richenthal's chronicle of the Council of Constance.[131] At the coronation of Pope Pius II (1458), the flax was presented and ignited three times: first in the middle of the central nave, then by the altar of Saint Maurice (in the left nave), and finally on the stairs leading to the apse (the *Scala Sancti Petri*).[132] The scene was painted by Pinturicchio for the Piccolomini Library of Siena Cathedral (1504–07): the master of ceremonies lights a bit of flax placed at the head of a cane and pronounces the words of the rite while turning to the pope, who is being carried in procession on the gestatorial chair.[133]

An additional notice is provided by Agostino Patrizi Piccolomini (1484–92). In his account the master of ceremonies, in accordance with tradition, burned the flax in the pope's presence and, while genuflecting, recited to him three times the words: "Holy Father, thus passes the glory of the world" *(Pater sancte, sic transit gloria mundi).* Immediately afterward, the pope moved in procession to visit the tombs of the Roman pontiffs in the nave that extends the chapel of Saint Gregory the Great.[134] To the symbolism of the transience of power, so splendidly represented by the burning flax, was added a gesture warning of the mortality of the pope's physical person in a symbolic prefiguration of his own incorporation into the line of deceased pontiffs.

As we have seen, the rite of burning the flax was incorporated into the Roman liturgy between 1064 and 1140. The chronology is not much different for that of the presentation of the ashes. In neither case is the history of the rite perfectly linear: on the contrary, each presents notable variations and contrasts. For the flax-burning rite as well, the role of the pope seems at first to have been exclusively active.

The history of the pontifical rite of the flax also demonstrates that, from the Gregorian reform onward, the humbling reserved for the pope was never forgotten. But certain critical moments, such as the central decades of the thirteenth century, influenced the rite's evolution, at times indeed changing it radically. The definitive incorporation of the flax into the ritual of the papal coronation ended up eliminating the ceremony celebrated at Easter, which drops out of the sources after the early fifteenth century.

Until then, the rite was still in use at the court of the German king, but seems afterward to have been abandoned. The Roman liturgy of papal coronations instead retained it down to modern times.[135] The rite of igniting the flax thus ended up being an exclusive symbol of the transience of the reigning pope's power. If the rite of the flax "for the pope alone . . . assumes its full significance,"[136] that was the result of a long and conflictual evolution.

The Lateran Chairs

It is now time to examine whether and how the ceremonies for installing newly elected popes at the Lateran incorporated symbolic gestures and objects concerning the person of the pope, understood in his human dimensions.[137]

This time Benedict's *ordo* (1140–43), which served as our point of departure for reconstructing the rites of papal humility (candle wax, ashes, flax), offers little help, for it does not contain an *ordo* for the pope's possession-taking of the Lateran. On the other hand, several elements of this ceremony instead show up for the first time in the lives of Paschal II and Honorius II (1124–30) in the *Liber pontificalis,* as well as in the first *Vita* of Bernard of Clairvaux.

ℰ

Paschal II was elected on August 13, 1099, in the church of San Clemente. The author of his *Vita* focuses on the ritual stages by which "the election was carried out," and thus his pontificate legitimized. These included the procession from the Vatican to the Lateran, where the pope formally took possession of the palace on the following day. The various phases of the ritual of Paschal's possession-taking of the Lateran are now—for the first time—carefully described:

> After the cardinals had dressed [the pope-elect] in the red mantle, and placed the tiara on [his] head, the pope was taken to the Lateran, accompanied by the crowd's singing. Then he was led from the piazza on the south side right up to the portico of the basilica of Our Savior, which is called Constantiniana. The pope dismounted from his horse and was placed first on the throne that stands there before the church, then taken inside to the patriarchal one. He then ascended to the palace and arrived at the two curial chairs. Here he was girded with a cincture, from which hung seven keys and seven seals so that, thanks to the seven gifts of the Holy Spirit, he might know with how much care to make provision for the governance of the holy churches over which he presides in accordance with God's will. Placed on both of these curial chairs, he was handed the papal crosier *[ferula]* and, already lord [of the palace], he brought the rite of election to completeness as he sat or walked about in the various rooms of the palace meant for the Roman pontiffs alone.[138]

The importance of the curial chairs is illustrated by the passage that immediately follows this description. During a vision, the Bishop of Alatri was said to have indicated that Rainerius would be the future pope (Paschal II), prophesying: "he will live and be seated" *(Vivet, ait, sedebitque).*[139]

Even though the pope had gone in procession to the Lateran already wearing the papal mantle and crown, the *Vita* of Paschal II still set extraordinary importance on the phase of his possession-taking of the palace, in which he was seated on chairs before the portico, in the basilica, and in an unspecified part of the palace. The first, in the portico of the basilica, has no name; the second was without doubt the marble seat *(sedes marmorea)* of the apse, which the biographer defines as patriarchal *(patriarchalis),* the pope's own seat. The pope sat on the other two in ascending to the palace, which suggests that in all likelihood they were located at the entrance. The newly elected pope—"already sovereign"—sat in various other parts of the palace, but the *Vita* says not a word about those seats *(sedes).*[140] Only for the chairs at the entrance to the palace does the author of Paschal's *Vita* note details of a ritual nature: while sitting, the pope was provided with "a cincture from which hung seven keys and seven seals"; and while seated, he received the papal *ferula* (crosier). The keys and seals symbolized the seven gifts of the Holy Spirit that were to guide the pope in the (wise) exercise of his government. Taking possession of the palace was a constitutive part of his election. It was "to bring it to a conclusion" that the pope entered the palace provided with the *ferula,* the visible symbol of his possession and dominion. "Already sovereign," he proceeded inside the palace to other less well specified sites.

The *Vita* of Honorius II is rather more succinct. After choosing Bishop Lambert of Ostia in the church of Saint Pancras (near the Lateran), the electors placed the newly elected pope on the chairs situated before the church of Saint Sylvester. The biographer Pandolfus provides two new details: the shape of the seats (a *sygma*), clearly identical to those described as curial by the author of Paschal's *Vita,* and their exact location in front of the church of Saint Sylvester. The name *symae* or *sygmae* recalls the nearly circular seat of the chair, whose form was similar to the capital letter *sigma* in Greek uncial script, which in Latin writing corresponds to a "C." The author of the *Vita* of Honorius II also aimed to make clear that it was the electors who placed "the pope on the two seats."[141]

For the author of the first *Vita* of Saint Bernard, the various phases of the ceremony of taking possession of the Lateran were "sittings" *(sessiones),* done in accordance with "ancient custom" *(antica consuetudine).* Here, too, references to ceremonial gestures served to underscore the legitimacy of Pope Innocent II, whose election in 1130 was carried out by "those who had remained on the catholic side." His rival, on the other hand—Anacletus II (Pietro Pierleoni, 1130–38)—was elected "by means of fraudulent machinations."[142]

For fuller descriptions of the ceremony of taking possession of the Lateran, we must await the later ceremonial books of Albinus (1189) and Cencius (1192), and the two *ordines* conserved in the codices at Basel and London.[143]

After the pope's death and burial, the cardinals gathered in a "solemn place" *(celeber)* to elect his successor. At the conclusion of the election, the archdeacon and the first of the deacons cloaked the pope-elect in a red cope and "conferred his name" upon him. Two of the eldest cardinals accompanied him to the stone seat called "dunged or bedunged" *(stercorata vel stercoraria),* located in front of the portico of the Lateran Basilica; the cardinals placed him on the seat "with honor" *(honorifice).* After being seated awhile, the pope-elect received three fistfuls of coins from the chamberlain's pouch, which he threw to the people, declaring: "This silver and this gold are not given me for my own pleasure; what I have, I will give to you." Then the prior of the Lateran Basilica, and one of the cardinals or his confreres, accompanied the pope to the "sacred altar of the basilica." Those who entered through the portico were greeted with the words: "Saint Peter has elected our Lord." After the church choir *(schola cantorum)* sang the *Te Deum Laudamus* the pope-elect, seating himself on the throne, received all the cardinals at his feet, and for the kiss of peace. Then, surrounded by cardinals, subdeacons, secretaries, and members of the choir, he left the basilica. Judges accompanied him as far as the "basilica" (or chapel) of Saint Sylvester. The pope's procession passed under the arch "where there is the image of our Savior who bled when a Jew struck him in the face." After this first encounter with (the blood of) Christ, the ceremony of the "porphyry" chairs took place.[144] Their placement before the chapel of Saint Sylvester was no accident. According to an ancient legend, Sylvester I was the pope who, at the command of Saints Peter and Paul, had healed the emperor Constantine of leprosy: the relics that the pope-elect now went to adore in the chapel of Saint Lawrence outside the Walls ("in Palazzo"), the *Sancta Sanctorum* ("Holy of Holies"), at the conclusion of the ceremony of possession-taking were believed to have been given to Sylvester by Constantine himself, along with the images of Peter and Paul placed above the altar.[145]

℮

Seated on the porphyry chair to the right, the pope-elect was handed the papal *ferula* and the keys to the Lateran (basilica and palace) by the prior of the basilica of Saint Lawrence outside the Walls (the *Sancta Sanctorum*). The pope then went to sit on the chair to the left, also of porphyry *(iusdem lapidis),* and handed the *ferula* back to the prior, along with the keys. While the pope-elect remained on this chair for a bit, the prior of Saint Lawrence girded him with a red cincture, from which hung a purple pouch containing twelve seals made of precious stone, and some musk. "Afterward the pope must seat himself on those two chairs, so that it seems that he is lying between [inter] two biers [lectulos]—that is, as though he were reclining [accumbat] between the preeminence of Peter, Prince of the Apostles, and the preaching of Paul, the Apostle of the Gentiles."[146] The pope-elect then received all the officials of the palace, first at his feet, then for the kiss (of peace). Next, the treasurer gave him some silver coins that he tossed to the people, declaring three times: "He scatters abroad, he gives to the poor; his righteousness endures forever" (2 Cor. 9: 9).[147] Advancing along that same long portico, he passed under "the icons of the apostles who reached Rome by sea, though brought by no one," and entered the basilica of Saint Lawrence outside the Walls (Sancta Sanctorum). There he remained a long time in prayer, "before his own special altar." He then entered his chambers, where he rested before going to dinner.

The following Sunday the pope-elect, accompanied by the palace clergy of all orders, and by Roman nobles, went to Saint Peter's to be consecrated by the cardinal bishops. After the consecration came the bestowing of the pallium. The archdeacon and prior of the basilica arranged it for him by inserting three gold pins into it; one in front, one behind, and one on the left side. On his head were placed three hyacinth stones. Thus adorned, he proceeded to the altar, where he celebrated mass. Meanwhile the cardinal deacon, the subdeacons, and the clerks (scriniarii) of the basilica intoned lauds. After celebrating the mass, the pope went to the stable where his decorated papal horse was being kept. There the archdeacon received the tiara (frigium) from the papal stable master (major strator) and crowned the pope. Once crowned, the pope then made his return to the Lateran in a cavalcade across the city, surrounded by the jubilation of the crowd. When they reached the palace, the cardinal priests descended their mounts before the pope, received his benediction, and intoned the customary laud. The judges did the same and accompanied the pope-elect to the palace, where he offered every prior of every order "with his own hand" (propria manu) the "due and customary presbytery."[148] The priors of the basilicas received double.[149]

The different stages of the ritual must be analyzed one by

one. Only in this way can we attempt to grasp the elements of ritual humbling that were meant to remind the pope of the mortality of his physical person, and of the transience of the power that had been entrusted to him at the moment of his election as Roman pontiff.

Sedes Stercorata

The stone seat located in front of the portico of the Lateran Basilica was defined in the ceremonial books we looked at earlier with an unusual name: bedunged *(stercorata* or *stercoraria).* The name does not seem to derive from popular sources. Rather, the ceremonial books copy out in its entirety the passage from the first book of Samuel (1 Sam. 2: 8), which declares that God "raises up the poor from the dust; he lifts the needy from the ash heap, to make them sit with princes, and inherit a seat of honor" *(Suscitat de pulvere egenum, et de stercore erigit pauperem, ut sedeat cum principibus et solium generale teneat).*[150] The biblical words "the needy from the ash heap" *(de stercore pauperem)* were already present in the eighty-fifth formula of the ancient day book *(Liber diurnus),* with which the new pope announced his own election.[151]

Was use of the seat a longstanding custom? It is hard to say. But certainly the biblical verse reappears in the sources, after long centuries of silence, precisely around the middle of the twelfth century. An English chronicler applied it to his compatriot, Adrian IV (1154–59), in a manner that echoes the rhetoric of humility that Saint Bernard had directed at Eugenius III.[152] The coincidence should be noted, for it may be indicative of the theme's emerging contemporary relevance, and certainly does not contradict the fact that the first explicit reference to the *sedes stercorata* ("bedunged seat") figures, as we have seen, in the late twelfth-century ceremonials of Albinus, Cencius, and others.

The significance of this symbol of humility, perhaps the most radical symbol ever applied to the Roman pontiff (by means of the connection between the seat and the word *stercus,* meaning dung, mud, filth, and even excrement), is obvious.[153] Having reached the summit of grandeur and wealth, the pope was obliged to recall his basic human condition and to humble himself.[154] Thus had done Abraham when he was admitted to "full colloquy" with God. Peter Damian had reminded Pope Alexander II of this in *De brevitate*. At the same time, the ritual effected a religious transformation of the newly elected pope, who could now occupy the throne of glory.[155]

The *sedes stercorata* stood on a marble base of the same period (or not much later), carved in high relief with serpents, lions, and dragons, images that were "a clear reference to the high medieval symbolism of the royal throne" that, inspired by a biblical passage, presented the sovereign as "the conqueror of monsters." [156] It was no accident that the London codex counted the *sedes stercorata* among the "imperial" thrones, and indeed compared it to those of porphyry.[157] It established a contrast between papal humility and the regal nature of the papal office.

The pope did not seat himself alone on the *sedes stercorata,* but was conducted there "with honor by the cardinals." The gesture reflected their exclusive right to elect the pope that had been sanctioned by the decree on papal elections of 1059.[158] By accompanying the pope to the bedunged seat in this manner, the cardinals ritually inserted themselves into the delicate balance of forces that always underlies the relationship between mortality and institutional continuity. Seen in this sense, the analogy with the papal rite of the ashes is perfect.[159]

Sitting and Lying

And what of the porphyry chairs? Did they possess features symbolizing mortality as well?

It should be noted at the outset that the name used by Albinus and Cencius, *porphireticae,* indicates that these two chairs were believed to be made of porphyry—the imperial marble par excellence—because "they have the same rosy color as porphyry." [160] In reality, the chairs were made of a kind of marble called "ancient red" *(rosso antico),* one that was nonetheless considered to be among the most precious and esteemed, and which had been in use in Rome since the time of the republic.[161] The form of the seat bottoms themselves, which the *Vita* of

Honorius II had already likened to the shape of the Greek sigma, made them resemble the seats of the public baths, which in all likelihood had originated at the nearby spas.[162]

The two "porphyry" chairs set before the Lateran palace constituted a sort of double throne. In Byzantium, as well, the imperial throne in the hall of the Consistory, elevated as it was by small porphyry steps and covered by a canopy suspended from columns, was really a double throne. On business days the emperor, dressed in gold, sat on the right; on high feast days he sat on the left, dressed in purple as a sign of the holiday's greater solemnity. For other official ceremonies two thrones were placed next to each other. That in which the emperor sat was the throne of Arcadius, while the "empty throne" was that of Constantine.[163]

In the *Vita* of Paschal II the chairs were still defined as "curial," a term that in ancient Rome had been used to designate the "thrones" of high magistrates. In Honorius II's *Vita,* instead, they are described as having the shape of the uncial letter sigma *(sygma)*—identical, therefore, to those of "porphyry."[164] That the transition from curial chairs to "porphyry" thrones was a feature of the *imitatio imperii* is confirmed by a fact having to do with their monumental character. Traditionally, when the pope celebrated the liturgical rites in the stational churches of Rome, he sat either on a portable seat (a cathedra or faldstool), placed in the atrium or in front of the church, or in the marble seat in the church's apse. On May 6, 1123, Alphanus, the treasurer for Pope Calixtus II and the principal negotiator of the Concordat of Worms, donated to the church of Saint Mary in Cosmedin a papal throne that he had had "restored." To an old marble seat, an imitation of a Roman magistrate's *(sella curialis),* had been added lions' paws at the fore of the armrests, taken from the ancient seat of a magistrate or even of a monarch. The "restoration" produced a kind of conflation between the magistrate's chair and the marble seat of state *(solium),* the model for which is to be found in the biblical image of Solomon's throne, "the only one that might permit a distinction between the traditional forms of the faldstool and the seat of state *[solium],* both of which could refer either to the person of the emperor or to a bishop." The throne in Saint Mary in Cosmedin "expresses the notion of imperial authority *[imperium]*" and "is an unmistakable symbol of the monarchic aspirations of the papacy," although we should not overlook the influence of the marble seat in Saint Peter's at the Vatican, decorated with two lions.[165]

ℰ

To the newly elected pope, seated on the porphyry chair to the right, the prior of the basilica of Saint Lawrence in Palazzo, from which depended the *Sancta Sanctorum,* presented the papal *ferula* and the keys. The *ferula,* a shepherd's crook different from the pastoral staffs of bishops, was noted as a papal insignia for the first time by Liutprand in his account of the deposition of Pope Benedict V at the Roman synod of 964: the pope removed his pallium and handed over the *ferula* that he was holding, which his rival in turn broke in half to signify that Benedict was no longer pope.[166] According to the *Vita* of Paschal II, the newly elected pope held the *ferula* while sitting on both these seats. "Already lord," he brought "to completion the rite of election as he by turns sat and walked about in the various parts of the palace reserved to the Roman popes alone."[167] The *ferula* was thus a symbol of power linked to the ceremony of taking possession of the palace. Albinus and Cencius also defined the *ferula* as a "sign of rulership and correction" *(regiminis et correctionis).* But the pope returned it when he moved to another seat. Thus, he was no longer holding it when he proceeded into the palace.[168] So also, the keys were no longer merely those "of the basilica and Lateran palace," since, as Albinus and Cencius put it, "the power of closing and opening, of binding and loosing, was given specially to Peter, the first of the apostles and, through him, to all the Roman pontiffs." Clearly referring to Matthew 18: 18, the keys, which until then had symbolized possession of the Lateran Palace, now bore the symbolic weight of apostolicity.

ℰ

Seated on the porphyry chair to the left, the pope-elect received a series of objects, presented as though symbolically concatenated. From a cincture hung a purse containing twelve precious stones and some musk. The cincture alluded to chastity and innocence of life. The purse represented the treasure *(gazofilacium)* that allowed the pope to be "the servant of the poor and of widows." The twelve seals symbolized the apostles. The original model was imperial: the Roman-Germanic *Pontifical* comments fully on the long passage of Exodus (28: 17–18), in which the twelve precious stones of the papal vestment stand for the twelve tribes of Israel.[169] The musk was added "to gather the aroma" of which the apostle had spoken (2 Cor. 2: 15, 16): "For we are in the aroma of Christ."[170] The newly elected pope must be "in the aroma of Christ" *(Christi bonus odor)*—that is, representing in his person the aroma of Christ's doctrine.[171] Purse, seals, and musk hung from the pope's girding cincture, as though to say that chastity and innocence of life were the indispensable prerequisites for the exercise of his new apostolic office.

℃

On another point, the *ordines* of Albinus and Cencius, and the Basel and London codices, are in complete agreement: the pope must "sit" and "seem to lie" on both chairs, or rather, first on the one to the right, then on that to the left.[172] He must sit as though lying between two biers *(lectuli)*. The seating of the pope on "porphyry-like" chairs at the entrance of the Lateran Palace was therefore a gesture located between two interpretive poles, and which had to represent both in a sequence that amounted to a distinct simultaneity.[173] Its funereal overtones were evoked by the image of the biers to which the ceremonial books refer. Even the author of the *Vita* of Leo X (1049–54) had deployed the image of "the bed on which he lay" *(lectulum in quo jacebat)* to describe the position of the dying pope.[174]

And further: the juxtaposition of the gesture of *sitting* on the throne and of *lying* in the tomb is present in Lothar of Segni's *De miseria conditionis humanae.* Referring to the powerful, the young cardinal warned: "He who once sat proudly on the throne now lies prostrate in the tomb."[175]

This is the sequence foreseen by the ceremonials of Albinus and Cencius for the "porphyry" chairs in the third and last phase of the pope's possession-taking of the Lateran Palace, and it is also that which, more than those that preceded it, was girded by the lofty symbolism of apostolicity and the *imitatio imperii.* To sit and to lie on chairs defined for the occasion as couches or biers *(lectuli)* were gestures that simultaneously signified a rite of passage to the apostolicity of the papal office (the primacy of Peter and the preaching of Paul), and a ritual anticipation of the death of the newly elected pope himself. The pope was thus born and died with the apostles.

ẽ

Two other innovations that can be traced to the twelfth century should now be considered. They line up perfectly with the two gestures—sitting and lying—presented to us by the Lateran rite of possession-taking.

In the centuries-long history of the lead seal that was traditionally hung by a hemp or silk cord from papal letters produced in the chancery, an important transformation occurred around 1100. The custom of placing images of the apostles Peter and Paul on the front *(recto)* of these seals goes back in fact to the pontificate of Paschal II (1099–1118). The portraits of the apostles were inscribed between a cross and the letters SPA (Saint Paul *[Sanctus Paulus]*) and SPE (Saint Peter *[Sanctus Petrus]*). On the back *(verso)* appeared the pope's name, written in its nominative Latin form with the appropriate Roman numeral. The papal seal, or bull, had thus attained a definitive form that remained practically unaltered down to modern times.[176] The mold of the lead seal associated the (name of the) pope with the images of the apostles Peter and Paul, thereby underlining the apostolic authority of the papal office: the pope *sat* among the apostles. Paschal II's pontificate is particularly important for our purposes because, as we have seen, his *Vita* in the *Liber pontificalis* is the oldest source that describes the elements of the ceremony of the pope's installation at the Lateran.[177]

Two or three generations later, in the second half of the twelfth century, we encounter a new legend in the sources, centered on the *bodies* of the apostles Peter and Paul. In the *Description of the Vatican Basilica (Descriptio basilicae Vaticanae)* that the canon Petrus Mallius wrote for Pope Alexander III, there appears an entirely new account: the Altar of the Confession in the Vatican preserved not only the body of Peter, but that of Paul as well.[178] This new view is important, for according to the most ancient traditions the bodies of the apostles Peter and Paul had been deposited in the basilicas dedicated to their respective memories, Saint Peter's in the Vatican, and Saint Paul's outside the Walls. The biography dedicated to Pope Cornelius (251–53) in the old and venerable *Liber pontificalis* recounts that their burials were taken care of by a certain matron named Lucina, who had "raised by night" the apostles' bodies from the catacombs.[179]

The legend was taken up again in 1192 by another canon of Saint Peter's, Romanus, who added an additional element: at the altar of Saints Peter and Paul, located before the Altar of the Confession in the Vatican, "had been weighed the precious bones" of the apostles Peter and Paul.[180] The coincidence—thematic as well as chronological—between a legend that assigned such great importance to the bones of the Roman apostles and the symbolism that can be discerned in the rite of the two Lateran chairs is unmistakable. In the rite of the pope's possession-taking of the Lateran, described by Albinus and Cencius (1189, 1192), was the newly elected pope not perhaps meant to sit between the two "porphyry" chairs representing the apostles Peter and Paul as if he were lying between two biers?[181]

The king of France also had to perform a gesture at his coronation that resembles that called for in the papal rite of taking possession of the Lateran. According to the *ordo* of Charles V (1364), indeed, the prince "who is to be crowned king must present himself seated and almost lying on a bed prepared for the occasion" *(sedentem et quasi jacentem supra thalamum).*[182]

The differences between the two gestures—pontifical and regal—are noteworthy nonetheless. The king arose, or rather, was born anew after being found "almost laid out." The active role of the king consisted in his rising up rather than lying down. In the royal French *ordo,* the gesture amounted to an inverted funeral rite: "The king's rising is not that of a cadaver headed for its final rest, but that of a body being reborn to new life."[183] The pope, instead, lay down as though he were *reposing (accumbat)* among the apostles.

Between the royal and papal gestures of reclining there exists the same difference as that between the famous saying "the king never dies" and the concept according to which "even the pope dies." The king has two bodies, the pope does not have two bodies.[184] The pope is born and *dies* in the apostles Peter and Paul.

ẽ

The final phases of the possession-taking of the Lateran confirmed the apostolicity of the person of the pope-elect and his
approach to Christ. Indeed, he entered the chapel of the *Sancta
Sanctorum* alone to adore Christ's relics.

    The archdeacon and prior of the basilica accompanied him
"along the entire portico under the icons of the apostles who
arrived by sea, though brought by no man," up "to the doors of
the most sacred basilica of Saint Lawrence that is called the *Sancta
Sanctorum.*" Albinus and Cencius recount that entering alone
"into the basilica, the pope-elect remains long in prayer before
his own special altar." The Basel *ordo* is more explicit: in the basilica of Saint Lawrence "there is the holy altar at which nobody
dares sing mass except the Roman pontiff, for hidden *(recondita)*
there are the umbilical cord and the Circumcision of the infant
our lord Jesus Christ with the milk of his mother in a golden
cross decorated with precious stones." [185] The *Descriptio Lateranensis Ecclesiae* also reports, already in the first version (written
just shortly after 1073), that in one of the "coffers is conserved a
cross of purest gold . . . in the center of which are the umbilical
cord and the foreskin of the Circumcision of Christ; the cross is
anointed with balsam, and every year the ointment is renewed
on the day of the Exaltation of the Holy Cross [September 14],
when the pope and the cardinals go in procession from Saint
Lawrence to the basilica of the Savior, called Constantiniana." [186]

ẽ

Roughly twenty years after Gregory X's (1272–73) ceremonial
book, Cardinal Jacopo Stefaneschi, an eyewitness to the coronation of Boniface VIII, celebrated in Rome on January 23–24,
1295, recorded the humbling significance of the Lateran chairs:
the pope ascended to the threshold of Peter "taken from the
ashes" *(de stercore sumptus)* and "born of dust" *(de pulvere nactus)*. [187]
During the papacy's sojourn at Avignon, the Lateran chairs were
not used because they had been left behind in Rome. That explains why the *Ordo XIV* and other fourteenth-century ceremonial texts never discuss them. [188] Agostino Patrizi Piccolomini
(1484–92) described the Lateran rite anew, but associated the

reclining position that the pope was to assume with the *sedes ster-corata,* rather than with the porphyry chairs.[189] Was this simply an error, or does it reflect complete incomprehension of the rite itself? According to Johann Burchard, on the other hand, Innocent VIII (1484–92) "stretched out" across each of the chairs: "Then the pope was led to the entrance of the chapel of Saint Sylvester, where two draped porphyry chairs had been placed. The pope sat down or, rather, he almost lay down, on the one on the right . . . ; then he got up from the aforesaid chair and moved toward the one on the left, where he again stretched out in the same manner."[190] Such a description agrees with the *ordines* of Albinus and Cencius, but offers no further interpretation of the symbolism. Whatever the case, the now definitive triumph of the coronation ceremony precipitated an inarrestable decline in the Lateran ceremony of possession, and an ever greater incomprehension of its symbolic significance. That explains, among other things, Leo X's (1513) decision to abandon the *sedes stercorata* entirely.[191]

ॐ

We have thus reached the end of a long ritual and rhetorical *iter* on the themes of the pope's physical mortality and the transience of power, which it is necessary to summarize, and to which we must address new questions.

1. First of all, we must ask ourselves whether it was right to choose Peter Damian's *De brevitate* as our point of departure. It seems that it was.

The monk from Fonte Avellana was the first to write about the ashes of the dead and about burning the flax, of humility and mortality, in a treatise that, moreover, was addressed to a sovereign pontiff. His discussion was original and amounted to a real discovery of the corporeity of the pope, understood in his specificity. Damian brought to light an institutional problem of enormous dimensions: the pope's bodiliness was a source of potential weakness (in life as well as death), but the same corporeity could also be an example for all Christians.

2. History proved him right. The rule of "Peter's years" retained its historical validity down to the nineteenth century, and

it was never forgotten. Since the eleventh century, every unusually long pontificate has required some justification in terms of the divine. Thus it was for Paschal II (1099–1118), Alexander III (1159–81) and even for Pius VI, who died in 1799. For the antipope Benedict XIII, the fact that he had "reigned" longer than Saint Peter provided grounds for his subsequent condemnation. Urban VIII (1623–44) was obliged to note that the legend of "Peter's years" was not an article of faith. But in 1871, when Pius IX celebrated the first twenty-five years of his pontificate, and thus reached "Peter's years" for the first time in the history of the papacy, commemorative plaques were put up in numerous Roman basilicas.

3. The speed with which, only a few decades after Damian's *De brevitate,* the theme of the pope's physical mortality and the transience of his power became ensconced in the Roman liturgy, and in authoritative sources such as the *Liber pontificalis,* is remarkable. Within a few decades, the Roman liturgy was endowed with a rich ritual apparatus centered on humbling the pope-elect. In the first ceremonial book of the post-Gregorian Roman church, Benedict's *Ordo XI* (1143–45), the pope's physical mortality was in fact at the center of three rites: the papyrus dipped in candle wax, the ash ceremony, and burning the flax. As we have been able to observe, the ceremonies of the ashes and the flax were adopted at Rome no earlier than 1064 (in the case of the flax) and 1091 (in the case of the ashes). But even the rite of the Lateran chairs, at least those features concerning mortality and transience, goes back no earlier than the last decades of the eleventh century. Only in the case of the papyrus pillow, for which there exists, moreover, only a single reference (that of Benedict), do we lack notices permitting us to date its adoption at the papal curia. Thus, all the papal ceremonials of the twelfth century devote considerable space to the humbling of the pope. This was a ritual program that embraced the entire span of the pope's life, from his election (taking possession of the Lateran) to his death (the papyrus cushion), and which was annually renewed on three liturgical occasions of special solemnity (Christmas, Ash Wednesday, and Easter) that were celebrated in Rome's three leading basilicas (Saint Peter's, Saint John Lateran, and Santa Maria Maggiore).

4. The rapid adoption of a ritual program concerning a theme that at first sight would scarcely seem flattering to the ruling pope requires an explanation.

Paradoxically, part of the answer is provided by the structure of the ritual of papal humbling itself: it emerged, in fact, not as a means of weakening, but of reinforcing, the institution of the papacy. It featured a rhetoric and rituality aimed at illustrating "that which is above," the superiority and universality of the papal office, by highlighting "that which is below," mortality and transience.[192] Let us not forget that Damian addressed his letter to Pope Alexander II on the eve of his victory over his rival for the papacy, Cadalus. In it, he affirmed that insofar as the pope was a man, he was destined to die; but inasmuch as he was a pope, he was the "universal bishop, prince of emperors, and king of kings" (universus episcopus, princeps imperatorum, rex regum), and "superior in honor and dignity to all those living in the flesh."

It is therefore in this apparent contradiction between the notions of physical mortality on the one hand, and the papacy's universality and supremacy on the other, that it seems we can locate the interpretive key to that complex rhetorical and ritual discourse on papal humbling that we have reconstructed from the eleventh century forward.

It was no accident that the ritual of the pope's humbling became fixed in Roman ceremonial customs at the same time that the papacy was embarking upon the imitatio imperii, a historical development with broad implications that assumed particular intensity from precisely the mid–eleventh century onward. The ritualization of mortality and transience established a counterweight to the imperial regality of the Roman pontiff, who was becoming ever more the "true emperor" (verus imperator). The sepulcher of Pope Sylvester II acquired its monitory role in contrast to the desire of a series of popes to be entombed, like emperors, in porphyry sarcophagi. In this instance, the contrast between mortality and power was reinforced by elements of an even magical nature, such as the sweating tomb and the rumbling bones of a dead pope. In the ritual of burning the flax, the pope-elect's role became passive relative to the growing importance assumed by the ceremony of papal coronation: only his assumption of a passive role could effect a perfect opposition between transience and the regality of the papal office. The examples could be multiplied. Thus, by the late fifteenth century, when the rite of taking possession of the Lateran had lost its original symbolic force, the coronation in the Vatican brought together the concepts both of transience and of mortality that had infused the Lateran chairs with ritual significance. Besides submitting to the traditional rite of burning the flax, the pope now had to visit the sepulchers of the deceased pontiffs as well.

5. Peter Damian's letter has led us to reconstruct a surprising rhetorical and ritual evolution centered on the person of the pope in his human dimension. Above all, we have seen the emergence of a rhetoric of "the brevity of life of the Roman popes," based on an undeniable historical fact: in the first millennium of the history of the papacy, no pope had ever ruled longer than the first pope, Saint Peter. Two avenues of ritual development then opened up before our eyes: they concern the themes of the pope's mortality, and of the transience of the power entrusted to him. For the papacy in the last centuries of the Middle Ages, brevity of life, mortality, and transience were all elements of a single dispensation. Each of these characteristics concerned the pope in his corporeity and humanity, even if they did not address his physical body in exactly the same way.

This imposing ritual travail was nurtured for the most part within the papal institution itself, and was fed by the constant and sustained attention of the "technical experts": the roles played by the canon Benedict, the compilers of the ceremonial books of the late twelfth century, Albinus and Cencius, and all those who codified in writing the various gestures and procedures, were decisive. Through their writings, innovations, and textual emphases, they assured that, rather than fading away, the ritual of humbling the popes was continually updated to accommodate new situations and circumstances.

Authoritative voices often intervened from outside the curia. Bernard of Clairvaux, mendicant writers like Antoninus of Florence and Sanchez de Arévalo, even chroniclers far from Rome like Robert of Torigny, contributed to keeping the rhetoric of mortality and transience alive. The sources that tell us about Sylvester II's warning sepulcher are English.

At this point one conclusion emerges on its own: the themes of the pope's physical mortality, and the transience of his power, concern the whole church, because the (body of the) pope belongs to the church universal. From this point of view as well, Peter Damian's intuition turns out to have been historically rich and exact.

6. The ritualization of such delicate concepts also provoked resistance from individual popes. The history of the ceremony of the ashes has appeared to us deeply marked by the ongoing quest to strike a balance between the ritual expression of the pope's physical mortality and respect for the lofty office he filled. At Rome, the rite of burning flax was not immediately embraced in the manner of Byzantium, but was put in a liturgical setting, in accordance with a twice-yearly calendric cycle (rather than thrice-yearly, as at Besançon), and the role of the pope was long exclusively active.[193] Funeral bones and marble stones were never presented to a pope. John the Deacon kept silent about Sylvester II's warning tomb, though he seems to have known about it.

An interesting case was noted by an anonymous ceremonialist and eyewitness. As we have seen, on Ash Wednesday, 1303, Boniface VIII accepted the ablution of the hands from the first of the cardinal bishops, but he does not appear to have received the imposition of the ashes. If this was the case, the pope indeed performed a rite of purification but not of mortality, while avoiding, moreover, a ritual submission to the representative of the College of Cardinals.[194]

That Boniface may have maintained a certain calculated impertinence concerning the rite of ashes is indicated by an anecdote recorded with a wealth of detail by the author of the *Annals of Genoa (Annales Genuenses)*. There we read that one Ash Wednesday the archbishop-elect of Genoa, Porchetto Spinola (1299–1321) of the Order of Friars Minor, finding himself in Rome, wished to receive the ashes from the pope. But rather than place them on his head, as the rite prescribed, Boniface threw the ashes in his eyes, justifying his action with a parody of the ritual's words: "Remember that you are a Ghibelline, and thus you will return to the ashes of the Ghibellines."[195] Boniface indeed stripped the archbishop of his office in the belief that Spinola had offered hospitality to his most bitter rivals, the Colonna cardinals. If the story is true, it shows that Boniface VIII ascribed a humbling significance to the ashes that was more political than religious, and for this reason, perhaps, tried to avoid the ceremony himself on Ash Wednesday, 1303.

7. Peter Damian had warned: the life and death of a pope are and must be a model for all Christians. Not only by the brevity of his life, but also by its exemplarity, a pope distinguishes himself from other sovereigns. In a pope, what counts is his complete humanity, including not only his mortal condition as a man, but also the perfection of his life. This is why in ancient Rome the sacred verbena boughs placed under the head of the deceased were an instrument of divinity, while in the analogous papal ceremony the papyrus dipped in candle wax was preserved until the pope's death, after having been "kissed with pious devotion" by him. The body of the pope was a body that transformed itself (it is born and dies apostolic, holy, and blessed) while retaining at the same time its own physicality (mortality).

The pope was different from other sovereigns because his power was of a double nature, temporal and spiritual. And from this arises another question: in the centuries that concern us, did the Roman church devote the same rhetorical and ritual attention to the purity of the pope's life as it did to the themes of mortality and transience? Are there not here as well basic issues for the history of the pope's body, deriving precisely from the particular nature of the papal office?

To address these new problems, we must turn briefly from the physicality of the pope to consider instead the historical evolution of his institutional role.

2 *Persona Christi*

Vicarius Christi

As we have seen repeatedly, Peter Damian, in his treatise *De brevitate* (1064), had defined the pope as the "universal bishop," "superior in honor and dignity to all those who live in the flesh," "king of kings," and "prince of emperors." Two years earlier, in his *Synodal Disquisition (Disceptatio synodalis),* he had expressed the hope that the "sublime persons" of king and pope might be conjoined in such a way that henceforth "the king shall be in the Roman pontiff, and the pope in the king."[1] This amounted to an appeal for reciprocal understanding between pope and emperor: "wrapped up in the divine mystery" and "almost incorporating each in the other," they were called upon to cooperate "in the divine example of the two powers—that is, of Christ."[2] At the same time, the papal person was inheriting a rich regal symbolism of a Christly nature.

Damian was also the first to apply the title *Vicarius Christi* ("Vicar of Christ") to the pope. Until then it had been reserved to the emperor as God's representative on earth.[3] In 1057 he wrote to Victor II (1055−57) that Christ told the pope personally that he had instituted him to be his vicar.[4]

Bernard of Clairvaux still used the title *Vicarius Petri* ("Vicar of Peter") in his letters to Pope Innocent II (1130−43) and in his writings prior to 1147. But after Eugenius III's (1145−53) ascent to the pontificate, he opted for *Vicarius Christi,* thus contributing to the title's historical affirmation. In his *De consideratione (On Consideration)* Bernard went further: Christ had designated one universal vicar, the pope.[5] An ancient tradition was thus broken. Until then, the title *Vicarius Christi* had been applied as well to other bishops and even to lay princes.

Elaborating on the notion, which was in fact quite recent, Bernard turned to a new corporal metaphor: "Let us now investigate as carefully as possible who you are and what person you temporarily represent in God's Church."[6] His response is in effect a long list of titles, which he applied to the pope in a crescendo that culminated with Christ: "You are a great priest, the supreme pontiff; you are the first of the bishops, the descendant of the apostles; for preeminence you are Abel, for government Noah, for the patriarchiate you are Abraham, for order Melchisadech, for dignity you are Aron, for authority Moses, for jurisdiction you are Samuel, for power Peter, and by anointment you are Christ."[7] In his capacity as pope, it is Eugenius's task to "arrange the members of the body of Christ," a "body that Paul himself describes to you in his truly apostolic language, applying it with marvelous harmony to the head."[8] Already, in 1130, to defend the legitimacy of "his" pope, Innocent II, and to denounce the actions of Innocent's rival, the legate Anacletus II (1130–38), Bernard had deployed a bodily image of tremendous christological power: Innocent II was the true pope because he was made of "the bones of his [Christ's] bones, and the flesh of his flesh."[9]

The influence of the abbot of Clairvaux was immediate. The title *Vicarius Christi* became a part of the language of the papal chancery during the pontificate of the first Cistercian pope, Eugenius III.[10] Huguccio of Pisa justified applying the title exclusively to the pope by asserting that "only the pope can be called Vicar of Christ, if one considers the authority that Christ gave to him alone."[11] At the end of the twelfth century, Innocent III (1198–1216) reserved the title *Vicarius Christi* exclusively to the office of the Roman pontiff and, taking up Bernard's metaphor, used it to bind the pope even more tightly to Christ by declaring: "the pope is him who is called upon to bear or to 'represent' [*gerere*] the person of Christ."[12]

Regality

Innocent III was perhaps the first pope to express his views on the limits that the physical dimension of his human nature placed on his actions as pope. His condition as a man belonged to a "state or order [that] we cannot increase."[13] The pope's humanity seemed to constitute the only limit on the fullness of his power. It was the physical and natural limits of his human condition that justified, according to Innocent, the dispatch of papal legates throughout Christendom.[14] He used an identical argument to explain as well the bishops' participation in the pope's fullness of power.[15]

With the ascent of Innocent III, the "fullness of power" *(plenitudo potestatis)* became a technical term used to define papal sovereignty.[16] Paralleling this development, the pope supported the concept with references to the corporal metaphor of the pope as head *(caput)* of the church:[17] "Just as in the human body the head alone possesses the fullness of the senses, in such a way that the other members participate in its plenitude, so also in the ecclesiastical body the other bishops are called the 'solicitous part' *[pars sollecitudinis],* while the sovereign pontiff alone assumes the fullness of power."[18] In the course of his pontificate, Innocent's declarations became ever more precise: "Peter is the only one who was called to enjoy the fullness of power. From him I received the miter of my priesthood and the crown of my royalty; he has established me vicar of Him upon whose habit it is written: 'King of kings and lord of lords, priest for eternity according to the order of Melchisedech.'"[19] The Christly origin of the pope's royalty was a key argument. After referring to Peter, the pope then spoke about papal royalty in the first person. Christ was the "king of kings and lord of lords" *(rex regum et dominus dominantium).*[20] Innocent IV (1243–54) also cited Christ's royalty to explain the succession of powers that God had used to govern men: "Until the time of Noah, God governed alone; he did so with ministers after the time of Noah, who was not a priest but performed priestly duties. The same was true of all those who succeeded to the governance of the Hebrews. This lasted until the time of Christ, who by right of birth was our King and Lord. Christ governs through his vicar, the pope."[21]

Ubi Papa, ibi Roma

According to a very ancient tradition, bishops were obliged to travel to Rome to carry out a visit *ad limina* ("at the threshold") of the tomb of the apostles Peter and Paul. The long-standing association of the words *ad limina* with the apostles began to shift around the middle of the twelfth century.[22] The transformation followed the same chronology of development that led, in the pope's case, to the abandonment of the title *Vicarius Petri* in favor of *Vicarius Christi.*

Gratian recorded the bishops' obligation to make an *ad limina* visit and highlighted its predominantly religious character (*reverentia,* reverence).[23] But in the *Summa* of Rufinus (1157–59), the religious act of visiting the tombs of the apostles had already been replaced by a visit to the pope, to whom the bishops were obliged to pay their respects *(reverentia).*[24] Rufinus's thought was quickly taken up by other important canonists. According to Stephen of Tournai (after 1160), the bishops were obligated to visit the church of Rome once a year.[25] Again, around 1160, the anonymous author of the *Summa Parisiensis (Paris Summa)* emphasized the fact that the bishops must carry out their annual visit—to the Roman curia—in communion with the pope.[26] In place of the tombs of the apostles the *Summa Parisiensis* thus substituted a juridical abstraction, the Roman curia.[27] A further definitive step was taken by Huguccio in his commentary on Gratian's *Decrees* (*Decretum,* 1188–91). By *limina,* he understood "also the Roman curia, wherever it may be."[28] Wherever it may be: in other words, wherever the pope is. The pope was the Roman curia.

Innocent III does not seem to have commented on the issue. Speaking of Peter, however, he located the papal office in a universal framework that was also spatial in nature: "Peter presides over all things in fullness and in breadth: he is indeed the vicar of Him to whom belongs the earth and all that it contains, and all who live upon it."[29] In the course of his pontificate, the identification between the person of the pope and Rome came to extend well beyond the narrow confines envisioned by the canonists. Arriving in 1207 at Viterbo, the neighboring city that in those days regularly hosted the Roman curia, Abbot Andreus Guglielmus declared: "I arrived at Viterbo and found myself in Rome!"[30] Several decades later Lyons, the city to which Innocent IV traveled in 1245 to hold a council, came to embrace "half of the faithful, arrived from every part of the world"; in other words, "another Rome" *(Roma altera).* The expression comes from Innocent's own biographer, Niccolò of Calvi.[31]

Following on what Huguccio had confirmed, Sinibaldo Fieschi (the future Pope Innocent IV) established an even more explicit identification between the *limina* and the whereabouts of the pope. By the phrase *ad limina* of the apostles, he meant "where the pope is" *(ubi papa est)*.[32] No one before him had gone so far. A few years later, Hostiensis (d. 1271) would coin a maxim on the subject, destined to become famous: *"ubi papa, ibi Roma"* ("where the pope is, there is Rome").[33] While he was still a professor at Paris, Hostiensis advanced an analogous argument in his *Golden Summary (Summa aurea)* (1253), taking as his starting point the ceremony of conferring on bishops the pallium for their offices, which was traditionally held at the altar of Saint Peter in the Vatican Basilica. The cardinal deacon or a subdeacon of the Roman church took the pallium "from the body of blessed Peter," or rather, from the niche called, in fact, "of the palliums," and placed it on the tomb of the apostle. According to Hostiensis, such a ceremony need not necessarily be celebrated in Rome, but could be held "wherever the pope may be." He gave two reasons. First of all, "because it is not where Rome is that there is the pope, but the contrary."[34] Second, because "it is not the place that sanctifies the man, but the man the place."[35] This latter image had been created by Gratian to indicate that it was personal piety, and not the office, that rendered its occupant holy.[36] As Hostiensis developed the argument, Gratian's notion was transformed to support the idea that it was no longer Rome, but the person—holy—of the pope that was the institution's spatial point of reference. *Ubi papa, ibi Roma.*

All this reveals an ability to express a variety of institutional developments and curial realities in abstract formulas: the continual and indeed forced evolution of the papacy throughout the second half of the twelfth century; the rise of the curia as the seat of administration and government of the church universal in the last decades of the century; a tighter ecclesiological relationship between the bishops of Christendom and the universal church; and the unchallenged universality of the papacy. Above all, the abstraction was supported by a total absorption of the Roman church into the person of the pope.

Hostiensis's metaphor would eventually serve to justify the papal residency at Avignon. According to Augustinus Triumphus (1270–1328), the pope "does not need to reside in a specified place, for he is the vicar of Him whose seat is heaven, and whose footrest is earth" (Isa. 66: 1).[37] For Alvarus Pelagius (1332), it was the Christly foundation of papal authority that legitimized the temporary rupture of the tie between the pope and Rome: "the church is the mystical body of Christ and the community of Catholics . . . it is not bound by the walls of a city [or, of Rome] . . . the mystical body of Christ is there wherever its head is, that is, the pope."[38]

Christ had not conferred his jurisdiction and power either upon a place or upon Rome, but upon Peter and his successors.[39] Thus for Baldus de Ubaldus: "where the pope is, there is Rome, Jerusalem, Mount Zion, and the common homeland."[40] The pope's person represented the universality of the church even in its spatial dimensions.

Pars Corporis Pape

In his *De consideratione,* Bernard of Clairvaux describes the institutional intimacy between pope and cardinals in physical terms of health and disease: "We come now to those who are at your side *[collaterales],* to those who help you *[coadiutores].* These never leave you, they are your intimates. Therefore, if they are good, you are the first to profit from their abilities, just as you are also the first to suffer from their defects if they are bad. You would be wrong to imagine yourself in good health if your sides hurt."[41] According to John of Salisbury, too, Eugenius III was "aware of the malady at his sides; in fact, this is how he used to refer to his aids and counselors."[42] But the image did not catch on, perhaps because it came into competition with that of the figure of the legate "bound to the side" *(legatus a latere)* of the pope, which was already an accepted term in the diplomatic and chancery language of the Roman church.

In 1167 John of Salisbury referred to the cardinal legate Pietro of Pavia as a "member of the Roman church" *(membrum Ecclesiae Romanae)* understood as a body.[43] The metaphor reappears in Otto of Freising's *Deeds of the Emperor Frederick I (Gesta Friderici I imperatoris),* in which the cardinals are portrayed as the "highest members" *(summa membra),* who must not detach themselves "from their head," the pope.[44] Imperceptibly, however, Otto places the term "member" *(membrum)* (meaning the cardinals), in relationship not to the "Roman church" *(Ecclesia Romana),* but to the pope. The cardinals make a *body (corpus)* with the pope. For the papal biographer Boso, as well, the cardinals "adhere to their head like members of his body *(membra sui corporis).*[45]

Innocent III was the first pope to use this corporal metaphor. In a letter of August 1198, he calls the cardinals "members of our body" *(membra corporis nostri)* and exclaims: "we are all [pope and cardinals] one body in Christ."[46] The phrase has biblical origins. Had Saint Paul not perhaps said that "we are members of his [Christ's] body"?[47] But the apostle's phrase embraced all Christians. The Innocentian formula instead created a double identification that applied exclusively to the hierarchy of the Roman church: the body of the pope, of which the cardinals were a part, made a body with Christ.

To the word "member" *(membrum)* the canonists preferred the formula "part of the body" *(pars corporis).* We find the first evidence of this in Bernardus Parmensis (mid–thirteenth century): "only the cardinals can be sent 'from the side of the pope' *[de latere pape],* in the strict sense of the expression, because they are called 'part of the body of the lord pope' *[pars corporis domini pape].*"[48] By the beginning of the fourteenth century, the expression "part of the pope's body" *(pars corporis pape)* was already a traditional phrase in canonistic literature.[49] The abandonment of *membrum* in favor of *pars* can be attributed to the influence of Justinian's *Code,* which defines the Roman senators as "part of the body" *(pars corporis)* of the emperor.[50] Were the cardinals not perhaps the senate of the church?

Hostiensis elaborated further on the intimate ecclesiological bond between pope and cardinals, deploying a new corporeal image: "Although the pope is head of the universal church and the faithful are his members in general, the pope is head of the cardinals in a special way, and the cardinals are his members. This body must be so united to him as not to require an oath of fealty or of obedience. He does not receive an oath from these cardinals because they are part of his viscera."[51] This new metaphor, a bit macabre, was born in the context of a culture that had discovered the physical interior of the body and the corpse, and found itself at ease there.[52] Moreover, Hostiensis carried his thought through to its conclusion: if the cardinals were "just like visceral organs to him" *(tamquam sibi inviscerati),* sick cardinals could not have blood drawn from a vein without a special papal license.[53]

Hostiensis interpreted the formula "part of the pope's body" *(pars corporis pape)* to support the jurisdictional prerogatives of the cardinalate. The cardinals were part of the pope's body because "all of the cardinals pass judgment together with the pope."[54] Even in the list of charges *(memorandum)* drawn up by the Colonna cardinals against Pope Boniface VIII, the cardinals defined themselves as "cojudges of the Roman pontiff, that is, members not only of the body of the church, but of its head."[55] All of the terms used by the Colonna cardinals were old, but not the emphasis, which was decidedly polemical.[56] The incorporation of the cardinals into the pope's person was meant to support their participation in the exercise of papal power, and to redefine their position of preeminence over the bishops. The debate may be considered, in a certain sense, to have reached its defining moment in a letter that Eugenius IV sent to Archbishop Henry Chichele of Canterbury, which was drawn from the code of canon law. In it, the pope declares that the cardinals are "the pope's assistants, and are justly called his brothers; they are 'part of his body, adjoining members of his body *[pars sui corporis, contigua sui corporis membra].*'"[57] The terms "members" *(membra)* and part *(pars),* which for centuries had separately accompanied the metaphorical incorporation of the cardinals into the person of the pope, here found themselves solemnly reunited.

Christly Visibility

Boso, Alexander III's biographer, describes the pope's triumphal return to Rome in March 1178, as follows: "Then everybody stared at his face as though it were the face of Christ, whose place on Earth he takes." It was the feast of Saint Gregory the Great preceding the fourth Sunday of Lent. The Romans greeted the pope with standards and crosses. Boso adds that "it is not recorded that this was ever done for any other Roman pontiff." Senators and magistrates, nobles and commoners held out olive branches in their hands and sang the customary lauds.[58] At the

end of the thirteenth century, during the ceremony of his coronation, Boniface VIII was preceded by a (white) horse bearing
a cross.[59] In the last decades of the fourteenth century, the cross
would be replaced by a monstrance containing the eucharistic
host.[60] Meanwhile, the tradition of sewing a cross on the pope's
ceremonial shoes had become established.[61] Even the announcement of the election of a new pope—"I announce to you the
great joy" *(Annuntio vobis gaudium magnum)*—echoed a phrase of
Saint Paul's that referred to Christ: "This is Jesus Christ whom I
announce to you."[62] Dante saw "Christ held prisoner" in Boniface VIII.[63] Alvarus Pelagius (1332) exclaimed: "Since the sovereign pontiff represents Christ and takes his place on earth, the
faithful who look at him with the eye of faith see Christ himself";[64] "the pope is indeed the successor of Adam, the first man,
and it is for this reason that God willed that the Vicar of Christ
be made, by a special office, in his image and likeness."[65] Finally,
for Antonio da Butrio (d. 1408), "That which is done by the
pope as vicar of God is interpreted as though it had been done
by God alone; the deeds of the vicar are seen as the deeds of the
Lord."[66]

Between the eleventh and the thirteenth centuries, the pope
became the unique *Vicarius Christi* as well as the *living* image of
Christ on earth.[67] And this is why, from at least the beginning
of the twelfth century onward, the manner in which the supreme pontiff celebrated the Eucharist was distinguished—even
in terms of visibility—from that of the other priests and bishops
of Christendom. To the question "Why does the Roman pontiff,
in performing Communion, observe another custom?" Lothar
of Segni, the future Innocent III, gave the following response in
his treatise *On the Sacred Mystery of the Altar (De sacro altaris mysterio):* "The Roman pontiff does not communicate where [the
bread of] the host is broken; he in fact breaks [the bread of] the
host at the altar, but communicates on the throne *[in cattedra];*
because Christ broke [the bread of] the host at Emmaus before
two disciples, but ate at Jerusalem before eleven apostles."[68] Toward the end of the century (1286) William Durant developed
Innocent's thoughts by explaining: "Being Vicar of Christ, the
supreme pontiff is the head of all those who live in the church
militant. Precisely because he represents Christ, the head of the

church, in a more perfect and solemn way, he is accustomed to communicate in a more elevated *[sublimior]* place."[69]

Infallibility

For the Anonymous of York, whose arguments, developed around 1100, constitute an essential point of departure for the reconstruction of the phenomenon of the "king's two bodies,"[70] the king was a "twinned person" *(persona geminata)* whose two parts were descended, one "from nature" *(ex natura)*, the other "from grace" *(ex gratia)*. One part resided "in his capacity as a man" *(in hominis proprietate)*, the other part "in spirit and virtue" *(in spiritu et virtute)*. In the first case, the king was "by nature an individual man" *(naturaliter individuus homo)*; in the second, he was "Christ, that is, a God-man" *(Christus, id est Deus-homo)*.[71] The king was God and Christ by grace; what he did, he did "not as a man."[72] The contrast between person and office is carried to extremes: the author went so far as to assert that even Christ, when he assumed human form, was at that time "weak."[73] For the bishops, the implications of this perspective were decidedly antihierocratic: the king in his office *(in officio)* represented both of Christ's natures; the bishop was therefore inferior to the king, because he represented Christ only in his human dimension.[74]

To the pope, the Anonymous applied a triple distinction. The pope possessed a multiplicity of *persons:* "Such a figure is not simple but multiple, and has several persons."[75] The pope:

> possesses the person of the supreme pontiff and of a man, as well as that of a homicide and of a sinner. . . . In his person as supreme pontiff he is above all men; in his human person he is their equal; in *his person as sinner* he is beneath other men. In the person of the supreme pontiff, he sins not but can remit sins; as such, he is to be venerated and honored above all other men, and to be judged by no one.[76] In his human person, even if he sins not, he cannot remit sins, and as such he must be venerated, honored, and also judged as a man. In his person as a sinner he is to be neither venerated nor honored, but judged as inferior to man. It is not in fact just to reverence and honor in the same way the apostle, the homicide,

and the adulterer, or rather, the most sacred order of the pontificate and the base crime of the homicide or the adulterer.[77]

Deploying a dialectic so radical as to give the impression
that he was engaged in a scholastic literary exercise, the English
writer wondered: is the pope the only person in the church who
must truly be obeyed? But whom should we obey? The pope as
a man or the pope in his apostolic *(apostolicus)* person? On this
point, too, the Anonymous's response reflects remarkable clarity
in terms of its distinction between physicality and office: "we
should not obey him as a man, because no such obedience is
owed to a man. Otherwise, such obedience would be due to
every man." Obedience was owed to the pope "in that he is apostolic, that is, sent by Christ."[78]

In a letter to the patriarch of Constantinople (Nov. 12, 1199),
Innocent III commented on the text of Luke 22: 32 in this manner: "And the Lord revealed that he had prayed for him, saying in the heat of passion: 'I have prayed for you, Peter, in order
that your faith may not fail and that you, once converted, will
strengthen your brothers.' This clearly means that his successors
have never deviated from the faith. . . ." According to the common view of the twelfth-century canonists, while praying that
Peter's faith should not fail, Christ had not promised Peter infallibility in the governance of the church—had Peter not perhaps
erred in his behavior toward the Jews, as Saint Paul had reminded
him (Gal. 2: 11)?—but rather for the grace of ultimate persever-
ance in the faith. But Huguccio and the twelfth-century decretists had given Christ's words a broader interpretation.[79] Identifying the person of Peter with that of the universal church, they
deduced that it was the church's faith (and not that of Peter or of
his successors) that would never fail: "'That your faith may not
fail' should be understood to mean finally and irreversibly, just
as, although he [Peter] may have failed for a time, he was afterwards made more faithful. In the person of Peter is to be understood the church, in the faith of Peter the faith of the universal
church that never fails totally, and will never fail until the day of
Judgment."[80] In his letter of 1199, Innocent III interpreted the
text from Luke more literally. And he tied together more tightly
than they had been in the past the idea that Christ, in his prayers,

had guaranteed the "indefectibility" of the faith of the universal church, and the fact that Peter and his successors had never deviated, and never would, from the catholic faith.[81]

"It is because the pope . . . is the image of Christ," observed Peter John Olivi (1295), that "some say that the pope is uncreated [increatus] and immense and unerring [impeccabilis] and infallible and omniscient like Christ."[82] The person of the supreme pontiff became the guarantor of the integrity of faith of the universal church: "It is impossible that God would concede to someone the full authority to decide doubts regarding the faith and divine law, and permit him to fall into error. And since he must not fall into error, he must be followed like a rule that never errs. And God has given this authority to the Roman pontiff."[83]

Christ's Two Natures

As the living image of Christ, the pope shared in Christ's two natures, human and divine. The argument had been used around 1100 by the Anonymous of York to define the "twin person" (persona gemina) of the king.[84] Innocent III, in a sermon given on the feast of Saints Peter and Paul, transferred it to the dignity of Peter.[85] But even here, it is necessary to await the end of the thirteenth and the beginning of the fourteenth centuries to observe how the "incorporation" of the pope into the double nature of Christ made it possible to justify the pontifical fullness of powers—that is, the spiritual and temporal power of the Vicarius Christi. Expounding on the papal power, Augustinus Triumphus (1270–1328) found there "a mixture of divine and human elements" and declared that "in the pope, power [potestas] is twofold: one—the power of orders [potestas ordinis]—is bound to the true body of Christ; the other—the power of jurisdiction and administration [potestas iurisdictionis vel administrationis]—to the mystical body of Christ."[86] Even in Giles of Viterbo's On Christian Government (De regimine christiano, 1302), the pope "is called Vicar of Christ, both as a man, because he is a priest, and as God and man, because he is a king; for this reason, and quite rightly, he is called Vicar of God."[87] The declarations of Alvarus Pelagius (1332) are also emphatic on this point: "Thus, as Jesus has two natures, so also his vicar general, and every individual pope, participates in a certain manner in Christ's two natures; in the divine nature in what regards spiritual matters, and in the human nature in what regards temporal affairs."[88]

Corpus Ecclesiae

Over the same span of time that has occupied us until now, other ideas and images that medieval ecclesiology had applied to the church were progressively transferred to the pope. In twelfth-century ecclesiology, the concept of church-Christianity was supported by a profound corporeal symbolism. According to the highest representative of this churchly metaphorizing, Honorius Augustodunensis, the "body of the church" *(corpus Ecclesiae)* was made up of seven members—eyes, hair, teeth, lips, knees, neck, the two shoulders—corresponding to the seven "orders of the elect" *(ordines electorum).* They were the seven members of the bride (the church), "praised by the groom [Christ] because they follow the precepts of Christ."[89] According to Lothar of Segni's (Innocent III's) treatise on the mysteries of the mass, it is the Roman pontiff, dressed in his liturgical vestments, who must be kissed in seven "parts of the body" (mouth, chest, shoulders, hands, arms, knees, feet) as a sign of reverence.[90] Once he became pope, Innocent went further. In a sermon he gave on the feast day of Saint Gregory the Great, he rigorously applied much of the complex symbolism of sevens, which Honorius Augustodunensis had reserved to the church's seven orders of the elect *(ordines electorum),* to the liturgical vestments of the pope.[91]

Innocent III developed the identification between the figure of the pope *(caput,* "head") and the churchly body in other directions a well. The infirmity of the church's members touched the pope in his body: when the church was sick, the pope was afflicted in his heart.[92] The pope made a body with the church.

It was for this reason, therefore, that in the symbolism of spiritual marriage, Innocent III innovated radically. The emphasis shifted from its traditional placement on the mystical marriage between Christ and his church to that between the bishop of Rome and the Roman church.[93] This ecclesiological conception is rendered visually in the mosaic of the apse of Saint Peter's, in the lower part of which Innocent had himself portrayed wearing the insignia of his office and standing slightly inclined before the Roman church—depicted as a young woman.[94]

Around 1300, Giles of Rome could say without hesitation that "The supreme pontiff who directs the summit of the church . . . can be called the church."[95] A few decades later, in the magnificent drawings of Opicino de' Canistri (d. 1334), a cleric at the papal court at Avignon, the figure of the pope is twice accompanied by an inscription identifying him with the "body of the church." In the first, the pope is designated as the "apostolic body of the church" *(apostolicum corpus Ecclesiae):* at the bottom, at the feet of the pope, a tiny figure represents the church of the laity that owes tithes to the "right hand of the mystical Christ."[96] The figure of the pope is analogous to that of Christ in an earlier drawing.[97] In the second, the pope is called the "body of the church militant" *(corpus Ecclesiae militantis):* the figure of a baby with a halo bears the inscription "son of man" *(filius hominis)*—that is, Christ.[98]

Mortality

As we have seen, from the twelfth century onward, the pope's person was increasingly identified with the church—that is, with Christ. The pope was no longer *Vicarius Petri,* but *Vicarius Christi,* and, moreover, Christ *visible* on earth. The "person of the pope" *(persona papae)* had succeeded in drawing to itself the traditional bond between Rome and the tomb of the apostles. Through the use of the concept of "the head" *(caput),* the figure of the pope had risen to become a privileged and exclusive *seat (sedes),* the guarantor of the "indefectibility" of the church's faith. The pope's body had become a metaphor that defined the intimate ecclesiological relationship between pope and cardinals at the summit of the hierarchy of the Roman church.

The rhetoric and ritual of humility that we reconstructed in the first chapter opposed the physical mortality of the pope's physical person to the superiority and universality of the office of the supreme pontiff. The pope's life was brief and his power transient, but as pope he was the "universal bishop" *(universus episcopus)* and "prince of emperors" *(princeps imperatorum)*—that is, "superior in honor and dignity to the human condition." During his life as pope, enclosed by insuperable boundaries set by God and history ("Peter's years"), the pope incarnated a "suprapersonality" of a Petrine nature.[99] But the nearer the pope came to Christ, the more the dissociation between the pope as man and the pope as "the person of Christ" *(persona Christi)* became indispensable. The argument was of such importance that, in the thirteenth and early fourteenth centuries, it was the popes themselves and hierocratic theologians who discussed it, certainly not to weaken, but rather to reinforce, the Christly foundation of the papal office. Thus, Pope Honorius III (1216–27) contrasted the perpetuity of the figure *(figura)* of Melchisedech, the prefiguration of Christ, to the mortality of his own physical person.[100] Referring to his predecessor, Innocent III, Honorius declared that "being mortal and unable to avoid death, he prepared himself with the arms of penance, desiring to dissolve himself and to be with Christ, in whom and through whom he wished to live and die."[101] Intimacy with Christ did not make the pope immortal.

Nicholas III also distinguished, in his letter of election (Nov. 25, 1277), between human mortality and the Christly perpetuity of his new office. Christ wished "to subject [his] perpetual vicariate to a continuity of ongoing successions: and although, in fact, the vicars [of Christ—that is, the popes] are bound toward the empire of death on account of their frail human condition, subject to the law of mortality, the office of the vicariate, immortal, remains forever, above and beyond the various substitutions."[102]

Augustinus Triumphus (1270–1328) recorded that "Peter and every pope after him succeeded Christ as his vicar in office and in power, not in person *[in officio et potestate, non in persona]*. . . . Neither Peter nor his successors are personally *[personaliter]* Christ's successors, and it is for this reason that they are called his vicars and ministers."[103]

For Alvarus Pelagius, the pope acted not preeminently *(non excellenter)*, like Christ, but as his minister *(ministerialiter)*: Christ's power lasted eternally *(eternaliter)*, that of the *Vicarius Christi* only temporarily *(temporaliter)*, although "in some successors [of Peter] this power [*potestas,* here understood in the sense of authority], lasts in the church down to the end of the centuries." [104] "Christ can judge not only that which is manifest, but also that which is hidden in the heart; the *Vicarius Christi,* although he is a pure man, cannot. Man, in fact, can see only that which is evident." [105] The need to demonstrate the difference between the person of the supreme pontiff and a physical person drove Alvarus to observe that "Christ was judged by Pilate not as a public person, but as a private one . . . before Pilate, [Christ] represented not the person of the pope, but that of a mere man." [106] The whole course of Alvarus's thought led him inexorably to a discussion of mortality and the brevity of the popes' lives. Its tone echoes Bernard of Clairvaux's *On Consideration (De consideratione):*

> Consider what the pope is, because he is a man; who he is, because he is a bishop. . . . A man is born, a bishop is made. . . . Insofar as he is born of a woman, he will live but a short time, because the popes live but a little while and their lives are filled with many miseries . . . more than for other men. . . . Consider him nude, because nude he came out of his mother's womb . . . he weeps at having been born . . . he does not think himself to have been created supreme pontiff, but to have been made of the vilest ashes.[107]

We ought not be surprised to find that, at the end of a chapter devoted to the history of the corporal metaphors that marked the evolution of the image of the pope from the Gregorian reform to the late thirteenth century, the theme of mortality again emerges so clearly. The analogy with what we have already had occasion to observe is perfect, because the problem presented itself in an identical manner. Because the pope was increasingly meant to *incarnate* the church, which is eternal, it was necessary to dissociate the physical person unequivocally from the institution.

But the fact that the pope had become the visible image of Christ on earth brings back a question that is basic to the history of the pope's body: how was the contrast between the potential frailty of the pope's bodily and human nature, and the Christly basis of the lofty office to which he had been called, treated within Roman ecclesiastical thought? Was the debate merely rhetorical, or did it also generate a rituality analogous to that which we have been able to observe in studying the theme of mortality and transience?

1   Bernardino di Betto, known as Pintoricchio. *Coronation of Pius II: The Ceremony
    of Igniting the Flax before the Pope*. Fresco: Siena, Cathedral, Libraria Piccolomini.
    Photograph courtesy of Scala/Art Resource, NY.

2 *Sedes stercorata* ("bedunged seat"). Rome, Saint John Lateran, cloister. Photograph courtesy of Istituto Centrale per il Catalogo.

3 "Porphyry" Chair. Vatican City, Vatican Museum, Gabinetto delle Maschere (museum photo).

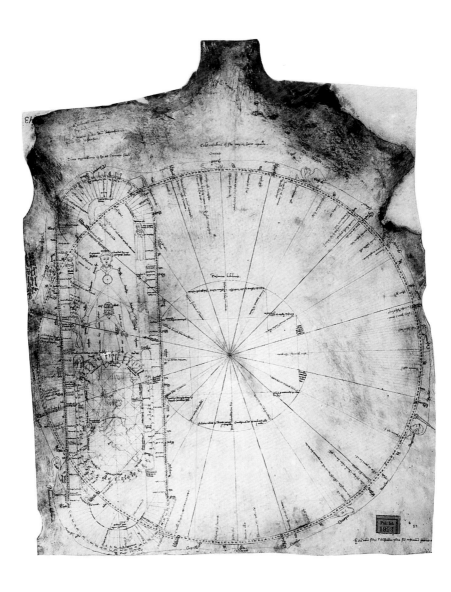

4 Opicino de' Canistri, drawing of the heavenly sphere and the terrestrial world (the vertical oblong on the left). The pope appears in the upper part of the oblong, with the inscription *apostolicum corpus Ecclesiae* ("Apostolic Body of the Church") written to the left and right of his head. The small figure beneath him represents the laity, from whom the clergy, the "right hand of the church," collect the tithe. *Liber de laudibus Ticinensis civitatis* (*The Book of Lauds of the City of Ticino*). Vatican Library, MS *Pal. lat.* 1993, fol. 17. Photograph courtesy of Vatican Library.

5 *The Emperor Constantine, on foot, leads Pope Sylvester I, on horseback, to Rome.* Fresco, Rome, basilica of the Quattro Coronati, oratory of Saint Sylvester. Photograph courtesy of Scala/Art Resource, NY.

6   Melozzo da Forlí, *Pope Sixtus IV founds the Vatican Library* [1475] *and names Bartolomeo Sacchi, known as Platina, to be its first librarian.* Fresco, Vatican City, Pinacoteca Vaticana. Photograph courtesy of Scala/Art Resource, NY.

mentu3 . Cum intentione nra in pñti compendio nõ sit nisi practica t
ncha designare cum adiuuamine illius q̃ ē trinus psonalt et unus ē
regnas p omïa secla seclor3 Amen.

Ll Jber de inuestigatione secreti oculti. —

VIA homo ē magis r
de mũdo et sua indu
sm q̃ ipe p sua na3 dc
animalibus brutis p s
q̃ in ipo est et ē inuesti
inuentituus secretor
nõ st amïalia bruta Et
res est grauis ad intel
magis gaudet q̃n int
Quo ergo inuestigatic
ti sit tanti amatu a
ē inuestigatu et ueni
multu gaudet et letat
de inuestigatione sit n
ta quã omes alie arte
suũ fine propterea su

ē magis amatu a uoluntate q̃ omes alie artes de rebus nalib3 et ideo pp no
tis inuestigationis dicti secreti ē intells magis alatus q̃ inuestigationes aliar3
ad destruendum intentiones eroneis quas archa istud secreti aliq habuer
do et practicando : Compommus isti tractati ut falsitas sit infima et uerit

7 *Presentation of an elixir to a pope* [Celestine V?], *whose tiara is being stolen by a
fox* [Boniface VIII?]. Florence, Biblioteca Nazionale, MS BR 72, fol. 273r.
Photograph courtesy of Biblioteca Nazionale Centrale di Firenze.

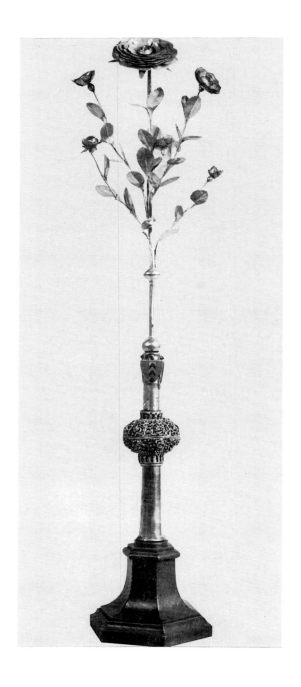

8   Golden rose given by Pope Clement V to the Bishop of Basel (1311). Paris,
    Musée de Cluny. Photograph courtesy of Giraudon/Art Resource, NY.

9 Tomb of Clement IV (details of the face of the gisant). Viterbo, church of San
   Francesco. Photograph courtesy of Alinari/Art Resource, NY.

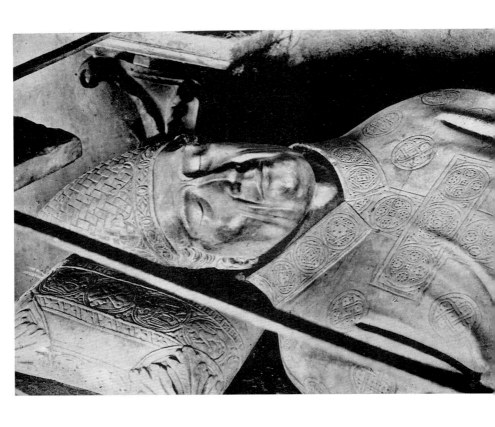

10 Tomb of Gregory X (detail of the face of the gisant). Arezzo, Cathedral.

11 *Hippocrates and Galen*. Fresco, c. 1230, Anagni, crypt. Photograph courtesy of Scala/Art Resource, NY.

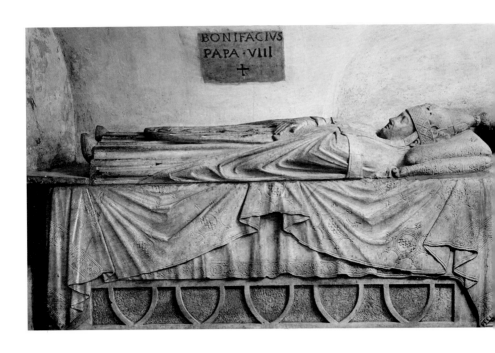

BONIFACIVS
PAPA · VIII
✝

12 Tomb of Boniface VIII. Vatican City, Saint Peter's, Vatican Grotto. Photograph courtesy of Alinari/Art Resource, NY.

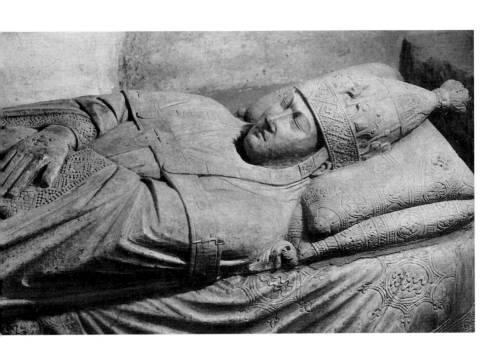

13 Tomb of Boniface VIII (detail of the face of the gisant). Photograph courtesy of Alinari/Art Resource, NY.

14 Bust of Boniface VIII. Vatican City, Vatican Palace, Sala di San Giovanni (Hall of Saint John). Photograph courtesy of Alinari/Art Resource, NY.

15 Commemorative statue of Boniface VIII. Bologna, Museo Civico. Photograph courtesy of Alinari/Art Resource, NY.

ngs eages fut ramenez en perpetuele
obseurte et fut extemete auec le roy dio.

le sixiesme chapitre contient les cas
daulcuns nobles malheureur et en
pou de paroles lauteur parle contre
les nobles orgueilleur. Et comme
ce ou latin. Dum post ꝫ c̄.

pres ce que ie eu descript e̅ bzief
le cas de didier noble noble

16 *Pope Joan gives birth.* Miniature from a manuscript of Boccaccio's *On Outstanding Women* (*De claris mulieribus*). Paris, Bibliothèque nationale, MS. *Lat.* 598, fol. 151. Photograph courtesy of Bibliothèque nationale de France.

3 Whiteness

Wax Lambs

To open up the field of ritual, a first path is provided by that same *Ordo XI* (1140–43) by the canon Benedict that was our point of departure in reconstructing the rituals of mortality and transience.[1] Benedict describes two ceremonies centered around lambs.

The first was celebrated on Easter Day. After holding the liturgical station at Santa Maria Maggiore the pope returned, crowned and in procession, to the Lateran. Dismounting his horse, he removed the tiara and entrusted it to his servant *(cubicularius)*, who placed it in a strongbox. The judges accompanied the pope as far as a room in which eleven stools and a chair were arranged around him, "symbolizing the twelve apostles who dined together on Easter Day at Christ's table." There, besides the dean *(primicerius)* and prior of the basilica, five cardinals and five deacons were seated. The pope first distributed the presbytery, then got up and went into another room to bless a roasted lamb; then he returned to the table. Here he took a piece of lamb and presented it to the prior of the basilica, saying: "What you are going to do, do quickly . . ." (John 13: 27);[2] then he put it in the prior's mouth. He gave the rest of the lamb to the other eleven, who were "reposing" (in the ancient manner) around the table.[3] In this reproduction of the Last Supper, the pope took the place of Christ, the prior of the basilica that of Judas, and the other eleven apostles were represented by five cardinals, five deacons, and the dean. This Easter Agape is recorded by the canon Benedict and by another *ordo* that reproduces his text.[4] Then, there are no further traces.

The second ceremony no longer had as its object a flesh and blood lamb, but wax lambs instead. The ceremony was not held on Easter Sunday and was divided into two phases: making the wax lambs and distributing them. The lambs were made on Holy Saturday before Easter, and distributed on the following "White" Saturday *(in albis):* "On Holy Saturday the archdeacon gets up in the morning and mixes oil and the year-old chrism into the pure wax; the acolyte prepares it, works it, and shapes it into the form of lambs that the pope distributes during the mass of Saturday *in albis.*"[5]

Unlike the Easter Agape, this two-phased rite of the lambs finds an exact counterpart in an earlier source, a Roman *ordo* of the ninth century: "In the Catholic church, in the city of Rome, at the first dawn of Holy Saturday, the archdeacon comes into the Lateran Basilica and pours some pure wax into a great vase; and he mixes in some oil and blesses the wax; then he models the wax into the likeness of lambs, and stores them in a clean place. On the octave of Easter these same lambs are distributed by the archdeacon to the people, who burn them at home as incense, and for fumigation as need arises."[6] The celebrant was the archdeacon; the wax lambs acted as talismans.

The similarities between these two *ordines* are surprising even as regards the days prescribed for the ceremony: Holy Saturday for the making of the lambs, Saturday *in albis* (or the octave of Easter) for their distribution. But their differences are notable as well. In the earlier *ordo,* it is the archdeacon who pours the wax into a vase, mixing it with oil; it is he who blesses the wax, molds it into the shape of the lambs (which he stores in a clean place), and distributes them to the people on the octave of Easter. Two centuries later, instead, according to Benedict, the archdeacon took part only in the first phase of the ceremony, which had been modified in other ways as well: in addition to the oil, the chrism (symbol of unction) was now added to the wax; making the lambs was entrusted to an acolyte; and on Saturday *in albis,* the distribution ceremony was no longer performed by the archdeacon, but by the pope. It should be noted also that to the eucharistic significance of the immaculate lamb—a sacrificial victim—Benedict now added that of baptism.[7] The wax lambs were transformed into instruments of purification: they allowed man to cast aside his "old tunic" and liberated him from the grip of the devil. The "lamb of God" *(agnus dei)* constituted a rite of passage, from the old to the new man. The point bears emphasizing, for it was now the pope, rather than the archdeacon, who took an active role in the phase of distribution.

The lamb ceremony reappears in Cencius's *ordo* (1192).[8] In the phase of making the lambs (Holy Saturday), the figure of the archdeacon has disappeared entirely: the lambs were now constructed by the "acolytes of the pope" who, moreover, had to receive the ten pounds of wax from the altar of Saint Peter and present it personally to the pope. The wax was therefore imbued with an explicit and powerful Petrine symbolism. The distribution continued to be divided into two phases. On Saturday *in albis,* in the basilica of Saint John Lateran, the pope offered the lambs made of chrism and wax "to the bishops, cardinals, and others, clerics as well as laity"; during the *agape,* the acolytes presented the pope with a large silver serving plate full of lambs; another was given to the chamberlain who gave it to the papal family *(familia).*[9] The first distribution took place in the basilica, in a solemn and public liturgical setting, among a community of bishops, cardinals, clergy, and laymen emblematic of the church universal; the second was restricted to the curial circle of prelates present at the *agape* and the papal family *(familia).*[10]

In the ninth-century *ordo,* the pope took the place of Christ and distributed a roasted lamb on Easter Day. In Cencius's twelfth-century ceremonial, the pope distributed lambs made of wax imbued with Petrine symbolism, and which contained not only oil but also chrism, the symbol of unction; the ceremony of the lambs appears to have been restructured around the person of the pope, who assumed a mystical mediating role. Rather significantly, the pope did not take part in making the lambs, because these represented the body-symbol of his Christly office; but it was he who, in union with Peter, distributed them to the church (bishops, cardinals, clerics, laity) and to the curia (prelates and the papal family).[11]

Two Roman liturgical books from the second half of the thirteenth century give us a view of a distribution ceremony that includes an unprecedented scene.[12] On Saturday *in albis,* the pope distributed the wax lambs to the bishops, priests, deacons, and people; celebrated mass; and then returned to the Lateran

Palace and the "house in which he must dine." Here, "he approaches his table, after having washed his hands and given the benediction; before the table prepared for him, the acolyte serving that week first takes the tablecloth, then the serving plate filled with lambs and, heading toward the door, declares out loud: 'These are the young lambs that announce the *Alleluia*. Now they come to the font. They are abundant in splendor *[claritate]*.'"[13] The acolyte bowed, then, advancing a bit, repeated the same words a bit louder. Approaching a few more steps, he arrived in front of the supreme pontiff, to whom he repeated more loudly still: "Lord, Lord, these are the lambs."[14] The acolyte then set the serving tray on the table. The pope, in turn, distributed the lambs to his *familia*—that is, to the members of the curia—first of all to the chaplains, then to the acolytes, and finally to all the others.[15] The pope's active participation was complete. Even the lambs meant for the *familia* were distributed personally by the pope, and no longer by the chamberlain, a further indication of the rite's steady and repeated emphasis on the person of the pope, who no longer escaped ritually in either the active sense (the distribution to the *familia*), or the passive (repetition in an ever louder voice).[16]

The pope's passive role, and the acolyte's recitation of the words of the rite, were new elements in what was now the centuries-old ceremony of the lambs. Moreover, the words were analogous to those prescribed by the rite of burning the flax as it was recounted for the first time by the Dominican Stephen of Bourbon, just a few years after the composition of the Roman missal.[17] Was this coincidence—thematic as well as chronological—purely accidental? What matters is that in both cases, the rite's visibility appears reinforced. Moreover, this ritual identity also created a sort of symmetry between the two leading Roman basilicas: the rite of the lambs was held every year in the Lateran, while flax was lit by the pope during the coronation ceremony held in Saint Peter's.[18]

ℰ̃

Thirteenth-century ceremonials prescribed that the papal arms and year of coronation be impressed on the wax lambs.[19] Already, according to Benedict's *ordo,* they were to be made of *year-old* wax mixed with chrism, the symbol of unction. We read in

Pierre Ameil's ceremonial (1385–90) that the popes "are accustomed to celebrate the ceremony in the first year of their coronation; then they repeat it every seven years."[20] Paride de Grassi, master of ceremonies under Pope Leo X (1513–21), established an even more explicit tie to the coronation: "On Saturday *in albis* of the first year of the pontificate the cardinals, bishops, and other high officials received, in their upturned miters, and according to their rank in the hierarchy, some disks of wax (small, medium, large)"; "on both sides of those disks was depicted a lamb, lying on the mystical book shut by seven seals, and having in its right paw the triumphal crossed standard. Below the figure were inscribed the papal arms, followed by the year of coronation."[21]

Because the rite was a memorial celebration of the papal coronation, the ceremonials increasingly emphasized the color white, symbol of innocence and purity. The wax had to be "clean and very white" *(munda et albissima)*, "white" *(alba)*, "new" *(nova)*, and "beautiful and clean" *(pulchra et munda)*, because *virgin wax* protects "against every human contagion."[22] Urban VI performed the ceremony of making the lambs at Santa Maria in Trastevere on April 16, 1379, the Good Friday of the second year of his pontificate; the distribution took place on "White" Sunday *(in albis)*, not Saturday.[23] The subdeacon sang the traditional verses before the pope, who was "covered by a veil of beautiful and very fine silk" that underlined the purificatory nature of a ceremony so closely tied to the sole person of the pontiff.[24] The sacristan assigned to make the lambs mixed some new chrism with year-old chrism before imprinting the appropriate formulas.[25] The pope blessed them as he did the candles on Candlemas (Feb. 2) when, seated on the throne, "he would pass out the candles—of virginal white wax—not only to those individuals present, but also to the princes and princesses of the world, great and small, according to the gradations of their dignity and rank."[26]

℃

In 1350, Clement VI distributed three wax lambs to every cardinal, and two to the other prelates.[27] The ceremonial notes that "by now it is traditional that the pope no longer celebrates mass on Saturday *in albis* at the ceremony of the lambs." This constriction of his liturgical role was accompanied by an increase in his activity at the distribution. Urban V (1362–70) would even send three "lambs of God" *(agnus dei)* to the Byzantine emperor John V Paleologus.[28] Along with the gift, the pope sent verses that begin by recalling the mystical union between balsam and chrism. Urban emphasized, furthermore, the redemptive significance of the lambs.[29]

A century earlier another French pope, Urban IV (1261–64), had made a gift to the queen of Navarre of some shoes and a cincture "which the Roman pontiffs traditionally use." He explained their symbolic value in a long accompanying letter.[30] To the question, "why do you wish, dearest sister, to receive from the Vicar of Christ his own cincture?" the pope replied with a long series of explanations, all centered on the symbolic significance of the cincture, the bridle of "human sensuality." He identified the shoes with those with which God had wished "to shoe the feet of the apostles"; being "already pure, the shoes keep their feet [from] the contagion of earthly dust and human glory"; "with these shoes on their feet they appear at the Easter dinner of the Lamb." The similarities here to the ceremony of the lambs are very close. The "clean and virginal" *(munda et virginea)* wax of the lambs also had to protect "from every human contagion"; and if the cincture was a "bridle on human sensuality," for the thirteenth-century liturgist William Durant the mixing of balsam and chrism (from which the wax for the lambs was made) symbolized the "senses of our body."[31] On the porphyry chair to the right, as well, the newly elected pope was given a cincture (symbol of chastity) and some musk (symbol of the "aroma of Christ");[32] from the cincture were hung twelve seals symbolizing the apostles. Purified by the ceremony of the lambs and by such symbols of innocence as the cincture and the shoes, the pope's life, like those of the apostles, was worthy of partaking of the Easter dinner of the lamb, and of being bestowed upon the church. And to "tell it" was a body-symbol.

In recounting the ceremony held on March 28, 1486, in the presence of Innocent VIII, Johann Burchard paused to emphasize the importance of the color white: "On Easter Tuesday seven great white baskets were prepared, full of lambs that had been blessed . . . then a large silver basin was filled with the purest water. . . . [T]he pope immersed the lambs in the water, baptizing them, and the bishops at his side assisted. . . . [T]hey took the lambs out of the water and carried them in basins to some tables that had been prepared for the occasion, covered with immaculate tablecloths."[33] Between 1447 and 1572 three different popes—Nicholas V, Paul II, and Gregory XIII—each promulgated bulls prohibiting that the whiteness of the lambs be altered and imposing the most severe penalties for noncompliance.[34]

ℰ

What does the ceremony of the lambs teach us?

To begin with, we may note the difference between the ninth-century *ordo* and the *ordines* of the twelfth century. In the first, the pope distributed a roasted lamb. Three centuries later, the former eating *(manducatio)* of the lamb, absent in Cencius's *ordo,* had been transformed into a symbolic distribution of the body-lamb. The lambs had to be made with wax of a Petrine nature, and with oils—chrism and balsam—required for unction; moreover they had to be impressed, like seals, with the pope's distinguishing features. The impression of the pope's name in the wax lamb fused the person of the pope with the body-lamb symbolizing Christ. By means of the lambs, the pope played a role as mediator for an "expanded community" of the whole church. The parallels with the institutional development we traced in the last chapter are compelling. From the mid–twelfth century onward, was the pope not ever more frequently defined as the *Vicarius Christi* ("Vicar of Christ")? Did Innocent III not declare that the pope was he who "bears," that is, "represents" *(gerere),* the *person* of Christ?

The rite's symbolic significance did not, however, invest merely the institutional figure of the pope. The lamb ceremony was indeed, as we have seen, also a memorial renewal of the reigning pope's coronation: the pope's life had to be "clean and virginal" *(munda et virginea)* like the wax of the body-lamb. Is it not about this double function of the lambs that the thirteenth-century sources speak to us for the first time? Was the "splendor of the lambs," announced three times in an ever louder voice, not at once a visible manifestation of the Christly basis of the papal office, and a solemn admonition to humility and purity? Grasped in its full implications, the rite's message thus emerges quite clearly: the visibility of the pope's Christly office had to be reinforced by the purity and innocence of his life.

The Golden Rose

Benedict's *Ordo XI* (1140–43) also describes the ceremony of the golden rose. Singing mass on the fourth Sunday of Lent *(Laetare Ierusalem)* in the basilica of the Santa Croce in Gerusalemme, the pope held a golden rose scented with musk and preached on the symbolic significance of the rose's red color and its fragrance. The prefect of Rome then accompanied him on foot to the Lateran Palace, where the pope gave him the rose.[35] Cencius (1192) adds that the rose was oiled with balsam before the pope sprinkled on the musk.[36] Eugenius III (1145–53) is the first pope whose interpretation of the golden rose has come down to us: the rose was a "sign of the Passion and of the Resurrection of our Lord Jesus Christ."[37] Alexander III (1159–81), when he sent the rose to the king of France, also emphasized its Christly nature, pointing to a relationship between the flower and the biblical verse "I am a rose of Sharon" (*Ego flos campi*, Song of Sol. 2: 1).[38]

Innocent III (1198–1216) and Honorius III (1216–27) interpreted the rose's symbolism in two important sermons. For the former, the golden rose symbolized not only Christ, but his double nature, because the gold corresponded to the divine, the musk to his humanity. The balsam was like the "rational soul" *(anima rationalis)* that conjoins divine and human nature.[39] For Honorius, who took up the argument where his predecessor had left off, the triple substance of the rose (gold, musk, balsam) symbolized the Trinity: the gold (power) signified the Father, the musk (wisdom) the Son, and the balsam (love) the Holy Spirit.[40]

Honorius III subjected the rose to an interpretation that was based to a surprising extent on the colors white and red. The white symbolized Christ's innocence and virginity; the red, his martyrdom and Passion. The virtue *(virtus)* of the rose cooled heat and served as medicine. Christ was a cooling element *(refrigerium)* in the dangers of life and upon the heat of the passions. Even the shape of the rose symbolized Christ: it was narrow at the bottom and wide at the top. Christ, too, had been poor on earth, yet filled with the entire world. Every Christian should hold terrestrial things of little account, but value so much the more that which is celestial.[41]

The newly elected pope received the musk that he was to sprinkle on the golden rose while he was seated on the porphyry chair to the left before the Lateran palace. The musk, which the twelfth-century ceremonials (of Albinus and Cencius) interpreted as a symbol of the "aroma of Christ," hung from the cincture along with the purse and the seals. The ritual gesture of putting the musk on the golden rose was therefore a symbolic commemoration of the beginning of his pontificate, a point also underlined by the fact that the rose was first anointed with balsam.[42] Other elements underscored the intimate bond between the rite and the person of the pope: he had to receive the golden rose in his chambers *(camera)* from the hands of the chamberlain, and he had to hold it during the whole procession, even when he was preaching on its symbolic significance.

℮

Like the wax lambs, the golden rose symbolized the nature of Christ; and it was for this reason that only his vicar was authorized to carry it in procession. Innocent III was explicit: "because only Peter has risen to the fullness of power." Thus it could be said that "the Roman pontiff represents this flower."[43] Never before Innocent III had the symbolic interpretation of the golden rose been used so deliberately by a pope to identify the figure of the supreme pontiff with Christ. But, as his successor Honorius III had occasion to say, possession of the rose also entailed innocence of the flesh and disdain for earthly goods.

In the interpretations of the first two popes of the thirteenth century, therefore, the ceremony of the golden rose symbolized the approach of the figure of the pope to Christ (the pope was the only one to use this Christly symbol); but, at the same time, it constituted a ritual of symbolic purification directed exclusively to the sovereign pontiff.

Red and White

Another thirteenth-century pope holds an important place in the complex history of the symbolism of the pontifical colors white and red.

In Gregory X's ceremonial (1272–73) the mantling *(immantatio)*—that is, the traditional cloaking of the newly elected pope in the red mantle—is inserted into a ritual scheme based on the colors white and red: "Immediately after the election, the prior of the cardinal deacons removes the mantle that he [the pope] is wearing and puts on his shoulders the Roman white *[alba romana]* . . . then he replaces the mantle on him and says: 'I vest you with the Roman papacy, that you may preside over the city and the world *[urbi et orbi].*' "[44]

Thus dressed, Gregory took part in the solemn celebration of the Te Deum, after which he returned to his chamber and there changed clothes in preparation for the distribution of the presbytery, and to participate in the small celebration with the cardinals.[45] Having removed his cope (that is, the red mantle) and (white) miter, the pope put on a second red mantle that the ceremonial calls the *mantellus;* then he put on two stockings of red cloth, little boots of the same, and half-leg "religious" boots of red leather. A red cloth miter was placed on his head. His habit had to be long enough to fold at the middle over the red silk cincture.[46]

White reappeared during Gregory's coronation ceremony: "The supreme pontiff and all the cardinals and other prelates and subdeacons, each according to his rank, put on precious vestments colored white." After reaching the portal or the steps of Saint Peter's basilica, the prior of the cardinal deacons (who had already cloaked the pope in his mantle) removed the miter from his head to replace it with the tiara, the "crown that is called a kingdom," while the people proclaimed *"Kyrie eleison."* Immediately after the coronation, the white cavalcade led the pope and his retinue to the Lateran: "Every cardinal and prelate advances riding a horse covered with a white cloth; the subdeacons, chaplains, clerks *[scriniarii],* and others ride adorned in their garments, but on uncovered horses. The pope rides a great horse, adorned and covered with scarlet, but only on the hindquarters; the front of the horse remains uncovered."[47]

ℭ

During all the phases of the coronation ceremony, therefore, the pope showed himself dressed in only two colors, white and red. The point should be noted, because it is the first time that a pontifical ceremonial paused to treat both colors so precisely and systematically in relation to the rites of enthronement.[48] It is also important because in all probability that *ordo* was written at the request of the pope himself.[49] Previous *ordines* referred only to one color, the red of the mantle (called also *cappa rubea* or *clamys*), in which the archdeacon or prior of the deacons cloaked the newly elected pontiff immediately after his election.[50]

The same goes for the pope's horse. For centuries, the only color discernible in the sources concerning the horse was that of white.[51] In Gregory X's ceremonial book, instead, for the first time a perfect, but inverted, symmetry associated the pope's clothes (white and red) with his horse's covering (white with red trim): the *ordo* does not mention (because it is quite obvious) the white color of the pope's "great horse," but it cites the red color of the cloth that was to cover the rear of the horse that the pope rode from Saint Peter's to the Lateran.[52]

त्

The pope's right to wear the red mantle dates back to the Donation of Constantine. The famous forgery asserted that the emperor had donated to Pope Sylvester I (314–35) "various imperial garments," including the "purple cloak."[53] Sylvester II (999–1003) was accused by Arnulf of Orleans of sitting "on the sublime threshold wearing a vestment radiating purple and gold."[54] This first mention of the use of the red pontifical mantle *(cappa rubea)* was long an isolated one. Peter Damian polemically asked the antipope Cadalus (1061–64), whose election he contested, "have you perhaps been redressed in the red mantle of the Roman pontiffs, as custom requires?"[55] Immediately after his election, Gregory VII (1073–85) received the red mantle: it is the first time that we find the practice confirmed in actual use.[56] Notices become more frequent in the period from Urban II (1088–99) to Alexander III (1159–81).[57] Bruno of Segni (d. 1123) records that "the supreme pontiff wears the tiara . . . and uses the purple . . . because the emperor Constantine in his time gave all the insignia of the Roman Empire to Blessed Sylvester."[58] The *ordines* of Albinus (1189) and Cencius (1192) both point out that immediately after his election, the archdeacon or prior of the deacons *mantled* the pope with the red cope.[59] In all these sources, therefore, the "mantling" *(immantatio)* is the ritual element that makes visible the legitimate ascent to the pontifical dignity, taking the place of the former enthronement.[60]

White is also an imperial color, of divinity. In the chapter dedicated to imperial vestments in the *Book of the Imperial Court (Libellus aulae imperialis),* included in the *Golden Writings on the City of Rome (Graphia aureae Urbis Romae),* the author lists, immediately after the cloak, the "very fine and white" *(subtilissimo et candidissimo)* linen shirt.[61] The model is of Byzantine origin. At Byzantium, the emperor wore a white silk tunic under the purple cloak.[62] Thus, a first point is clear: the oldest papal ceremonial that took note of the white color of the newly elected pope's vestment was written at the behest of a pope who justified his decision to have himself crowned in Saint Peter's by citing the Donation of Constantine, and who transformed the coronation into an autonomous ritual element that assumed precedence over the possession-taking of the Lateran. The conjunction is revealing, for it indicates that the red and white colors of the papal vestments were features of the *imitatio imperii* ("imitation of empire").[63] Is this not, moreover, the reason for the growing interest that the papacy accorded over the course of the thirteenth century to the white horse, a symbol of power that had never figured among the insignia given by Constantine to Pope Sylvester I?[64] Describing Gregory IX's cavalcade across Rome on Easter Monday (April 12), 1227, just three weeks after the solemn ceremonies of his enthronement (March 21), his biographer emphasized in an entirely unprecedented manner his horse's raiment: the pope mounted a horse "adorned in precious fabrics."[65] And, in an extremely polemical passage, he accused Emperor Frederick II of wishing to blemish the "brilliantly white glory of the horse" *(equorum candidata gloria)* that awaited the Roman pope.[66] The horse also stands out among the "imperial adornments" *(ornamenta imperialia)* in the frescoes of the chapel of Saint Sylvester in the Roman church of the Quattro Coronati (1246), which were a political manifesto against Frederick II. There, Constantine holds the bridle of Pope Sylvester's white horse.

The colors white and red were not, however, intrinsic only to imperial symbolism. The red color of the papal cloak was also inspired by the scarlet vestment of the high priest in the Old Testament. The model derives from a passage in Exodus (28: 1–43), which we find abundantly described in the Roman-

Germanic pontifical and in one of Innocent III's sermons devoted to Gregory the Great, himself an emblematic figure of the
Roman pontiff.[67]

The same is true of white, a color that no other *ordo* until
then had paused to consider at length. Rather, in Gregory X's
ceremonial, the pope was invested "in city and world" *(urbi et
orbi)* only after being dressed in both the red mantle and the Roman white *(alba romana)*—that is, in a rochet, a white linen garment that the Fourth Lateran Council had reserved to the use of
bishops: "The pontiffs [here meaning bishops] are to wear white
garments in public and in church, unless they are religious [that
is, monks]."[68] The rochet is a garment worn exclusively by prelates with jurisdictional powers. The pope's double red and white
vestment was therefore completely in harmony with what Innocent III himself had affirmed: "I have received from him
[Peter] the miter of my priesthood and the crown of my royalty;
he has made me Vicar of Christ, on whose garment it is written:
'King of kings and lord of lords, priest for eternity according to
the order of Melchisedech.'"[69] Referring to Pope Sylvester I,
had Innocent not perhaps defined him as "a priest not only great,
but the greatest, sublime in his pontifical and royal power"?[70]

Is it not, therefore, significant that in Gregory X's ceremonial the symbolic identity between vestments and tiara should
be so complete? In the thirteenth century, the pope wore the
cope (or red mantle) and the rochet (or Roman white) whenever
he was portrayed wearing the tiara. The tiara represented not
only the temporal power of the pope, but the spiritual power of
the pontifical office as well.[71] A conclusion emerges by itself: the
pope's red mantle and the white habit symbolically united the
Roman pontiff's *plenitudo potestatis* ("fullness of power").

White and red are Christly colors. Had Rupert of Deutz not described Christ as "white in sanctity and red in Passion"?[72] Even
Christ's sepulcher had been defined by the colors red and white,
symbols of martyrdom and divinity.[73]

This is why red and white are the colors of the church. Had
Saint Jerome not applied to the church the white attire of the
supreme priest of the Old Testament?[74] In his *On the Mysteries*

(De mysteriis), had Saint Ambrose not developed the idea that the church "had received white garments," or rather "the pure garments of innocence"?[75] According to Honorius Augustodunensis, one of the subtlest theologians of the first decades of the twelfth century, "the cheeks of the church blush with sin . . . (but) become bright red on the outside with charity, and white on the inside with chastity."[76] For the anonymous twelfth-century author of a commentary on the apocalypse, even the white horse represented the church.[77]

Already, Gregory VII had warned in his "Dictates of the Pope" *(Dictatus papae)* in the Avranches codex (end of the eleventh century) that "only the pope may use the red cope as a sign of imperial authority and martyrdom."[78] The pope's red mantle was in fact the scarlet or purple robe that the soldiers draped over Christ in the court before putting the crown of thorns on his head.[79]

Just as the red color of the papal mantle was a symbol of Christ's martyrdom, and the purple could be identified with his blood, so also the Roman white *(alba romana)* that the Roman pontiff put on was a Christly symbol.[80] In the Donation of Constantine, the magnificence of the white cloth of the tiara explicitly recalls Christ's resurrection.[81] Recording in the third person the moment of his election to the pontificate, Pius II recalled having "put on the white tunic of Christ."[82] As an ancient papal diary puts it: "The pope must have the pure white clothes of celestial persons, so that the splendor of his celestial office may be manifest to the people."[83] Whiteness was luminosity.

The fact, therefore, that Gregory X's ceremonial, so concerned to emphasize the universality of the papal office,[84] should have been the first to highlight the pope's white and red garments reflects a very specific historical and ecclesiological situation: the white and red colors made it clear that the pope was the *Vicarius Christi,* the living image of Christ on earth. And because the pope "bore" or "represented" *the person* of Christ, who is the church, the pope too had to be dressed in the colors that symbolized the church. Was it not on red, white, and its opposite, black, that Lothar of Segni, the future Innocent III, based the construction of his entire liturgical system of the Roman church?[85] Were white and red not the colors of the standard of the church, the first references to which date precisely from the thirteenth century?[86]

℮

Several years after Gregory X's ceremonial, William Durant offered, in his *Rationale of the Divine Offices* (*Rationale divinorum officiorum,* 1286), the oldest symbolic interpretation of the white and red papal attire: "The supreme pontiff always appears wearing a red mantle on the outside; but underneath he is dressed in a bright white garment: because whiteness symbolizes innocence and charity; the red on the outside symbolizes compassion . . . the pope indeed represents the person of Him who for our sake stained his own garment red."[87]

Two points need to be cleared up right away. First of all, for the great Dominican liturgist, the pope is *always* dressed in white and red. This emphasis on routine accords with Gregory X's *ordo,* according to which, in the various stages of the coronation ceremony, the pope always wears the Roman white, in church (during the Te Deum), in public (the distribution of the presbytery), during mass with the cardinals, and even in his chamber, where the pope must wear the rochet over white linen garments. In circumstances not requiring the red crimson mantle, the pope used the red mantlet or mozzetta.

But what were the reasons for such a deliberate and unprecedented emphasis on the pope's continually wearing a white garment? The answer is basically quite simple: if the pope is *always* the living image of Christ on earth, does he not *always* have to wear white? Urban V turned to this very argument to explain why the pope *always* has to wear the white rochet: he indeed "represents in the church universal the divine person of Christ; thus the white exterior of the rochet [that is, of the Roman white] symbolizes the pope's natural interior purity."[88] Agostino Patrizi Piccolomini, in his ceremonial (1484–92), considered wearing a white garment daily a papal duty never to be set aside: "in the clothes that are not sacred, worn over the rochet, the pope uses nothing but red; under the rochet, the pope always wears a white toga and red socks with sandals decorated with golden crosses." Even on the iconographic level, the pope's double white and red attire became traditional from the thirteenth century onward.[89]

The formula coined by William Durant was not entirely
new. Already, in the view of Honorius III (1216–27), for example, the figure of the priest was two-sided: the exterior recalled ordination (that is, power *[potestas]*), the interior, sanctity. God had given both to Pope Sylvester, "not only great but
outstanding, whom He adorned with the garments of the virtues
and raised to the summit of the Apostolic See." [90] But Durant
applied the concept specifically to the pope's double *royal* attire.
The "external garment" (the red mantle) was now a symbol
exclusively of Christ's martyrdom, the Christly basis of the papal office; and the whiteness of the "internal garment" referred
uniquely to the innocence of the pope's life (and to his charity).
Such a line of argument suggests the need for consistency. The
"external garment" had to be reinforced by an equally Christly
interior purity. The symbolism of the pope's *interior* garment,
which Durant described as "pure white" *(candidus),* is entirely
analogous to that of the wax lambs: the life of the pope—the
persona Christi—had to be as "clean" *(munda)* and "virginal" *(virginea)* as the lambs, pure as his own white garments.

In these same years even the pope's horse, an ancient symbol of
power deriving from imperial origins, was subjected to a symbolic reinterpretation in terms of purity and the innocence of
life. Saint Bonaventure (d. 1274) observed that "on feast days the
cardinals ride horses draped with white cloths, while the pope's
horses are always white and sometimes covered with silken
cloths." [91] The white horse signified the flesh, the white cloths
purity: pope and cardinals had to overcome the flesh and not be
dominated by it; their flesh had to be pure. The fact that the
pope's horses were sometimes draped in silken cloths meant that
he had to possess (also) the symbolic virtue (humility) of the
silk. [92] According to Durant, too, the horses ridden by bishops on
their election day "have to be white, or at least covered in white,
to signify that the prelates' bodies have to be pure and chaste."
Only the chaste and the pure could follow Christ. [93]

None of this should surprise us. The debate on the purity of
the pope's life was then a subject of considerable relevance. In
Gregory X's *Vita,* the theme of papal austerity and "cleanliness"
(munditia) is a historiographical topos: the pope kept "his flesh

pure of every contagion."[94] For his immediate predecessor, the French pope Clement IV, the chronicles also underlined elements of austerity.[95] According to his epitaph in the Roman church of Saint Lawrence outside the Walls, Cardinal Guglielmo Fieschi, nephew of Pope Innocent IV, was "whiter than a swan"; and on the boss of the cape worn by Adrian V (d. 1276) in the gisant of his tomb is impressed a "lamb of God" *(agnus Dei)*.[96] According to Hostiensis, the cardinals who had received their red caps from Innocent IV in 1245 were "obliged to lead lives worthy of the name of Christian, inasmuch as that is what is denoted by the color red"; but as regarded the innocence of their lives, they had to be "whiter than snow."[97] It is scarcely surprising, then, that in the context of such intense discussions, carried on in terms of symbolic purification, there emerged the first indications of the highest ideal vision of the pope articulated in the Middle Ages, that of the "angelic pope" *(papa angelicus)*. In 1267 Roger Bacon wrote that forty years earlier it had been prophesied that a pope would come to reform the church, end the schism with the Greeks, and convert the Tartars and Saracens.[98] During the long papal vacancy of the years 1268–71, some verses spread the hope that the next pope would be "a holy man, father of the poor, illuminated by God, a chosen vessel who will have rejected the treasures of the world."[99] According to Salimbene, in 1271 (the year in which Gregory X was elected), other verses were supposed to have announced the coming of "a man of forty years . . . holy . . . of angelic life."[100]

On May 13, 1250, at Lyons, the city that had hosted the Roman curia since 1245, Cardinal Giovanni Gaetano Orsini read out in consistory, almost on the spur of the moment, a memorandum that the great English scholar and bishop of Lincoln, Robert Grosseteste, had delivered just beforehand to three cardinals and to Pope Innocent IV (1243–54) himself. The text contains one of the most severe denunciations of curial politics that had ever been pronounced at such an exalted level. At a certain point, the argument focused on the person of the supreme pontiff:

> Those who preside over this holy see assume the person of Christ in a most unique way among all mortals; it is necessary, therefore,

that in them [the popes] the works of Christ should shine forth in the highest manner, and that there be in them nothing that might be contrary to Christ's works. And on that account, just as the Lord Jesus Christ is to be obeyed in all things, so also everyone must submit to those who preside over this holy see, inasmuch as they assume the person of Christ, and insofar as they preside there in truth. If any one of them—may it never come to pass!—should assume the habit of their relatives, or of the flesh itself, or of the world, or of any other thing that is not Christ . . . then anyone who obeys him manifestly separates himself from Christ and from his body, which is the Church, and from him who meanwhile is head of this see, inasmuch as he assumes the person of Christ. . . .[101]

And, he added: "Even if they do not commit other sins, those pastors who fail to proclaim the person of Jesus Christ, whose person they assume, are among the Antichrists." [102]

The pope was either Christ or Antichrist. As the *persona Christi,* the pope was everything; in his own flesh he was no longer anything.[103] To be the *persona Christi* the pope must, among other things, divest his own flesh. Herein lies the great historical interest for us of the remarkable English bishop's memorandum. Never before had the potential dichotomy between the *person of Christ* and the *person of man* been submitted for consideration by a Roman pontiff in such radical terms. Far from speaking in the abstract, Grosseteste directly addressed his comments to Pope Innocent IV—that is, to the representative of a papacy that by now had won the political battle against Emperor Frederick II, and that was sustained by the highest hierocratic consciousness.[104]

White and Black

According to Gregory X's ceremonial (1272–73), the pope could sing mass on November 2 dressed in black and violet "as he pleases." [105] The *Ordo XIV* (1328), however, specifies that on that occasion "the pope is not accustomed to celebrate the mass for the dead, not even for an important king";[106] the pope put on not black liturgical robes, but the red mantle, open in the front, and a plain (that is, without pearls or gold) white miter.[107]

According to Agostino Patrizi Piccolomini's ceremonial (1484–92) as well, on November 2 the pope did not celebrate, but wore the red mantle or a simple cope of the same color; the cardinal who said the mass instead wore black vestments.[108]

At the end of the sixteenth century, the pope did not celebrate mass on the anniversary day of his predecessor's death.[109] Angelo Rocca (1545–1620) records that at Ferrara, in 1599, Cardinal Ottavio Paravicini (1552–1611) performed the mass of the anniversary of the deceased cardinals in the absence of Pope Clement VIII (1592–1605), "who is not accustomed to take part."[110]

Likewise, on Ash Wednesday, according to Agostino Patrizi Piccolomini, the pope put on not black vestments, but wore a violet-colored stole and a red cope.[111] The pope's abandonment of black liturgical attire on Ash Wednesday had already become a tradition by the time Pierre Ameil composed his ceremonial (1385–90).[112]

At Avignon, the pope celebrated in black only on Good Friday.[113] The logic was faultless: that was the day on which Christ's death was commemorated. On the other hand, and for the same reason, during the octave of Easter the pope wore only white garments, symbols of Christ's resurrection.[114]

The definitive acceptance of the pope's double-colored attire—white and red—thus ended up eliminating black liturgical dress from the pontifical ceremonial. The pope represented the *person* of Christ, the "eternal pontiff," and as such could have no direct contact with death. The chronicle of Sens records that when one of Honorius III's (1216–27) servants *(cubicularius)* got sick, "As soon as the pope saw that he was on the threshold of death . . . and while the attendants, in preparation for his death, were making all the arrangements for his funeral and absolution, the pope, commending him to God, went away."[115]

In the late sixteenth century, in two works dedicated to Pope Sixtus V (1585–90), the symbolic significance of the colors of the pope's clothing—internal and external—were reexamined. The Spanish theologian Alessandro de Torquemada dedicated to the pope a long treatise on the primacy of Peter, centered on the rays of "light of the hierarchy of the church militant."[116] The pope's entire adornment could be interpreted symbolically. The twenty-first ray illustrated the "white and purple vestments of the supreme Roman prelate." [117] The argument unfolds along the lines of the formula devised by William Durant, but with new accents. Herod had dressed Christ in white as a sign of derision; for this reason, the "church . . . decreed by a most just law that the leader of the church should be dressed in that same color (white) in which its redeemer was covered in infamy and shame. Indeed, only this color, pure and minimally stained, and only him, symbolize cleanliness, purity, and integrity. As head of the Roman church, the pope has the duty of maintaining the catholic faith with an integrity resplendent of life . . . it is most absolutely necessary that he be dressed in white." [118] The pope wore "red on the outside" because he represented the person of "Him who in his eternal benevolence offered his life and turned the 'garment of his body' [corporis indumentum] red." And because the "pontiff of the Catholic church . . . represents the person of the lamb of Christ, ever most gentle and obedient, it is fitting that his red garment should be encircled by the pallium which, in its whiteness, symbolizes that purity of soul, innocence and purity of life, with which the priest must be equally adorned." [119] Dressing in white and red (purple), that is, "the external 'appearance of the body' [corporis apparentia] that the Pythagoreans call epiphany [epiphania], means that the [Roman] pontiff should shine throughout the Christian world with the clear white ornaments of purity and charity." [120] In the climate of the Counter-Reformation, the person and office of the pope were absorbed into a total and complete symbolism of purification, the indispensable premise for the most universal "appearance of the body" possible. The pope's epiphany throughout the Christian world presupposed "the clear white ornaments of purity and of charity." The program was irreversible: it was, in fact, "the church itself that ordered its head to dress himself in the garments that Christ had worn during the Passion," red on the outside, and white underneath.[121]

In these same years Angelo Rocca, a future papal sacristan (1595–1620), asked in a treatise: can the pope wear green vestments? He answered in the affirmative, and his argument concerns corporeity. The green of the emerald is "a symbol of virginity, because (the emerald) will shatter unexpectedly if it is worn by a person who engages in 'sexual intercourse' [rem veneream]." [122] The pope should therefore wear liturgical garments colored green, the symbol of hope. The discussion then opens out into a consideration of the symbolism of the pope's white and red garments. As Durant had already asserted, the pope wore only white and red vestments. He indeed took "the place of Him whose spouse sings: My beloved white and red" (Song of Sol.: 5). The white was a symbol of divinity, the eternal light. The pope wore white because he represented "our pontiff and lord, Christ" and (in fact) "the immutability of the divine nature." To such an enthusiastic assimilation of the pope to Christ's divine nature Rocca added, on the other hand, an undeniable insistence on the symbolism of white in terms of purity. White was the color that purified the pope's "flesh and mind." For this reason, the pope *always* wore white clothes: "at home as well as in public, none of the pope's undergarments *(subtanee)* should be other than white; even the linen garment called the rochet must always be pure white"; "it is fitting that the garments nearest the pope's body should always be white, nor can this principle be subject to any sort of modification." [123]

Angelo Rocca's views depended upon positions that we saw emerging for the first time clearly and explicitly in the thirteenth century. From the time of Gregory X's ceremonial (1273) onward, the pope's double colors—red and white—hearkened back to the *imitatio imperii* but served even more to symbolize the pope's *plenitudo potestatis* and the Christly nature of his office. By that time, the pope had definitively become the *Vicarius Christi*—that is, the *persona Christi*—and the pope's body the institutional reference point of the Roman church, as in the ecclesiological concept that defined the cardinals as *pars corporis papae* ("part of the pope's body"). For William Durant, the red recalled Christ's martyrdom; the white, purity and innocence of life. This image was the outcome of an exquisitely scholastic form of argumentation: the pope's exercise of his office, symbolized by his wearing the red mantle on the outside, must agree with the whiteness of his "interior garment." [124] A direct line therefore connects the liturgists of the thirteenth century with those of the late sixteenth: the white garment symbolized the Christly basis of the papal office and the reigning pontiff's innocence of life.

The flowering in the thirteenth century of such deliberate references to the pope's red and white garments in fact amounted to a victory for white, a color to which the earlier sources had not paid much attention. White's victory was even broader and more profound in the period of the Counter-Reformation. For Sixtus V's liturgists, white made possible the *corporis apparentia* of the pope—that is, it symbolically purified the pope's life and manifested the fact that he was the *persona Christi*.

The emphasis on white clothes also complemented the development of the rite of the wax lambs that we reconstructed in the first part of this chapter. The whiteness of the pope's daily garments, and the symbolism of the body-lamb, were meant to resolve symbolically the possible conflict between the pope's potentially fragile corporeity and the lofty office he was called to fill.

But then, all this would lead us to conclude that from the eleventh century onward, with moments of great intensity, as in the thirteenth century, the pope's body was the object of a double ritual and rhetorical order: whiteness was supposed to ensure symbolic purification, while the theme of mortality and transience, which has held our attention from the outset, was meant to remind the pope of the inevitability of death.

$\widetilde{\mathfrak{C}}$

A new question thus emerges by itself: this double discourse, which has seemed so forceful and constant in terms of ritual and rhetoric—how did it manifest itself at the moment when the pope's *real* death arrived? What strategies did the Roman church devise to resolve those problems that so often had been ritualized by the liturgy of mortality and transience while the pope was still alive? How, then, did the Roman church confront that "moment of terror" that Peter Damian had spoken about? How, in the end, did those elements of "majesty" *(maiestas)* and innocence— which had been located ideally in the figure of the pope from the mid–thirteenth century onward—survive in memory and in the apostolic succession of the deceased popes? Having seen the means by which the living pope's body was constructed, we must try now to see how that order to which the carnal metaphor attached could be deconstructed without being demolished.

PART II

The Pope's Death

4 New Spaces and Times

Protecting the Palace

As for rites of mortality, so also for the death of the pope himself, we must turn our analysis back to the mid–eleventh century and, more precisely, to the pontificate of Leo IX (1049–54). Two episodes illustrate the depredations that often followed in the wake of a bishop's or a pope's death. The first did not actually occur in Rome itself; but the papal letter concerning it is important for our purposes, not least because its author was Peter Damian, whose observations on mortality and the pope's death have accompanied us from the very beginning of this study.

ℰ

What had happened? Around 1049, after the death of their bishop, the inhabitants of Osimo, a little town in the Marches near Ancona, had invaded and plundered the episcopal palace, cut down the vines and shrubs, and burned the peasants' houses. It is impossible to tell whether the popular fury was provoked by some misdeed committed by the deceased bishop. The fact remains that the ruling pope, Leo IX himself, found in it a pretext to have Damian draw up a severe indictment of a practice that he here described as a "perverse custom" (*perversa consuetudine*). The letter, which dates from the first year of Leo's pontificate (1049), contains a long discussion of the illicitness of such pillaging.[1] Damian's argument is based on the contrast between the physical mortality of a prelate and the immortality of Christ, "the bishop of all our souls," the "immortal spouse of the church," to wit, the "eternal pontiff."[2] This amounted to saying that though the bishop was dead, there remained the church—that is, Christ. It should be emphasized right away that this papal letter is of great

historical interest, for it is the first to present such a clear distinction between the physical person (of the bishop) and the perpetuity of the church.

In the second episode that concerns us, Leo IX was again the
main protagonist. On the morning of April 18, 1054, already
gravely ill, the pope had a vision announcing his imminent death.
He directed the clerics who had come to Saint Peter's to have his
marble sepulcher brought there, then ordered that he be carried
into the basilica on the very bed in which he was lying.[3] Scarcely
had the news been spread about, then the Romans ran to the
Lateran to despoil the palace, "as they were accustomed to do."[4]
The author of Leo's *Vita* adds, however, that "thanks to the
merits and virtues of the blessed prelate, no one succeeded in
entering the area of the palace. Seized by terror, the Romans
turned back in shame."[5] It was then, in Saint Peter's Basilica,
seated on his bed awaiting death, that Leo delivered a sermon
devoted entirely to the respect due to the church's goods, in harmony with his program to defend the "liberty of the church"
(libertas Ecclesiae).[6]

Before exploring the historical significance of these two episodes, it is necessary to recall that notices of the depredation,
spoliation, and pillaging of property belonging to deceased prelates go back a long time. We hear of them from the very first
centuries of Christianity. Already, in 451, the Council of Chal-
cedon had threatened to strip of their offices clerics who made
off with the goods of a deceased bishop.[7] In 533, the Council of
Orleans tried to repress the undue appropriation of a deceased
bishop's goods by making the custody and protection of the episcopal residence the direct responsibility of the bishop called to
preside over his burial. Here, too, the objects of these strictures
were exclusively the clergy.[8] A decree of the Council of Valence,
in 546, likewise imposed on clerics, accused of having invaded
and seized the goods of a bishop at the end of his life, the duty of
defending and preserving the deceased bishop's goods.[9] In 615,
the Synod of Paris reiterated the respect due the last testaments
of bishops and clerics, and threatened the guilty—clergy or
laity—with excommunication from "ecclesiastical consortium"
and from "association with Christians."[10] On the other hand,

the Council of Chalons, in 650, prohibited bishops and arch-deacons from appropriating the property of deceased priests or abbots.[11] The Council of Toledo of 655 was the last to deliberate on this issue. Its ninth decree falls into the tradition of the Council of Valence: responsibility for maintaining custody of a deceased bishop's goods fell to the bishop in charge of his burial.[12]

Clearly, these measures were aimed almost entirely at repressing the abuses of clerics who had lived with or near the deceased bishops, and at placing the episcopal residence and church under the protection of the bishop who had been called to preside over his burial. Between the fifth and the seventh centuries, only one conciliar decree, that of Paris in 615, explicitly referred to laity participating in the looting of deceased prelates' goods.[13]

In this centuries-long saga of robbery and spoliation, one historical fact cannot but surprise: it is actually necessary to wait until 885 before we come upon clear references to depredations of the Lateran Palace taking place on the occasion of the pope's death.[14] Pope Stephen V (885–91), when he took solemn possession of the Lateran in the company of bishops, the imperial legate, and the Roman senate, found that sacred vases, jewels, and precious liturgical ornaments had been stolen from the wardrobe (*vestiaria*) of the holy palace—even the famous golden cross that Belisarius had given to Saint Peter![15] The papal biographer wrote a dramatic account of the episode. Even the cantine and the granary had been found empty: to provide for the ransoming of prisoners and the support of orphans, widows, and the poor, the pope had had to appeal to the generosity of his own relatives.[16] This artful mise-en-scène of the desolated palace had the purpose of underlining the pope's determination to halt such sackings, which itself seems to have been an innovation. Before a number of illustrious witnesses (bishops, imperial legates, the senate), Stephen solemnly declared that he would have all these matters investigated, "so that everyone would realize that nothing like this had ever been attempted before then."[17]

᷒

Unwillingness to tolerate episodes like this shows up again only twenty years later, and confirms the reality of the problem. In 904 a Roman council determined to suppress the custom of sacking, after the pope's death, the Lateran Palace, city, and surroundings. The decree speaks of a "most evil custom" that "has been growing," and that was not exclusively Roman.[18] "Ecclesiastical censure" and "imperial indignation" were to be combined to repress it.[19]

In the European context, the Roman decrees of 885 and 904 were not isolated developments. A few years earlier, the imperial capitularies of Pavia (876) and of Quierzy (877) had sought to check the pillaging of bishoprics and abbacies on the deaths of their occupants.[20] Two popes, Stephen V (885) and Formosus (891–96), issued privileges to Archbishop Fulk of Rheims to protect his church from similar abuses.[21] Fulk, in turn, appealed to the king of France to take measures assuring that the temporal goods of the bishopric of Laon would not be plundered at the death of Bishop Didon.[22] In 909, the Council of Trosly denounced the habit of the "more powerful" (potentiores) of taking possession of deceased bishops' goods "as though they were the personal property of the prelate, which runs counter to every law."[23] Appealing for the emperor's intervention, the Roman council of 904 perhaps wanted to revive a tradition of which we find an echo in a capitulary promulgated in September 824 by Lothar, the son of King Louis the Pious, in the aftermath of the disorders that had accompanied the death of Pope Paschal I (d. Feb. 11, 824) and the election of Eugenius II (Feb.–May 824): Lothar took charge not only of the election and of maintaining public order, but decreed that "the depredations that usually occur" were forbidden "whether the pope is living or dead."[24]

Though the repression of such abuses was not new, it is nonetheless true that in the Roman documents (885–1054), the custom of pillaging was now set in a framework of rising reprobation and ritual struggle that ended up reaching, much more than elsewhere, theoretical levels of great historical interest. As we have seen, Stephen V promised to recover everything that had been stolen, insisting that his act represented an innovation; the council in 904 likened the sacking of the papacy to that of bishoprics, and requested imperial protection in strong and decisive tones. But only the letter of 1049 concerning the pillage at Osimo opposed the sackings on the basis of an explicit consideration of physical mortality and institutional continuity. More-over, the idea was formulated with extreme clarity: the church's permanence was grounded on the theological bedrock of the immortality of the "eternal pontiff," Christ. In 1054, it was the merits and virtues of the dying Pope Leo IX that in the end confounded and halted the Romans who had run to despoil the Lateran Palace. In both instances, the aim of protecting the "pontifical goods" was supported by an institutional abstraction or, if we like, a depersonalization of the rupture caused by the death of a bishop or of the Roman pontiff.

These features are essential for our purposes, for they consti-tute the very soil, the *humus,* from which emerged, a few years later (1064), Damian's discussion of the "brevity of life" that we have already had occasion to examine. An identical form of ar-gumentation is unmistakable: as a physical person, the pope is destined to die, but the institution of the papacy is perennial.

℮

After the pontificate of Leo IX, there follows a long hiatus in the documentation on the plundering of papal goods after a pope's death. The subject reappears unexpectedly only at the beginning of the thirteenth century: the English chronicler Matthew Paris records that ten days before his death, Honorius III (1216–27) was carried, "exhausted and half-dead," to a "high window" (of the Lateran) and shown to the Roman people, who had begun to "unleash themselves against the pontifical goods." Attempting to convince the Romans that the pope was still alive, the Roman curia hoped to avert the traditional sacking.[25]

The reason for such a long silence is perhaps to be sought in the fact that, between Leo IX and Honorius III, many popes died far from Rome.[26] Does this mean the Roman people abandoned themselves to pillaging "pontifical goods," and scenes of disor-der, only when the pope's death occurred in the city?[27] It seems not at all unlikely. The spontaneous violence the sources tell us about cannot but be related in some way to the pope's physical presence in Rome, and to the speed with which news of his death was disseminated.

For the rest, the episode narrated by Matthew Paris was an isolated one: for the entire thirteenth century, we have no other sources on the pillaging of the "palace" by the Roman people after the pope's death.[28] In fact, after Honorius III and through the end of the century, the vast majority of popes died outside of Rome because of the constant movement of the Roman curia.[29] Even for the Avignon period (1308–78), there are no notices of popular depredations of the Apostolic Palace after the popes' deaths.[30] On the contrary, in the papal funeral ceremonials of Avignon (Pierre Ameil, François de Conzié—the first in the history of the papacy), safeguarding the "palace" against outsiders aroused no particular concern among the officials (chamberlain and cardinals) charged with guaranteeing the proper conduct of affairs during a papal vacancy.[31]

In the second half of the fifteenth century, when the popes' deaths again occurred more often in Rome itself, the chronicles speak to us with renewed frequency of tumults and public disorders.[32] News of a papal death continued to produce "chaos," but, so far as can be seen, robbery and sacking no longer centered on the "pontifical goods," as they had in the Middle Ages (885, 1054, 1227).[33] On the death of Sixtus IV (Aug. 12, 1484), groups of youths headed for the palace of Count Girolamo Riario, the pope's nephew, and devastated it so thoroughly that not a door or window was left intact. Others ran to Castle Giubileo, where Countess Caterina Sforza Riario's estate was located, and "stole a hundred cows and all the goats and many pigs, asses, geese, and roosters that belonged to the Countess; among which was a great amount of salted meat, and round Parmesan cheese." When they returned to Rome, they forced open the granaries of the churches of San Teodoro and Santa Maria Nuova. At Sant'Andrea delle Fratte, meanwhile, Battista Collerosso and his sons attacked the shop of a baker, killing him.[34] In the summer of 1559 (Aug. 8), after learning of the death of Paul IV, the Romans

> ran to the prisons, broke down the doors, and set everybody free; they did the same to the Inquisition, saying that many were imprisoned there for reasons other than heresy; still, they did not release the heretics before making them first swear devotion to Holy Church and the Christian faith: which they did to keep the heretics quiet, and so as not to show themselves contemners of

religion. . . . On the same day, the people ran to the Campidoglio, smashed the marble statue that had been dedicated to him three months earlier, and knocked the mitered head off its shoulders, which the children then rolled all around the city, trampled on and mocked by everyone: finally, they threw it into the river.[35]

On July 11, 1590, hearing the news of Sixtus V's death, the Jews who held their market on Wednesdays in Piazza Navona hurried to collect their merchandise and flee, fearing pillage.[36]

Clearly, the fifteenth- and sixteenth-century sources grounded in social reality speak often of robbery and plunder; the episodes we know about indeed concern Roman palaces belonging to noble families tied to the world of the curia, but not the Apostolic Palace. On this point there is agreement with the ceremonials: Agostino Patrizi Piccolomini (1484–92) prescribed that the cardinals should avoid every tumult "whenever the pope's death happens in Rome," but said nothing about the necessity of protecting the "palace."[37]

The history of Roman pillages linked to the popes' deaths raises some general points worth recapitulating.

1. In pillaging the "palace," the Roman people ritualized the idea that part of the "pontifical goods" were their own property and should therefore be restored to them at the pope's death. Recall that the papal rite of taking possession of the Lateran itself confirmed this notion: seated on the *stercorata* (bedunged) seat, the newly elected pontiff threw three fistfuls of coins to the Roman people, declaring: "This silver and gold have not been given me for my own pleasure; what I have, I will give to you."

2. The papacy's struggle against this sort of plundering began before the Gregorian reform. The first episode in fact goes back to 885. The date merits attention. Still, it is only later, under Leo IX, that the Roman sources contain clear evidence of reflection on the distinction between the pope's physical person and the institution of the papacy. To defend the "pontifical goods" amounted to saying that although the pope dies, the church itself is eternal. In his letter on the events at Osimo, had Leo IX not forcefully opposed the sacking of the bishop's palace with

the idea that Christ is the "immortal spouse of the church" or, rather, the "eternal pontiff"?[38] This suggests that the protection of the "palace" was chronologically the first institutional area in which a conscious and explicit distinction was made between the pope's physical mortality and the permanence of the papacy.

3. This centuries-long struggle came to fruition in the thirteenth and fourteenth centuries. Working in its favor were a number of circumstantial factors, above all the frequency with which thirteenth-century popes were elected and died outside of Rome. The prolongation of the papacy's residence at Avignon in the fourteenth century (1308–78) further impeded the revival of traditional sackings, whose spontaneity and impetuousness were tied in some way to the deceased pope's physical presence in Rome.

4. But the principal check derived from the affirmation of the papacy's universality, which by the thirteenth century had become a political reality that extended beyond ecclesiology. Peter Damian had already warned that the pope's death was a "moment of terror" of universal dimensions that concerned all of Christendom. From the Gregorian reform onward, the pope's death increasingly concerned the church universal. Could the Roman people still hope to appropriate goods that now belonged not only to the bishop of Rome, but to the universal church?

5. In the first decades of the thirteenth century, besides protecting the "palace," the papacy also managed to force the emperors to renounce the right of spoils with respect to ecclesiastics.[39] The papacy's victory on the matter of the *ius spolii* ("right of spoils"), a manifestation of its *plenitudo potestatis* ("fullness of power"), coincided, moreover, with the expansion of the curial practice of drawing up testaments.[40] The oldest papal *licentia testandi* ("license for drawing up a will") sent to a curial prelate (Cardinal Pietro of Piacenza) is a letter from Celestine III (1191–98).[41] The doctrine that underlay the *licentia testandi* was based on the concept that part of the late prelate's goods belonged to the church. This distinction naturally applied to the pope as well.

A common element thus underlay both the papacy's effort to protect the "palace" from popular plundering, papal pretensions on the matter of the *ius spolii,* and the curia's doctrine on testaments: the death of a curial prelate, even more that of the pope, had to take place under the control of the Roman church in both the private and institutional ("suprapersonal") spheres. The pope dies, but the church is eternal.

Burial with Honor

Leo IX had wished to await death lying on his bed in Saint Peter's Basilica. That very morning, he ordered his marble sepulcher to be brought in.[42] A few decades later, the author of the *Vita* of Paschal II (d. 1118) informs us that before being buried with the due obsequies and honors, and carried into the Basilica of the Savior (the Lateran), the pope's corpse, "covered with balsam," was dressed again in sacred vestments according to the instructions of the *ordo*.[43] In the *Vita* of Paschal's immediate predecessor, Urban II (1088–99), there appears a fleeting but significant note on the honors of his burial: "his body was borne, through Trastevere on account of his enemies' plots, to the church of Saint Peter, as is traditional, and there buried with honor."[44] The *Vita* of Paschal's successor, Honorius II (1124–30), deliberately recalls the antiquity of a Roman *ordo* used to define the honors due to the popes' corpses.[45] The same is true of Pietro Guglielmo's *Liber pontificalis* (1142), which ends precisely with the *Vita* of Honorius II: twice it underlines the failure to carry out the proper pontifical funeral rites.[46] The author's lament, coming after the events, is a punctilious ceremonial critique: the pope's body was transported from the Lateran to the monastery of Saints Andrew and Gregory by "lay hands"; the body was dressed only in a shirt and sleeves; the coffin lacked sheets. Never before does one encounter in the *Liber pontificalis* such deliberate emphasis on the liturgy of the funeral and the pope's remains, here described with the learned word for cadaver, *gleba*.[47] The entire passage, sustained by a play on the words "bearing" and "carried away" (*deportanda, deportata*), serves to underscore the existence and relevance of a ceremonial of funeral honors that applied exclusively to the case of a pope's death. This is the *ordo* about which the *Vitae* of Paschal and Honorius spoke, which prescribed the preparation with balsam and the dressing of the body, as well as the solemn participation of the "fathers" *(patres)*, that is, the cardinals. This is important: the *Liber pontificalis* had traditionally indicated only the location of the pope's tomb.[48]

Less than a century later, in the *Liber pontificalis* of Boso, papal chamberlain and cardinal under Popes Adrian IV (1154–59) and Alexander III (1159–81), explicit references to ceremonial funeral honors at the pope's death appear in such a systematic manner that it is necessary to speak of a topos. This in itself provides indisputable confirmation of the existence, traditional by the second half of the twelfth century, of rites and funeral ceremonies reserved exclusively to the Roman pontiff.[49] Notably, the series of examples begins precisely with the life of Leo IX, the first of the reforming popes of the eleventh century.[50]

All this confirms that between the last decades of the eleventh century and the first decades of the twelfth, a long path was quickly traveled. The *Liber pontificalis* enables us to follow the tracks, first in that brief notice of the "honorific" burial of Urban II, then in an explicit reference to the existence of an *ordo,* and in the description of several elements constituting the (new) ceremonial. The need to draw ever more attention to papal funerals, reinforced by ceremonial honors, entailed a valorization of the corpse as well as of the tomb.

These developments in Roman funeral rituals inscribed themselves, moreover, into a ceremonial context that included the courts of other European sovereigns. Sources for the kings of France also cite "royal funeral customs" for the first time at the beginning of the twelfth century (1129).[51] In England, a more precise ceremonial is evident in the second half of the century. Henry II (1154–89) was the second king to be buried in the clothes he had worn at his consecration. Indeed, on that occasion, according to a chronicler, the royal funeral was conducted "according to royal custom" *(more regio).*[52]

Burial and the Electoral Process

Another point must immediately be brought into consideration. The concern for the pope's burial, so clearly evident in the sources, also had an institutional motivation: to guarantee the proper transfer of the *potestas papae* ("power of the pope").

To cast doubt on the legitimacy of Hildebrand's election to the papacy (April 22, 1073), his detractors pointed out that he had been elected "even before the body of his predecessor had been buried."[53] Bonizone of Sutri replied to these accusations in his *Book to a Friend* (*Liber ad amicum,* c. 1080), explaining that Hildebrand had been assisting at the burial of Alexander II at the very moment in which the "concurrence of the clergy" that carried him to election became manifest.[54] Again, in 1130, Cardinal Chancellor Aimeric's initiative to proceed to the election of his candidate, Innocent II, without waiting for the funeral of Honorius II, was taken by the supporters of his rival, Anacletus II, as additional proof of the election's invalidity.[55]

For the history of papal burials, the interest of the tragic events of 1130 lies in the broad reflections that emerged from within the College of Cardinals. Even before Honorius II was dead, the cardinals agreed that on account of the "hatreds and animosities that pervaded the city of Rome," they should begin thinking about the election of his successor. Some of them pointed out that "the election of a successor cannot be undertaken while the Roman pontiff is still living or, if he is deceased, before he has been buried," and appealed to existing canons. Others noted, instead, that the urgency of the situation made it advisable to modify the canons. They nevertheless agreed that in the future, under pain of excommunication, no move to elect a successor would be permitted "while the pope remains unburied."[56]

The old canons to which the cardinals referred prescribed that the process of electing a successor begin on the third day after the pope's death. The basic text, Boniface III's decree of 607, spoke only vaguely about burial: the word *depositio* (deposition) could even have been interpreted as synonymous with death.[57] On this point, the text had not been modified for centuries. We encounter the concept again in the decree of the 1059 Lateran Synod, according to which the election of a successor must take place "when the pontiff of this universal Roman church is dead."[58] But a generation later, around 1098, Cardinal Benno, in transcribing the Bonifacian text, substituted for the word *depositio* the more precise term *sepultura* ("burial").[59] The fact should be noted because, as we have seen, the contemporary *Vitae* of Paschal II and Honorius II were the first to speak of an autonomous *ordo* for papal funerals.

℮

When, after the death of Pope Celestine III (Jan. 8, 1198), a part of the College of Cardinals left the Lateran for the more secure Settizonio Palace to begin the process of electing his successor, Lothar of Segni (the future Pope Innocent III) was among those who remained at Saint John's to take part, with some degree of ostentation, in the funeral of the deceased pope. According to his papal biographer, Lothar "wanted to be present with some of the other [cardinals] at the funeral obsequies of his predecessor, [which were celebrated] in the Constantinian Basilica."[60] Forty years after Innocent III's election, the death of Gregory IX (1241) opened up one of the most dramatic vacancies of the Apostolic See: with deliberate violence, the Roman senator Matteo Rosso Orsini shut the cardinals in that same Settizonio Palace in which Innocent III had been elected.[61] The Milanese Goffredo Castiglioni got sick just three days after his election as Pope Celestine IV (Oct. 25, 1241). Terrified, some of the cardinals sought refuge at the papal villa of Anagni, from which they scolded their "Roman" colleagues for not having dared to participate in the pope's obsequies, or to turn to their important family connections in Rome to organize his burial with the honors that tradition required.[62]

We may therefore draw a provisional conclusion. The ostentation shown by Hildebrand (Gregory VII) and Lothar of Segni (Innocent III) in wishing to participate in the last rites of their predecessors; the protest of Anacletus II's electors against the chancellor Aimeric; and the fact that, in the midst of myriad difficulties and disturbances, the cardinals who had retreated to Anagni in 1241 still found time to polemicize against the neglected observance of honorable papal funeral rites, all point in the same direction: the election of a new pope had to take place not only after the death, but after the—honorable—burial of his predecessor.

Letters of Election

This deep institutional bond between death, burial, and the election of a new pope began to figure ever more visibly as well in the formulary of the letters with which newly elected pontiffs traditionally announced their election. The chronology unfolds over the same arc of time that has concerned us until now: the phenomenon in fact emerged around the mid–eleventh century and became firmly established in the course of the thirteenth.[63]

One of the very first reforming popes of the eleventh century, Stephen IX (1057–58), replied to Archbishop Gervais of Rheims, who had congratulated him on his accession to the pontificate (Aug. 2, 1057).[64] Alexander II (1061–73), instead, announced his election on his own initiative. The reference to his recent election, however, is succinct: he did not even mention his predecessor's name explicitly.[65] Elected on September 1, 1073, Gregory VII sent out fully four letters announcing his election—to Henry IV of Germany; to Desiderius, abbot of Montecassino; to Prince Gisulf of Salerno; and to Guibert, archbishop of Ravenna.[66] An announcement of the death and burial of his predecessor follows.[67] This seems to confirm that Hildebrand's highly visible participation at Alexander II's funeral was a deliberate and conscious gesture.[68]

The sequence (death of the predecessor, burial, election) established for the first time by Gregory VII reappears, without notable variations, in the letters of Calixtus II (Feb. 2, 1119) and Anacletus II (Feb. 24, 1130).[69] Celestine II (elected Sept. 26, 1143) and Eugenius III (elected Feb. 15, 1145) added the *dates* of their predecessors' deaths.[70] Writing to the archbishop of Genoa (Sept. 26, 1159), Alexander III informed him of his predecessor's date of death (Sept. 1), of his burial (Sept. 4), gave the place (Saint Peter's in the Vatican), and paused even to note the length of the deliberations that had led to his own election (three days).[71] The chancery's precision was no doubt motivated by the fact that Alexander's election was being contested. His rival, Victor IV, was less precise: but even his letter of election (Oct. 28, 1159) refers to the death and burial of his predecessor, two elements that by now had become traditional.[72]

In the letter he sent on January 9, 1198, announcing his

election to King Philip Augustus of France, Innocent III did not specify the date of his predecessor's burial, but underlined its honorific character.[73] This was not a coincidence pure and simple. Writing to the king of Jerusalem on July 25, 1216, Honorius III also affirmed that the cardinals had indeed met to discuss the succession the day immediately following Innocent III's funeral and the deposition of his body with honor in the tomb.[74] The letters of election of the line of thirteenth-century popes from Gregory IX (1227) to Martin IV (1285) continued to describe these two phases—funeral rites and burial of the corpse—but generally substituted for the reference to honors a general citation of custom—"according to custom" (*juxta morem*), "as is becoming" (*prout decuit*), "according to law and custom" (*prout est juris et moris*), "due" (*debita*)—a clear sign that the "honor of funeral obsequies" (*honor exequiarum*) had by now become a tradition.[75]

In this long but fairly straightforward diplomatic evolution, a new step was taken by the papal chancery under Nicholas IV: besides the obsequies and entombment of the corpse, the electoral letter of this first Franciscan pope, addressed on February 23, 1288, to the archbishop of Sens and his suffragans, paused in fact to note the identity between the place of election and the deceased pope's residence.[76] The same point reappears in the letter with which Benedict XI announced his election to the archbishop of Milan (Oct. 31, 1303); the chancery formula had been brought into conformity with Gregory X's constitution *Ubi periculum* ("Where There Is Danger," 1274), which ordered the cardinals henceforth to proceed to the election of a new pope in the same place where his predecessor had died. The constitution had at first been suspended, then finally confirmed, by Celestine V (1294).[77] The definitive acceptance of Gregory's constitution halted, for what concerns us, the diplomatic evolution of the papal letters of election. There were scarcely any innovations in the Avignon period.[78]

A Time of Mourning

The solemn transport of Eugenius III's corpse from Tivoli to Saint Peter's in the Vatican took place the same day as his death

(July 8, 1153). The funeral cortege took "the public street, following a central route through the city." Clergy and people took part en masse. In describing the event, the papal biographer Boso speaks in terms of "mourning and of sorrow," unusual in the long tradition of the *Liber pontificalis*.[79] Their significance went well beyond momentary emotion. The death of the pope meant mourning—mourning for the whole church.

The thought found an even more explicit formulation in the *Vita* of Gregory IX (1227–41).[80] His sumptuous enthronement in the Lateran allowed the church to "change its lugubrious clothes" and, at the semidestroyed walls of the city *(Urbe),* to recover in part "its ancient grandeur."[81] The pope's death began a time of mourning for the church. The ascent of a new pontiff, instead, constituted a "rebirth" *(rinascita)* for the church. Recording Innocent IV's election (June 25, 1243), the *Vita* of Gregory X (1271–76) used the idea of the "widowhood of the Roman church" in a new manner, which it completed in turn with the image of the spouse, "integrally" reunited with the election of a new pope.[82]

Taken as a whole, the elements that have come to light so far are varied, but also convergent. Let us review them again: the insistence of the *Liber pontificalis,* from the *Vita* of Urban II onward, on the honorific character of the pontifical burial; the reference in Paschal II's *Vita* to the use of balsam in preparing the deceased pope's body; the express desire of Hildebrand (Gregory VII) and Lothar of Segni (Innocent III) to be able to attend the burials of their deceased predecessors; the outrage (expressed in the *Vita* of Honorius II, and by the cardinals during the 1241 vacancy of the Apostolic See) at the failure to observe pontifical funeral rites and gestures; the theme of the widowhood of the Roman church, especially pronounced in the thirteenth century; the progressive and systematic insertion of accounts of their predecessors' burials into the letters with which newly elected popes announced their election; and the birth, finally, of an autonomous pontifical funeral *ordo.* These are themes that, together with chronology, all point in the same direction: from the mid–eleventh century the Roman church accorded growing attention to the death and burial of the pope. The rhetorical and ritual emphasis on the "honors" due the deceased pope was part of a broad and deliberate process of distinguishing between the pope's physical mortality and the permanence of the papal institution.

Funeral Rites

We should now ask ourselves whether and how such a radical distinction was ritualized within the framework of papal funeral ceremonies. But to do so we must wait until the fourteenth century. For the first complete pontifical funeral ceremonial comes two and a half centuries after the first reference to the existence of such an *ordo* in the *Vita* of Paschal II (d. 1118).[83] Its author is Pierre Ameil, who was present at the papal court from the pontificate of Urban V (1362–70) until his own death on May 4, 1401.[84]

ℰ

Ameil's ceremonial distinguishes sharply between three spaces: the pope's private chamber, the chapel, and the church. In his chamber, the dying pope spent the last moments of his life, which the ceremonial codified in the words and gestures it assigned to him. It was in the papal chamber that the corpse was washed and dressed. The chapel was a semipublic place for the exposition and visitation of the body. The public funeral was celebrated in the church. Two processions conveyed the corpse from the chamber to the chapel, and from the chapel to the church. There were thus three places for three different purposes: the preparation and visitation of the body (in the papal chamber, or *camera*); the liturgical vigil for curialists and religious (in the chapel); and the solemn obsequies (in the church). The period of time assigned for all three of these phases was nine days. The administrative and ritual responsibilities were assigned above all to three agents: the papal chamberlain, the penitentiaries, and the cardinals.

The role of the chamberlain had a double purpose, private and public. It was his job, in fact, to protect the "papal goods" *(bona pape)* from every offense *(insultum),* and he could, during the entire vacancy, live in the *camera* with the *familia* (papal aides). At the moment when the pope's corpse was taken out of the chamber and into the chapel, the chamberlain had to receive immediately all the keys in the possession of the *cubicularii* (servants) and summon the first cardinals, by age, from the orders of bishops, priests, and deacons, to turn over to them all the pope's jewels, together with the inventories.[85] Only the sacristan was exempt, "because the office is perpetual."[86] In the trip from the chamber to the chapel, only the chamberlain, the household *(domus),* and the *familia* were authorized to wear black caps and to accompany the pope's corpse.[87] The chamberlain had to "see everything"—that is, "accompany the body"—but only if he was not a cardinal;[88] if, on the other hand, he was, "he is to dress neither in black, nor red, nor green, but in other colors."[89] On this point, Ameil provides an exact and detailed list of the members of the *familia* who must wear black.[90]

While the pope was still in his death throes, the penitentiaries read him the office of the dead, the seven penitential psalms, and other prayers contained in their manual. The Friars of the *Bulla* (Seal) or of the *Pignotta* had to wash the corpse with "cold water and good herbs" that the *cubicularii* had prepared; the barber had to shave his head and beard. His body was then washed again with white wine (warmed with fragrant herbs and good vernaccia) provided to the workers by the servants in waiting or the papal wine stewards. The chamberlain or the sacristan had to give them balsam to oil the corpse, "and even the hands." The penitentiaries had to redress the pope's body, after "having almost seated it," "with sacred vestments, almost all of red; that is, with white sandals, cincture and belt, fanon, stole, short tunic *(tunicella),* maniple, dalmatic, gloves, chasuble, and pallium taken from the body of Peter."[91] They folded the fanon over the pope's head and shoulders as though he were going to celebrate mass, and put the berretta and white miter (without pearls or gold) on his head.[92]

Two or three days before the pope "loses speech," the chamberlain had to convene the cardinals so that the dying man might dictate his testament in their presence and elect his place of burial.[93] Still in their presence, the pope had to make the profession of faith. The cardinals were to pardon him if he had failed in any way in the exercise of his office.[94] The pope had to "commend the church" to the cardinals, so that they might make provisions in peace and quiet to select a new "pastor"; indicate, if he thought it appropriate, or in accordance with his conscience, the name of whom he considered fit to govern the church; commend "all his familiars"; turn over all of the goods, treasure, and jewels of the Roman church; and give an account of all the credits (as well as debts) contracted by the Roman church, so that his successor might satisfy them.[95] Finally, to the cardinals the pope conceded "some pardons . . . in the forum of conscience" *(in foro conscientie)*.[96] Immediately after the pope's death, even before the body had been washed and dressed, the ceremonial prescribes that the cardinals visit the corpse. But then they had to "withdraw."

Throughout the entire period of the corpse's preparation and semipublic display in the chapel, the cardinals could not be present, nor could they put on the vestments ordinarily associated with their ecclesiastical rank. If, for example, the obsequies were held in the chapel, any cardinals who wished to attend personally had to remain seated in one of the rear benches, dressed in a wool cloak, without vestments, and without wearing any red.[97]

During the novena the cardinals were to wear neither black, nor red, nor green, but some other color.[98] Only for the masses of the novena were they to put on black copes.[99] The cardinals' mourning was liturgical, defined to coincide with the period of the official funeral. On the first day of the funeral ceremonies, while the bier—called the *castrum doloris* ("fortress of sorrows")—was surrounded by the pope's familiars, dressed in black, and by the chamberlain (provided he was not a cardinal), the members of the College of Cardinals remained standing in the choir.[100] They then had to celebrate the funeral offices following a rigid hierarchical order. The order of succession—cardinal bishops, priests, and deacons—could not be broken for any reason; whoever did so lost his place.[101]

The body and the bier—the *castrum doloris*—were laden with visible signs of the pope's former majesty *(maiestas)*: the pallium had to have "touched the body of Peter"; the penitentiaries had "to fold the fanon on the head and around the shoulders as though (the deceased) were to celebrate mass"; the cover of the mattress had to be red silk; on it were to be laid two gold cloths held together; the bier itself was covered with a black or blue-violet *(iacintino)* silk cloth "bearing the arms of the pope and of the Roman church"; analogously, on the bier were placed—during the exposition in the chapel—two cushions made of gold cloth and bordered with silk, one under the pope's head, the other under his feet.[102]

The pope's barber was forbidden to carry away the shaving box containing the razors and silver basin, but the new pope was obliged to give him ten or twelve florins. The basin had to stay in the pope's chamber *(camera)* with the razors and the shaving cloths.[103] These were personal objects, the last to have touched the body of the deceased pope, whose head and beard the barber had shaved.[104] A second article explained that sometimes the popes' bakers and wine stewards wished to obtain the tablecloths on which the pope had eaten for the last time, or the casks from which he had had his last drink; but these should never be turned over to them, "because they have their own salaries."[105] The objects that had touched the pope's body were thus transferred to the institution against the payment of an honorarium *(gagia)*.

The text of Ameil's ceremonial is the first in the history of the medieval papacy that contains a detailed description of the ceremonial forms to be observed during the transport and burial of a Roman pontiff. Including over one hundred articles, the section on the pope's death is the first of a long series of appendices to the liturgical *ordo* preceding that devoted to the conclave.[106] This attention to ceremonial is concerned, deliberately and officially, with a span of time encompassing the pope's final illness, the ceremonial procedures having to do with the preparation of the corpse, the exposition in the chapel, and official obsequies, as well as the conclave.

Already, the *Vita* of Paschal II had recorded that the pope died after receiving extreme unction and having "made confession."[107] The author of Gelasius II's (d. 1119) *Vita* added other details. The pope, "struck unexpectedly by a malady the Greeks call pleurisy, called together many of his brothers from every region, made confession, and took communion."[108] Calixtus II's (d. 1124) *Vita* also emphasized the fact that the pope "had gone to rest in the Lord," that is, after making confession and arranging all his affairs.[109] For the thirteenth century, information on the popes' preparations for death is scarce. A continuator of Bernard Gui informs us, however, that before dying at the castle of Soriano, Nicholas III (d. 1280) summoned "into his presence all the cardinals and curialists residing at Viterbo."[110] The first complete description of the scene of a pope's confession and preparation for death is that of Benedict XI.[111] The text was meant to be an exact account of what happened at the pope's death (July 7, 1304). Compared to Ameil's prescriptions, there are no significant differences.[112] Devotional and institutional gestures are blended together. The pope confessed himself and received communion in the presence of the cardinals; he called for extreme unction and received it devoutly from the cardinal bishop of Albano; the profession of faith also served implicitly to authenticate the orthodoxy of the pope's action; the dying pope exhorted the cardinals to concord. After the description of the pope's selection of a burial site (the Dominican convent in Perugia), there follows an article dedicated entirely to the cardinals, whom Benedict absolved from every excommunication, irregularity, and sin. Along with other prescriptions concerning the papal *familia,* the goods he had had when he was still a cardinal, and the books in his possession, other elements confirm the general impression of the document as a whole: in its substance and structure, it was indebted to thirteenth-century curial and papal testaments.[113]

If, at first sight, one might think that the scene of the pope's preparation for death fits into an idealized vision of Christian death, in fact, as we find it described, it was a moment more of special ecclesiological—rather than spiritual—importance. The entire phase turns around two key moments, private and public. The pope was called upon to confess his sins. Indeed, for Pierre Ameil, author of the oldest papal funeral ceremonial (1385–90), the pope, "being the light of the whole universe, must give an example to all kings and princes, laymen and clergy, who turn to God in their infirmity and open up their consciences; he must do so, because he is the head of all Christendom."[114] The dying pope must also, however, "commend the church" to the members of the College of Cardinals. The preparation for death was a public affair that sanctioned the cardinals' responsibility as institutional agents in the transfer of the *potestas papae.*

č

The distinction between physical mortality and the permanence of the papal institution is also at the center of the second ceremonial on papal funerals by François de Conzié, papal chamberlain for forty-eight years (1383–1431).[115] The vice chancellor, whose office ended with the pope's death, had to receive from the hands of the sealers the molds of the bulls, which he wrapped in strong canvas and upon which he impressed his own seal to prevent any more letters being sent out. The prior of the cardinal bishops then convened all the cardinals resident at the curia, who assembled solemnly in one of the palace chambers to attend a ceremony at which the mold bearing the deceased pope's name would be broken to pieces. The vice chancellor would turn over the mold to be destroyed, along with a hammer specially prepared by the bullators. The other mold, reproducing the images of the apostles Peter and Paul, was to be left "whole and undamaged" and placed in the same canvas that, closed and sealed by the vice chancellor, would be turned over to the chamberlain, who kept it until the election of the new pope. The vice chancellor could keep the canvas, but only after it had been sealed by the prior of the cardinal bishops and by three priors of each order of cardinals.[116] The cardinals were thus guarantors of the transfer of the *potestas papae.* For the same reason, the lamb with the "seal of the fisherman" was given to the College of Cardinals on the pope's death.[117]

Conzié specified further that, during the novena, the cardinals should wear cloaks of a dark color, but not black, lined with gray or dark blue, except those who were related to the late pope or had been raised to their offices by him.[118] The distinction between the two categories of curialists who were authorized to wear mourning or not was clearly formulated: "It should be known that mourning clothes are not to be worn on account of the pope's death by those who hold perpetual offices in the curia. . . . Those, instead, who hold nonperpetual offices which end with the pope's death . . . may wear mourning so long as, besides these offices, they do not hold lesser perpetual offices."[119]

The chamberlain's role remained unchanged. He had to have all the doors of the Apostolic Palace closed immediately, except one for necessary services, which likely conformed to normal practice at Avignon.[120] In prescribing the extraordinary measures necessary for maintaining public order, Conzié said not a word about protecting the "palace."[121]

℃

But must the cardinals wear mourning? On this point, an interesting development is observable between the texts of Ameil and Conzié. According to the former, during the public funeral for the pope (the novena), the cardinals could not put on habits of black or red (nor even the intermediate color green). The cardinals were to wear black copes only when they celebrated the masses of the novena. Conzié, instead, distinguished between those cardinals who were relatives of the pope and had been put in office by him, and the others: only the former could wear black cloaks, the others, instead, "may wear dark-colored cloaks, but not black." This distinction, which would persist down to modern times, reflects a new and refined sense of the difference between the physical nature of the pope, mortality, and the perpetuity of the church.

In this respect, there is a certain correspondence with the history of the funeral rituals of the French kings. The presidents of the Parlement of Paris did not have to wear mourning "because the crown and justice never die."[122] The practice is attested for the first time in 1422, on the occasion of Charles IV's funeral, but a miniature portraying the funeral cortege of Queen Joanna of Bourbon (d. 1378) takes us back—and this is important for our purposes—to the age in which the oldest ceremonials of papal funerals were drawn up.[123]

℃

It is necessary to conclude once again. To the questions posed at the outset, the analysis of the two oldest ceremonials of pontifical funerals has allowed us to respond with a certain clarity. The distinction between the physical person of the deceased pope, and the institutional permanence of the papacy, is the cornerstone on which we have been erecting the entire history of the death of

the pope from the Gregorian reform onward. If the funeral ceremonials of the late fourteenth century contain a few innovations
from the Avignon period, in their essence they reflect an older
ritual and rhetorical development that we have also attempted to
reconstruct for what concerns the theme of mortality. The pope
dies, but the church is eternal.

From this centuries-long ritual development that led to the
creation of a new ritual space—the novena—there also emerges,
however, another essential feature: an ever-growing interest in
the body of the deceased pope. Recall the scene of the dying Leo
IX having himself carried into the basilica of Saint Peter's. Think
of the rhetorical emphasis on the "honors" due the deceased
pope. Participation at the pope's burial could became a source of
legitimacy or of conflict in the election of his successor. Based
on the twelfth-century *Liber pontificalis,* it is possible to speak of
a genuine historical revaluation of the corpse and of all that per-
tained to it.

But we should also ask ourselves now whether there is not a
contradiction between these two characteristics. Or, instead, is
the contrast only apparent? To answer these questions, undoubtedly important, we must reconstruct above all the ritual journey
on which the pope's corpse was taken as it moved one by one
through the various moments in its passage from exposition to
the grave.

5 The Corpse

Nudity

There is a famous episode surrounding the corpse of Innocent III, the first pope of the thirteenth century. It is recounted by Jacques de Vitry, one of the most renowned preachers of the epoch, who would eventually become cardinal bishop of Tusculum (1229–41). In 1216 he was obliged to travel to Perugia, where the Roman curia was then in residence, to be consecrated bishop of Acre. As chance would have it, he arrived the day after Innocent III had died (July 16, 1216). The pope was not yet buried. His corpse had been displayed in the cathedral of the city, but during the night (July 16–17) some people had "furtively" stripped it of the precious vestments in which it was to have been entombed. The cadaver had been abandoned in the church almost nude *(fere nudum),* in an advanced state of decomposition *(fetidum).* Jacques concludes that he was thus able to confirm with his own eyes how "brief and vain [is] the illusory splendor of this world." [1]

Needless to say, Jacques's testimony reflects the rhetoric of mortality and humility that we have been reconstructing from the outset of this study. But his words may also be compared to those that Lothar of Segni, the future Pope Innocent III himself, had used in speaking of the "misery of man." The agreement with Innocent's *De miseria conditionis humanae (On the Misery of the Human Condition)* may not be word for word, but the similarities are nonetheless striking.[2] The analogy deserves to be highlighted, because it touches several essential points: nudity, the stench of the cadaver, and the transience of power.

ꝛ

What sort of nudity are we dealing with? What is the meaning of the words "almost nude" *(fere nudum)* that Jacques uses to describe the state in which Innocent III's corpse had been abandoned? Should the nudity of the pope's corpse be taken literally? Some reservation seems justified on this point, because medieval terminology tended to identify nudity with transparency and whiteness: "almost nude" might mean not so much nudity in the strict sense, as that the pope was left dressed only in his white shirt.[3] Certainly, Jacques's "sullen words" contrast sharply with the prestige of a pope whom the English chronicler Matthew Paris was ready to call "the astonishment of the world" *(stupor mundi),* and whom modern historians do not hesitate to pronounce "the most powerful in the Middle Ages."[4]

That said, there are no clear grounds for doubting the veracity of the tragic event.[5] Nor does it diminish the validity of Jacques's account to set it against the silence on the nocturnal spoliation of Innocent's corpse from the only other eyewitness to his death and burial.[6]

ċ

The theme of nudity appears a second time in the thirteenth century in relation to another powerful pope, Innocent IV, who died at Naples on December 7, 1254.

The first testimony we should examine is that of the Franciscan chronicler Salimbene of Parma, which comes, however, several decades after the pope's death. Salimbene recounts in his *Cronica (Chronicle,* 1284) that the Fieschi pope "remained nude on the straw and abandoned by everybody, in accordance with the custom of the Roman pontiffs when they die." The deceased was looked after not by untrustworthy papal custodians, but by the "Teutonic" friars, who even took care of washing the pope's body. According to Salimbene, the two friars addressed the pope as follows: "It is true, Lord Pope, that we have sojourned in this land for many months, desiring to speak with you and to discuss with you our problems. Your servants would not even permit us to enter and see you in person. Now they care nothing about looking after [your corpse], because they have nothing left to gain from you. Nevertheless, we will wash your body."[7]

Curiously, another Franciscan, the pope's biographer, the Umbrian Niccolò of Calvi, bishop of Assisi, reports instead that

"Friars Minor and Preachers and many other religious, even members of the secular clergy, passed the night next to the bier of the deceased father, and assisted him with lauds and prayers."[8] The contradiction between Niccolò's and Salimbene's accounts seems complete, and leads one to think that the deceiver may have been the author of Innocent IV's *Vita*. In describing nocturnal vigils attended by so many, Niccolò may have distorted reality "out of some sense of pious respect, or for some other reason."[9]

Who was telling the truth, Salimbene or Niccolò of Calvi?

That the latter might have wanted to conceal part of the truth would have been in the nature of things. After all, he was writing just a few years after the pope's death, when at least one of the two Fieschi cardinals, the pope's nephews, was still alive.[10] But how can it be imagined that a papal biographer, who had lived for decades at the Roman curia (he was Sinibaldo Fieschi's chaplain and confessor before his ascent to the papacy as Innocent IV), would describe in such minute detail a scene that bore no relationship, even in theory, to the papal ceremonial? In short, Niccolò may have dissembled, but the ritual and liturgical gestures he refers to could have taken place. And this is already a lot, given the extreme rarity of thirteenth-century sources on papal funeral customs.

℮

But should the problem be posed in precisely these terms? That is, were Salimbene and Niccolò of Calvi really talking about the same thing?

If we look closely, Salimbene seems in fact to have had in mind the period immediately following the pope's death: Innocent IV had been left nude on the straw, and only thanks to the solicitude of the Friars Minor did his body get washed; abandonment and nudity were a "custom of the Roman pontiffs when they die."[11] That undoubtedly means that, for the Franciscan Salimbene, the corpse had been abandoned nude before being prepared, dressed, and exhibited. For Salimbene, the pope's nudity came immediately after his death.

Niccolò of Calvi, instead, was thinking of the nocturnal vigil, a moment that has to be kept separate from that which preceded it, and which it followed. Understood in this sense, his testimony is perfectly consonant with the oldest papal funeral ceremonial, that of Pierre Ameil, which we examined earlier.

℃

Before drawing conclusions, we should look at another source, which also happens to be Franciscan. The episode in fact derives from the oldest chronicle of the English Franciscans, whose composition precedes that of Salimbene's *Cronica* by several years.

But let us take matters in their proper order. In his *On the Coming of the Friars (De adventu Minorum),* the Franciscan Thomas of Eccleston records fully three times the decrees issued by Innocent IV concerning the conflict that pitted the mendicants against the secular masters of the Parisian *Studium.* According to Thomas, the promulgation of these decisions, unfavorable to the mendicants, caused the pope to lose the gift of speech, which he recovered only thanks to Saint Francis.[12] The English chronicler then relates a notice he received from one of the familiars of Alexander IV (1254–61), the pope who had suspended Innocent's notorious decrees on the very day of his election:[13] while he was still a cardinal (and protector of the Franciscan order), Alexander had predicted the sudden death of his predecessor, Innocent IV.[14] The Franciscan chronicle continues, affirming that "In truth, at the death [of Innocent IV], all his familiars abandoned him, except the Friars Minor. The same thing happened to Gregory [IX], Honorius [III], and Innocent [III], at whose death Francis was present."[15] At this point, Eccleston's discussion of the pope's death takes a more general turn: "Brother Mansuetus used to say that no mendicant, indeed no man, dies in so miserable and vile a way as does any pope."[16] The story ends with the legendary disappearance of Frederick II on Mount Etna, which amounted to another attempt, in effect, to demonize one of the most powerful and determined enemies of the Friars Minor.[17]

℃

Thomas of Eccleston and Salimbene must be read together not only because of their chronological proximity. Both of them clearly belonged to the same historiographical tradition of open polemic against the memory of Innocent IV. The abandonment that might befall a pope's corpse at the moment of death served to construct the *damnatio memoriae* ("damnation of the memory") of a pope (Innocent IV) who had acted against the order's interests.

Thomas and Salimbene both allude to a custom of abandoning the pope's corpse, and this is a point to bear in mind. To this custom, moreover, the Franciscans opposed a discourse that tended to guarantee the pope loving care of his corpse. They went so far as to create a series of abandonments of the bodies of deceased popes, who were then protected by a double sort of Franciscan mediation: the mythical presence of Saint Francis at Innocent III's funeral, and the devotion with which the Friars Minor were supposed to have washed, prepared, and kept vigils over the corpses of those popes who had most favored their order since its foundation: Innocent III, Honorius III, and Gregory IX.[18]

The purpose of these accounts was twofold: first, to emphasize the custom of abandonment in order; second, to establish the Franciscan order as custodian of the deceased pope's body. Such a strategy would have made no sense, unless abandonment and nudity indeed had some basis in reality already.[19] The Franciscans made themselves the mediators of a powerful rhetoric of mortality, one that could even produce a *damnatio memoriae,* but which effected at the same time an operation of posthumous and devout appropriation of the pope's body with respect to the bodies of the deceased popes, even of a pope considered an enemy of the order.

ℰ

That the *damnatio memoriae* directed against Innocent IV was part of a strategy inspired by the mendicant orders is confirmed by an *exemplum* that we encounter only in Franciscan and Dominican collections. This episode, too, put the nudity of a cadaver at the center of attention. But this time, the subject was a cardinal rather than a pope, one who died accidentally at Assisi on May 25, 1253, just a few months before Innocent IV.

The cardinal bishop of Albano, Pietro of Collemezzo, the victim of a sudden fall, was reported to have been abandoned, stretched out and almost dead, by the members of his *familia* who hurried to plunder horses, vases, and various furnishings. The friars who arrived on the scene were reported to have seen someone violently pull off his miter and chasuble, abandoning the cadaver nude.[20]

This *exemplum,* too, aimed to effect a *damnatio memoriae,* for reasons that are not terribly difficult to uncover from the cardinal's biography. Cardinal Pietro of Collemezzo was, in all likelihood, the principal supporter at the curia of William of Saint Amour.[21] His death occurred during one of the most critical phases of the conflict at Paris between the secular and mendicant clergy. In April 1253 the secular masters had decided not to accept any more teachers *(magistri)* who had not first sworn to uphold the statutes of their corporation. That effectively shut the mendicant masters out of the Paris *Studium.* A month after the death of Pietro of Collemezzo, on July 1, 1253, Innocent IV instead sided with the mendicants, and ordered the seculars to allow them access to professorships in the *Studium.* The *damnatio memoriae* of Cardinal Collemezzo was thus a demonstration "in reverse" of the mendicants' victory, made possible by the death, no doubt divinely inspired, of the greatest curial supporter of the Parisian secular masters. An unexceptionable contemporary source confirms it. In his *On Bees (De apibus)* the Dominican Thomas of Cantimpré made the message clear: "what happened to the unfortunate cardinal was the just judgment of God: he wanted to punish a bishop and cardinal of the Roman curia who had mortally tyrannized over the Friars Preachers and the Minors in equal measure."[22]

℘

After a silence of more than two centuries, sources that speak to us about the abandonment and nudity of the pope's corpse suddenly appear again around 1500.

Shortly before dying, Pope Julius II (1513) granted an audience to Paride de Grassi, the papal master of ceremonies. The pope remembered "having seen many popes who, once dead, were immediately abandoned by relatives and servants, and preyed upon even for indispensable things, such that they were left lying there in a shameful way, downright nude with their private parts exposed, a thing which, for someone of authority— of majesty *[maiestas]*—as elevated as that of the papacy, was scandalous and degrading."[23] To prevent such a thing happening after his own death, the pope wanted to pay him in advance.

The audience conceded to Paride de Grassi is the only one in the entire history of the medieval and Renaissance papacy in which a pope discussed his own burial with his ceremonialist. This unique text reveals a paroxysmal anguish at the thought that in dying, "the pope returns to being a man." To Paride de Grassi, who suggested that, in accordance with tradition, he have his corpse wrapped up in a white shirt, Julius replied affirmatively, provided the "white cloth used to wrap his corpse was gilded with gold." The dressing of his corpse had to make visible the signs of his former majesty. The pope refused the nudity of the corpse: the golden borders transformed the whiteness (and therefore the nudity) into glory. At the end of the audience, Paride de Grassi asked the pope to confirm his arrangements in the presence of two members of the curia.[24]

℣

Let us say immediately that Julius II's "fears" were fully justified. At the death of Sixtus IV (Aug. 12, 1484), the master of ceremonies, Johann Burchard, had had to overcome innumerable obstacles in carrying out the ceremonial of dressing the corpse:

> The abbot of San Sebastiano, the sacristan, took the bed and all its adornments although, considering my office, these things properly belonged to me. Everything else was stolen, so to say, in an instant, no sooner than the corpse had been carried out of the room. And indeed, despite all my hunting from the sixth to the tenth hours, I was unable to find either oil or a handkerchief, or any sort of receptacle, in which to put the wine and the water scented with herbs to wash the corpse; and not even socks or a clean shirt to dress it.[25]

The corpse of Alexander VI (d. Aug. 18, 1503) was also left unattended "all night, with two torches, without anyone keeping the vigil: and this despite the fact that the penitentiaries had been called to recite the office of the dead."[26] The deceased pope even became an object of ridicule. The next day, Sunday, around midnight, the corpse was carried into the Chapel of the Febbri, where

> it was set down by the wall, in a corner to the left of the altar. The job was given to six very crude men who joked and cursed the pope and his corpse, and two joiners, who made the bier too narrow and too short. Without torches or lights, without anyone

bothering to take care of the corpse, they squeezed it into the box, forcing it in at the mitered end, and covered it with the old rug already mentioned. This is what I was told by Camillo Crispolti, a benefice-holder at St. Peter's.[27]

A few months later, instead, dressing the corpse of Pius III (d. Oct. 18, 1503) was not a problem:

> The pope was washed, dressed, and carried into the antechamber where, on a bed, the mattress of which had been covered with green velvet, he was dressed in the sacred vestments, with the sole exception of the pectoral cross, which was not there, and for which I substituted a cross made with the dangling cinctures, held in place with four pins. He was then transferred to the Hall of the Parrot, and placed upon the table. Meanwhile, in the antechamber and in the Hall of the Parrot, the penitentiaries said the office of the dead without interruption. The cardinals had convened in the Hall of the Pontiffs, then they passed into the Hall of the Parrot, reciting the "Our Father" . . . and they kissed the pope's feet.[28]

In dressing the corpse of Sixtus IV, Burchard admitted to having made a mistake: "having been a member of the order of Saint Francis, he should have been buried in the Franciscan habit, wearing the sacred vestments of the pontiff on top."[29] The problem even provided the stimulus for a broader reflection on the pope's mortality:

> It should be noted that this morning, while dressing the deceased, we made a mistake. He should actually have been wearing, under the sacred vestments, the habit of the Franciscan order, to which he belonged, and not the pontifical. Thus, too, in his own time, was dressed Alexander V, also a member of the order of St. Francis. And the reason for this is that a man, at death, loses every human form of hierarchical superiority; on that account, Sixtus should have been buried in accordance with his human condition preceding his apostolic appointment.[30]

Paride de Grassi's comment on the same matter is even more detailed:

> When [a religious] is elected [pope] he must, for the rest of his life, take off the regular habit in order and put on the apostolic, the same for all the popes: the papal habit is indeed unique, for it

follows the rule of no single order; indeed, as the highest pontiff, he is in truth considered greater than any other man *[maior homine]*; although he is not subject to any rule and cannot be obliged in life to abandon the regular habit, that not withstanding, as the Vicar of Christ he is above the human condition. Once dead, therefore, the pontiff, because he ceases to be the Vicar of Christ and returns to being a man, for this reason, for his burial, he must be dressed, carried, and interred with the habit he was accustomed to wear before the Apostolate, when he was still a man. It is true, however, that the corpse of the deceased must wear, in addition to the regular habit, all the pontifical vestments as well, with which, in life, he was accustomed to celebrate the mass.[31]

Around 1500, then, the concept by which the pope, "dead, returns to being a man," was formulated with renewed firmness by the masters of pontifical ceremonies themselves. The theme was then undoubtedly relevant. According to one of the prescriptions in Agostino Patrizi Piccolomini's ceremonial, not found in any earlier *ordo,* the dying pope was expressly invited to repeat the words pronounced during the coronation ceremony: "Holy Father, thus passes the glory of the world" *(Pater sancte, sic transit gloria mundi).*[32]

In another passage of his memoirs, Burchard wrote that the pope's corpse "in private, is placed nude on a slab [to be] washed and cleaned."[33] In substance, this note agrees with Salimbene's testimony of three centuries earlier, concerning the "custom of the Roman popes when they die." For Salimbene and Burchard, abandonment and nudity overtake the pope's corpse immediately after his death, before it is washed and dressed. Salimbene refers to abandonment and nudity as a custom; Burchard speaks about them as of a situation of normalcy. In both cases, the abandonment and nudity of a pope's corpse was an event of an almost ritual nature, implicitly supporting the view according to which "even the pope dies." Thus it is true that the abandonment and nudity of the pope's corpse proved that "the pope did not have two bodies or substances like a king, but only a natural body, that is born and dies. What remained was Christ, it was the Roman church, the Apostolic See, but not the pope." "The king never dies" *(Le roi ne mert jamais),* "the pope dies" *(papa moritur).*[34]

Such a direct line of thought should not cause us to lose

sight of the fact that the themes of mortality and the transience of power went through periods of particular intensity. The chronology of the sources indicates as much, concentrated so strikingly as they are in the thirteenth and late fifteenth centuries—that is, precisely in the periods of the papacy's greatest strength. But even in this regard, the sources on nudity convey important messages, because they concern—certainly not by chance—powerful popes and hierocrats like Innocent III, Innocent IV, and Julius II. Such a radical emphasis on nudity, and on the possible abandonment of the corpse, obviously served a "humbling" purpose and reestablished a sort of equilibrium.

ẽ

Burchard's notices should also be kept in mind because they teach us that around 1500 the depredations and thefts by members of the papal *familia* continued to take place when a pope died. On this point, the contrast with the courts of other sovereigns is striking: there seem to be no further notices of the abandonment and spoliation of the bodies of the French kings beyond the middle of the twelfth century.[35]

The hostility of Burchard and the other masters of ceremonies to the spread of such customs indicates that, in some quarters of the curia, there were forces capable of offering some resistance. True, as far back as the thirteenth century, the papacy had tried to curb the recurrent pillaging by the papal *familiares* by offering them cash payments in lieu of the objects that by tradition they might appropriate on the pope's death. Moreover, an ever greater number of curial offices were considered permanent; their holders did not have to resign at the pope's death.[36] Nevertheless, the notices considered here (to which could be added others from later periods) demonstrate abundantly that although the Roman curia succeeded, between the thirteenth and fifteenth centuries, in protecting the "palace" from looting by the Roman people, institutional efforts to bring a halt to the robberies by curialists and familiars were not crowned by any great success.[37]

The reason is really quite simple: the exercise of papal and curial power continued to be based on personal bonds of loyalty that were inevitably dissolved at the death of the lord. Under these circumstances, the members of the papal entourage could not but experience the pope's death as a tragic moment of rupture, not least because nepotism also presupposed broad changes of personnel with every new election. Contrariwise, the phenomenon of robbing the garments and objects that had belonged to the deceased popes began to decline only in relatively recent times with the progressive establishment of impersonal professional relationships concurrent with the modern bureaucratization of the Roman curia.

Display

The stripping of Innocent III's corpse took place while it was on display in the cathedral of Perugia. Astonishing as it may seem, even in this respect the episode narrated by Jacques de Vitry constitutes an important documentary discovery. The public display of a pope's corpse is not in fact attested in other, older sources.[38] The Roman pontifical of the twelfth century prescribes that "after the soul has left the body, the deceased's body should be washed, then cleaned, placed in the coffin, and carried into church."[39] The corpse therefore seems still to have been hidden from view. In describing the transfer of Eugenius III's (1145–53) mortal remains from Tivoli to the Vatican on the same day as his death, Boso instead emphasizes the fact that the funeral cortege, accompanied by a busy throng of clergy and people, followed the "public street" and "crossed the city."[40] This reflects an unmistakable (and new) interest in according the corpse greater visibility.

Aside from the episode narrated by Jacques de Vitry, we must wait until the second half of the thirteenth century for additional details. In that period, the ceremony of putting the pope's corpse on public display is partially represented on the funeral monuments of several popes and cardinals. The tomb of Cardinal Ancher of Troyes, nephew of Pope Urban IV, still preserved today in the Roman church of Saint Praxides, is the first of the Roman funeral monuments in which the deceased lies on a funeral cover embroidered with clearly funereal heraldic motifs (roses and fleurs-de-lis).[41] On the pediment of Boniface VIII's sarcophagus (carried out by Arnolfo di Cambio around 1296), whose remains were transferred to the Vatican Grotto after the destruction of the old basilica of Saint Peter's, a double layer of cloths is visible: that on top displays medallions bearing the arms of the Gaetani family.[42] The use of personal coats of arms shows up on the tombs of cardinals, like that of Guglielmo Fieschi.[43] Mentioned for Pope Urban IV, we find them for the first time on the funeral monument of Honorius IV.[44] Pierre Ameil's ceremonial (1385−90) prescribes covering the pontifical coffin with two gold cloths bearing the arms of the pope and the Roman church, and directs that the popes' corpses should be displayed on two cushions covered with gilded cloth, the same length as the catafalque.[45] None of the gisants of the late thirteenth-century popes and cardinals failed to include one or two cushions of this type, which seem to be covered with ornamental fabrics. The sculptures represent the dignitaries (popes, cardinals) dressed in the liturgical vestments that we find described in thirteenth-century ceremonial texts.[46]

The ceremony of publicly displaying the corpse contrasts with the nudity and danger of abandonment discussed above. It was perhaps even to highlight this contrast that Jacques de Vitry deployed such an emphatic rhetoric of mortality. The public display of the body, which during the thirteenth century had already become a ritual element in the funeral ceremonies of knights and high dignitaries in Italian cities, must in fact be viewed in the much broader context of imitation *(imitatio)* of Roman antiquity: the exposition was a means of glorifying the deceased.[47] At Byzantium, the body of the emperor, dressed in his coronation gowns, was displayed in the hall of the nineteen Acubiti.[48] King Philip II Augustus of France (1180−1223) was also displayed wearing the clothes in which he had been crowned, and with the royal insignia, at a time when the practice was becoming general throughout Europe.[49]

But the difference is only apparent. If nudity was a way of saying that at death the pope "returns to being a man," the display of the corpse served as a means of glorification, as well as providing public authentication of the pope's death.

Embalming

To make possible prolonged public exposition of the corpse, it was necessary to turn to ever more precise and complex embalming procedures.

The oldest testimony on this point is offered by the *Vita* of Paschal II (d. 1118), though it does not seem to bear directly on the ceremony of public display. The papal biographer says simply that the pope's corpse was "covered with balsam."[50] Moreover, this seems to be an isolated case. For at least two centuries, no other source enables us to know whether and how the popes' corpses were embalmed.[51]

In the first papal funeral ceremonial, instead, Pierre Ameil (1385–90) carefully describes the phase of preparing the corpse:

> Once the pope is dead, the penitentiaries, with the Friars of the *Bulla,* if there are any, or else of the *Pignotta,* with water, and with good herbs that the servants *[cubicularii]* or aides of the papal chamber *[camera]* must prepare, will wash the body well, and the barber will shave his head and beard. Thus washed, the apothecary and the said Friars of the *Bulla* will close all his apertures tightly with wool *[bumbasio]* or flax *[stupa];* the anus, mouth, nostrils, and ears, with myrrh, incense, and aloe (if it can be had): his body should then be washed again with white wine, warmed with fragrant herbs and good vernaccia, which the servants in waiting or, indeed, the wine stewards, must provide the workers. Then his throat should be filled with aromatics and especially with wool, and the nostrils with musk. Lastly, his whole body should be rubbed down and anointed with good balsam, even his hands. The chamberlain, or rather the servants *[cubicularii]* attending in the chamber, or the sacristan, who take care of the balsam, if they have it, should make it available.[52]

The operation was entrusted to members of the curia: penitentiaries, servants, almoners.[53] The embalming was of the "external" type: neither incisions nor an opening were made in the corpse. It was the procedure described by Guy de Chauliac in his famous manual of surgery, which nevertheless contains a long and detailed chapter on the "care of deceased bodies."[54]

The personal physician of Clement VI (1342–52), Chauliac (d. 1368) mentions a second procedure, however, for preparing the "bodies of the dead" *(corpora mortuorum),* which involved opening the abdomen to remove the vital organs.[55] He acknowledged that he had obtained this information from "the apothecary Giacomo, who had embalmed many Roman pontiffs."[56] The tradition was therefore already relatively well established

among curial customs. "Internal" embalming required employ-
ing specialized personnel: the preparation of the body was no
longer entrusted simply to curialists (penitentiaries), but to a
professional (the apothecary).[57]

℮

According to Guy de Chauliac, embalming should prevent the
face's putrefaction for a period of eight days.[58] Pietro Argellata,
Chauliac's student and a renowned professor of surgery at the
University of Bologna (1397–1421), declared himself satisfied to
have succeeded in embalming the corpse of Alexander V, who
died in Bologna, so as to be able to preserve him for eight days.
The face, hands, and feet were left free, because "the hands and
feet have to be seen, just like the face." [59] On this point, Henry
of Mondeville (d. 1320), surgeon of King Philip IV the Fair of
France, offers valuable confirmation:

> In preparing cadavers there are three ways of proceeding. Some
> cadavers merit little preparation to preserve them from corruption,
> or indeed none at all; such is the case for the bodies of the poor,
> and for certain wealthy people if the inhumation is to be carried
> out within three days in the summertime, or within four days in
> winter. Others indeed require some amount of preparation; this is
> the case with men of medium standing, such as soldiers and bar-
> ons. Finally, there are those who must be entirely preserved with
> their faces uncovered, such as kings, queens, supreme pontiffs, and
> prelates.[60]

This agrees entirely with Ameil's funeral ceremonial: the deceased pope's face was covered when the body was displayed in
the chapel, uncovered during the public display in the church,
then covered again when the corpse was laid in the coffin. At
death, the pope "returns to being a man" (face covered), but his
death must be "visible" (face uncovered).[61]

The funeral monument of Adrian V (1276) in San Francesco
alla Rocca in Viterbo allows us to move back a few decades. The
head, hands, and feet appear as the three key elements of the
gisant. An imaginary line "begins" at the head, reaches its apex
in the hands "sliding" toward the observer, and terminates in the
feet "rotated" toward the inside of the monument. The structure
of the sculpture presupposes an almost completely horizontal

positioning of the gisant, privileging a view of the hands. The vertical slant of the four dangling tassels of the cushion also suggests that the funeral bed was designed to be placed in a horizontal position.[62] All that seems clear: Adrian V's funeral statue reproduces the essential elements of a papal funeral bed at the moment of his public exposition, which must leave visible precisely the face, hands, and feet. Also, according to Pierre Ameil, as well, the chamberlain or sacristan had to give some balsam to the apothecary and the Friars of the *Bulla* to oil the corpse of the deceased pontiff, "and even the hands."[63]

℃

If we accept the testimony of Guy de Chauliac and the other leading surgeons of the fourteenth century, the embalming of the pope had a very specific aim: to assure the conservation of the corpse for a period of eight days, coinciding with the duration of the novena. From this point of view, it is hardly surprising that the sources take us back to the beginning of the fourteenth century, the most likely period also for the introduction of the novena into the papal funeral ceremonial.

The public display of the pope's corpse was indeed a characteristic of the *imitatio imperii* ("imitation of empire"), and made visible the lofty office filled by the deceased.[64] Displaying the dead pope with his hands, feet, and face uncovered served above all, however, to guarantee the public authentication of his death. Embalming and displaying the pope's mortal remains were therefore inseparable processes, of fundamental importance also in the process of transferring the *potestas papae* ("power of the pope").

Burial

How, in turn, was the pope's corpse dressed for its deposition in the tomb? Two documents enable us to respond with a certain degree of precision. These are reports that were drawn up at the opening of the tombs of Gregory VII (1073–85) and Boniface VIII (1294–1303), whose pontificates fall, moreover, at the two ends of the chronological period that concerns us.

The precision of these accounts is unequal. The detail of the document on the opening of Gregory VII's tomb, which took place in Salerno in 1578, is much inferior to that of the notarial instrument drawn up on October 11, 1605, by the canon Giacomo Grimaldi, when Boniface VIII's sepulcher in the Vatican Basilica was opened up.[65]

In this second report, the following passage is important:

> [Boniface VIII] had on whole stockings that covered his legs and thighs, in accordance with the custom of those times; the inside was colored red, and at the top they had silver buckles. The soutain, instead, was white; the rochet long down to his heels, made of cloth of Cambrai, and on the breast, behind the legs, and at the ends of the sleeves, were gold and silk embroideries representing the mysteries of the life of Jesus Christ, and its length descended to his feet. The stole that he wore at the collar, about five palms long, was bound with a tassel of brocaded fabric with silver and black silk. The maniple of gold and silver fabric, worked in waves, of black silk, and purple, three palms long. The sandals, colored black, pointed according to the gothic style, without crosses, worked in "flower of silk." The pontifical habit of black silk with narrow sleeves, brocaded, with lions of silk cloth and gold in a blue field. The dalmatic of black silk cloth, with similar brocade work, embroidered with roses, with two dogs at the feet. The pontifical socks of black silk. The chasuble broad and long, of black silk with curious designs. The fanon was like the one used today. The pallium of very fine white silk with crosses. The gloves of white silk made with well-done needlework, and decorated with pearls. The hands were crossed, the left placed upon the right, and on the accustomed finger there was a ring with a sapphire of great value: finally he had on his head the miter of white damask, a palm wide and long.[66]

All of the vestments required by Pierre Ameil's ceremonial for dressing the pope's corpse show up in Giacomo Grimaldi's description, in which appear moreover the rochet, the sapphire ring, and a note on the placement of the hands in the form of a cross. The agreement could not be more complete. Even the manner of crossing the fanon on the alb around the neck is described identically in the two documents. This means that Pierre Ameil's ceremonial indeed reflects long-standing ritual customs that were respected at least on the occasion of the burial of Boniface VIII. Grimaldi describes, among other things, "crosses [affixed] to the pallium with black silk, as they are worn by Roman pontiffs today, and golden pins bearing precious sapphires, one at the center of the breast and the other on the left arm, still intact."[67] Similar pins appear on the gisants of Honorius IV (d. April 3, 1287) and Boniface VIII (d. Oct. 11, 1303).[68] According to Pierre Ameil, as well, the crosses on the pallium had to be attached with three pins, in accordance with custom.[69]

Special attention must be paid to the colors. Only the reverse of the stockings and the cincture were colored red; the soutain, rochet, pallium, gloves, and miter were white. The greater part of the vestments was black: the bow of the stole, the maniple, the sandals, the papal habit, the dalmatic, the socks, and the chasuble. In the sixteenth and seventeenth centuries, the pope's squire followed the funeral bed riding a black horse.[70]

According to the 1578 report on the corpse of Gregory VII,

> the body of the aforesaid pope [was found] as it had been, entirely intact, with the nose, teeth, and other members of the body. He was wearing a simple pontifical miter, to the bands of which crosses were attached. For vestments he had a silken stole woven with gold, with golden ornaments, in which were inscribed some letters, to wit, *Pax Nostra* [Our Peace]. He had gloves woven of silk, of admirable beauty, of gold and pearls, with a cross above, and on his ring finger he had a gold ring without a gem. He wore a red chasuble woven of gold, a silken tunicle, frayed stockings, these too woven of gold and silk, with crosses over the feet, that reached almost to the knee. He had a golden cincture, and a veil placed over his face. There appeared still to be some vestiges of the pallium, and many crosses were attached to his clothes, in such a manner that nothing necessary to the pontifical garments appeared to be lacking.[71]

The report does not specify whether Gregory VII was wearing black-colored clothes, but the phrase "and a veil placed over his face" echoes Ameil's ceremonial ("and they should fold the fanon on his head"): the face of the deceased pope was covered when it was displayed in the chapel, uncovered when it was displayed in church, but it was covered again when the corpse was placed in the casket.[72]

Saintly Bodies

Before the eleventh century, the *Liber pontificalis* mentions miraculous events and healing scenes at the death of a pope on only two occasions. To the sepulcher of Pope Silverius (536–37) "ran the sick, and they were healed." [73] Pope Martin I (649–53) "died in peace, like Christ's confessor, and performed many miracles down to our days." [74] For the next several centuries, the most absolute silence was observed. The situation changed with the death of Leo IX (April 19, 1054). Suddenly, there was talk of miracles taking place around his tomb. [75] A century later, in his *Description of the Vatican Basilica (Descriptio basilicae Vaticanae)* addressed to Pope Alexander III (1159–81), the canon Petrus Mallius gives the generic title of saints to the popes buried there, and speaks of "saintly bodies." [76] With the death of Honorius III (March 18, 1227) began a long series of miraculous events and cures. His porphyry tomb in the basilica of Santa Maria Maggiore was an object of public devotion. [77] In Niccolò of Calvi's *Vita* of Innocent IV (d. Dec. 7, 1254), the formulas already sound like a topos. [78] The deceased Clement IV (d. Nov. 29, 1268), who had arranged to be buried in the Dominican church of Santa Maria in Gradi, also "began to perform miracles"; "crowds of people, moved by his sanctity and his miracles, swarmed to his corpse to see it, touch it, and kiss it." [79] In the *Vita* of Gregory X (1271–76), the account of the miracles that took place "near his sepulcher" amounts to a "book of miracles" *(liber miraculorum)* of the hagiographical genre. [80] The long list was transcribed onto a table, and placed at his sepulcher in the cathedral of Arezzo. [81] At the death of Martin IV (March 28, 1285), the public display of his corpse in the Perugia cathedral was accompanied by scenes of healing. [82] According to a chronicler who claimed to have been present at these events,

> People afflicted with various maladies, especially of sight, joints, hearing, and speech, remained prostrated around the bier on which the pope's body had remained for several days. They were seen and assisted by numerous clerics and laity; many were healed. The series of miracles had not yet ended by May 12, the day on which this writing was set down; on the contrary, every day miracles were mercifully performed by God on behalf of the multitude

of the faithful who flocked there; and he who wrote these things also saw them.[83]

The deceased pontiff had chosen to be buried in the church of Saint Francis in nearby Assisi. Honorius IV (1285–87), who was named executor of the testament by his predecessor, ordered his transfer from the cathedral in Perugia.[84] But the Perugians, "so as not to be deprived of a saintly body, and lose a treasure," lodged various appeals and stalled for time.[85] Already, in 1279, the commune had incorporated into its statutes a monetary fine of twenty-five lire against anyone who "might dare to offend the sepulcher of Pope Urban IV." Even more than the incidents of depredation, the Perugian injunction is precious testimony to the fact that, for a city like Perugia in the thirteenth century, the presence of the tomb of a pope in the cathedral was a treasure to protect and defend.[86] On the death of the Dominican pope Benedict XI (d. July 7, 1304) as well, "miracles began to be announced," described in a book of miracles *(liber miraculorum)* that, however, has not survived.[87] At Avignon, the tomb of John XXII presents an extraordinary analogy with Gothic monstrances of relics. The bones of the pope repose in a gold reliquary.[88]

Veneration, cult, scenes of healing, quarrels. As surprising as their multiplicity is the chronological concentration of a series of episodes that began at the death of Honorius III, and became especially numerous in the third quarter of the thirteenth century. Different sorts of phenomena in fact fit together with a certain coherence: the rites of humility served to remind the ruling pope that his life as pope was brief and that his power was transitory; the rites and rhetoric of purification reminded the reigning pope that the lofty office that brought him near to Christ had to be upheld by the purity and innocence of his own life. Contemporary notices suggest that in the central decades of the thirteenth century, this coherence extended even beyond death: at death, the pope "returns to being a man," but he continues to belong to the apostolic series of saintly bodies of Peter's successors.

On this point, the funeral monument of Clement IV (1265–68), preserved today in the Franciscan church in Viterbo, reveals some very interesting possibilities.[89] The recumbent figure of the pope portrayed in his gisant—the first on Italian soil with features that seem drawn from real life—represents the face of an old man with his eyes closed. Its realism portrays not so much the old age of the deceased, as physical mortality itself. Rejecting all of the attributes of physical beauty, the image of Clement IV's tired and aged face expresses the very truth of death.[90] Above the gisant, Hedwig, the saint Clement IV had canonized at Viterbo in 1267, appears as a mediator between the pope and the Virgin Mary. On the pediment was placed a statue that an old source identifies as Saint Peter. The hypothesis seems plausible, because on the monument of Adrian V (1276) we also find the figure of Saint Peter in a similar position, here representing the immortality of the papacy. "Even the pope dies," but the "pope's power" *(potestas papae),* Petrine, is eternal.

The verisimilitude of Clement IV's gisant is perhaps to be attributed to the thought of the master general of the Dominicans, Thomas Aquinas, which is a new indication of the interest of the Friars Preachers in the pope's body, understood in terms of its mortality.[91] But to this most distinctive accentuation of the idea that "even the pope dies" should be contrasted, in these same decades, the equally vigorous popular devotion to Clement's body and sepulcher, for which the canons and Dominicans of Viterbo competed, seemingly operating on two fronts that were not, in fact, contradictory: the physical mortality of the pope, and memory reinforced by an aura of sanctity.[92] The same can be said for the case of Gregory X (1271–76). His *Vita* is the first of the thirteenth-century papal biographies to provide a list of the deceased pope's miracles, and also the first to emphasize the pope's "cleanliness of flesh" *(munditia carnis)* while he lived. Here we find an echo of the themes advanced by Peter Damian: the pope offered his life, his teachings, and his death "usefully to us as an example"; he died "as a magnificent conqueror of the world, of the flesh, and of the devil; thus he was made a consort and fellow of the angels."[93]

℮

The popes also belonged in the memory of the apostolic succession. The concept was not new, but only in the thirteenth century, as has been shown, did it find conscious expression at various levels: rhetorical, ritual, monumental, and devotional. Around the mid–thirteenth century, the papacy in addition devoted an annual liturgical commemoration to the memory of the deceased popes (and cardinals). The decision was made by Alexander IV (1254–61) in August 1259: from then on, every September 5 the pope, assisted by the cardinals, solemnly celebrated an anniversary mass for his deceased predecessors and cardinals. The office took place in various chapels during vigils and at vespers, with nine lessons and "with notes" *(cum nota)*. That day, the pope offered meals to two hundred poor, while each cardinal provided for another twenty-five.[94]

Alexander IV's decision was unprecedented, but some indications suggest that the desire to celebrate the memory *(memoria)* of the popes and cardinals had somewhat deeper roots. In the register of the dead *(obituarium)* of the canons of Saint Peter's at the Vatican, the long list of popes whose anniversaries they observed begins chronologically with Eugenius III (1145–53).[95] In the formularies of the papal chancery, the practice of accompanying the names of deceased popes with the phrases "dearly departed" *(bone memorie)* or "of holy memory" *(sancte memorie)* seems to date back to the pontificate of Innocent III.[96] In his collection of sermons, Pope Honorius III included that which he delivered on the feast of the "papal confessors."[97] On July 16, 1228, Gregory IX, returning to Perugia, celebrated there "magnificently" the anniversary of his (not immediate) predecessor Innocent III, who had died in the city on July 16, 1216.[98] Marino Filomarini's collection of papal letters contains one that Pope Innocent IV sent to all the churches of every religious order so that they might celebrate his anniversary in perpetuity with a solemn office. The formulary emphasized human mortality.[99]

At death, the popes joined the succession of the deceased pontiffs. Is this the reasoning that led the Roman church to preserve and venerate the *praecordia* (vital organs) that had been taken, in the course of their "internal" embalming, from the popes'

bodies? From the sixteenth century onward, the *praecordia* of embalmed popes (Julius II, Clement VII, Paul IV, Pius IV, Pius V) were in fact systematically deposited in the grotto of the Vatican Basilica.[100] On the death of Sixtus V (Aug. 27, 1590), which took place in the Quirinal Palace, "his *praecordia* were carried to the neighboring church of Saints Vincent and Anastasius, it being the Palatine parish. . . . There, down to Leo XII (1823 –29), were entombed only the *praecordia* of the popes who had died in the Quirinal Palace, and although by his order the church is no longer the parish of the said palace, he directed not only that the *praecordia* of the popes who had ended their lives in the Quirinal should be deposited there, but also those who died in the Vatican." In 1757, Benedict XIV had an underground chapel built beneath the high altar of the church to conserve, "in a well-sealed mortuary vase," the *praecordia* of the popes whose names were recorded in marble inscriptions, placed in the walls of the high altar.[101]

6 Perpetuity

Novena

The time has come to turn our attention to the funeral ceremony of the novena, so-called because it extended over a period of nine days.

Before reconstructing its history, it should be recalled that for many centuries the pope's body was usually buried on the same day as his death.[1] The election of a new pope could be held only after a three-day period had elapsed since his death (and burial).[2] At the beginning of the thirteenth century, the period between the pope's death and his burial continued in this tradition. According to Honorius III's letter of election, and a contemporary source, his predecessor Innocent III had died in Perugia on Saturday, July 16, 1216, at the ninth hour, and had been buried the next day in the Perugian cathedral, in the marble sepulcher located near the window of the altar of Blessed Herculanus. The funeral was held, "as tradition requires, in the presence of seventeen cardinal bishops, priests, and deacons, and of many other archbishops, bishops and prelates, and of a multitude of clergy and laity."[3] Honorius III's funeral was also held, "according to custom," the day immediately following his death (March 18, 1227).[4] Celestine IV, who died only seventeen days after his election (Nov. 10, 1241), was also buried the day after his death.[5]

In the last decades of the thirteenth century, the period of time between death and burial suddenly got longer. John XXI (Peter the Spaniard), who died on May 20, 1277, the victim of a collapsed ceiling in a room he had ordered constructed in the papal palace at Viterbo, was buried six days after his death.[6] Something outside the ordinary also occurred at the death of

Nicholas III. The pope died on August 22, 1280, at Soriano. The funeral was held on Sunday, August 25, in Saint Peter's Basilica. It is true that the period of time between his death and burial was due in part to the need to transport his corpse.[7] The notices of two independent chroniclers that Martin IV, who died at Perugia on March 28, 1285, was buried only four or five days afterward, on April 1 or 2, is supported by a letter.[8] The author, an eyewitness, tells us that the pope's corpse was displayed for several days.[9]

ℰ

These developments unfolded around the time that Gregory X (1271–76) promulgated his historic constitution, *Ubi periculum* ("Where There Is Danger"), creating the modern conclave.[10] The cardinals were henceforth required to wait no longer than ten days before proceeding to elect a new pope.[11]

Ubi periculum in fact opened up a new ritual space, but one whose development was nevertheless gradual. It is well known that to overcome the hesitations and resistance of cardinals illdisposed to accept the uncomfortable enclosure of the conclave, Gregory X had had to turn for support to the bishops present at the Council of Lyons.[12] His severe constitution, published twice on the same day, November 1, 1274, for universal dissemination and for the *studia* of the universities, seems to have been observed during the three vacancies of 1276, but was then suspended, if not actually revoked, by Popes Adrian V (1276) and John XXI (1276–77).[13] Celestine V, elected pope on July 5, 1294, reinstated it on September 28 of the same year.[14] His successor, Boniface VIII, was in effect elected after ten days.[15]

We do not know whether the ceremony of the novena was held at the death of Boniface VIII. Ferreto de' Ferreti of Vicenza indicates, however, that the pope's funeral was conducted "in accordance with ancient tradition" *(de more vetusto)*.[16] This could be an indication that the "new rite"—the novena—was not used. Is this perhaps also the meaning we should assign to Ptolemy of Lucca's words, that Boniface VIII "was buried with less reverence than the pontifical dignity required"? *Ubi periculum* was, however, scrupulously observed. Benedict XI was in fact elected on October 22, 1303, eleven days after the death of his predecessor (October 11).[17]

In the *Vitae* of the Avignonese popes Clement V, John XXII,

Benedict XII, Clement VI, and Innocent VI, there are no references whatsoever to the novena; and yet, on the death of Clement VI (1342–52), the novena was celebrated.[18] All the *Vitae* of Urban V (1362–70), except the first one, instead begin by referring explicitly to the novena of his predecessor, Innocent VI (1352–62).[19] The *Vita II* of Gregory XI, who died in Rome on March 27, 1378, does the same.[20] Only a few decades later, Pierre Ameil included in his ceremonial book (1385–90)—which we analyzed in previous chapters—the first description of the novena that has come down to us.[21]

℃

Even the papal novena must be attributed in some degree to the papacy's *imitatio imperii* ("imitation of empire"). This is suggested by the fact that it was probably introduced during the interregnum, and by the fact that with the pontificate of Gregory X, as has been shown, the papal coronation rose to become an autonomous ritual element.[22] In Byzantium, moreover, relatives of the emperor dressed in mourning for nine days after the deaths of their wives, brothers, and sons.[23] The chronicle of Nikophoros Gregoras, written in the early fourteenth century, recounts that when the emperor Andronikos II was buried (1328), the funeral ceremony lasted nine days.[24]

As for the ceremony of displaying the body, however, so also for the novena, the deep-seated reasons were nevertheless ecclesiological and institutional in nature. The novena made it possible to render two bodies visible: the corpse of the deceased pope, to be displayed publicly with his face uncovered, and the "body of the church" *(corpus Ecclesiae),* represented in an equally visible manner by the College of Cardinals. Not by chance, Gregory X began his ceremonial by recalling Peter Damian's concept of the "brevity of life": "the life of every sovereign is brief, and on that account it often comes about that the Roman pontiffs, who hold the primacy of the subcelestial hierarchy, end their lives within a brief space of time." And he emphasized the necessity of guaranteeing institutional continuity: "such a lofty hierarchy cannot be *headless,* as though it were a monster."[25] Only a few years before, Hostiensis had forcefully reiterated that, before proceeding to elect a new pope, the cardinals had the duty to take care of the burial of the "defunct body."[26]

☙

At this point it should immediately be recalled that the debate on the powers of the cardinals during a papal vacancy reached its climax precisely in the last decades of the thirteenth century.[27]

Harking back to the doubts expressed by those who wondered whether the *potestas papae* ("power of the pope") was transferred to the College of Cardinals during a papal vacancy, Matthew Paris cites a letter that had been sent by seven cardinals, including the future popes Innocent IV and Alexander IV, on July 25, 1243, to an English abbot, concerning an ecclesiastical benefice. According to Matthew, the cardinals prefaced their decision by declaring "that the power [*potestas*] resides with them during the vacancy of the Apostolic See."[28] Hostiensis conceded decision-making power to the cardinals only "in questions of great, evident, and immediate necessity,"[29] refuting the notion that at the pope's death "the cardinals are without a head: that is not true, because they have the real and general head of the church, that is, Christ."[30] Around 1300 the canonist Johannes Monachus, a favorite of Boniface VIII, declared unambiguously: "During the vacancy of the Apostolic See, the 'plenitude of power' [*plenitudo potestatis*] resides among the cardinals."[31] So also did Giles of Rome: "Some say that the church never dies. Indeed, when the see is vacant [*sede vacante*], the papal power remains in the church, or rather, in the College of Cardinals."[32] And again, Peter John Olivi (1295) declared: "And certainly, when the pope is dead and has not yet been replaced, the principal authority to govern the entire church lies with them [the cardinals]."[33] Saint Francis had promised obedience not only to the "pope and to his successors, but also to the Roman church," by which should be understood the College of Cardinals, "who are properly and antonomastically the seat of the Roman church."[34] After the death of Benedict XI (July 7, 1304), the cardinals felt able to affirm that the "power and authority of the Roman pontiff, when the seat is vacant, remains with the College of Cardinals of the holy Roman church."[35]

The arguments of the theologian Augustinus Triumphus (1270–1328), called the Anconan, were in certain respects conclusive: the "power of the pope is perpetual," but "it cannot be perpetuated in the pope himself, because even he dies [*ipse moritur]*, just like other men." It was necessary, therefore, that the pope's power be "perpetuated in the college." Christ was the head of the church, and consequently "the power of the pope is perpetual, because it remains always in the College, that is, in the church, which belongs to Christ, its incorruptible and permanent head." [36] During the limited period of a vacancy, the College of Cardinals was the church: "The College of Cardinals can be compared to the pope, like a root to a tree or to a branch: just as the power of a branch or tree that flowers and produces fruit remains in the root when the branch or tree [is] destroyed, so it appears *[videtur]* that the papal power remains in the College (of Cardinals), that is, in the church, when the pope dies: in the College as in a proximate root, in the church of prelates and other faithful as in a remote one." [37] For Alvarus Pelagius, as well, when the pope dies "the body of cardinals *[corpus cardinalium]* and the whole church have as a general head of the church, truly and really, Christ who lives." [38]

ぞ

If the College of Cardinals represented the church during a vacancy, its responsibility naturally increased over the papal chamberlain and penitentiaries who were called upon to perform key duties during the vacancy. Clement V (1305–14), in fact, decided that the offices of chamberlain and penitentiaries should not "expire on account of the pope's death": moreover, he conceded to the cardinals the right to nominate, in the event of his death, a new chamberlain or new penitentiaries. [39] Around 1300, therefore, the functions of the chamberlain and penitentiaries were increasingly regarded as constituting permanent offices, whose occupants did not cease to hold them at the pope's death. [40] For this reason, during a papal vacancy the penitentiaries' letters had to bear the formula "By the Authority of the Roman church which we exercise" *(Auctoritate sancte Romane Ecclesie, qua fungimur)*. [41] These were significant changes because, in the preceding period, when the pope was alive, the chamberlain had generally been defined as being "of the lord pope" *(domini pape)* and not "of the holy Roman church" *(sancte Romane Ecclesie)* or "of the sacred palace" *(sacri palatii)*, like other officials; [42] the cardinals and curialists had to confess to the pope's penitentiary, "because he represents the person of the pope in matters of penance." [43]

All these measures solidified the ecclesiological prestige of the cardinalate, and were at the same time supported by a clear sense of the continuity of the Roman church.[44] It may even be said that these decisions, taken as a whole, constituted a culminating point in distinguishing between the pope's physical mortality and the permanence of the institution, the first glimmerings of which, as has been said, date back to the mid–eleventh century. More than two centuries later, the Roman church disposed of juridical instruments *(Ubi periculum)*, ritual spaces (the novena), and ecclesiologial arguments (concerning the cardinalate) that enabled it to face with a certain equanimity the pope's death, that period of "emptiness" (the vacancy) that Peter Damian had defined as a "moment of terror."

℮

At the beginning of the fourteenth century, reflection on the contrast between human mortality and institutional permanence was of considerable contemporary interest. One of the greatest civilian lawyers intervened in the discussion. According to Johannes Andreae (1270–1348), "he who holds the [office of the] papacy or the dignity is corruptible; the papacy [itself], instead, the dignity or authority *[imperium]*, is eternal." [45]

A few generations later, in his commentary on the *Decretals* (1393–94), Baldus de Ubaldis would recall that "only the pope is the vicar of Jesus Christ on earth . . . although the pope possesses the natural characteristics of a man *[naturalia hominis]*, nevertheless he also has a certain solemnity that permits him to act in virtue of the heavens *[in virtute coelesti]*." [46] The pope was like the emperor: "The emperor in his person may die, but the dignity itself, that is, the authority *[imperium]*, is immortal; just as the supreme pontiff dies, but the supreme pontificate does not die." [47]

To underscore the difference between the physical persons of the emperor and the pope, and the perpetuity of the empire and the papacy, Baldus contrasted the figures of emperor and pope with that of the king, whom he declared to be institutionally different. Unlike the former pair, "two things combine in the king: the person and what he signifies *[significatio]*; and that signification, which is something pertaining to the intellect, miraculously *[enigmatice]* perseveres forever, though not corporeally; for let the king be deficient with regard to his flesh, he nevertheless functions holding the place of two persons."[48] This amounted to saying that "the King survives the king."[49] On the other hand, the pope and the emperor could not have "two bodies," because the papacy and the empire were by definition nondynastic. "Even the pope dies," and at his death the *potestas papae,* eternal, passed to his successor through the College of Cardinals, which represented the church during the limited period of the vacancy. It was for this reason that when they held consistories during a vacancy, the cardinals had to sit in such a way as not to leave the pope's place empty.[50]

Elections and Sackings

Besides time, space too appears to have been filled ritually by Pierre Ameil in the oldest papal funeral ceremonial (1385–90).

The protection of the palace was the chamberlain's responsibility. He had to have all the doors of the Apostolic Palace closed immediately, excepting one for necessary services.[51] On the whole, this must have been in keeping with normal practice at Avignon. In the ceremonial book he wrote just slightly later, François de Conzié records the cardinals' obligation to entrust the custody of the city to a captain: Conzié made the problem of public disorder a central concern. But because it was a problem that had now been resolved institutionally, Conzié said not a word in relation to the pope's death about the need to protect the papal palace.[52] Reading these Avignonese ceremonials confirms the conclusion to which we were led by our reexamination of the accounts of the sackings of the "palace": no source after the first decades of the thirteenth century explicitly refers to a real or potential sacking of the papal "palace" originating from the outside (that is, from the people).

In the thirteenth century, only seven of the nineteen popes who succeeded from Innocent III to Boniface VIII died in Rome: Honorius III (1227), Gregory IX (1241), Celestine IV (1241), Innocent V (1276), Honorius IV (1287), Nicholas IV

(1292), and Boniface VIII (1303). When—after a century—a conclave was again held in Rome in 1378, the sources speak anew of pillaging, no longer in relationship to the death of the pope, Gregory XI, but rather as accompanying the election of his successor, Urban VI.

The cardinals who met in conclave at Saint Peter's were, at a certain point, terrorized by the growing tumult of the Romans. The *Vita II* of Gregory XI recounts that these disorders provoked fears that "all the Northerners and Frenchmen" would be killed or taken prisoner. The cardinals convinced the Roman cardinal Francesco Tibaldeschi of Santa Sabina, popularly known as the "Cardinal of Saint Peter," to keep a lookout at the entrance of the conclave. Tibaldeschi had a window opened, and pleaded with the crowd to be quiet and wait a little longer; he then assured them that the cardinals intended to satisfy their desire (for the nomination of a Roman cardinal as pope). But those further back in the crowd demanded to know what was happening. They were told: "It is he, lord cardinal of Saint Peter" *(Dominus cardinalis Sancti Petri)*. The crowd seems to have understood this to mean that the "Cardinal of Saint Peter" was the new pope, and shouted: "We have a pope, the cardinal of Saint Peter" *(Papam habemus cardinalem Sancti Petri)*. They then scattered throughout the city, chanting "long live Saint Peter" *(Viva, viva, Sancto Pyetro)*. Many moved on to the cardinal's residence, "plundering and destroying everything." [53]

These events are confirmed by the interrogations that followed the outbreak of the schism. They relate that Cardinal Orsini, attempting to placate the crowd, had appeared at one of the windows where the conclave was meeting that looked out on the second courtyard of the Vatican. Turning to the people, he shouted: "Be quiet, because you have a pope!" "Who, then?" they asked. "Go to Saint Peter's," he replied. Some of the Romans took this to mean that the new pope was the "Cardinal of Saint Peter" and ran to Tibaldeschi's house to sack it. [54]

℮

The sources dealing with the pillaging of 1378 do not say whether this was a custom. But this is how Adam of Usk describes a second case that we know of, in which the goods of a cardinal elected to the papacy were sacked. Describing the events surrounding Innocent VII's election (Oct. 17, 1404), the English chronicler reports:

> The pestiferous Romans rose up in two parties, Guelfs and Ghibellines . . . laying waste to each other with massacres, robberies, and murders, each insisting on the creation of a pope from their own party, but neither of them being able on account of the aforesaid to take control of Saint Peter's or the conclave. Whence their partisanship caused the election of one who belonged to neither of their factions, that is, Innocent VII from Sulmona. When his election was announced, all the Romans broke into his house and, in accordance with their rapacious custom, or rather, to speak more truthfully, snarling with depravity, plundered everything, leaving nothing but the bars on the windows.[55]

Another reference to sacking the private residence *(domus)* of a newly elected pope appears in Jacopo d'Angiolo's letter to Manuel Chrysolaras of Constantinople on the election of Gregory XII (Nov. 30, 1406).[56]

℮

The first official reaction to this (new) ritual of pillaging came from the Council of Constance (1417). The conciliar assembly tried to repress not only the spoliation of the goods of the cardinal elected pope, but also those of the electing cardinals.[57] The principal victim of the plundering was the pope-elect who, as the conciliar decree cautioned, was considered to have reached the "summit of wealth"; but the popular impetuosity set its sights somewhat on all the cardinals, at least those most vulnerable. Sometimes, as in 1378, even a misunderstanding (entirely unintentional?) about the name of the successful candidate could come into play.

Aeneas Sylvius Piccolomini, the future Pius II (1458–64), wrote an account of the looting that took place on the election of Pope Nicholas V (1447) that seems to exemplify the phenomenon. The pope-elect was Cardinal Parentucelli, but the residences sacked included those of the Colonna, the cardinal of Capua, and the cardinal of Bologna. Piccolomini even seems to hint that the people were not entirely misinformed: "it is the poor man's fortune to lose only a little."[58] He then adds that, immediately after the announcement of his own election to the pontificate (Aug. 19, 1458), his cell was stripped of silver and books "in accordance with a vile custom." As for his home, the people immediately ran there to plunder it:

> Then the cardinal's servants sacked Aeneas's cell and, following a shameful custom, carried away his money—what little there was—his books, and his clothes; at the same time, the vile and infamous rabble not only pillaged but literally tore to pieces his house in Rome, carrying away even the stones. Several other cardinals suffered similar damage, and that because, while the people stood by anxiously waiting, rumors flew about, and now this and now that cardinal was indicated as the pope-elect: the rabble then ran to his house and looted it.[59]

One cardinal, when the name "Genoese" was heard instead of "Sienese," lost a good part of his belongings.[60]

℮

The persistence, if not indeed diffusion, of the rite of pillaging led Leo X to promulgate solemn new prohibitions during the public session of the Fifth Lateran Council on March 16, 1516. Paride de Grassi recorded the scene: the bishop of Mileto received a note from the pope's hand and went to the pulpit to read it out. The pope protested "the Romans' custom of breaking into the house of the cardinal who has been elected pope; then, pretending that this or that other person has been elected, they plunder his house and furnishings as well."[61] Rather than emphasizing the antiquity of the ritual, the bull instead underscored its relative newness.[62]

The conciliar and papal measures did not halt the rite, which raged for at least another two centuries.[63] In his *On the Cardinalate (De cardinalatu),* the most important fifteenth-century treatise on the office in its various aspects, including the domestic, the curialist Paolo Cortesi suggested putting a guardroom at the entrance of the palace to prevent sacking.[64] During the conclave that followed the death of Pope Marcellus II (May 1, 1555), when rumor got out of the election of the "cardinal nephew" Alexander, "the people went to sack the palaces of these Farnese lords," "and scarcely could the constable *[Caporione]* resist them."[65] In October 1559, when the (unfounded) news was

spread of the election of Cardinal Ercole Gonzaga, the abbey of
Felonica (near Mantua), of which he was the commendatory,
was razed to the ground, and its orchard and gardens leveled,
with the abbot's own consent, by the locals and the monks.[66]

℘

Why do the sources only tell us about this sort of plundering for
the first time in 1378? Why did the looting take place not after
the pope's death, but only when news got out of the election of
a new one, or of a cardinal believed to have been elected? Why
did the rite always and only involve the goods of a cardinal?

1. As we saw above, the Romans' custom of plundering the
pope's palace after his death is attested for the last time in 1227:
the dying Honorius II was shown from a high window of the
Lateran Palace, "exhausted and half alive," to the Roman people
who had begun "to unleash themselves upon the papal goods."[67]
The Roman curia's frequent moves in the thirteenth century, and
its prolonged residence at Avignon in the fourteenth, had enabled the papacy to protect "the palace" from popular pillaging
when the pope died. In 1378, none of the sources tell us about
sacking the "palace" after the pope's death.

The fact, therefore, that the oldest evidence of pillaging the
goods of a cardinal elected pope emerges in 1378—that is, at the
first conclave celebrated in Rome in almost a century—is no accident. This was a real ritual innovation, possibly meant to take
the place of the older—but now impossible—rite of sacking the
"papal goods" after the pope died.

2. Pillaging the goods of a cardinal elected pope was even a
rite of passage.[68] By allowing himself to be despoiled, the neo-
elect abandoned the "former man" and symbolically ascended to
a new "suprapersona."[69]

On the other hand, in looting the palace of the man believed "to have ascended to the summit of wealth," the Roman
people appropriated the goods that the newly elected pontiff
was required to distribute—symbolically and literally—during
the possession-taking of the Lateran, both to the Roman people
and to the members of the curia. This is why even the pope-
elect's attendants joined in the looting, indeed plundering the
cell in which the conclave itself had been held. The rite there-

fore performed a function completely analogous to the Lateran possession-taking ceremony, because it constituted a symbolic appropriation of the goods entrusted to the new pope.

But in 1378, when Urban VI was elected, was the original symbolic significance of the Lateran rite still truly perceptible? Had the possession-taking of the Lateran not entered a phase of progressive decline in 1272, when Gregory X decided to make the coronation in the Vatican a constituting and autonomous act? It should also be recalled here that the Lateran chairs had not been transported to Avignon, and thus it had not been possible to use them there in the coronation ceremonies. Did the spoliation of the goods of the cardinal elected pope, attested for the first time at the first conclave celebrated in Rome after three centuries of the papacy's absence, thus not perform the role of replacing the now declining Lateran rite?

3. By 1378, the institutional role that had been entrusted to the cardinals as far back as 1059 was firmly established. The cardinals were now the undisputed guarantors of the transfer of the *potestas papae*. Indeed, the cardinals *were* the church during the limited period of the papal vacancy.

By focusing on the goods of the cardinal-elect, and the cell in which he had been elected, the rite symbolically removed the elect from the college—signaling, that is, that from now on it was his responsibility alone, as the pope-elect, to guide the church in the fullness of power.

College! College!

As we have seen, in Pierre Ameil's view the chamberlain occupied a position of great prestige. A century later the situation had changed. For Agostino Patrizi Piccolomini, it was the cardinals who should take charge of the inventories, even before the pope had died. Once news had gotten out that the pope had reached the end of his life, a commission of three cardinals, chosen from among the three orders, had the responsibility, together with the chamberlain, of compiling an inventory of all the goods in the papal palace. The chamberlain, deprived of the right of initiative, dropped into a subordinate position.[70] The cardinals' central role in the various phases of the papal burial rite was underscored by the fact that, from the very outset, Patrizi Piccolomini called them "the highest men" *(summi viri)* or members of the (church's) "senate" *(senatus)*.[71] They were to send out letters to the princes and leading prelates informing them of the pope's death, a responsibility not anticipated by Ameil. They must use the "apostolic style," and address the recipients "as though [the sender of the letter] were the pope." All responsibility for the Apostolic Palace now fell to them. They were to use their authority to prevent every disturbance, *whenever the pope's death may occur in Rome,* a reference to the Romans' very distinctive customs (and for this reason absent from Pierre Ameil's ceremonial, which reflects rather more the situation at Avignon).[72] It was the cardinals' responsibility to indicate "when the obsequies will begin" (that is, the novena).[73] Also revealing is Patrizi Piccolomini's note that, during the novena, the singers should turn to face the "chorus of the cardinals" *(chorum cardinalium)*.[74] The candles around the pope's catafalque should be lit only when a cardinal advanced to celebrate mass.[75]

℃

In Ameil's time, the novena included the period of exposition of the corpse and its burial. The first mass took place immediately after the corpse had been transported from the palace.[76] That the cardinals were required, after the daily sermon, to visit the corpse, "if it has not been buried," clearly indicates that the deceased would not yet have been buried at the beginning of the novena.[77] This is further confirmed by the accounts of the Apostolic Camera for the burials of Clement VI (1342–52) and Innocent VI (1352–62).[78] But in the second half of the fifteenth century, the period of the public display of the pope's corpse in church and, consequently, the length of time separating its arrival in church from its burial, appears instead to have been reduced to the minimum necessary—a single day. Johann Burchard, a scrupulous observer, ever alert to changes in papal rites and ceremonies, noted: "formerly it was usual to leave it for three days."[79]

Moreover, the sources reflect growing impatience with the public display of the pope's corpse, because of commotions exacerbated by popular devotion.[80] The body of Eugenius IV, prepared with balsam, was presented to the people for only a day.[81] Penitentiaries placed the corpse of Sixtus IV, dressed in sacred vestments, on the bier, "in order that it may be publicly displayed." [82] The scene was described by Burchard:

> At first the corpse was set before the high altar, raised, then lowered a bit, with the head turned toward the altar, and the feet sticking out of a closed iron grate, in such a way that those who wanted to could kiss them. Later on the grate was opened, and the deceased was moved closer to the altar, so that everyone could enter and exit freely; nevertheless we posted some guards, so that no one could steal the ring or anything else. It remained there until about one at night.[83]

Of the display of the corpse of Alexander VI, the same master of ceremonies records:

> But the Bishop of Sessa, fearing that allowing the people free access might give occasion for scandal [for fear, that is, that someone among those who had been injured by the pope might be able to avenge themselves], had the bier moved again from the aforementioned place to the entrance of the chapel, between the stairs: with the feet turned and pointed toward the grating and the doors, in such a way that they could be touched by hand through the grating itself. There it remained the entire day: and the gate remained closed the whole time.[84]

The sarcasm with which Burchard was pleased to describe the state of decomposition of Alexander VI is especially revealing. No one before him had dared go so far:

> During this whole time the pope had been left, as has been said, within the railing of the high altar, with four torches burning around him. His face had become ever more horrible and dark, to the point that around the twenty-third hour, when I saw him, he was the color of a very dark cloth or, if you will, of a negro. The face was swollen, the nose was swollen, the mouth was gaping wide while the tongue, swollen to twice its size, filled the whole space between the lips: this was such a horrible spectacle that everyone said they had never seen anything like it.[85]

Holding the novena appears to have been increasingly separate from the burial of the pontiff's corpse. This is indicated

already in the sources on the death and burial of Pope Innocent VII (d. Nov. 6, 1406).[86] Sixtus IV died on August 12, 1484;
the body *(corpus)* was carried into church on August 13 and immediately buried; the "obsequies," that is, the novenas, began on
August 17 and continued to August 25.[87] Innocent VIII's death
also took place during the summer (July 25, 1492). Stefano Infessura indicates that on August 5 the obsequies *(exequie)* had
ended. That means the novena had begun on July 28.[88]

Becoming more autonomous of the "royal" burial of the deceased pope, the novena became a ritual time reserved for the
cardinals, whose participation now followed a strictly hierarchical order: the cardinal bishops opened and closed the ceremony.
Moreover, once the pope's body had been displayed and buried,
the novena was celebrated around the empty catafalque *(castrum
doloris)*. This made it necessary to create an illusion by simulating
the presence of the corpse: two footmen dressed in mourning
stood at the feet of the two sides of the *castrum doloris,* continually and calmly moving fans bearing the papal arms, as though
to shoo away flies.[89] The oldest evidence of this feigned representation of the corpse goes back to the death of Eugenius IV
(Feb. 23, 1447). Its source of inspiration was perhaps of ancient
origin. In a famous passage of his *Roman History,* Dio Cassius
describes the wax statue of the emperor Pertinax, who died in
193, before which "a young slave shooed away flies with a fan of
peacock feathers, as though the prince were already dead."[90] But
we do not know when the rite was incorporated into the papal
funeral ceremonial. Aeneas Sylvius Piccolomini, an eyewitness
to Eugenius's funeral, offers a malicious comment on the practice, conceding nonetheless that it was done by custom.[91]

ℭ

The fiction of the fans was adopted also for the funerals of cardinals. Patrizi Piccolomini's ceremonial (1484–92) is the first to
talk about them: "around the *castrum doloris* [of the cardinals],
two pallbearers of the deceased cardinal move two fans with la-
borious calm, both made of black silk and bearing the cardinal's
arms, as though they had to chase away flies even in a wintry
climate."[92]

This is but one example of the imitation of papal funeral
ceremonial with which the history of cardinals' funerals is

brimming.[93] The first suggestions of a special interest in particularly ornate funerals for cardinals date from the thirteenth century.[94] Pierre Ameil's ceremonial contains a long notice on cardinals' funerals, comprising over thirty articles, almost all of them
concerning liturgy.[95] The celebration of a funeral novena by the
cardinals first appears in Cardinal Guglielmo Teste's testament
(Avignon, 1326).[96] But this is an isolated notice. After a documentary silence of almost fifty years, references to novenas become increasingly frequent in testaments from the last years of
the Avignon period (1372, 1373), and even more so during the
schism (1384, 1397, 1402, 1407, 1410, and 1422).[97] All of the
testators were French. But these were still funerals of a private
sort. There is not a trace of novenas in the funeral description for
Cardinal Ardicino de Porta of Novara (d. April 9, 1434) that appears in an addition to Ameil's ceremonial.[98] In the second half
of the fifteenth century, instead, an important development took
place. The novena was no longer celebrated, as it had been at
Avignon, at the place of entombment, but now provided instead
the ceremonial framework for the cardinals' official funerals. As
in the papal funeral ceremonial, the *castrum doloris*—the catafalque without the corpse of the deceased—was now an indispensable necessity.[99] Toward the end of the century, Patrizi Piccolomini's ceremonial now described the novena as an essential
element in the official funeral rites of the cardinals, one in which
the other members of the college were required to take part.[100]
By the sixteenth century, moreover, the novena had become the
exclusive prerogative of popes and cardinals.[101]

A few days after the burial of Alexander VI, on August 24, 1503,
the cardinal of Naples organized a meeting of the cardinals, the
so-called Congregation, in his palace. Burchard described it as
"singular" that the hosting cardinal "had worn throughout the
entire meeting a violet mantlet that touched the ground." To his
colleagues who asked why he was dressed this way, the cardinal
of Naples replied, "because I am cold." [102] But was this the real
reason? The violet mantlet established a hierarchy among the cardinals, and challenged the basic ecclesiological notion that during
a papal vacancy the church was represented—collectively—by
the whole College of Cardinals.

On September 9, 1503, the cardinals of Naples and Saint Peter in Chains entered Rome "to the joy and triumph of everyone" *(cum magna letitia omnium et triumpho)*. Many carpets had been laid down outside Castle Sant'Angelo. The Roman people greeted them, shouting: "Church! Church! College! College!" *(Ecclesia! Ecclesia! Collegio! Collegio!)*.[103] The cardinals—the *College*—were the *church*.

The cries of "Church! Church! College! College!" proclaimed the church's permanence; they amounted, that is, to an updating of the juridical maxim that "the dignity does not die" *(Dignitas non moritur)*, first articulated in the twelfth century. They prefigured those that would soon be applied to the figure of the king: "The king is dead! . . . Long live the king!" *(Le roi est mort! . . . Vive le roi!)* or "The king never dies" *(Le roi ne meurt jamais)*.[104] Of course, the pope did not have two bodies like the king; the pope's physical body was destined to die: but the church, represented by the College of Cardinals during the vacancy, was eternal.

Nudity, saintly bodies, perpetuity: these are the three essential moments that signal the ritual voyage upon which the pope's corpse was conveyed in the centuries that concern us. They only seem contradictory. Dying, the pope is nude, because in death the pope "returns to being a man"—that is, he loses the *potestas papae*. To the pope's mortality, which the theme of nudity or the macabre descriptions of the late fifteenth-century masters of ceremonies were happy to underline, however, there contrasts a strong historical consciousness of the church's permanence, which the ceremony of the novena managed to ritualize perfectly. But the opposition between mortality and perpetuity, though powerful, did not exhaust the history of the pope's death, because the deceased pope's body belonged virtually to the series of saintly bodies of the successors of Peter.

The questions we raised in opening this section on the history of the pope's death were numerous. Is there a relationship between the ritual and rhetorical discourses that accompanied the life of the reigning pope from the Gregorian reform onward, in

terms of mortality, transience, symbolic purification, and the
royal death of the pope? In what way were the papal funeral rites
influenced by them? In short, what were the deep-seated institutional motivations that drove the Roman church to create a
pontifical funeral ritual? We seem to have reached the moment
for summarizing, and for attempting to pose some new questions.

1. From the mid–eleventh century onward, the theme of
mortality and transience that Peter Damian had so forcefully set
out in his treatise, *De brevitate,* never left the ceremonial and
rhetorical life of the Roman church. The metaphor of "Peter's
years" and the rites of mortality (burning the flax, the ash ceremony) retained their validity down to modern times. Even the
body of the deceased popes served to underpin the "humbling"
reserved for the reigning pontiff. One thinks of Sylvester II's legendary sweating sepulcher and rumbling bones, meant to signal
the imminence of the pope's death. One thinks also of what Bernard of Clairvaux wrote to Pope Eugenius III (1145–53): "Let
your own predecessors warn you: the end of your office is as
certain as it is near." Moreover, according to the coronation rite
of the late fifteenth century, the newly elected pontiff had to visit
the sepulchers of the deceased popes after being subjected to the
burning of the bands of flax.

A first point therefore emerges clearly: the correlation between the discourse of mortality reserved for the ruling pontiff,
and the history of the pope's death, is exact. Along an identical
chronological line, which begins with the first reforming pontificate of the eleventh century (Leo IX, 1049–54), the history
of the pope's death has in fact appeared to be sustained by a
common element: the conscious will to distinguish between the
pope's physical person and the pontifical office. The protection
of the "palace" from popular plundering, the funeral monuments
of the thirteenth-century pontiffs, and the Avignonese funeral
rituals of the late fourteenth century all bespeak the conviction
that "even the pope dies." At death, "the pope returns to being
a man."

2. Peter Damian raised not only the life but also the death
of the pope to a level of superiority and universality. The pope's
death was a "moment of terror" that concerned the whole of

Christendom: "when the pope dies, the universal orb is deprived of a common father"; those who were disturbed by the death of such an exceptional and singular personage "fear in their trembling viscera the end of their own lives." In the ensuing decades, the sources tell us that the pope's death was an event of universal dimensions that needed its own ritualization: the first signs of the existence of an autonomous pontifical funeral ceremonial *(ordo)* indeed date back to the beginning of the twelfth century, a period in which concern for the honors of the pontifical burial did nothing but grow.

3. The genesis of an honorific funeral ritual specifically reserved for the pope's death reflects a deep realization of the papal institution's perpetuity. In his letter to the inhabitants of Osimo (1049–50), Leo IX had opposed the sacking of the deceased bishop's goods by invoking the "eternal pontiff," Christ. For a complete ritualization of such a fundamental ecclesiological development it is necessary to await the novena, a new ritual space that emerged in the last decades of the thirteenth century, following Gregory X's historic decision (*Ubi periculum,* 1274) ordering the cardinals to delay no longer than ten days to begin the conclave. The ceremony of the novena showed itself capable of making visible not only the pope's death, but also the perpetuity of the church, represented for the restricted and provisional period of the vacancy by the College of Cardinals.

The emergence of the novena was the culmination of a line of thought on the pope's death that had begun at the dawn of the reforming papacy of the eleventh century, in a historical period that saw the affirmation, in the 1059 decree on papal elections, of the cardinals' exclusive right to elect the Roman pontiff. From the mid–eleventh century onward, the cardinals became the guarantors of the institutional continuity of the papacy.

As we have seen, already according to the *ordines* of the late twelfth century (Albinus and Cencius, 1189, 1192), the pope-elect did not sit alone on the *sedes stercorata* at the Lateran, but was placed there "with honor by the cardinals"; the gesture anticipated the role that the cardinals would be called on to play at the pope's death. The rite of the ashes also aimed to resolve with the greatest equilibrium possible the inevitable tension between

mortality and respect for the office; at the same time, it consecrated the institutional prestige of the College of Cardinals. The
message of these rites is clear: the *pope's body* is destined to die,
but through the entire period of the vacancy, the *corpus Ecclesiae*
(body of the church) is entrusted to an institutional *body*, the
"body of the cardinals" *(corpus cardinalium).*

Giles of Rome, who declared that the pope "can be called
the church," is also the theologian who identified the cardinals
with the church (during the period of the vacancy): "Some say
that the church never dies. Indeed, when the see is vacant *[sede
vacante],* the papal power remains in the church, that is, in the
College of Cardinals." At death, the pope "returns to being a
man." The *corpus Ecclesiae,* which the pope had represented in
life, was transferred at his death to the College of Cardinals, because they *were* the church for the limited period of the vacancy,
but they would return to being "part of the pope's body" *[pars
corporis pape]* immediately after the election of his successor. This,
too, is a metaphor that asserted itself forcefully in the course of
the thirteenth century.

As Augustinus Triumphus (1270–1328) observed, the power
of the pope "is perpetual," but "it cannot be perpetuated in the
pope, since even he dies just like other men." It was necessary,
therefore, that it be "perpetuated in the college," which was
(temporarily) the church. In the oldest papal funeral ceremonial,
Pierre Ameil's, it was to the cardinals that the pope must "turn
over the church" in the last moments of his life. In 1503, during
the vacancy of the Apostolic See, the Roman people cried out:
"Church! Church! College! College!" *("Ecclesia! Ecclesia! Collegio! Collegio!")*

The cardinals' rights during a vacancy would never have
been able to diminish those of the papal "fullness of power"
(plenitudo potestatis), but decisive compensations came to be created in the ritual sphere, in concert with the prestige that the
cardinals achieved between the thirteenth and fourteenth centuries. The historical developments tied to the deaths of the
popes in the last centuries of the Middle Ages were underlaid by
a balance of forces, latent but real, between the institution of the
papacy and the ritual—and therefore, ecclesiological—pretensions of a cardinalate ever more conscious of its prerogatives.

4. The papacy's long removal from Rome helped assure ever more effective protection of the "palace" when the pope died. In this regard, the fact that the last notice of the Romans' habitual sacking of the "palace" on the pontiff's death goes back to 1227 is no mere accident. The curia's growing mobility in the thirteenth century, and its long sojourn at Avignon in the fourteenth, brought an end to an ancient folkloric custom. The protection of the "palace" confirmed the victory of an emphasis on continuity entrusted to a College of Cardinals ever more conscious of its institutional authority during vacancies of the Apostolic See.

The growing prestige of the College of Cardinals within the institutional structure of the church may also have contributed to the birth of a popular ritual that we find recorded only with the papacy's return to Rome in 1378: by stripping the newly elected pope of the goods he had held as a cardinal, the rite created a "new man"—sanctioning, that is, the neo-elect's ascent to the "fullness of power" and the end of the vacancy during which the cardinals had represented the church.

5. At death, the pope lost power *(potestas)*. This is why the part of the mold used for sealing papal bulls that bore the late pope's name was destroyed, and the pope's body was placed in a coffin with his face covered. During the public exhibition of the corpse that preceded its burial, instead, the pope's face had to be uncovered, along with his hands and feet. The body of the deceased pope had to be able to be "seen" as well as "touched."

The bones of John XXII repose at Avignon in a golden reliquary. The body of a deceased pope could in fact be an object of devotion, and appear as a saintly body. The concept of sanctity that the Gregorian reform had succeeded in applying to the figure of the pope was thus transferred to the body of a deceased pope.[105]

The frequency of cultic episodes around the popes' corpses increased with the first of the reforming popes of the eleventh century, Leo IX, and reached a climax precisely in the second half of the thirteenth century. If the pope was the living image of Christ on earth, should his *life as a pope* not be supported by an equally Christlike purity? Is this not what we are being told by the histories of the rite of the wax lambs, of the pope's white clothes, and of the ideal vision of the angelic pope? But were innocence and purity things that, like power, the pope lost at death? No: on the contrary, the *saintly bodies* about which the sources of the period speak to us so often prolonged beyond death the *saintliness of life* that precisely then was being proposed as a model to the reigning pope, with the aid of an unprecedented and complex rhetorical and ritual discourse of purification promoted especially by the mendicant orders.

They were entirely complementary to the rite of enthronement at the Lateran: sitting and lying on the porphyry chairs, the newly elected pontiff was *born* and *died* in apostolicity. From this point of view, the embalming of the popes—ever more frequently documented from the beginning of the fourteenth century—was, after all, an act that also defied the corruption of a virtually saintly body.[106]

A common thread therefore runs through the entire history of the pope's body that we have reconstructed in the first two parts of this book. The reflection on the pope's person, understood in its physical dimension—which presents itself for the first time in such a mature and explicit manner in Peter Damian's *De brevitate,* addressed to Pope Alexander II (1064)—was only deepened and amplified in the following centuries, helping to shape all spheres: liturgical, institutional, spiritual, and anthropological. From the very first of the reforming pontificates of the eleventh century, a rich rhetorical and ritual apparatus, elaborated above all within the church itself, displayed ever more clearly the difference between "that which is above" and "that which is below"—juxtaposing, that is, the pope's physical mortality with the perpetuity of the pontifical office, and attempting at the same time to enfold the pope's entire life within a transparently *angelic* dimension. To be worthy of being the *persona Christi,* the pope had to "undress himself of his own flesh" (Robert Grosseteste): the visibility of the Christly basis of the person of the supreme pontiff had to be supported by an equally luminous appearance of the body *(corporis apparentia)* (Angelo Rocca).

In this centuries-long development, the thirteenth century holds a special place. All the most important features emerge at this point with special clarity, interwoven with a new complexity. At the beginning of the century, Jacques de Vitry paused to consider the nudity of Innocent III's corpse. A few decades later, the deceased pope's nudity became a basic argument underlying papal "humbling" and the *damnatio memoriae*. The Franciscan Salimbene (1284) described the abandonment and nudity of a pope's corpse as a genuine *custom (consuetudine)*. Only in the late fifteenth century did the theme of nudity reemerge with renewed vigor.

On the other hand, in the thirteenth century the pope's body rose to become an institutional metaphor, and the institutional figure of the pope came to be identified with the two natures of Christ. At the end of the century, the theologian Giles of Rome went so far as to declare that "the pope can be called the church." If the pope represents the church—Christ—must he not subject himself to even more visible humbling? Is it therefore only a coincidence that in the thirteenth century the distinction between person and office was a dominant theme, as demonstrated by the papal letters of election, the funeral monuments, the oldest gisant on Italian soil (that of Clement IV), the discussions of the pope's death understood as mourning for the church, or, finally, the incisive Franciscan rhetoric on the abandonment and the nudity of the pope's corpse?

No ceremonial book corresponds perfectly to reality, but in essence the *ordines* of Pierre Ameil (1385–90) and of François de Conzié (1383–91) describe gestures and rites whose precedents can in large part be documented. The rationalism with which the late thirteenth-century ceremonials tend to insert the deceased pope's closest aides into an institutional framework (transforming the custom of appropriating objects last touched by the pope's body into a system of money payments) was perhaps the result of an evolution belonging to the Avignon period. But the key element of the entire ceremonial, the distinction between the physical mortality of the Roman pontiff and the perpetuity of the institution, finds perfect documentary confirmation in the thirteenth-century narrative sources as well as in the papal funeral monuments of the period. Even the exposition of the pope's corpse is not attested in the medieval centuries before the thirteenth. The display was at once a means of glorifying the deceased and of publicly authenticating the pope's death. That led, around 1300, to the adoption of ever more artificial and sophisticated procedures of embalming, aimed at guaranteeing the perfect conservation of the corpse for the period of the novena.

℃

It is in light of these conclusions that we must now confront a third aspect of the history of the pope's body, that of its physical *corporeity* in the strict sense. This raises problems that we have touched on only fleetingly in the preceding pages, all directed at studying images and metaphors that found their expression in the world of rituals and symbolic events. Here, the inquiry must instead turn to the manner in which the Roman pontiffs experienced their physicality in real and cultural terms. At its center we will find above all the care of the body, which we will seek to grasp, however, in various manifestations and aspirations that extend well beyond simply preserving physical health.

The sources enable us to attempt this investigation only from the beginning of the thirteenth century—which, in this field as well, presents strikingly original features with respect to what preceded it. And it is precisely the wealth of documentation that induces us to concentrate exclusively, in the third part of this book, on problems related to the thirteenth century. Our intention is in fact not so much to rewrite the history of the relationship between the pope and medicine within the framework of a *longue durée* (the last centuries of the Middle Ages, for example), as it is to determine whether the problems of physical corporeity intersected with the ritual and rhetorical discourses on mortality and transience that we have encountered in the first two parts of this work.

PART III

Corporeity

7 Recreatio Corporis

Mobility and Holidays

Over the course of a century, from Innocent III to Boniface VIII (1198–1303), the papal curia was absent from Rome for nearly sixty years. Except for Celestine IV, who reigned only seventeen days (Oct. 25–Nov. 10, 1241), none of the thirteenth-century popes spent his entire pontificate in the eternal city.[1] Eleven of the nineteen of them passed more than half their time outside Rome. Six never went there at all. This was true of all three of the French popes—Urban IV (1261–64), Clement IV (1265–1268), and Martin IV (1281–85)—whose itineraries brought them only to the provinces of the papal state. Celestine V (1294) never left the kingdom of Sicily, where he had been a subject before his elevation to the pontificate. Boniface VIII (1294–1303) spent nearly half his pontificate outside Rome, above all at Anagni.[2]

In the eighteen years of his pontificate, Innocent III (1198–1216) spent thirteen summers outside Rome.[3] The departures generally took place between April and June, and always before the feast of Saints Peter and Paul.[4] Only in the years 1199, 1200, 1204, 1205, and 1210 did he spend the entire summer in Rome. The reasons were owing to force majeure: in 1204 and 1205 the pope was tied up by political disorders in the city; in 1210 he had to confront Otto IV.

Of course, the popes had not waited until the thirteenth century to begin spending their summers outside Rome. In his *Vita* of Paul I (757–67), Anastasius the Librarian emphasizes the fact that the pope died during the summer (June 28) in the monastery of Saint Paul outside the Walls, where he had sought shelter from the intense summer heat.[5] Popes stricken with malarial fever also sought relief and shelter outside Rome. When he fell ill just a few days after his election (July 1, 1048), Damasus II had himself brought to Palestrina to breathe cleaner air, but he died there on August 9.[6] Stephen IX also came down with malaria, and left Rome for Montecassino, where he spent the entire winter of 1057–58.[7] In asking Nicholas II (1059–61) to be relieved of his episcopal duties, which he no longer felt able to exercise due to his advancing age, Peter Damian sent the pope a tetrastichic poem he had composed a few years earlier on the fevers of "Rome, devourer of men."[8] Gregory VII spent three summers (1074, 1075, and 1076) at Laurino, near Salerno.[9] In 1116, the Roman curia left the city to spend the "insufferable" *(impatientem)* summer in the vicinity of Campagna and Marittima.[10] After the Council of Benevento (1117), weakened by the summer heat, Paschal II (1099–1118) sought refuge in Anagni.[11] Calixtus II sojourned in Velletri, Veroli, and Anagni during the summer of 1122, and returned to Rome only in October.[12] In the second half of the twelfth century, the presence of the papal court in the pleasant cities of Lazio suddenly became more frequent. Eugenius III (1145–53) had a palace built at Segni.[13] On March 15, 1155, in preparation for the summer, the bishop of Veroli rented a house situated on Monte San Giovanni from the cardinal-count of Campagna.[14] Adrian IV (1154–59) left Rome at the beginning of May, accompanied by the emperor Frederick Barbarossa. But at Pontelucano (June 1155) an epidemic forced the emperor to return to Germany *(ad propria).*[15] The following year the pope, coming back from Benevento, headed to Narni, then to Orvieto, a city that no pontiff had visited before him; with the arrival of winter (Oct.–Nov.), "he descended toward the agreeable and populous Viterbo."[16] In 1159, the pope decided to spend the summer at Anagni, where he died on September 1 of the same year. In a letter of 1167–69, Alexander III thanked the people of Veroli not only for their loyalty, but also for the graciousness of their reception.[17] Lucius III (1181–85) spent nearly all of his pontificate outside Rome, at Segni, Anagni, Sora, and Velletri.

Only with the pontificate of Innocent III, however, did the alternation between winter residence in Rome and summer sojourns in agreeable cities of the papal state become the norm. This was a real change. In the last decades of the twelfth century, the popes had spent long periods outside Rome, but in the cities of northern Italy (Verona, Ferrara, and Pisa), to which they were constrained to go by political considerations and matters of church administration. Celestine III (1191–98), on the other hand, remained in Rome throughout all seven years of his pontificate.[18]

The new schedule that Innocent III imposed on the papal curia was immediately embraced by his successors. Honorius III (1216–27) and Gregory IX (1227–41) spent winters in the Lateran Palace, for centuries the popes' official residence, but left Rome with almost annual regularity at the beginning of summer.[19] Though he was elected in Perugia on July 18, 1216, Honorius III waited until the end of August to make his return to Rome. He spent only four summers in the Lateran Palace (1218, 1221, 1224, 1226). And in one of his letters of June 1226, he complained that he was unable meet with the cardinals, who were themselves absent from Rome "on account of the inclemency of the climate."[20] In August of the same year he conceded a judicial adjournment "on account of the absence of the cardinals and the proctors," who had received permission to leave Rome to avoid "the summer heats."[21]

From Innocent III onward, the winter-summer alternation was so regular that in his *On the Marvels of the City of Rome (De mirabilibus Urbis Romae),* the Master *(magister)* Gregory casually defined the Lateran as "the pope's winter palace."[22] The expression used by the author of this most original guide to medieval Rome is the only one of its sort, and cannot but take us back to the first decades of the thirteenth century. After 1226, and for the rest of the century, no pope spent an entire summer in Rome.

℃

The mobility of the papal curia in the thirteenth century was unquestionably a development with broad implications. The curia was transferred more than two hundred times. In ten cities of the papal state—Anagni, Assisi, Ferentino, Montefiascone, Orvieto, Perugia, Rieti, Segni, Tivoli, and Viterbo—the thirteenth-century popes spent nearly forty years in all.[23] In the twenty years from 1260 to 1280, the Roman curia resided almost uninterruptedly in Viterbo, the city in Lazio that was also the seat of the longest vacancy of the Apostolic See (1268–71).

Such frequent moves required impressive logistical organization. Transferring the curia involved hundreds of different people: the members of the papal family (*familia*, around two hundred), the cardinals and their assistants (*familiares*), lawyers and proctors, the merchants who followed the court (*mercatores Curiae*), the chancery scribes, bishops making their *ad limina* visits, prelates who had come to Rome on business, penitents, pilgrims, and so forth. At least five or six hundred people, attached to the curia directly or tied to it by professional interests, regularly accompanied the pope on his moves.[24] The organizational responsibilities fell to the Apostolic Camera. Between the lines of the rare surviving thirteenth-century account books can be read an explicit desire to assure the popes and other members of the curia a pleasant trip and comfortable accommodations. Officials were sent ahead to look after the delivery of furniture for the papal camera, and to secure the safekeeping of the treasury. In preparation for Boniface VIII's arrival at Anagni in May 1299, a cleric of the camera and a "papal doorkeeper" (*ostiarius pape*) went ahead "to fit out and distribute the dwellings." A certain Zaone was charged with preparing the lodgings (*hospitium*) of the cardinal chamberlain, while two attendants brought the "goods of the chamberlain's quarters" (*roba camere camerarii*). Again, in October 1302, two attendants were sent ahead of the curia to Rome "to prepare the residences." The Apostolic Camera took care to have repairs and improvements made along the roads. On September 28, 1302, it paid three *lire* and eight Provençal *soldi* "to repair the road from when the pope rode through"; for the return trip from Anagni to Rome in autumn 1302, seventeen "freebooters" (*ribaldi*) were hired to "prepare the road." The pope had available an awning that the cameral account books call a "butterfly" (*papilio* or *papilius secretus*). In October 1299, Boniface VIII ordered Master Niccolò of Piglio to have a platform prepared so that he could more easily mount his horse. Boniface also had at his disposition a richly decorated carriage.[25] The cities had to commit themselves to providing free hospitality to the high officers of the curia. The communes were required to set a ceiling on rents. The control of prices was entrusted to tax officials named by both parties. Around the mid–thirteenth century, a rent could quadruple when the Roman curia arrived in a city of the Lazio region around Rome. In 1266 Clement IV, called on to calm a real estate market that had reached full boil, decided that rents should be reduced by 75 percent in the case of a (papal) vacancy of the Apostolic See; but a private lease of 1279 reveals only a more modest reduction of 50 percent. Again, in 1311, when the curia was set up at Avignon, a testament from Viterbo presupposed that the pope's return would produce a doubling of rents.[26]

♥

Some of the popes' trips were connected to the exercise of temporal power.[27] Alexander III spent fully twenty-six months (1179–81) living in the palace at Tusculum "as lord."[28] Innocent III left for Campagna and Marittima in 1208 to shore up the papacy's feudal holdings. While he was leaving Agnani, the most faithful of his vassals, Count Giovanni of Ceccano, who had already sworn fealty to the pope in 1201, joined him with a party of fifty knights. Richly dressed, they escorted the pope with honor and much brandishing of weapons. At Giuliano, the count held a joust among his knights from nine in the morning to dinnertime. At Fossanova, a protonotary of the king of Sicily announced to the fanfare of trumpets the arrival of Riccardo, brother of the pope, count of Sora. At San Germano, the midpoint of the trip, Innocent III summoned a parliament of the barons to order the affairs of the kingdom of Naples as far as Faro. At Ferentino, on October 6, Riccardo of the counts of Segni swore a solemn oath of vassalage to his brother the pope.[29]

Boniface VIII took advantage of the court's movements to visit castles and villages in Lazio belonging to his own Caetani family. The fact was regularly noted by the Aragonese ambassadors. On September 11, 1299, the proctor of the king of Aragon wrote that the pope "went off to his castles."[30] Similar comments appear in the dispatch of October 1, 1299, announcing the pope's return to Rome.[31]

In numerous cases, moreover, the popes had to leave Rome — or were unable to reenter it — because of conflicts with Emperor Frederick II or political disorders in the city itself. But a thorough analysis of the dates of the curia's departures and returns indicates unmistakably that the real motives for the popes' regular alternation between winter residence in Rome and summer sojourns in the comfortable cities of the papal state cannot be assigned to political concerns. In nearly two-thirds of the cases, the papal curia left Rome in the months of May or June. The move never took place before Easter.[32] The curia's departure generally took place in conjunction with a particularly important liturgical feast, such as Ascension or Pentecost.[33] Likewise, the dates of return are, on the whole, homogeneous: in two-thirds of the cases, the pontifical court set itself in motion to return to Rome between October and November. The conclusion is self-evident. More than anything else, the mobility of the thirteenth-century Roman curia was due to the desire of the popes and members of the papal court to avoid the discomforts of the Roman summer every year.

Every now and again the prolongation of a conclave required the cardinals to remain in Rome during the summer, on which occasions the effects on health could be disastrous.[34] Gregory IX died in the Lateran on August 21, 1241, quite likely the victim of malaria. Senator Matteo Rosso Orsini then enclosed the eight cardinals in the Settizonio Palace on the Palatine Hill. That caused the death of the English cardinal Robert of Somercotes; but Goffredo Castiglioni, elected Pope Celestine IV, also died only seventeen days later. Several of the cardinals sought refuge at Anagni before his burial. During the ensuing vacancy, the cardinals Sinibaldo Fieschi (the future Pope Innocent IV) and Riccardo Annibaldi fell gravely ill.[35]

When Innocent V died on June 22, 1276, the cardinals quickly reached agreement in naming his successor. With the Roman summer already at the gates, the new pope, Adrian V (Ottobono Fieschi), ordered the immediate transfer of the pontifical court to Viterbo. There, however, the pope died only a month after his election (Aug. 18, 1276).

Honorius IV died in Rome of gout on April 3, 1287, in the palace he had had built for his family (the Savelli) on the Aventine Hill. Discord among the cardinals prevented the rapid election of his successor. With the arrival of summer, malaria decimated their ranks: six were killed, five more got sick, and four others abandoned Rome for refuge in more agreeable and healthy localities. Girolamo Masci, bishop of Palestrina, alone remained at Santa Sabina. By keeping a fire burning continually in his rooms to purify the infected air, he managed to survive the pestilential vapors. The return of autumn again delayed the election of the new pontiff. Nicholas IV was elected only toward the end of winter, on February 22, 1288.[36]

Again, after the death of Nicholas IV, which occurred in the springtime (April 4, 1292), the cardinals were unable to reach agreement quickly on the election of a new pope. With the onslaught of summer, the majority of them sought refuge in Rieti and Anagni. Only three stayed behind in Rome, one of whom died of malaria.[37]

ℭ

From the very first years of Innocent III's pontificate, the sources on the *recreatio corporis* ("restoration of the body") become more numerous. Innocent himself talked about it in a sermon he delivered during the festival of the golden rose: "You should know, beloved, that the corruptible body cannot bear up under continual strains unless the remedy of restoration *[recreatio]* is interposed from time to time."[38] In 1209 "Pope Innocent III temporarily left Rome on account of the summer climate, which was contrary to his body."[39] On the other hand, the stays at Segni (1212 and 1213), so beloved to Innocent, who enjoyed there the company of his own family, were considered *arid* by his chaplains, who by now had become accustomed to the pleasures of more comfortable summer residences.[40] In 1205 Innocent had to stay in Rome through the summer months, but allowed several of his curialists to await the return of a milder climate elsewhere, and thus to avoid the dangers of the "[malarial] fevers" that were going around Rome.[41]

In 1202 Innocent decided to pass the summer at Subiaco. The organization of the papal court was described by an anonymous curialist in a letter (Aug. 6–Sept. 5, 1202) that is suffused with an extraordinary admiration for Subiaco's idyllic countryside. The author, close to Cardinal Deacon Hugo, the future Gregory IX (1227–41), reveals himself to have been a true nature-lover who delighted in being able to savor its hygienic and sanitary virtues.[42] His allusions to the architectural audacity of the Sublacan hermitage, and to the pictures in the rooms, reflect cultural interests and a refined spirit of observation.[43] Tents were readied to accommodate the pope and his court. To the south were set up the "smoke-filled tents" of the head pontifical cook, who bore the biblical nickname "Nabuzardan"

(Nebuzaradan); to the east was the apothecary, who in the morning could best examine urine thanks to the rising sun; the market
was situated to the north.[44] The pope's residence was called a
"little tabernacle" *(parvum tabernaculum).* To it "was reserved the
best position"; in other words, it was situated in such a way that
it was exposed as much as possible "to the warmth of the sun."[45]

The *Deeds (Gesta)* of Innocent III and Riccardo of San Germano twice underscore the fact that the pope spent an entire
summer outside Rome.[46] The biographer of Gregory IX (1227–
41), on the other hand, speaks regularly of the pope's summer
removals, which he attributed to reasons of hygiene and sanita-
tion. In 1232, the pope happily *(feliciter)* passed the greater part
of the winter at Anagni before moving on to Campagna and
Marittima.[47] In 1227, he wanted to spend the summer at Anagni
"on account of the menace of the suspect quality of Rome's summer air."[48] In June 1230, he came to Anagni "in search of the
indulgence of a more clement air," fearing "the outbreak of an
incendiary summer";[49] the following year, again in June, he
abandoned Rome "moved by the suspicion of a now imminent
summer";[50] in autumn 1236, he moved from Rieti—considered a dangerous place for rheumatism—to Terni, a city the papal biographer describes as "filled with watercourses, with trees
spread about everywhere," and where he had a palace constructed "abounding in comfort";[51] in June 1238, he hurried to
reach Anagni to "avoid the harm of suspect air"; the return to
Rome (Oct. 1238) was decided upon when "the perils of summer
were already disappearing."[52]

Yearning for the pleasures of *recreatio corporis* even became in
these years an element in the polemical exchanges between pope
and emperor. A curial letter preserved in the collection of chancery formulas of the papal chaplain Albert of Behaim, whose
composition goes back to the period of the first Council of Lyons
(1245), denounced Frederick II for having laid siege to Rome,
thus aggravating the physical condition of the pope, "who was
accustomed to restore himself during the summer with more sa-
lubrious air."[53]

Commenting on Innocent IV's reentry from Lyons in 1251,
his biographer, Niccolò of Calvi, recorded that it was "a tradition that the popes return to Rome at the beginning of winter."[54] On the other hand, the curia's removal to Assisi on

May 25, 1254, was justified by the fact that "it is a tradition that the pope passes the summer outside Rome."[55]

In the time of Alexander IV (1254–61), two of the most brilliant papal notaries of the period, Giordano of Terracina and John of Capua, competed in a playful exchange of letters. John exposed the defects of Subiaco with witty realism and displayed his preference for Anagni, which he indeed called "regal" (regalis). Giordano instead painted Subiaco in an idyllic light. It was "a blessed land . . . elegant in every convenience." The "generous right hand [of the Almighty] supplied it with an abundance of all those goods that contribute to the profit and comfort of both the soul and the body."[56] In July 1262, Urban IV (1261–64) wanted to move from Viterbo to Montefiascone to avoid the ardors of the unrelenting heat.[57] Martin IV (1281–85) had a palace constructed there.[58] Referring to the transfer of the court from Anagni to Trevi del Lazio between August 27 and 31, 1299, the king of Aragon's proctor noted that Boniface VIII had left Anagni "for the sake of restoring his body" (causa recreationis corporis sui),[59] an expression the pontiff himself would use in a letter of September 1, 1299, to the king of England.[60]

Fear of Contagion

Speaking of the stench of cadavers in his De miseria conditionis humanae (On the Misery of the Human Condition), Lothar of Segni (Innocent III) deployed images drawn not from the old monastic tradition of contemptus mundi ("contempt of the world"), but from descriptions in the contemporary medical literature of Salerno. This was true of the pestilential stench of the cadavers as of the yeasty putrefaction of worms. The similarities to the Salernitan Questions (Questiones Salernitanae) cannot pass unnoticed.[61] The school of Salerno also taught that "reptiles and flies, and thus also serpents, are generated by putrefaction from external heat, and are therefore contrary to human nature and kill it."[62] It may be added that in the last decades of the twelfth century, the school of Salerno also accorded considerable interest to the Aristotelian texts on "spontaneous generation."[63]

In the letter of the anonymous curialist on the stay of Innocent III's court at Subiaco (1202), the author described the nature of the flies, audacious insects that "disturb human comfort with such importunity," with details that cannot but be the fruit of attentive reading and observations. Their noxiousness was due to their nature, choleric rather than phlegmatic.[64] For Pier delle Vigne, the dangers of mosquitoes and the vapors of the Roman summer heat became an argument to frighten away prelates who wished to come to the council convoked by Gregory IX in 1241: "And should you by chance come to Rome, what would await you but new dangers? Unbearable heat, putrid water, coarse and unhealthy food, heavy air, an enormous number of mosquitoes, an abundance of scorpions, and a race of dirty, evil, and violent men! Beneath the city are subterranean caverns filled with poisonous vermin that come out in . . . the summer."[65] The same biographer of Gregory IX speaks of an incredible invasion of snakes within the city walls, and emphasizes the tragic consequences of illness and death caused by the decay of their corpses.[66] The idea that the pestilential corruption of the air was caused by serpents and monsters that lived in the earth's depths was also expressed by the author of the *Practical Breviary (Breviarium practicae),* an outstanding observer of the environment around the Roman curia.[67]

The *Vita* of Gregory IX graphically records, moreover, the pope's efforts to reduce the putrid effluents in the Roman streets that polluted the city's air.[68] Putrefaction indeed rose to become a literary topos: the struggle against the rebels who had taken over the Cartularia Tower was compared to the necessity of checking the putrefaction caused by an untreated wound;[69] heresy was described as a contagious disease.[70] Even the letter written by the cardinals who had sought refuge at Anagni after the death of Celestine IV (1241) speaks of "disgusting putrefaction, heavy odors, and stench" *(pudendas putredines, fetida pondera, fetores).*[71] That the theme was of great contemporary concern is demonstrated, finally, by the fact that the putrefaction of corpses, "full of worms and stench," was the subject of rhetorical exercises in the chancery letters of those close to the papal court of Gregory IX.[72]

ℭ

The attention to corpses and their stench is present also in the treatise *De retardatione accidentium senectutis (On Delaying the*

Misfortunes of Old Age), which we will take up in a bit. The author, connected to curial circles in the first decades of the thirteenth century, posited a precise relationship between the putrefaction of corpses and malarial fever. The "pestilential vapor" *(vapor pestilentialis),* which here undoubtedly means malaria, had purportedly been spread among the Greeks (in the Byzantine Empire) because of the many corpses that had been left abandoned after a "tremendous battle in Ethiopia." The information came from Avicenna.[73] From the outset, *De retardatione* attributes the causes of old age "to the multiplication of the living, who infect the air around us,"[74] an idea that Roger Bacon would repeat almost literally in his "Letter on the Secrets of Nature" *(Epistola de secretis naturae).*[75]

In his *Book on Particular Matters (Liber particularis),* Michael Scot also devoted extensive treatment to malaria, "a corruption of the air that is not evident everywhere, but which moves about hidden from region to region, then settles down and maintains itself,"[76] which reinforced Frederick II's concern with problems of infected air. In his *On Governments, Routes, and the Goals of Wayfarers (De regiminie et via itineris et fine peregrinantium),* written for the emperor in 1227, Adam of Cremona emphasized the problem of polluted air and the means of purifying it.[77] In this regard, the osmosis between the papal court and that of Frederick II seems complete.[78]

Fear of contagion was undoubtedly one of the papacy's great preoccupations throughout the thirteenth century. On February 27, 1264, Urban IV (1261–64) created a commission to examine Pierre de Rossel, a professor of theology at Paris, who was suspected of having leprosy. It comprised two of the pope's personal physicians, Raymond of Nîmes and Remigius, as well as Cardinal John of Toledo, an expert in medical and alchemical problems.[79] The agreement reached between the Apostolic Camera and the commune of Viterbo in 1278 for the Roman curia's arrival in the city called for the elimination, for hygienic reasons, of the nauseating pools of linseed oil.[80] Seen in this context, the accounts claiming that Martin IV (1281–85) summoned to Rome a doctor, Hugh of Evesham (who was then made a cardinal), to find a way of combating the Roman malaria, do not seem far-fetched.[81]

The Pleasure of Water

The anonymous author of the letter on the stay of Innocent III's court at Subiaco (1202) wrote, among other things:

> we are residing . . . above a most beautiful lake. . . . The lake is worthy of every praise; it often shows itself in blue colors when the wind agitates its waters, as though they were ocean waves, though they are very different from the ocean in the taste and quality of their water. When the water is calm, we should wish to stroll upon it in spirit, as though nature could be identical with its image; for it resembles a meadow, though obviously lacking flowers. What more is there to say? The more we delight in admiring it, the more we suffer from not being able to approach. . . . These places are located on some most beautiful islands, which invite human nature in a marvelous way to the most pleasant recreation. Here and there the water runs and separates along various streams. Here it flows gently, there it is pushed along by a rapid current; here it makes a "gurgling" noise, there it remains silent in transparent clarity; and there, further, for lack of the rigors of the cold, it boils and rises as in a kettle.[82]

This long panegyric to water ends with a direct reference to the person of the pope himself: "The water is beloved to the third Solomon [that is, Innocent III], who willingly thrusts in his holy hands and uses it as a cold 'gargle' [to refresh himself]. Thus, the water comes to the rescue of man's double necessity, and with a double effect. For it serves, indeed, to wash off externally what is contrary to human sensibility because of its filth; internally, the water eliminates that which resists its dominion, thanks to a gracious 'moisturization.'"[83]

The British chronicler Gerald of Wales also reveals an unexpected interest in water on the part of Innocent III. The archdeacon of his diocese, having come to Rome to handle some legal matters, Gerald encountered the pope at the "Virgin Spring" (Fonte Vergine), where he "used to come regularly to take walks" (spatiandi causa). Located south of Rome, not far from the Lateran, the spring was "most beautiful," rich in "clear fresh waters, artistically enclosed by equal-sized stones," and there "flowed from it a pleasant and abundant stream toward the fields." The archdeacon found the pope "seated near the source of the spring, a bit apart from the others."[84]

Already, a few decades earlier, in August 1167, Alexander III had been seen having lunch at the foot of Mount Circeo, "at a spring that from then on was called 'papal' [papalis]." The episode contrasts with the politically troubled nature of that trip: the pope had fled Rome, where he was being "held hostage" by the Emperor Frederick Barbarossa, thanks to some ships sent him by the king of Sicily.[85]

Under Innocent III, as well, the new spring discovered at Spoleto beneath the city walls was immediately named "the papal spring" (fons papalis).[86] At Ferentino, Innocent had an "excellent and most beautiful" fountain constructed in 1203.[87] At Viterbo, some old chronicles date to 1217 the discovery of "quite virtuous hot water." The spring was given the name "Water of the Crusade."[88]

The presence of numerous thermal baths was undoubtedly the real reason why Viterbo became the city in which the Roman curia passed ever more time in the thirteenth century.[89] Matthew Paris records that Gregory IX "had many gallstones, he was very old and needed the baths in which he was accustomed to restore himself at Viterbo."[90] The waterfall that Witelo used to visit with his curial friends to study the causes of the rainbow was located by Bagno dello Scoppio, near Viterbo.[91] It is scarcely surprising, then, that well-off prelates turned their attention to this city in making real estate investments. The astronomer and physician Campano of Novara (d. 1296) had an important residence built there, where he spent the last years of his life. The aging doctor and astronomer had obtained permission from Boniface VIII (then Cardinal Benedetto Caetani) to leave the curia in 1288.[92]

℮

Mobility, fear of contagion, the celebration of water: these were all aspects of a single phenomenon that the sources reveal with great clarity starting from the pontificate of Innocent III, in this as in many other things a profound innovator. Innocent inaugurated the annual withdrawal of the curia from Rome, but also theorized the *recreatio corporis* on an occasion, moreover, that was quite unusual: the sermon on the golden rose. On this point, the contrast with the pessimistic and austere doctrine of his *De miseria conditionis humanae* is notable.

Such open pursuit of a convenient *recreatio corporis* suggests sensibilities that cannot be reduced simply to the desire to flee the Roman malaria. Even if we allow that the centuries-long endemic presence of the Roman malaria may have been going through a phase of recrudescence in the twelfth and thirteenth centuries, mobility, fear of contagion, and pleasure in water were features of a new sensibility regarding corporeity.

To satisfy such evident needs for *recreatio corporis,* the Roman curia made unhesitating use of the possibilities offered by the emerging papal state. The alternation of residences willed by Innocent III, and his "refoundation" of the papal state, were entirely complementary. Viterbo, which hosted the papal court more often than any other locality in Lazio or Umbria, also had more thermal baths than any other city in the papal state.

No matter how one looks at it, hygienic and sanitary concerns were the underlying reasons for the curia's striking mobility in the thirteenth century, even in instances in which more urgent political problems would appear to provide surer explanations for the phenomenon.[93] The constant movements of the thirteenth-century papal court are the reflection of a new court life, as well as of a perception of space, and of logistical efficiency, quite rare in those days within Europe for their breadth and sophistication.[94] A conscious "holiday culture" became a central feature of the rhythm of life at the papal court from the very first years of the century.

New aspirations for a comfortable *recreatio corporis* induced the Roman curia to experiment with prolonged absences from Rome. Attracted also by the comforts *(amoenitas)* of cities like Viterbo and Orvieto, the French popes of the thirteenth century avoided coming to Rome at all. To justify such frequent recourse to this new type of mobility, juridical and ecclesiological thought also came to affirm in the course of the thirteenth century that "where the pope is, there is Rome" *(ubi papa, ibi Roma).* For the abbot of Andres, Viterbo was a second Rome because the pope resided there; but the chronicler did not forget to underline that Innocent III had gone there to escape the Roman summer, so contrary to his body.

The new Arabic studies of the body also appear to have been of decisive importance. Intellectuals and scholars immediately brought them to the attention of other members of the papal court in order to overcome, among other things, fears and obsessions on matters such as contagion and infection. In this regard, the Roman curia appears to have been in perfect osmosis with the court of Frederick II; indeed, in certain matters (such as the winter-summer alternations of residence), the documentation puts the papal court ahead. And when, in the last decades of the thirteenth century, the papacy could again reside regularly at Rome, the palace constructed by Innocent III on the Vatican Hill was transformed into a comfortable and "luxurious pontifical residence" by Nicholas III and his successors (1280–1300). "In a garden of grand dimensions" were planted "trees of every type." [95] The first Vatican gardens even included an impressive park of exotic animals. [96]

8 Cura Corporis

Doctors and Prescriptions

The pontificate of Innocent III is the first for which it is possible to prove the existence of a "papal doctor": Master (*magister*) Giovanni Castellomata bears the title of "doctor to the pope" (*medicus pape*) in the testament of Marie, countess of Montpellier and wife of King Philip II of Aragon, drawn up at Rome on April 20, 1213.[1] Castellomata was a notable figure. As we will soon see, the author of the oldest Western treatise on delaying old age credited Castellomata with persuading him to write his work.[2] In the first half of the thirteenth century, the Castellomate were one of the most influential families of Salerno,[3] a point that confirms the vital ties between the papal court and the Salerno school of medicine, which probably went back much further than what the sources tell us. In his poem on prescription medicines,[4] Giles of Corbeil, doctor to the French king Philip Augustus (1180–1223), sings the praises of a renowned doctor from the school of Salerno, Romuald, who can be identified as the homonymous archbishop of Salerno (d. 1181).[5] In underscoring his fame as a doctor, Giles emphasizes the high regard in which he was held at the papal curia as an "author on medicine" and "patron of life."[6] Around 1200, prestige acquired at Salerno could lead to a cardinalate. Giovanni of San Paolo, author of the compendium *Flowers of Diets (Flores Dietarum)*—a treatise of clear Salernitan stamp—may perhaps be identified as the like-named cardinal.[7]

More generally, medical knowledge and a cardinal's career were by no means incompatible in the first decades of the thirteenth century. The Subiaco letter that we have already

encountered speaks of a "master" who "enjoys an excellent reputation with the third Solomon," to wit, Innocent III. The author had already prescribed to his reader, "Master Romanus,"
that he abstain from "all those things that might cause him to
lose weight."[8] The doctor was quite likely Romano Bonaventura, the future cardinal deacon of Sant'Angelo (1216–36) and
bishop of Porto (1236–43).[9] Besides the identity of names, it
should be noted that the "sermon on penitence" *(sermo de poeni-
tentia)* by "Master Romano, Cardinal" *(Magister Romanus cardinalis)* bears an affirmation that reveals particular interest in
medicine.[10]

Moreover, the author of the Subiaco letter readily cites
Galen and "Hippocratic authority."[11] It is difficult not to think
of the portraits of Hippocrates and Galen that were painted in
the cathedral crypt at Anagni. They are important not only for
their unusual iconography. The frescoes' patrons are to be sought
among the canons of the Anagni cathedral, who enjoyed such
strong ties—through a whole series of personal and family
connections—with the courts of Popes Innocent III and Gregory IX. Such was the case of Rinaldo of Jenne, who would be
elected Pope Alexander IV in 1254.[12]

ℭ

According to the author of the *Deeds of Innocent III (Gesta Innocenti III)*, the pope acquired a home *(domus)* for his doctor *(medicus
pape)* in the neighborhood of the new Vatican Palace.[13] The hos-
pital of Santo Spirito in Sassia that he founded was primarily intended for the care of popes and cardinals.[14] Innocent may also
have been the first pope to speak so frequently in the first person
of his own maladies, and of the limits of his human condition.[15]
The pope often used medical terms and definitions in his writings.[16] He referred, for example, to the opinions of those "who
write about the things of nature," and particularly to those of
doctors *(physici)*. From the first group, he accepted as "reasonable" *(rationabiliter)* the idea that the moon is cold and damp, and
that the sun possesses "the tranquility of the animal virtues"; he
recorded the opposition of the second group to the idea that
"water with wine is transformed *[transubstantiatur]* into blood."[17]
Innocent knew how to talk about the flesh of lepers, not in a

figural sense, but with a clinical eye; he could define the various types of fevers, describe the endurance of pains, and so forth.[18] Even the sermons he delivered on occasions of the highest importance (his consecration ceremony; the opening of the Fourth Lateran Council) are filled with medical references.[19]

We know, moreover, that Innocent's name is indissolubly linked to the rebirth of medieval anatomy: the oldest evidence of medical examinations being carried out for legal purposes indeed comes from references contained in two of his letters, written in 1209. In both cases, the papal judgments were made in accordance with procedural requirements meant to clarify the causes of accidental deaths, and to assign ultimate responsibility. In the first case, the pope asked medical experts to carry out an examination (not an autopsy in the strict sense) of the cadaver of a homicide victim; in the second, he ordered that a verdict by surgeons and doctors, who had examined (but not opened) the cadaver of a young victim, be publicly announced.[20] These important documents demonstrate Innocent's clear and precise understanding of medical issues, and signal the fundamental role that the canon law would be called upon to play in the development of intellectual and judicial techniques that would eventually lead to medical autopsies for legal purposes.[21]

Innocent III's pontificate exemplified the new relationship between medical knowledge and curial prestige, the diffusion of medical works within cultural circles and the papal curia, and the attention devoted to new forms of knowledge concerning the body, above all anatomy. Similarly, the presence of David of Dinant at Innocent's court appears in a new light.[22] This papal chaplain was none other than the homonymous natural philosopher and Aristotelian who was condemned by the Synod of Paris in 1210.[23] The author of a treatise on anatomy, David's detailed descriptions of geographical and natural features of the Mediterranean world, of Palestine and Sicily, also suggest that he had spent considerable time in southern Europe.[24]

℮

Over the course of the thirteenth century, interest in medical studies grew steadily among curial circles. The proposal that Master Richard of Wendover, Gregory IX's doctor, should be identified with Ricardus Anglicus, author of one of the most important thirteenth-century treatises on anatomy, seems entirely valid.[25] It was during Innocent IV's pontificate (1243–54) that the Dominican Tederico, son of the doctor Hugo of Lucca, composed the first version of his most important work—the *Surgery, or The Daughter of the Prince (Cyrurgia seu Filia principis)*—at the request of a fellow member of his religious confraternity, Andrés Albalate, bishop of Valencia (1248–79), whom he had served as chaplain.[26] Later on, at the beginning of the fourteenth century, Henry of Mondeville would credit the papal doctor Guglielmo of Brescia with inspiring the work.[27]

Richard of Fournival's *Biblionomia* lists 125 titles on medicine by 36 different authors, preserved in 30 codices.[28] For the formation of this extraordinary collection of medical works, the chancellor of Amiens's permanent residence in Italy was undoubtedly crucial. Richard had been brought into the *familia* of the English cardinal Robert of Somercotes (1239) as a chaplain.[29] As a master and subdeacon, he obtained Gregory IX's authorization to practice surgery until he was ordained a deacon.[30]

Those rare sources that enable us to glimpse with some precision the nature of a thirteenth-century curialist's career concern figures who engaged in medical activities at the papal court. Campano of Novara appears for the first time at the curia as the chaplain of Pope Innocent IV's nephew, Ottobono Fieschi, cardinal deacon of Sant'Adriano al Foro from 1252 to 1276, then Pope Adrian V (July 11–Aug. 18, 1276). Campano arrived there with his scientific reputation already firmly established by the commentary on Euclid's *Elements* that he had completed between 1256 and 1259.[31] By the time he died in 1296, after thirty years of curial life, he was very rich. The *familia* at his service included fully six people. Campano owned an important palace in Viterbo. His landed holdings were appraised by the Aragonese ambassador as worth more than 12,000 florins. This is the size of the gift that Cardinal Gerardo Bianchi of Parma, Campano's last protector and the executor of his testament, promised Pietro Caetani, Boniface VIII's nephew, to help him rebuild the Torre delle Milizie.[32] Campano's wealth cannot have come from his family or benefices. We should deduce that it was accumulated over the course of his long career as an astronomer and astrologer, as well as a doctor, within a papal curia that by the second half of the thirteenth century had become quite well-off.

Campano is famous above all for the important scientific works that he produced in the field of astronomy over the thirty years that he was attached to the Roman curia, among them the difficult *Theorica planetarum (Theories of the Planets)* commissioned by Urban IV (1261–64).[33] But in the membership roll of Nicholas III's *familia* (May 1278)—the only document of this type that has survived from the thirteenth century—his name is accompanied by the title of "physician" *(phisicus)*.[34] The author of the *Breviarium praticae (Short Guide to Practice),* who knew the curial environment quite well, provides the prescription used by "Master Campano" *(Magister Campanus)* to make pills that "he was accustomed to take every day," and which "he cannot do without."[35]

In the preface to his *Key to Healing (Clavis sanationis),* Simon of Genoa thanks Campano for encouraging him to write it and recalls having sent him a copy for his opinion.[36] The most important lexicon of medical terminology produced in the Middle Ages, Simon worked on it for nearly thirty years, collecting terms from the vast Greek, Latin, and Arabic medical literature and undertaking numerous voyages. Of this vast labor, Simon, who ended his curial career as the doctor of Pope Nicholas IV (1288–92), has left us a document of exceptional interest in his preface: an inventory of the codices he consulted, some of which were in his possession at the time he wrote the work. It is an impressive list. Simon was the only one of the thirteenth-century encyclopedists who knew both versions of the Latin text of Dioscorides's *On Medicine (De medicina).*[37] Among the works he cites that were subsequently lost is Demosthenes's *Ophthalmology (Ophtalmikos),* of which we do not even know the original Greek text. The codex Simon saw was damaged at the beginning, like that which Pope Sylvester II (999–1003) had ordered copied from a manuscript in the library of Bobbio.[38] Under the entry *kirtas,* in a discussion of papyrus and its medical uses, Simon describes his visits to the libraries of Roman monasteries in search of ancient texts, where he saw papyrus books and privileges *(privilegia)* in an unintelligible writing.[39] It is therefore not without significance that a doctor of Simon's caliber should have acknowledged the medical abilities of Campano of Novara.[40]

The sums of money paid out by the executors of the cardinals' testaments to doctors were considerably greater than those that went to other members of the deceaseds' *familiae*.[41] The Hungarian cardinal Stephen explicitly asked his executors to compensate the doctors who had tried to cure him.[42] At the redactions of the testaments of the cardinals Conte Casate (1287) and Thomas d'Ocre (1300) that took place only a few days before their deaths were present three and two doctors respectively, several of them of European-wide fame.[43] A couple of them did not belong professionally to the papal court; their presence was therefore circumstantial—owing, that is, to the nature of the cardinals' maladies and deaths. In his testament of February 22, 1302, Cardinal Gerardo Bianchi left fifteen and ten florins to two of Charles II of Anjou's doctors, Giovanni of Tocco and Iacopo of Brindisi.[44] He left money to four other doctors as well, obviously for services rendered immediately before his death.

To compensate Giovanni of Procida for assisting him in his convalescence, Cardinal Giovanni Gaetano Orsini, the future Pope Nicholas III (1277–80), sought to help him recover some property in the kingdom of Naples that had been confiscated because he supported Manfred of Germany. The cardinal wrote personally to Pope Clement IV, asking him to intervene with Charles of Anjou. Clement agreed, while complaining that he had not himself received the medicine that the learned doctor had promised him.[45]

℮

Prescriptions to clarify vision are said to have been prepared by Albertus Magnus for Pope Gregory (IX?).[46] Master John of Toledo—probably the same as the homonymous cardinal—praised the electuary that Innocent IV is said to have had prepared for his eyes to help restore his vision.[47] The author of the *Breviarium praticae* refers to the "pills that Pope Alexander [IV?] and the King [of Sicily] took every day before and after lunch, which work against cataracts, clear the vision, sharpen the hearing, expel superfluities from the body, and can be taken without changing the diet," as well as "the cream sent by the king of France to Pope Gregory IX [which] serves [to cure] fistulas, ulcers, abscesses, and every kind of hardening."[48] On the other hand, Philip the Fair's famous surgeon, Henry of Mondeville, who knew the medical circles around the papal curia quite well, transcribes in his work a prescription that Boniface VIII apparently acquired from a certain Anselm of Genoa, only to resell it to the king of France.[49]

℃

Before the end of the twelfth century, references to doctors at the curia are practically nonexistent. Thirteenth-century sources, instead, allow us to identify more than seventy doctors serving popes and cardinals.[50] They are spread evenly across the entire century. Comparable documentation does not exist for any other European courts of the period. And even in Rome, there were innovations. The doctors who served the curia had prestigious names. They found support there, and accumulated riches. The aid that the Fieschi family gave Campano of Novara over several decades assumed the form of scientific patronage. Medical activity could facilitate curial ascent. That the famous doctor, Peter of Spain, was elected Pope John XXI in 1276 can be taken as emblematic. The papal court was also an important center for the production of medical works and their diffusion throughout Europe. Richard of Fournival, the author of *De retardatione accidentium senectutis (On Delaying the Misfortunes of Old Age),* and perhaps also Gregory IX's personal doctor (named Richard as well), were all part of that very restricted circle of thirteenth-century intellectuals whose names are in various ways linked to the introduction of Avicenna in the West.[51] At Urban IV's table, where philosophical and scientific disputes took place that were described by Campano of Novara (in the dedication of his *Theorica planetarum*), medicine was also discussed.[52]

Such an intense web of medical interest points also to a new sort of institutional consciousness. The pope had a body whose health deserved the best remedies available, which should be prescribed by the most authoritative doctors of the age. At the same time, the pope's health was an object of attention in every part of Christendom because, were it fragile, it could impact negatively on the life of the church; a pope's delicate health was a source of potential disturbance. Both of these features emerge clearly from the thirteenth-century sources; and this, too, was new. At the end of September 1208, at Anagni, a (false) rumor of Innocent's imminent death spread rapidly.[53] Honorius III was said to be in frail health.[54] In 1276, before June 22, the general council *(Consiglio generale)* of San Gimignano sent an emissary to Rome to find out about the state of Innocent V's health, "for he was said to be ill."[55] On July 24, the abbot of Westminster and Henry of Newark informed Edward I of England that Innocent V had died in Rome on June 22, despite the efforts of his doctors.[56] The cardinal and doctor John of Toledo attempted, in vain, to cure the dying Innocent IV.[57] According to a Roman chronicler, Martin IV's personal physicians were unable to diagnose the malady that led to his death.[58] The description of the final stages became well-known.[59]

For the first time in the history of the papacy, therefore, we witness in the thirteenth century the setting in motion of an organic and complex logistical operation, both cultural and economic, devoted to the *cura corporis* ("care of the body") of popes and cardinals. The phenomenon presents elements even of an obsessive nature, similar to those we encountered in the *recreatio corporis* ("restoration of the body"). Is it not perhaps odd that from the very first decades of the century, the sources speak to us ever more frequently of the popes' illnesses, and of the presence of doctors at the beds of deceased popes? Under the year 1252 in his *Greater Chronicle (Cronica maiora),* Matthew Paris records the ivory cross that the master *(magister)* and "papal physician" *(phisicus pape)* Richard received from the dying Gregory IX: "the cross was very dear to the pope, who wanted to give it to someone equally dear to him."[60] Fully eight doctors took turns around the deathbed of Cardinal Gerardo Bianchi, among them some of the most illustrious luminaries of medical science of the time.[61] During the vacancy opened up at Perugia on July 7, 1304, by the death of Benedict XI, the cardinals, considering that "the power and authority of the Roman pontiff remain with the College of Cardinals during a vacancy of the see *[sede vacante],*" decided to relax the closure of the conclave to permit, among other things, "doctors with medicines" to come visit them.[62]

Appearances

An anonymous chronicler, an eyewitness of Innocent III's last days, speaks favorably of the pope's voice. It "was so sonorous that everyone could hear and understand it even though he spoke softly." [63] Moreover, Innocent is described as handsome *(pulcher)*, though the author also emphasizes that the pope's countenance *(aspectus)* was "much respected and feared by all." [64] The biographer of Urban IV also notes his "clear voice" *(clara quoque voce)*, and the pope's physical "beauty," in the context of a description that, rather significantly, fuses bodily models ("a charming face *[venustus facie]*), naturalistic observations ("a cheerful countenance" *[hilaris vultu]*, "medium tall" *[mediocris corporis]*), and moral characteristics ("a strong heart" *[corde fortis]*).[65] A few years later, a contemporary Roman chronicle highlights the handsome face and resonant voice of Nicholas III (1277–80).[66] In describing Nicholas III's physical appearance, an independent source, the Dominican Ptolemy of Lucca's *New Ecclesiastical History (Historia ecclesiastica nova)*, uses a similar turn of phrase: Ptolemy calls Nicholas III "the composite" *(el composto)*, "because he was one of the most handsome clerics on earth." [67] The epitaph to the Orsini pope itself exalts his physical beauty.[68] The inscription is devoid of religious content: rather, it repeatedly invokes the concept of "fame." [69] A few years earlier (1261–65), Henry of Würzburg, author of the *Poem on the Condition of the Roman Curia (Carmen de statu Curie Romane)*, one of the most important poems on life at the papal court in this period, had described—albeit ironically—Cardinal Ancher of Troyes (1262–86), the nephew of Pope Urban IV (1261–64), as a model of beauty.[70]

The problem needs to be set in a broader context. An important contrast has been observed between the effigy of Honorius IV (1285–87), sculpted by Arnolfo di Cambio, and what we know of the pope's actual physical appearance. Arnolfo's statue exudes a "marvelous serenity." [71] But according to Ptolemy of Lucca, Honorius was so crippled (by gout) in his hands and feet that he could not celebrate mass without a crutch. His brother, too, was so stricken by the disease that he had to be carried from room to room.[72] But the contradiction is only apparent. In the central decades of the thirteenth century, the idea had already taken hold that in public the body of the sovereign should express serenity, equilibrium, and decorum. Speaking of John XXI (1276), Ptolemy of Lucca records that the pope, "though a man of great learning, was of modest distinction; he was impetuous in speaking, meek only in his habits"; because "it was easy to approach him, his defects were manifest to all. But this runs counter to the teaching of the Philosopher [Aristotle], who declares that the 'prince's private affairs' [*facta principum personalia*] should not be set before men's gaze, but only his public deeds, for which the prince must answer before the people, as Valerius Maximus wrote."[73]

The epitaph "composite" that Ptolemy of Lucca applied to Nicholas III was also used by the author of the *Secretum secretorum (Secret of Secrets)*.[74] The body's aesthetic was a basic requirement for the image of a sovereign: "It is indeed necessary that you be a spiritual man of good looks and decorum."[75] The *Secretum secretorum* is a sort of "mirror of princes," presented in the guise of a letter that Aristotle supposedly wrote in old age to his ex-student Alexander the Great, to tell him about a "secret," filled with images and mysterious examples to prevent its being stolen by unworthy persons. It is a heterogeneous sort of *summa* mixing medical advice, moral instruction, and tips on healthy living useful in helping the sovereign maintain his physical well-being. The first part concerns the qualities that distinguish a good king, as well as norms and prescriptions that should govern his comportment. The second is devoted to the maintenance of health. In the third part the author discusses alchemy, the properties of stones and plants, and justice as a universal principle of order.[76] The fourth is dedicated entirely to physiognomy, a new science that seems to have fascinated the thirteenth-century elites.[77]

Ptolemy of Lucca's charge that John XXI was too generous in allowing access to his person was echoed in the *Secretum secretorum*, a work in which poisons are discussed at length, as well as the necessity of not putting all trust in a single doctor, and of consulting an astronomer.[78] And these were also central concerns at the court of the thirteenth-century popes.[79] Should any of this surprise us? After all, Philip of Tripoli, translator of the complete version of the *Secretum secretorum* that circulated in the West around the 1230s, must be identified with the curialist Philip, nephew of Honorius III's vice chancellor and patriarch of Antioch from 1219 to 1225.[80] In granting him a canonry in Tripoli (May 17, 1227), Gregory IX recalled that he had cared for his uncle, who had recommended him personally *(viva voce)* to Honorius.[81]

ℰ

The oldest certain reference to the *Secretum secretorum* can be found in a collection of letters of the papal legate Albert of Behaim, containing those he sent between 1241 and 1255, many of them written while the Roman curia was staying at Lyons (1245 – 50).[82] William of Moerbeke (d.1286), too, well-known for his translations of Aristotle, would have been deeply influenced in his studies on the philosophy of light and vision by the *Secretum secretorum*, a work on which Albertus Magnus had commented at length.[83]

Can we fail to note in this regard that in his *Perspectiva (Optics)*, finished during his long curial sojourn, Witelo distinguishes twenty-nine different kinds of beauty?[84] His work is "valid above all for the aesthetic sensibility that permeates it." It constitutes a decisive affirmation of the Aristotelian and Thomistic theory of the superiority of form over color. Thanks to Thomas Aquinas, Witelo was able to establish some distance from his model, Alhazen. The coincidence is important: while staying at Viterbo, Aquinas himself became interested in various aspects of optical issues.[85] In his dedicatory letter to the *Perspectiva*, Witelo recalls the studies of the philosophy of light that his Dominican friend, the papal penitentiary William of Moerbeke, was forced to abandon due to the burden of his curial duties. Moerbeke had translated Hero of Alexandria's *Catoptrics (Catoptrica)*, which Witelo used in his *Perspectiva*.[86]

Witelo also recounts often visiting a waterfall near Viterbo to study the phenomena of the refraction of light.[87] We know, moreover, that on February 7, 1277, he was present in Viterbo to witness a testament drawn up for Cardinal Simone Paltanieri of Monselice. This is the only firm date we have of Witelo's stay at the curia. Its historical value lies in enabling us to establish that the two leading students of optics in the thirteenth century lived contemporaneously at the papal court. Witelo's *Perspectiva* and John Peckham's *Perspectiva communis (General Optics)* in fact present in virtually identical language a phrase concerning the lesion of the crystalline lens *(tunica* or *humor glacialis),* considered fatal to vision. Witelo and Peckham also present in an identical manner, using even the same terms, an argument deriving from Alhazen that is not found, with the same modifications, in any other treatise on optics circulating in the Latin West during the thirteenth century. On this account, it is reasonable to conclude that one of them had to be copying the other. Peckham had been called to the curia in the autumn of 1276 to teach theology at the *Studium curiae.* The great scholar and future archbishop of Canterbury appears to have used his time there (1276–78) to complete the revision of his *Perspectiva minor (Lesser Optics).*[88] A decade before Peckham's arrival in Viterbo another leading English scientist, the famous Franciscan Roger Bacon, had sent Pope Clement VII a treatise on optics, his *On Rays (De radiis).*[89] In the decade 1267–77, the papal court at Viterbo was therefore the principal European center for the production and transmission of works devoted to optics. The ruling pope himself, John XXI (1276–77), was a specialist in problems of vision. Peter of Spain was in fact the author of one of the most important medieval treatises on ophthalmology, *On the Eye (De oculo).* It is probable, moreover, that he finished the work during the long period he spent at the curia before ascending to the pontificate.[90]

Light, vision, corporeity. Aesthetics became a basic requirement of the sovereign's external appearance in the thirteenth century. These were new ideas. The Western elites became aware of them through texts like the *Secretum secretorum,* the complete version of which was translated by a curialist, Philip of Tripoli, and to whose diffusion the circles around the papal court made a signal contribution. But the papal court also played an essential role in disseminating the science of vision in the last decades of the thirteenth century. During these years, Arnolfo di Cambio, one of the greatest artists tied to the world of the Roman curia, analyzed blindness from real life in one of his works, in a way that amounts to the realistic representation of trachoma. The "Master of Isaac" painted the "corneal cloth," one of the serious complications produced by trachoma, as a kind of third eyelid. The scarred retraction of the eyelid, caused by the trachoma, appears exactly represented in Isaac's eyelids, swollen and reddened around the rims, and without lashes. We have here a case of scientific curiosity that must be set in that climate of passionate interest in the visual sciences that so strongly characterized the cultural life of the papal court during the second half of the thirteenth century. After all, ophthalmology, optics, and the philosophy of light were among the principal objects of study of that extraordinary "Viterbo circle," composed of scientists on the order of Campano of Novara, Peter of Spain, Witelo, John Peckham, Simon of Genoa, and William of Moerbeke.[91]

9 *Prolongatio Vitae*

Delaying Old Age

On May 5, 1122, Calixtus II (1119–24) received in audience a patriarch from the Indies named John. He reportedly told the pope about a city named "Hulna" *(Civitas . . . Hulna),* the site of the apostle Thomas's tomb, the balsam from which would cure every sick person who went there on the day of the saint's anniversary.[1] On September 27, 1177, Alexander III decided to send his own doctor, Filippo, to "Prester John." The pope's letter to "Our beloved son in Christ, John, illustrious and magnificent king of the Indies" *(karissimo in Christo filio Iohanni, illustri et magnifico Indorum regi)* may be a reply to the famous "Letter of the Prester John," which was already circulating in the West at that time.[2]

In the imaginary realm of Prester John, filled with abundance and prosperity, all physical and moral decay were absent: "Whoever uses this fountain three times while fasting will be freed of every infirmity, and his life will remain as it was when he was thirty-two years old." In his kingdom, reports the "Letter of Prester John," there are "stones that the eagles [symbols of immortality] bring us regularly, thanks to which we can rejuvenate ourselves and recover the light."[3]

At two crucial points in the papacy's rise to political supremacy—the 1122 Concordat of Worms and the 1177 Peace of Venice with Emperor Frederick Barbarossa—Prester John's "utopia," so richly suggestive for the myth of bodily incorruptibility and immortality, seems to have held a particular fascination for the those in the highest circles of the papal curia.

ℭ

Lothar of Segni (Innocent III) devoted two chapters of his first book, *De miseria conditionis humanae (On the Misery of the Human Condition)*, to old age. His rhetoric on the discomforts of senescence is powerful and effective, but remained grounded in traditional images.[4] More interesting is his passage concerning the brevity of life. The author, then thirty-five years old, began by observing: "we read that at the beginning of the human condition men lived nine hundred years and more." But then, when "the life of man began to decline, the Lord, speaking to Noah, set a new limit on life of one hundred and twenty years" (Gen. 5: 3). Thereafter, "only very rarely did men enjoy long lives; and because the [length of] human life became ever shorter, the Psalmist declares: 'The years of our life are threescore and ten, or even by reason of strength fourscore; yet their span is but toil and trouble'" (Ps. 90: 10 [Vulgate 89: 10]).[5]

In accordance with tradition, Lothar found in the Flood a point of rupture so far as human life spans were concerned: the circumstances that had permitted the long-lived patriarchs to live up to 900 years and more were unrepeatable. But though he considered it "very rare" that life might still last as long as 120 years, it was not impossible. Moreover, Lothar did not explicitly link to original sin the idea that the human condition since the Flood had witnessed a progressive and constant shortening of life. Finally, his conclusion has a nostalgic flavor: "Now my few days will shortly end"; "few now reach sixty, very few seventy."

The continual shortening of life spans, however, put a check on any vain delusions concerning the *prolongatio vitae* ("prolongation of life"). On this point Lothar was in agreement with the Salerno school, which denied the possibility of prolonging life.[6] It should be noted again, however, that Lothar's reflections on old age were not mere substitutes for more overt references of a theological or spiritual nature. And this means that, though he was inspired by the literary tradition of the *contemptus mundi* ("contempt of the world"), Lothar also innovated. His arguments rest, in fact, on a naturalistic vision of the physiological history of man that, by 1200, an educated person could find in the writings of the Salerno school and in recent translations of Aristotle's works, above all his *On Generation and Decay (De generatione et corruptione)*.[7] After all, Lothar, who had studied at the Paris *Studium* in a period of particular intellectual vivacity, seems to reveal a clear interest in medicine, which he even enjoyed showing off in the sermons he delivered after his rise to the papacy.[8]

Even the oldest treatise devoted entirely to aging and the prolongation of life leads us back to Rome. In the chapter in which he talks about the problems of air, the author of *De retardatione accidentium senectutis* (*On Delaying the Misfortunes of Old Age*) in fact recalls having "seen a mountain in the vicinity of Rome, where the climate and the plants are of such a quality that sick animals become healthy again after having grazed there a while."[9] Deferring to the medieval custom of referring to illustrious figures who could confer authority and protection, he declares that he was induced to compose his treatise by the "force of persuasion" *(ad suasionem)* of two "wise men" *(sapientes).* The first was "Johannes Castellioniati," who we can easily identify as Giovanni Castellomata, already Innocent III's doctor.[10] The second was Philip, chancellor of the University of Paris (d. 1236), a figure the author could have met at Paris, or at the papal court during one of the chancellor's two known curial sojourns.[11]

But there is more. The oldest codex of *De retardatione* contains the version addressed to Pope Innocent IV (1243–54).[12] Furthermore, its conclusion *(explicit)* gives the name of the author, identifiable only as "the master of Castle Gret" *(dominus castri Gret).* A very similar name—"the master of Castle Goet" *(dominus castri Goet)*—appears as well in Abbot Ivo of Cluny's (1256/7–75) list of books: that codex, now lost, contained the version of the "Letter on the Misfortunes of Old Age" *(epistola de accidentibus senectutis)* that had been sent to Emperor Frederick II (1194–1250).[13]

We do not know whether *De retardatione* was written originally for the pope or for the emperor.[14] The beginning *(incipit)* of the work could be adapted to either: the short version of it in fact calls the recipient "Lord of the World" *(Domine mundi),* of a "doubly noble line" *(ex bina nobili stirpe),* which could apply as well to Emperor Frederick II, the son of Henry IV and Constance of Altavilla, as to Sinibaldo Fieschi (Pope Innocent IV), a descendant (on both sides of his family) of the high Ligurian nobility.[15] That the treatise may have been sent to both Innocent IV and Frederick II is a further indication of that cultural osmosis that seems to have linked the papal and imperial courts in the fields of the natural sciences and medicine.[16]

De retardatione mistakenly came to be considered the work of Roger Bacon.[17] Already, toward the late thirteenth century, codices attributed it to Arnald of Villanova and Raymond Lull. Marsilio Ficino used it for his *Vita longa (Long Life).*[18] The attribution to Bacon emerged only in the fifteenth century, among a very restricted group of English manuscripts that, moreover, show considerable hesitation on this point. The treatise was published many times in the fifteenth and sixteenth centuries under the names of Arnald of Villanova, Raymond Lull, and Roger Bacon. In modern times, however, thanks to renewed interest among English cultural circles in the *prolongatio vitae,* the ascription to Bacon was the only one that survived. *De retardatione* continued to be transcribed in England, where it was even published in an English translation by the successful editor Richard Browne (1683). The originality of the treatise, so rich in cultural novelties, continued to fascinate the European elites for several centuries, well after Marsilio Ficino's fifteenth-century rewriting of the myth of the *prolongatio vitae.*

The author believed that he had made a great discovery, to which he devoted long studies.[19] He wanted to offer the Western elites (the emperor, the pope, the chancellor of the University of Paris) a system of thought rich in innovation. From this derived his emphasis on the fact that the possibility of prolonging life "was held in little esteem by the Caldeans and the Greeks, because it had not come down to them, or because it had been buried by the Ancients."[20] For this latter reason, of the three "ways" that conduced to retarding old age—the conservation of peace, the *regimen sanitatis* ("healthy regimen"), and the *prolongatio vitae*—the third was the most difficult, but also the most effective.[21]

In the High Middle Ages, belief in the possibility of prolonging life was based on texts from classical antiquity and the Old Testament. The myth turned on three basic elements: time, space, and magical ingredients—distant and inaccessible. Medical learning retained the idea that men had been able to live longer lives in remote periods of the past, before the Flood. Genesis relates the history of patriarchs who had died only after several hundred years. Had Methuselah not lived as much as 960 years? Even Saint Augustine had explained in his *City of God* that, indeed, "the years of those patriarchs must be reckoned by the same standard as our own."[22] Numerous legends, of which we find traces in the medieval maps that have come down to us, attributed exceptionally long lives to peoples living in regions located on the edge of the earth, in most distant Asia.[23] The idea of the possibility of rejuvenation thanks to some marvelous substance found an effective vehicle in the famous medieval legend of Alexander the Great. Four venerable old men had shown Alexander three miraculous fountains, capable of turning death into life, of conferring immortality, and of restoring youth. Alexander and his companions jumped in and were restored to the condition of thirty-year-old men, the ideal age in the Middle Ages, analogous to the number of years lived by Christ. But the differences between this legend and *De retardatione* are also notable. In the thirteenth-century treatise, the basic elements of the myth of the *prolongatio vitae*—space, time, ingredients—are no longer inaccessible, but are instead available *here* and *now*. For the first time in the Latin West, the vision of the *prolongatio vitae* was set forth within a framework of *science* and *observation*.

❦

The theme of the progressive—physiological—shortening of life is central to *De retardatione*. Getting old means progressively losing two of the four elements that compose the human body (heat, moisture) in favor of the other two (cold, dryness).[24] The important thing is to have medicines available that are not subject to decay, and can therefore delay the loss of "innate heat" *(calor innatus)* and the "escape of moisture" *(resolutio humiditatis)*. From some of these it is possible (indispensable) to extract their power *(virtus)*.[25] Knowledge of the substances that can delay old age is *occult,* because he who possesses the secret of all their properties sooner or later transgresses the divine law; it follows that only the "wise in speculation" *(sapiens in speculatione)* and the "expert in the ways of things" *(expertus in operatione),* can derive "noble and sublime" profit from such substances.[26]

The list of occult substances *(occulta)* is the centerpiece of the entire treatise. Its character, at once didactic and deliberately obscure, assured it lasting success; as late as the mid–sixteenth century, the doctor Tommaso Rangoni of Ravenna proposed it repeatedly in almost identical terms to three successive popes; thanks to these elixirs, he claimed, they would live to 120 years, and thus see "Peter's years."[27]

The first of the occult substances *(occultum)*—gold—lies hidden in the earth; the second—amber—swims in the sea. The third—the viper—slithers on the earth; the fourth—rosemary—grows in the air; the fifth—"the vapor of youth" *(fumus iuventutis)*—derives its origin from the "noble animal"; the sixth—human blood—comes from the long-lived animal; the seventh—aloe wood—comes from an Indian plant.[28] The most important *occulta* seem to have been gold, amber (or pearls), and the "square stone of the noble animal" *(lapis quadratus nobilis animalis),* because they retarded the loss of natural moisture, kept it tempered with the natural heat, and never underwent change "caused by their makeup" *(ab eorum temperantia).* Gold was undoubtedly the most important cultural novelty; *De retardatione*'s author was aware of it, but limited himself to describing its capabilities without losing himself in symbolic speculation.[29]

One of the most important sources of inspiration for both the potable gold and the "alchemic element" was undoubtedly the *Secretum secretorum (Secret of Secrets),* which *De retardatione* uses (it was the first Western work to do so) in the most complete version.[30] The *Secretum secretorum* devotes considerable space to the *prolongatio vitae* and initiates an entirely new discussion around the "body of the sovereign," aimed at the elites of the Latin West. The *prolongatio vitae* lies within two spheres, private and public, because in it the well-being of the sovereign comes to be fused with the prosperity of the community over which he presides.

The convergence is important: as has already been shown, to locate the birth and diffusion of the complete version of this work of Eastern origin, we must return to the environment of the Roman curia in the early thirteenth century.[31]

Immortality

That the greater part of the manuscript tradition might suggest Roger Bacon as the author of *De retardatione* is not entirely without logic. Ultimately, the centuries-long attribution to the Oxford Franciscan of a work that laid the foundations of the

Western myth of the *prolongatio vitae* is justifiable. Bacon had dedicated considerable space to the problems of rejuvenation and the prolongation of life in his major works, particularly those he addressed to Pope Clement IV (1265–68).[32] He came into contact with Clement when, as cardinal bishop of Sabina, the future pope was staying in the north of France, waiting to cross to England to carry out a legation that promised to be politically delicate and complex. After reaching the summit of the papacy in 1265, Clement wrote Bacon several times from 1266 onward asking for his writings. Bacon admits working intensely following the Epiphany of 1267 to satisfy a pope who, moreover, had asked him to keep the matter secret, probably because a decree of the chapter general of the Franciscans (Narbonne, 1258) had prohibited any publication outside the order and any direct communication with the papal court.[33]

Ĉ

There are some notable differences between *De retardatione* and Bacon's writings on the *prolongatio vitae*. But within the space of a generation, Bacon was able to assimilate the new ideas on the body presented in *De retardatione,* and to incorporate them into his extraordinarily audacious and coherent "theology of the body."[34]

Bacon's theses can be summarized as follows: to reach the full natural span of life set by God and nature, man can avail himself of the marvelous powers of astronomy, alchemy, and optics *(perspectiva)*. Human nature's immortality is not owing solely to the resurrection; man's immortality is natural: that is, it concerns the body as well as the soul. It is true, Bacon explained, that "for the sake of the body, man was by nature immortal, which means that he cannot die or be subject to death except because of sin; at the resurrection of the dead, all men will be immortal, not only the saints, but also the damned." But it was also true that "the immortality of the human race is natural; and therefore it is not surprising that as the soul is rational, so also the body is immortal." Bacon emphasized that even though man had fallen into sin, he had nevertheless been able to live naturally *(naturaliter)* for a period of a thousand years, as demonstrated by the existence of the "long-lived patriarchs." Only later had life bit by bit become shorter so that, according to the Psalmist, the days of our years could not exceed seventy years (Ps. 90:10 [Vulgate 89:10]). "Certain strong people can reach eighty, but their labor and sorrow increase accordingly, as we see by the light of a revealed faith." The corruption that led to death was therefore against nature. Indeed, the causes of this "acceleration of death" *(festinatio mortis)* should not be sought only in sin. "It is manifest that this was due to an error in man's caring for his health." The degeneration was therefore owing also to the fact that man, expelled from the earthly Paradise, had not followed the rules of the *regimen sanitatis*.

"The fathers did not observe moderation in eating and drinking, in sleep and awakeness, in movement and repose . . . no mortal kept to moderation, neither the doctors nor the rich, not even the poor: it was thus that the fathers corrupted themselves from the very outset in their 'constitution' . . . and it was thus that the fathers produced corrupt sons who were themselves corrupted by their own conduct, producing in their turn sons doubly corrupted." One after another, the succeeding generations "accelerated and multiplied the corruption and shortening of life," as "we can see and confirm in our own day." But "the corruption and shortening of life can be eliminated so that men may live to the full limit established by God and nature. For surely it was neither God, nor nature, nor design that instituted this corruption, but man's own stupidity." Bacon discerned the means of checking old age in the "experimental sciences": astronomy, optics, and alchemy. These experimental sciences "can repair the defects of the regimen of health *[regimen salutis]* that every man contracts at birth."

Astronomy and perspective must be used to calculate and facilitate the focusing of the stellar and solar rays—of the superior virtues—on precious stones and marvelous herbs, as well as on foods and drinks "at table or elsewhere" *(in mensa sive alibi)*. The observations of the astronomer and the tools of perspective—that is, optics—could thus work together to "render starlike" the foods and drinks, spices and medicines, stones and herbs used by men worthy of perpetual health and a prolongation of their life, in order that the "defective regimen" *(defectus regiminis)* contracted from infancy could be repaired immediately, and to delay the passions of old age, or at least mitigate their effects when it was no longer possible to check their onset. The alchemist, moreover, must prepare the gold by "igniting and dissolving" *(calcinando et solvendo)* it, so that it could be used in food and drink. Thus transformed into human nature, it would serve against every infirmity, assure continuous good health, and prolong life, especially if it was suitably prepared under the rays of the sun and the stars, and received their virtues. Thanks to alchemy, and in particular to the use of potable gold, the body could reach a perfect equilibrium, which Bacon defined as an "equal constitution" *(equalis complexio)*. "The experimenter extends his experience further and orders the alchemist to prepare him a body of equal constitution." [35] This perfect equilibrium was brought about by the fact that all the elements were equal with respect to virtue; no element dominated another, as was the case, instead, of fire in choleric people, air in the sanguine, water in the phlegmatic, and earth in the melancholy. The body, thus "composed of equal humors," "cannot by any means be corrupted" *(non potest corrumpi aliquo modo)*. Arriving at equality *(equalitas)*—that is, the uncorrupted *(incorruptio)* body—was for Bacon not only a possibility: achieving an equilibrium of the elements *(complexiones)* meant arresting the body's progressive corruption and, consequently, slowing, if not indeed halting, the body's inevitable aging. This condition of incorruptibility was the same as that of gold, a material composed to the highest degree of an "equal constitution" *(equalis complexio)*. In gold none of the elements dominated the others; rather, through the action of fire, the gold "increases its perfection." In a body that had recovered this equilibrium, no corruption *(corruptio)* was possible.

For Bacon, seeking the equilibrium and harmony of the body served not only to prolong physical life, but to "prepare it" for eternal life: "In fact, God, thanks to his natural virtue, will make from the ashes of the dead a body of equal constitution, from which will be constituted the bodies at the moment of resurrection, in such a way that every man, damned or saved, will be revived . . . and he will be unable to suffer any corruption whatsoever." In the scheme of salvation, "equality" *(equalitas)* was not only humanly and technically possible but, indeed, necessary. Rejuvenation—prolonging life with the help of experimental science and, above all, potable gold—meant rediscovering a harmonious balance that could prevent and check the growing corruption to which the human organism was subject because of original sin and the abandonment of healthy living *(regimen sanitatis)*. Recovering this state of corporal incorrupti-bility was the essential condition for approaching the uncor-rupted state of the resuscitated body, or rather, in the end, of a rejuvenated body in the beyond. To be, that is, like Adam, who was "nearly equally constituted" *(prope equalem complexionem)* and could have remained immortal.

℮

Bacon's whole line of thought was based on *De retardatione* and the *Secretum secretorum*. Thus he is interesting not because he provides new information, but because he presents a system of thought, the fruit of a conscious assimilation of cultural elements that had entered the West a generation earlier. In this respect, the entire historiographical tradition surrounding Bacon and the *prolongatio vitae* needs to be corrected. His rewriting of the myth of the *prolongatio vitae* contains implicitly the idea that man is not only responsible for his own body, but has a power over nature. Even here, Bacon adapted and transformed a recent acquisition of medieval culture: the idea that "science" possesses the means of achieving human mastery *(magisterium)* over the forces of na-ture. Alchemy could enable man to seize the keys that unlocked nature, whose infirmities could be cured by an elixir, a word that had now entered and become a part of the Western vocabulary.[36]

The Oxford Franciscan's system of thought seems in certain respects to be almost Taoist: for this reason, some have wondered whether Bacon's views on the *prolongatio vitae* might not be the result of the contacts that, around the mid–thirteenth century, began to link the Latin West and the Far East.[37] But the hypothe-sis of a direct Chinese influence has to be set aside: on the one hand, Bacon got his information from *De retardatione* and from the *Secretum secretorum;* on the other, Bacon was able to construct his "theology of the body" from within the cultural framework of Western Christianity itself.

Never before in the Christian culture of the European West had the myth of a possible prolongation of life been incorporated into such a rich system of thought, supported by a genuine the-ology of the body. In the works he wrote for the pope, Bacon provided the highest possible theological justification for bodily care based on the concept of an elixir, one capable of converting alchemy (and the other experimental sciences of which he was an ardent defender) into an instrument of salvation.[38]

℘

Theories and experiments with elixirs were at the core of that complex web of corporal interests that underlay the history of the papal court from the very outset of Innocent III's pontificate. Innocent spoke of old age in terms that differed from the traditional *contemptus mundi,* inaugurated the annual alternation between the curia's winter and summer residences, established a residence *(domus)* for the papal doctor *(medicus papae),* reflected on the *recreatio corporis* ("restoration of the body"), knew the medicine of the Salerno school, and had among his chaplains a scholar of anatomy, David of Dinant, and as his personal doctor a Salernitan, Giovanni Castellomanta, whose name is tied to the oldest Western treatise on how to delay old age. Not only were all the basic texts of the thirteenth-century rewriting of the myth of the *prolongatio vitae*—from *De retardatione accidentium senectutis* to the writings of Roger Bacon—of keen interest to the circles of the thirteenth-century papal court; a considerable part of the medical and paramedical culture of that period was in fact devoted to the desire for a possible prolongation of life. Such was the case of the *Secretum secretorum,* the full version of which was translated by the nephew of Honorius III's vice chancellor. Bacon's own ideas on the *prolongatio vitae,* based on the much celebrated experimental sciences (optics, alchemy, astronomy), found an unexpected reception in the thirteenth-century scientific movement at Rome. In the decade 1267–77, Viterbo was the European capital for optics. Light and macrobiotics were inseparable. Light had to preserve, by means of Bacon's "starlike" foods, the innate heat *(calor innatus),* whose conservation was the basis of the *prolongatio vitae.* Campano of Novara was for two or three decades a professional astronomer in the service of the popes, the first we know of in the history of the papal court. The cardinals John of Toledo and Hugh of Evesham were considered authorities *(auctoritates)* in the field of alchemy. That a doctor (Peter of Spain) elected pope (John XXI, 1276) should have studied firsthand the problems of the *prolongatio vitae* and of macrobiotics is entirely emblematic: in his *Summary on the Preservation of Health (Summa de conservatione sanitate),* Peter of Spain examined the action of the motions of the higher bodies as the cause of the shortening of human life;[39] in his *Knowledge of the Soul (Scientia de anima)* and *Expositions on the Book of the Soul (Expositiones in librum de anima)*, the great doctor and philosopher showed how light could be "truly the central element in all of microbiotics";[40] in *On the Eye (De oculo)*, he gave a prescription for renewing sight.[41] The insinuations of the French chronicler Guillaume of Nangis must therefore be taken seriously: "Pope John [XXI], although he had believed he could extend the duration of his life by many years, and had even declared it regularly in front of many people, died unexpectedly."[42]

In Bacon's view, the power of understanding the experimental sciences should be reserved to those with the duty "to rule themselves and others" *(regere se et alios).*[43] These were secrets to be entrusted only to the very few *(paucissimi)* and kept from the view of the masses *(vulgus)*. The techniques of making elixirs were instruments in the service of the body of the sovereign. Even in the *Secretum secretorum*, the sovereign's long life is identified with the prosperity of the society over which he presides. Just as the founders of alchemical knowledge were identified as most ancient philosopher kings, so also the recipients of these projects and techniques of transformation were identified as those who held power.

In the culture of the thirteenth century, besides the emperor, the pope could be counted among the very few. The pope, too, had a body and deserved to have his life prolonged by means of gold and Bacon's experimental science. To the pope, also, should be reserved the techniques of long life resulting in the multiplication of biological time. Indeed, to the pope even more than to other sovereigns, because from no other thirteenth-century sovereign court, not even that of Frederick II, is it possible to assemble such a rich mass of information on the hope of prolonging life.[44] The cultural osmosis observable between the two courts indicates that even in corporeal terms, the thirteenth-century popes wanted to live like emperors.

ॐ

But had Peter Damian not taught that on account of the brevity of his life the pope's body was different from those of other sovereigns? Did the thirteenth-century popes' aspirations for a possible prolongation of life not contradict the rhetorical and ritual discourse on mortality that we have reconstructed from the Gregorian reform onward? And again, did the pope's life not have to be supported by symbolic purification in terms of innocence and purity? For Peter Damian, the pope's life was the shortest, but (must be) also the most intense.

Contemporaries did not fail to note the contradiction. Indeed, it is the liveliness of interest in corporeal matters that seems to explain the passion surrounding the debate that erupted in the second half of the thirteenth century around the pope's body on both sides of the issue, mortality and symbolic purification. In 1250, Robert Grosseteste cautioned Innocent IV that the pope "must undress himself of his own flesh" to be worthy of being Christ on earth. Franciscans and Dominicans developed an emphatic rhetoric on the nudity of the pope's corpse. Those who commissioned the gisant of Clement IV, the recipient of Roger Bacon's theories on the *prolongatio vitae,* directed the sculptor to portray the marks of old age on the pope's face. Bacon, moreover, was the first to talk about an angelic pope, in a period in which the ancient symbols of imperial power (the red mantle, the white horse) were being reinterpreted in terms of purity and innocence of life. In the ideal image of the angelic pope, corporeity was the transparent image of purity and innocence. Even Bacon's theory of the *prolongatio vitae* aimed at situating the use of the elixir in a spiritual framework: it was a "tool of health" *(instrumentum salutis)* and should therefore prepare the body for glory. Was it not also because of his suspected use of the elixir that the sudden accidental death of John XXI provoked amazement and gave birth to a legend? At his death, the pope was said to have exclaimed several times: "And what will become of my book? Who will finish it?" But according to others, the pope died dictating a "perverse and heretical" work.[45]

PART IV

❦

Boniface VIII

10 The Body in Images

Apostolicity and *Plenitudo Potestatis*

Between January 24, 1295, and May 6, 1296, certainly before December 1296, Boniface VIII ordered the construction of a majestic "mausoleum" in the central nave of Saint Peter's Basilica, against the rear of the facade.[1] This was no mere tomb, but a chapel with a shrine *(sacellum)*. The chapel resembled a baldachin with an octagonal cupola supported by four columns. The sacellum was girded at its base by an iron chancel screen. The pope's sepulcher was mounted on the rear wall of the chapel in a niche draped with a curtain. Two angels drew it apart, thus revealing the pope's gisant, placed on a sarcophagus decorated with his Caetani family arms.

Above the sepulcher, the mosaic attributed to Jacopo Torriti was still admired in the sixteenth century: in the upper center were portrayed the Mother and Child with the apostles Peter and Paul at their sides; in the lower portion, beneath the Madonna, the mystical "empty throne" of the apocalypse was surmounted by a long cross and flanked by two palm trees.[2] The pope was represented with his own name *(Bonifatius VIII)*, like Innocent III in the mosaic of the apse of Saint Peter's Basilica, which may have served as a model.[3] Boniface appears dressed in a mantle, with the "kingdom" *(regnum)* on his head and the keys of Saint Peter dangling from his hand, kneeling before the Madonna and the baby Jesus, "with his hands clasped so that they almost touch those of the one and the other that are extended toward him."[4] Saint Peter stands over him with his hands resting on the pope's shoulders, about to present him to the Mother and Child.

Two decades earlier another pope of Roman origins, Nicholas III (Orsini, 1277–80), had had a chapel built in Saint Peter's in honor of Saint Nicholas, ordering the daily celebration of three masses.[5] Nicholas III had named his chapel after the patron saint of the diaconate of which he had been cardinal (Saint Nicholas in Carcere Tulliano), and who had inspired his choice of name as pope. Boniface VIII, too, who had been made a cardinal by Nicholas III, chose as the patron of his funeral chapel a pope— Boniface IV (608–15)—who bore his same name as pontiff; a pope, moreover, who was buried inside Saint Peter's Basilica.[6] We know for certain that Boniface VIII wanted to have the new chapel built in honor of a Boniface "confessor and pontiff."[7] This means that the pope "passed over another Boniface, a martyr who, unlike the pope, enjoyed a liturgical cult in the Vatican Basilica, celebrated on the anniversary of his martyrdom, May 14."[8]

According to the tradition of the *Liber pontificalis,* the collection of official papal biographies, Boniface IV (608–15) was the pope who had obtained permission from the emperor Focas to transform the Pantheon into a Christian church. The episode did not escape the notice of Siegfried of Ballhausin, the only contemporary of Boniface VIII to describe his funeral monument.[9] Here it is worth noting that relics of Boniface IV had been placed in two Roman churches, in moments of exceptional importance for the relations between papacy and empire. An arm of Boniface IV had been taken from his Vatican sepulcher and placed, together with the relics of other saintly popes, in the altar of Saint Mary in Cosmedin, consecrated by Pope Calixtus II (1119–24) on the eve of the Concordat of Worms.[10] On the same day Alphanus, Calixtus's chamberlain, had donated to the church of Saint Mary in Cosmedin a papal throne that he had had "restored" to make it "an undoubted symbol of the monarchic aspirations of the papacy."[11] Calixtus made a second decision concerning Boniface by having his sepulcher transferred to the interior of Saint Peter's Basilica.[12] In 1246, other relics of the martyr pope Boniface were placed in the chapel of Saint Sylvester beside the Roman church of the Quattro Coronati.[13] The chapel was then frescoed with scenes drawn from the life of Pope Sylvester I and the Donation of Constantine, a "political manifesto" meant to remind Emperor Frederick II of the temporal and political superiority of the papacy.[14]

Boniface VIII therefore preferred to honor a pope (Boniface

IV) rather than a saint (Saint Boniface Martyr); a pope, moreover, whose relics had been translated to the interior of Saint
Peter's Basilica, but also to other Roman churches at moments
of particular significance in the papacy's relations with the empire (1123, 1246). This impression is in no way diminished by
the fact that Boniface VIII had the relics of other saints added
to the corpse of Boniface IV.[15] Boniface IV's remains bore signs
of manifest political symbolism. Why else would Boniface VIII
have had an altar built in that pope's honor in the cathedral of the
Papal City—the new city that was supposed to take the place of
Palestrina, the nearby center of power of his Caetani family rivals, the hated Colonnas?[16]

č

In Boniface's gisant, probably the work of Arnolfo di Cambio,
the face exudes serenity. His "classic calm is the serenity that
overcomes death."[17] Several years before, in 1282, the same Arnolfo had represented the deceased cardinal Guillaume de Braye
with the marks of old age.[18] The stiffened body presents a "hag-
gard old face in an exhausted eternal sleep"; a body and a face
that contrasts with the youthful acolytes who "draw the final
curtain on death."[19] Even more striking is the contrast with another famous papal funeral statue: compared to Boniface's, the
gisant of Clement IV seems almost petrified by old age and
death.[20]

   According to Bernard Gui, "the pope had a monument built
for himself and an image done in stone as though he were
alive."[21] Boniface's face on the gisant is therefore an image that
fuses eternity with the present without, however, negating it;
it is visibly a "portrait" done from "life" of a person still "living."[22] And it was this novelty that sparked scandal and per-
plexity among contemporaries.[23] For the court poet Bonaiuto of
Cosentino, the sepulcher's program was an aspect of Boniface's
glory. The marble sepulcher that he had built for himself enabled
him, the "father of fathers" *(pater patrum)* and "vigilant judge of
the world" to "turn back the times."[24]

   The gisant is "discovered" not by acolytes but by angels, as
though to say that the pope—living—stands between God and
men, almost like an angel himself. Had Peter Damian not said

that the pope is "above the human condition in honor and dignity"? Had Innocent III not declared that the pope stands "between God and man"?[25] The notion was applied to the pope in verses by the English poet Geoffrey of Vinsauf: "You are neither God nor man: almost 'neutral' between them both," or, indeed, "wholly above men."[26] Hostiensis (d. 1271) confirmed that the pope, "greater than man *[maior homine]*, is less than the angels insofar as he is mortal; but he is superior to them in power and authority."[27]

Boniface VIII's portrait from life prefigures immortality (the resurrection), but at the same time "embodies" a physiognomy—that of the still-living pope—in the person of the supreme pontiff. The gisant, placed in a chapel that the pope wished to be "the visible and concrete representation of his pontificate," is the image of a body in "the office of the papacy."[28]

While the priest celebrates mass, his gaze falls on the sarcophagus; the gisant is so visually absorbed into the liturgical celebration that it "imprints itself almost as a negative in the modeling of the sarcophagus and the gisant."[29] Looking at the gisant, the priest "sees" not only the deceased, but the pope as the living image of Christ. Is it not in this sense that the "revolutionary relationship between tomb and altar" should be interpreted in Boniface's funeral chapel?[30]

Translations of the popes' bodies to the interior of Saint Peter's were not a new thing.[31] But this was the first time that the "saintly" body of a pope was put in an altar in a pontifical funeral chapel. A funeral chapel with the body of a saintly pope (Boniface IV) and two images of a pope still living (Boniface VIII): the first, as a gisant, serenely dead but still living, in mystical intimacy with the Eucharist;[32] the second, that of the kneeling pope being presented to the Virgin by the Prince of the Apostles. In both representations, Boniface bore the symbols of his office: the tiara, the mantle, and the keys of Saint Peter.[33]

Boniface VIII's gisant was placed above a sacellum containing the bones of another pope (Boniface IV), and beneath a representation of the same Boniface VIII kneeling before the Madonna and the baby Jesus, presented by Saint Peter.[34] The insertion of a gisant with a portrait done "from life" between the saintly body of a pope and Saint Peter established a verticality that smacks of self-legitimation.[35] The circumstances surrounding the chapel's construction bear this out. The order to build a chapel dates back to the very first months of Boniface's pontificate. Celestine V was in flight, and there was some fear that he might retract his renunciation of the papacy.[36] His pilgrimage to the church of Collemaggio was generating popular support that Boniface sought by every means to check.[37]

Boniface had not been elected to succeed an already deceased pope. The decision to transfer relics from another pope's body to his own funeral chapel thus served as a means of reestablishing a line of apostolic succession—literally, of dead bodies—that had momentarily been interrupted. For Boniface, the absence of his predecessor's dead body, seen from the standpoint of legitimacy, could have presented a problem. For by the last decades of the thirteenth century, the linkage between death, burial, and the electoral process had taken on the character of an indissoluble institutional nexus, so strong as to favor lengthening the papal funeral ceremony, the indispensable premise for the birth of the novena.[38]

Pope-Saint

In 1299, the Franciscan cardinal Giacomo Caetani Tommasini, son of Boniface VIII's only sister, donated to the church of San Clemente a tabernacle, perhaps also the work of Arnolfo di Cambio. In the tympanum, a pope in a tiara and a halo is presented kneeling before the Mother and Child, represented in the center. That pope-saint could be Saint Peter or, more likely, Pope Saint Clement, the patron of the church.[39] But what matters here is the fact that the pope's face seems to bear the features of Boniface VIII. The statue of "Saint Clement" would therefore be a crypto-portrait of Boniface.[40] If, in the funeral chapel at Saint Peter's, Boniface's gisant counted among the series of deceased pontiffs thanks to the relics of a papal saint, at San Clemente he was inserted or, indeed, "reincarnated," in the "body of a pope-saint"; conversely, the sanctity of a papal saint was transferred to a reigning pope, represented in his living likeness and bearing the attributes of power.[41]

Imitatio Imperii

In the middle of the Lateran field *(campus lateranense),* Boniface VIII had the Loggia of the Benedictions constructed with a double order of arcades open to the plaza. Controlling three heavily trafficked streets and facing the hospices run, even if indirectly, by his declared enemies the Colonna, the loggia was painted with frescoes that were long seen as being related to the benediction of the Jubilee, above all because of their inscription.[42]

But recent research has revealed the numerous difficulties in this identification of the loggia with the Jubilee.[43] The fresco seems instead to be an illustration of Boniface VIII's papal coronation as it was described by Stefaneschi.[44] Boniface wears the red imperial mantle and the double-crowned tiara; he is preceded by a small canopy (which alternates with the Caetani arms on the parapet of the second order of the loggia) and the cross held high to the left. On the first order are represented tiaras and keys. The members of the curia are all dressed in white. Standards can be seen among the people. The prefect of Rome wears red and gold *gonelle*. The fourth figure in the fragment, a monk with a beard (seen in profile between two columns of the pulpit) seems to be Celestine V, who is departing, as in Stefaneschi's verses.[45] If these hypotheses are correct, the Lateran fresco is the oldest public iconographic illustration of a papal coronation, and it is the first time that the canopy, a symbol of imperial power, was represented in relationship to a living pope.[46]

It should quickly be added that the presentation of Boniface at the "baldachin" is the last of three scenes. Although the others—the baptism of Constantine and the foundation of the Lateran Basilica—have been lost, they were part of an iconographic tradition that we can still see in the portico of Saint John Lateran and in the frescoes of the chapel of Saint Sylvester by the church of the Quattro Coronati.[47] The manner in which Boniface blesses the crowd harks back to a Constantinian iconographic matrix. The same is true of the disposition of the serial rows of figures in the upper register, featuring a sharp distinction between the pope and his court on one side, and the people on the other. The horizontal cover of the "baldachin" from which the pope faces is a feature that can be compared to one of the reliefs of the obelisk of Theodosius in Constantinople, which Boniface and his entourage could have known about either directly, or indirectly through studies of "antiquity."[48]

In the fresco of the Lateran loggia, Boniface VIII thus appears as the restorer of the Lateran—that is, as a second Constantine. The person of the pope, represented with his physical features, incarnates the temporal superiority of the papacy to the empire.

Una et Sancta

The bust of Boniface VIII found today in the Vatican Grottos was also produced, in all likelihood, by Arnolfo di Cambio, perhaps for the Jubilee.[49] A contemporary—Siegfried of Ballhausin—saw it in 1304 next to Boniface's sepulcher.[50] More than the moment and location of its original site, it is important to remember that the Vatican bust is the first documented and identifiable sculptural portrait of a living pope that was placed in a church;[51] it is the first statue of a pope blessing with his right hand and holding the keys in his left;[52] it is the first statue of a pope wearing a three-circled tiara; it is the first statue of a living pope placed next to the sepulcher of a pope; and, finally, it is a statue that bears remarkable similarities on an artistic and monumental level to the bronze statue of Saint Peter in the Vatican Basilica, to which it is "almost identical from the standpoint of workmanship."[53]

There is yet another feature that distinguishes it: never before had a tiara been depicted of such height, rising a full cubit.[54] Its circular form represents the shape of the globe. The sphere is a perfect body, symbolic of the macrocosm. A cubit was the measure used on Noah's ark.[55] In Boniface's famous bull *Unam Sanctam* ("One Holy"), Noah's ark was the prefiguration of the church.[56] Just as Noah guided the ark/church, so the pope is the ruler of the church, *one* and *holy*. Boniface used this argument in a letter of October 9, 1299, in which he recalled the pardon granted to the Colonna family.[57] Boniface saw the "One holy church" *(Una sancta Ecclesia)* embodied in the papacy, "indeed, in his own person."[58] Its gestures, objects, and symbolism (the benediction, keys, tiara) therefore make the Vatican bust an extraordinary monument in the "self-production of memory" and of "living images" that is unprecedented in the history of the medieval papacy's self-representation.[59]

Jurisdiction and Unity

At the beginning of October 1290, the cardinal legates Benedetto Caetani and Gerardo Bianchi arrived at Rheims to resolve a conflict that had dragged on for years between the archbishop and the canons: episcopal officials were accused of having sequestered houses and lands that belonged to the canons, destroying among other things the wall of one of the chapter's gardens. The canons had reacted by suspending the use of the organ in the cathedral and all participation in liturgical celebrations. October 1 was the feast of Saint Remigius, the patron of the cathedral, and it is easy to imagine that such a suspension of the divine offices, imposed on the lesser cathedral clergy as well as the laity, must have seemed especially severe.[60] The cardinals nevertheless managed to get the liturgical "boycott" suspended for their solemn entry into the city, for the period of their stay in Rheims, and until the case was settled. Exactly two months later, as they had promised, the legates promulgated their sentence (in the Abbey of Saint-Cloud at the gates of Paris).[61] At the end of the document, an appendix required that both parties (the archbishop and canons of Rheims) should have a silver statue built, representing a cardinal bishop (Gerardo Bianchi was the bishop of Santa Sabina) and a cardinal deacon (Benedetto Caetani was cardinal deacon of Saint Nicholas in Carcere Tulliano). The various dignitaries would be identified by their different liturgical vestments. The chasuble and pontifical insignia would distinguish the cardinal bishop; the dalmatic, the cardinal deacon. Both would wear miters, according to the tradition, already established by the thirteenth century, which allowed all the cardinals, regardless of distinctions of rank, to wear the miter. But to prevent any doubts about the identity of the cardinals, their names would be inscribed on the statuettes with their titles: *Gerardus episcopus Sabinensis, Benedictus Sancti Nicolai in Carcere Tulliano diaconus cardinalis.* These two statues, worth at least 500 Turinese lire, were to be set on the high altar during mass in all the solemn feasts of the liturgical year. Moreover, the archbishop and canons were forbidden to sell or lend them out. The sources do not enable us to say whether the statues were actually produced.

A dozen years later Benedetto Caetani, now Boniface VIII, found himself involved in a similar conflict as pope. This time it concerned the canons and bishop of Amiens. As at Rheims, the Amiens canons reacted to the bishop's efforts to recover his ancient rights with the traditional "cessation of the divine offices" *(cessatio a divinis)*. The bishop reacted by having the church bells rung, celebrating a solemn pontifical mass "out loud" *(alta voce)*, then placing the canons under an interdict.[62] On December 4, 1301, Boniface intervened in the conflict, summoning both parties to come to Rome within two months.[63] On this occasion again, as he had done in 1290 when he was still a cardinal, Boniface ordered the construction of two statuettes. The analogy with the Rheims case is complete, so much so that the pope repeated almost verbatim the text of the 1290 sentence.

Once again, both parties were obliged to have a statuette constructed, not only of silver, but of silver gilded with gold. The bishop's statue was to represent the pope; that of the canons, the Virgin Mary. Each statue would have had to be worth 1,000 Parisian lire—that is, double those of Rheims. As at Rheims, they were to be placed on the high altar during great liturgical solemnities. The pope even required that the bishop and canons deposit, as a guarantee, 2,000 lire with the abbey of Saint-Corneille in Compiègne.[64] Boniface's instructions were carried out: a 1347 inventory of Amiens cathedral indeed lists "two large silver statues gilded with gold, which are placed on the altar during the high feasts." By the mid–fourteenth century, however, the memory of Boniface's orders had faded, and the pope of the "papal statuette" was identified with Gregory the Great, the emblematic pope of the Middle Ages.

Twice then, Benedetto Caetani, as a cardinal and as the Roman pontiff, ordered that statuettes representing himself should be placed on altars on solemn liturgical occasions. The differences are not important and point simply to the fact that the Rheims statuettes were to depict cardinal legates, those of Amiens a pope. It made sense that the former should be made of silver, the latter gilded with gold. The minimum value doubled, from 500 lire for the cardinals to 1,000 lire for that of the pope.

It is of fundamental significance that these orders were issued at the conclusions of conflicts between bishops and cathedral canons. The statuettes symbolized—by means of the images of the two dignitaries—the jurisdictional power of the pope, which established and maintained the unity of the church.[65] This was a power that manifested itself to express the universality underlying various local situations. Herein lies the originality of the statuettes of Rheims and Amiens: they expressed in the concreteness of an image the ecclesiological concept whereby the pope "can be called the church" (Giles of Rome).[66] On this point there is no difference between the statuettes of the cardinals and that of the pope. The cardinals were intimately bound up institutionally with the pope; they were "part of his body."[67] Indeed, we may say that the statuettes ordered by the cardinals constitute an exceptional "visual" confirmation of the ecclesiological and institutional prestige to which the College of Cardinals could aspire at the end of the thirteenth century.[68]

But having the statuettes placed on the altars—was this not idolatry? King Philip the Fair's lawyers, assigned to draw up a list of accusations to justify the French process against Boniface's memory, did not let the opportunity slip: "In order to erect a most damned perpetual memorial to himself, he had his silver images [the statues] put up in churches, thus inducing men to idolatry."[69]

Was Boniface VIII an idolatrous pope? In the strict sense, no. The Rheims and Amiens statuettes were intended ultimately to *represent* the jurisdictional power of the Roman church, and to symbolize its unity. But it is also true that in these statuettes the individual (whether cardinal or pope) was to a certain extent conflated with his office. The statuettes produced an undeniable identification between personality and office.[70] By having the statues placed on the altars, Boniface did not make himself guilty of idolatry per se, because his gesture was in concert with ecclesiological views, audacious but orthodox, that were so prominent in the last decades of the thirteenth century. But by seeking to *embody* the Roman church and his jurisdictional power in such an eccentric and inflammatory way, Boniface indeed inserted his image and memory into a framework of immortality.

11 Physiognomy and Immortality

Cura Corporis

During Boniface VIII's pontificate, the sources on the subjects of medicine and the *cura corporis* ("care of the body") expand and bring together all the aspects of corporeity that we have seen unfolding in the preceding chapters. The alternation between winter and summer papal residences that had begun to drop off under preceding pontificates was renewed by Boniface and became regular, more than it had ever been before in the thirteenth century.[1] Not even the crusade against the Colonna family (August 1298) prevented the pope from passing the summer at his beloved Anagni. No fewer than seven doctors succeeded one another in Boniface's *cura corporis* over the course of his nevertheless brief pontificate.[2] This was the highest figure of the entire thirteenth century. The relations between the pope and his "court physicians" ran from exasperation to unbounded praise. Anselm of Bergamo, who had perhaps taught at Bologna before being called by Boniface to the curia,[3] unexpectedly abandoned him for reasons the sources do not reveal. The pope flew into a rage, had him pursued, and revoked the feudal holdings he had granted him (in the castellany and territory of Medicina).[4]

Boniface's new doctor, Arnald of Villanova, managed to cure his illustrious patient of pains his kidney stones had been causing him for decades.[5] This was the disease that would overtake the pope after the French assault at Agnani and that, with immense pains, would carry him to his death.[6] During the summer of 1301, Boniface enclosed Arnald in the castle of La Scurcola in Lazio, ordering him to write his treatise on "The

Regimen of Health" *(De regimine sanitatis)*. The work so pleased the pope that in the presence of several cardinals he exclaimed: "This man is the greatest scientist in the world . . . and we didn't even know it!"[7] At more or less the same time (July 1301), while the sun was in the sign of Leo, Arnald gave the pope a gold seal to protect him against the disease of the stone. The cardinals were amazed that a doctor suggested such remedies, and that the pope accepted, indeed, bragged about them. Boniface was reputed to have declared that Arnald "made me gold seals and a *bracale* [a sort of waistband] that I wear, and they free me of the pains of the stone and many others."[8] The pope's belief in talismanic powers should perhaps be ascribed to the growing influence of astronomical science in thirteenth-century European culture. After all, it may have been Boniface VIII who saved Peter of Abano from the persecution of the Dominicans of Saint-Jacques in Paris.[9] The Paris sojourn of this learned doctor and astrologer in fact took place during his pontificate.[10]

Peter's treatise on poisons, composed for an unnamed pope, may actually have been written for Boniface.[11] In it, the author speaks of a translation requested by the Agnani pope.[12] In these same years, the convert from Judaism, John of Capua, translated an important treatise against poisons (the *Liber antidotarius Albumeronis*) for the archbishop of Braga, Martin of Oliveira, who was then living at the curia.[13] There was a real fear of poison at Boniface's court: never before do the sources refer to the presence in the papal treasury of unicorns or serpents' tongues used to "taste" *(assazum)* food and drink. Such "magic knives" were credited with the power of chasing away possible poisons.[14]

John of Capua was asked by Boniface's doctor, Guglielmo of Brescia, to translate Maimonides's *Dietetics (Dietetica)*.[15] He concluded his dedication with an appeal to the pope to have his work deposited "in the papal archive with the other books on medicine," a striking indication of the prestige that Boniface's library enjoyed in the field of medicine. For no other thirteenth-century pope was the translation of medical texts pursued so feverishly as it was under Boniface VIII. In 1295 another papal doctor *(medicus papae)*, Accursino of Pistoia, translated Galen's *On the Properties of Foods (De virtutibus cibariorum)* from Arabic into Latin in Rome.[16]

Elixir

Such manifest interest in the *cura corporis* would itself be enough to give historical weight to the charge Arnald of Villanova leveled against Boniface VIII, that he worried less about "the zeal for Christ and health of souls, than about bodies." [17] Boniface's pontificate was remarkable in another respect as well: no other papal court in the Middle Ages furnishes such abundant evidence of the circulation of ideas on the *prolongatio vitae* ("prolongation of life").

In *De vita philosophorum (On the Life of Philosophers)*, a work generally attributed to Arnald of Villanova, the author, after singing the praises of potable gold as a medicine useful for healing leprosy and bladder stones, and for restoring and rejuvenating the body and preserving memory, then cites two figures as witnesses. The first, a certain "Lord *[dominus]* Hugo," reputedly swore that potable gold "is the greatest secret among the natural medicines" *(est maxime secretum in medicinibus naturalibus)*. The second, the "Lord Cardinal of Toledo" *(dominus cardinalis de Toleto)*, "is said to have quaffed down potable gold at meals along with his fellow cardinals throughout his entire cardinalate. They considered the gold to be the best and greatest secret known to them and in their possession." [18] The "Cardinal of Toledo" may have been the Cistercian John of Toledo, who enjoyed wide renown as an astronomer and alchemist. [19] Along with another English cardinal, Hugh of Evesham, he appears in medical-alchemistic treatises as a sort of authority *(auctoritas)* in the field of alchemy, above all in its relations with medicine. [20]

Even the treatise *On Wines (De vinis)* offers a recipe for potable gold, declaring:

> Many modern nobles, and above all the prelates, have pieces of gold boiled with their food; others imbibe gold with food or with other confections; others consume it in the form of limited gold, as in a confection called *diacameron*. . . . Some are in the habit of keeping a bit of gold *[frustrum auri]* in their mouths . . . others dissolve it into drinkable water, of which a moderate amount every year is enough to preserve health and prolong life. . . . Those who keep it in their mouths do so not without

reason; it has in fact been demonstrated that keeping silver in the mouth extinguishes thirst.[21]

The gold could be consumed by boiling it or by stripping it off coins. The latter method was used by Clement V (1305–14): after his death, caskets were found in the papal treasury containing florins from which had been peeled the gold that the pope, on the advice of his doctors, routinely took with his meals.[22]

We do not know whether *De vita philosophorum* was written by Arnald of Villanova or not.[23] But it is certain that the esteem the Catalan doctor enjoyed with Boniface VIII must also have depended on the fame that he had acquired in the field of the *prolongatio vitae*. Arnald devoted an important treatise to old age (*On Extreme Moisture [De humido radicali]*) and transcribed almost verbatim the *De retardatione accidentium senectutis* in his *On Preserving Youth and Delaying Old Age (De conservanda iuventute et retardanda senectute).*[24] Moreover, Arnald began his *Against the Stone* (*Contra calculum*, 1301–2), addressed to Boniface VIII, with an impassioned defense of "extreme moisture" *(humidum radicale)* as the indispensable precondition for the *prolongatio vitae.*[25] Such detailed attention to these problems was not required by the treatise's specific purpose. Should we therefore be surprised if, among the criticisms that the disillusioned doctor later aimed at Boniface VIII, "wanting to live long" holds first place?[26]

The accusation should be compared with two other bits of evidence that cannot be treated in isolation. According to the accusations drawn up by the French in their process against Boniface, the pope was reported to have preferred to the greeting "God give you eternal life" that of "God give you a good and long life."[27] Moreover, in one of the verses of Jacopone of Todi's famous invective against Boniface, the spiritual Franciscan framed the hated pope in the following manner:

> You thought for a greeting life to prolong
> Year, day, nor hour a man cannot hope for
> We see that for sin life is exterminated
> With death growing near then man thinks to beware.[28]

At first sight, these seem to be notions drawn from the tradition of the *memento mori*. But Jacopone's reproach that Boniface "thought for a greeting life to prolong" deserves to be taken literally. The word *greeting (per augurio)* here means "with magical techniques," which cannot but refer to making the elixir discussed above, and cannot but call to mind the abundant evidence concerning the relations between Boniface VIII and alchemists.[29] After all, Arnald of Villanova himself was supposed to have discussed alchemical problems with the pope in a series of queries *(quaestiones)*.[30] This is confirmed, moreover, by the testimony of Johannes Andreae. After declaring Arnald of Villanova "the greatest doctor and theologian in the Roman curia," the great civil lawyer, who well knew the environment of the papal court, added that "Master Arnald of Villanova had also been a great alchemist, who was willing to subject the little rods of gold *[virgulae auri]* he made to every form of verification."[31]

ℰ̃

The role played by the thirteenth-century papal court in the field of the *prolongatio vitae,* so new for the European elites, was thus essential. Figures like Innocent III's former doctor, Giovanni Castellomata; the *dominus castri Goet* (or *Gret*), author of the *De retardatione accidentium senectutis;* the translator of the complete version of the *Secretum secretorum,* Philip of Tripoli, nephew of Honorius III's vice chancellor; as well as, obviously, the Franciscan Roger Bacon all contributed decisively to rewriting the Western myth of the *prolongatio vitae.* In the space of a few decades (c. 1230–70) Europe's elites, above all Emperor Frederick II and Popes Innocent IV and Clement IV, put new weapons into the field of combat against old age.

The proposals of the *dominus castri Goet* and of Roger Bacon were different but complementary. The first tried to show that the *prolongatio vitae* was a science available here and now. The experimental sciences promoted by Bacon were supposed to secure the body's harmony and longevity, and at the same time to serve man's entire eternal destiny. In both visions, the elixir emerged as a "tool of health" *(instrumentum salutis),* and the body became the vehicle of its own uninterrupted history stretching into the hereafter. The elixir produced thanks to the experimental sciences inserted "man's whole destiny into an unbroken continuity between nature and the supernatural."[32] For Bacon, *aequalitas* ("equality") meant the psychosomatic perfection of men. The perfect body obtained through alchemy, besides being perfectly tempered itself, possessed the capacity to bring about a similar perfection and harmony in all the bodies with which it was brought into contact. *Aequalitas* seems in fact to have been the same as immortality. Bacon's view of longevity amounted to the structural equivalent of that material immortality that was the aim of the search for an elixir in Chinese and Indian alchemy.[33]

A few decades after Bacon had sent his works to Pope Clement IV (1265–68), a Genoese doctor, Galvano of Levanto—a married layman closely tied to the noble Ligurian family of the Fieschi, who in the thirteenth century produced four cardinals and two popes (Innocent IV and Adrian V)—wrote one of the oldest treatises on the *ars moriendi* ("art of dying").[34] In one passage, he set up a curious contrast between Andromache and Christ. Christ had risen from the dead to assure the immortality of the human race. Andromache, on the other hand, had consumed substances (aromatic herbs, balsam, opium, snake's flesh) that would enable him to "live on after death in the memory of man."[35] For Galvano, then, the elixir—composed of ingredients that recall the *occulta* of the *De retardatione accidentium senectutis*—was a tool of immortality. The "unbroken continuity" that for Bacon was above all spiritual in nature here reveals itself laicized. The elixir was no longer (only) a "tool of health" *(instrumentum salutis),* but at the service of *memory,* that is, of the "myth of glory."[36]

Such markedly protohumanistic features might make Galvano's *ars moriendi* appear to be a work of the mid–fourteenth century.[37] In fact, Galvano actually wrote it at the end of the thirteenth, for members of a papal court who had already had the opportunity to absorb the *De retardatione accidentium senectutis* and Bacon's ideas on the *prolongatio vitae*. Moreover, the only manuscript of Galvano's *ars moriendi* still in existence comes from Boniface VIII's library.[38] Though this is not in itself proof that Boniface actually read it, the point is by no means negligible.

The concern for bodily integrity is at the center of the famous decretal that Boniface VIII promulgated for the first time on September 27, 1297.[39] With *Detestande feritatis* ("Of Loathsome Savageness"), Boniface aimed solemnly to forbid the dismembering of corpses for the sake of transporting them, a practice that he declared to be an abomination in the eyes of God, contrary to human sensibility, and against common piety. Bodies should be buried at the place of death or near it, "in time" *(ad tempus),* that is, to allow for natural decomposition. In *Detestande feritatis,* moreover, the body rises to the level of memory before men, and on that account must be "cared for like a temple, and must suffer no violence after death." [40] This is suggested, moreover, by the only contemporary comment on Boniface's bull. The alert jurist and cardinal Jean of Lemoine explained that for Boniface "the human body, that is, its face, is figured in the celestial likeness, and can neither be marked nor disfigured." [41] Boniface's interest in the body therefore extended to a concern for the survival of the body's own physiognomic individuality— that is, for a body that would continue to have its own history in the hereafter. The *physiognomy* that Boniface wanted to defend was the "unbroken continuity" reminiscent of Bacon. As in Bacon and in Galvano of Levanto, bodily integrity and immortality were inseparable. In the entire history of the medieval papacy, this is the first time that the sources allow us to witness an anthropological effort directed so strongly at the survival of the body's own integrity and individuality.

Such a marked concentration of images in themselves, and of corporal concerns, must be seen in relationship to the debate that arose in the thirteenth century around the pope's body. It is important, because in the last decades of the century, as we have seen, the initiatives concerning the pope in his physical dimension, of mortality and symbolic purification, show themselves to have been numerous and profound, perhaps like never before.

The face of Boniface VIII's gisant breathes the calm serenity of immortality; the image of Clement IV, instead, bears the traits of old age and physical decline. According to the Dominican Martin of Troppau, it was no longer the moisture of his sepulcher but the rumbling of Pope Sylvester II's bones that warned the living pope of the imminence of his death. In these same years, the deceased pope's nudity became a recurring theme in a series of Franciscan and Dominican case studies *(exempla).* At death, the pope "returns to being a man." His life as pope is brief, and his power transitory. Clement IV's epitaph, which Boniface VIII could have read at Viterbo, records that the dying pope, "successor and heir of Saint Peter," was now only ashes.

But had Boniface not pursued a different strategy? The
Bonifacian images bespeak the unity of the church, the pope's
holiness, and the Roman papacy's jurisdictional power and superiority to the empire. This was no longer the typology of
a pope, but of an individual physiognomy that *incarnates* the
pontifical office. Here lies the real historical novelty of the Bonifacian statuary. But there is also a common thread running
between Jean of Lemoine's commentary on *Detestande feritatis,*
Bacon's theories on the *prolongatio vitae,* Galvano of Levanto's
observations on Andromache, and all of Boniface's statuary:
physiognomic integrity. The survival of memory itself was incorporated into a framework of "unbroken continuity" between
life and death. For Boniface, bodily practices and their rendering
in images therefore sustained a common ideal of immortality,
one that could not but appear to contradict the rhetorical and
ritual tradition of humility whose evolution we have followed
from the Gregorian reform onward. For did Boniface's effort to
orchestrate the survival of his *physiognomic memory* not contradict
the idea that in dying "the pope returns to being a man"? And
did Boniface VIII not "wish to construct a glorious memory for
himself," defying the belief that "even the pope dies" *(ipse papa
moritur)*?

The aim of the rhetoric and ritual of mortality born in the
dawn of the Gregorian reform was simple and straightforward:
to dissociate the physical person of the pope, which is mortal,
from the papal office, which is eternal. But did Boniface's systematic production of images of himself, imposed on statues
meant to express the church's universality in its various jurisdictional, political, and ecclesiological dimensions, not aim instead
at fusing the individual and the office? This identification of
the physical person with the office—had Benedetto Caetani not
been seeking it already as a cardinal, and even more so during his
pontificate?

In the Spiritual Franciscan Peter John Olivi's letter, which
we have already encountered in discussing infallibility, he lashes
out against those who think "that the papacy is something indel-
ible and inseparable from the substance of the humanity of him
who ascends to the papacy; so that just as in the consecrated
host which, while retaining its 'accidental' features, nevertheless
remains Christ, so also, as long as the pope's humanity remains,

[some believe that] Christ and Christ's papacy remain in him sacramentally." [42] Olivi then moves to a direct attack: "If, therefore, the pope or the bishop are the image of Christ in some respects [quoad aliquid], are they the image of Christ in all respects [quoad omnia]?" Finally, the subtle Franciscan theologian inquires: if the pope (as an institutional figure) "is the image of Christ eternal and immutable . . . must the pope also [as a person] be eternal and immutable?" If this were true, it would mean that "after the pope's death another pope cannot be substituted, since it is clear that after Christ's death another Christ cannot be substituted." [43] Never before had the danger of a potential fusion between the pontifical person and the institution been put in such explicit terms. Does Olivi's irony not itself suggest that the problem had by then become real? His letter dates from the very first months of Boniface's pontificate (1295). Was this simply a coincidence? After all, the growing identification of the figure of the supreme pontiff with the church (that is, with Christ) reached a climax around the end of the thirteenth century. But the more the person of the supreme pontiff approached Christ, and was identified with the church, did the fusion between individual and office not risk becoming a danger for the institution of the papacy?

At its core, is this not also what the legend of Pope Joan is talking about? [44] The figure of a mother, Pope Joan died giving birth to a son. The legend incarnated an illicit desire: the perpetuation of a pope's body. In life, the pope represented the church—Mother Church *(Ecclesia Mater)*—but he "cannot be perpetuated in the church, because even he dies, just like other men." [45] The pope did not have two bodies like a king. [46] In dying, the pope "returns to being a man"; he *undresses* himself, that is, of the person of the supreme pontiff. This is why, when dead, the pope is nude. [47] The power of the pope, instead, was "perpetual, because it remains still in the College of Cardinals, that is, in the church, which belongs to Christ, its incorruptible and permanent head." [48] Around 1300, the pope was the church; but only in life, not after his death.

It should be observed that the legend of Pope Joan spread widely after 1250, thanks to Dominican writers who showed yet again their ongoing interest in the pope's body. In the following decades, precisely while Benedetto Caetani was serving as a papal notary and cardinal, several extraordinary episodes of popular devotion took place at the deaths of a series of popes (1268–85), which were echoed by an equally heated debate on the purity and innocence of life of the Roman pontiff. These were particularly intense years. But well before, Peter Damian had warned that the pope was distinguished from all other sovereigns both for the brevity of his life and for its exemplarity. Sitting and reclining on the porphyry chairs at the Lateran, the pope was *born* and *died* among the apostles; and the symbolic objects of his office (purse and seals) hung from a cincture, the symbol of chastity. It was the holiness of his life that made the pope a participant among the *saintly bodies* of the apostles even beyond death, not an illicit desire for immortality, much less a desire to identify himself with the papal institution. Because, in dying, the pope "returns to being a man." This was confirmed by a line of reflection—rhetorical and ritual—on the physical mortality of the (body of) the pope that, by the time of Boniface VIII, had already been alive for two and a half centuries.

The history of the pope's body begins from the moment the sources speak to us of the relationship, ever complex and at times potentially conflictual, between the pope's physical nature and the papal institution.[1] As we have seen, this history comes into view during the pontificate of Leo IX (1049–54) and, more generally, from the central decades of the eleventh century onward. Peter Damian's treatise, *De brevitate* (1064), the first medieval text devoted exclusively to the figure of the pope seen in this dual perspective—physical and institutional—was in fact our point of departure.

Another point has likewise emerged rather clearly: from the time that the problem of the pope's body became an object of written commentary, the sources do nothing but expand. Indeed, the problem itself never ceased to inspire commentaries and proposals, polemics and critiques, at the center of the Roman church and throughout the rest of Christendom. Masters of papal ceremonies, writers and thinkers, theologians and moralists, members of the mendicants and lay saints such as Catherine of Sweden and Catherine of Siena, as well as doctors and alchemists, devoted sustained attention to this sovereign body on three points of paramount importance: the relationship between the pope's physical mortality and the perpetuity of the church; the need for a symbolic purification of the pope's body; and an aspiration (individual and collective) for the pope's perfect health (and long life).

This concern is intimately bound up with the nature of papal power in the Middle Ages and in modern times; it is also a reflection of one of the principal innovations by the advocates of the Gregorian reform: the pope belongs to the church, in life as in death, not only in the "person of the pope" *(persona papae)*, but also as a private individual. It was this realization that led to the rich rhetorical and ritual discourse that we have attempted to reconstruct. The history of the pope's body therefore provides a unique vantage point for understanding the institutional, ecclesiological, and political evolution of the papacy down to our own time for a perfectly simple reason: once the pope as an institutional figure became, between the eleventh and thirteenth centuries, the *incarnation* of the universal church as well, the physical aspect of his private person had to be subjected to ever more rigorous ritual and symbolic analysis and control.

The sources that reveal the various elements of this apparatus have to be sifted with care from among a variety of different sorts of documents. Valuable information can lie hidden inside ceremonial books, letter collections, and the treatises of ecclesiastical writers such as Peter Damian and Bernard of Clairvaux. Theological and canonistic literature, treatises on medicine or surgery, or again literary and poetic works (celebrating this or that pope, but also engaging with Rome itself) can all have a bearing on the history of the pope's body. The subject is so vast that everything concerning the papacy, either directly or indirectly, ought in principle to be consulted and read attentively.

But even a patient and detailed collection of texts could never be exhaustive. This is why it has seemed advisable in this epilogue to indicate a few texts that might undoubtedly have been included in one or another of the chapters of the original Italian edition, had I known of them beforehand.

They come for the most part, not coincidentally, from the thirteenth century. In various chapters we have seen the richness of the debate then unfolding around the pope's body in each of the aspects we have considered. That this was due to the general cultural environment, to a scholastic century that loved to classify and formulate every problem systematically, can scarcely be denied. That such a phenomenon should be seen in close relationship to the extraordinary political and ecclesiological rise of the papacy between 1200 and 1300 goes without saying. After all, Boniface VIII, the last pope of the thirteenth century, seems to have lived in a climactic manner the tensions between physical mortality and the perpetuity of the institution, between the brevity of life and immortality.

If the thirteenth century is important, it is because the con-
tradictions that informed the history of the pope's body then appeared with such surprising clarity. To recapitulate: in the second
half of the eleventh century, for the first time in the Middle Ages,
the pope's death became the focus of attention of specific rituals
that were features of a broader course of reflection on the relationship between the pope's physical nature and the institutional
continuity of the church. The pope's death was an important
benchmark for the reforming papacy, manifesting a clear awareness of the distinction between the pope's physical nature and the
perpetuity of the church. This awareness found an entirely natural expression in the rhetoric and ritual of mortality, the origins
of which date precisely to the mid–eleventh century. In 1064,
Peter Damian addressed a treatise to Pope Alexander II on the
brevity of the pope's lives that is remarkable in itself. Near the
end of the treatise, Damian informs the pope of the rituals of
humility used in imperial coronation ceremonies at Byzantium
(the presentation, in one hand, of a vase containing the bones
and ashes of the dead; and, in the other, a braid of fine-combed
flax, its threads hanging gently behind). Around 1140, in the first
Roman ceremonial book written after the Gregorian reform, the
rite of burning the flax is present in the Roman ritual, alongside
two other rites (the ashes and the presentation of the papyrus to
the pope), all aimed at reminding the pope of his physical mortality. No other sovereign of the time had the right to such an
apparatus. Nevertheless, it was not until the thirteenth century
that the discourse on the pope's mortality became suddenly more
incisive, notably with the appearance of a new theme, the nudity
of the pope's corpse, which we have been able to reconstruct
through the texts of Jacques de Vitry, Thomas of Eccleston, and
Salimbene of Parma.[2]

But Thomas and Salimbene were not the originators of
the theme. We now know that the pope's nudity was a central
theme in a sermon that Cardinal Eudes of Châteauroux delivered on the day of the first anniversary of the death of Innocent
IV (1243–54), in the first year of Alexander IV's pontificate
(1254–61).[3]

In speaking of the pope, Eudes turned to Aaron, a figure
emblematic of the Great Priest, and a prefiguration of Christ.

After a lengthy treatment of the mourning with which Aaron was honored after his death, the cardinal asked: "what happened to Aaron at his death?" His answer focused on the theme of nudity. Aaron had, in fact, been "stripped *[nudatus]* . . . of his vestments. . . . Thus it came about, literally, that the popes were denuded *[Sic ad litteram nudantur summi pontifices]*." Eudes went on to explain why: "The popes are stripped of their power. They are striped of all the temporal glory that they had *(Nudantur potestate sua. Nudantur omni gloria sua temporali quam habuerunt)*." At death, the pope loses his power *(potestas)*. Just as "Eleazar, Aaron's son, put on the vestments [of his father], so the successor of the sovereign pontiff puts on his [predecessor's] vestments. Nor did Eleazar ever doubt that he too would be stripped *[nudatus]* of the vestments he had put on." The pope was "nude" not physically, but because (immediately upon death) he no longer metaphorically wore the vestments that made visible the office he had held throughout his pontificate. As we have seen, for Jacques de Vitry, Innocent III's corpse was "almost naked"—not because it was nude physically, but because he had been stripped of the precious vestments *(vestimenta preciosa)* in which he had been dressed for solemn public display in the cathedral of Perugia.[4]

Nudity applied also to the cardinals, added Eudes, himself a member of the college: "We will be stripped *[nudabimur]* before we know it of the cardinalate and of all the other dignities with which our predecessors were dressed, and who were themselves stripped." The warning was above all of a moral order: "Let us fear, therefore, to be found also without the clothing of virtue, the garments of good deeds, and the garments of our chaste vows, for we will be stripped of our dignities, honors and riches, and of power *[potestas]*; for those who are found nude of these garments will not be admitted to the marriage of eternal joy."[5]

Eudes took up the theme of nudity again, more briefly, in another sermon delivered on the anniversary for popes and cardinals instituted by Pope Alexander IV.[6] On the other hand, in a sermon delivered during the vacancy following the death of either Alexander IV (1261) or Urban IV (1264), he returned to the theme of the brevity of the popes' lives and of "Peter's years," using—though not always citing—Peter Damian's *De brevitate*. The issues are framed identically: the term of life *(terminus vitae)* is indicated only for the pope, not for any other holder of power

(nulli enim existenti in potestate). Repeating one of Damian's assertions, he added that many "kings, bishops and princes have, in
contrast, ruled for forty and even fifty or more years. But no
pope can be found who has reigned longer than twenty-five years
besides the Blessed Peter. And yet [was Eudes here inspired by
Innocent III's example?] certain young men, aged less than thirty
years, have become popes. More than anyone else holding power,
the popes should have death ever before their eyes." [7]

Even before coming to the theme of nudity, Eudes discussed
the "transfiguration" of Aaron at Mount Sinai. The theme of
light enabled him to insert the pope, understood here in his institutional dimension, into a Christly perspective of great ecclesiological significance: "Because the image of God should shine
forth in the pope more than in any other man, his clothes must
be white as snow. His face should shine like the sun. Indeed, men
are recognized by their faces. It is by their faces that we recognize
their wills. . . . This is why, literally *[ad litteram]*, the pope wears
white clothing under his vestments. Only at his death are the
pope's clothes black." [8] This text represents a certain innovation,
since it precedes by a generation William Durant's symbolic interpretation, destined to become classic, of the pope's white vestments. [9] That the debate on the symbolic value of the pope's
white vestments was so important when Eudes delivered his sermons explains rather well, moreover, the fact that Gregory X's
ceremonial, which dates from the years 1273–74, was the first to
emphasize the whiteness of the pope's vestments at his election.

The contradiction between nudity and whiteness was, to be
sure, only apparent. They were, in fact, complementary. Nudity
referred to an essential institutional fact: "even the pope must
die," while only the church (that is, Christ) is eternal. Whiteness
was a metaphor (and a vestmental fact) that expressed the idea
that the pope must be worthy of being the image of Christ on
earth, and of incarnating the church. [10]

The two notions were complementary for another reason as
well. As Peter Damian had already observed, the pope's death
constituted a "moment of terror" for the whole of Christendom,
because it was a death that required a renewal that was, above all
in the High Middle Ages, potentially threatening for the papal
institution. At its core, the whole institutional and ritual history
tied to the pope's death, the different stages of which we have

been able to follow from the eleventh to the fifteenth centuries, had as its aim the elimination of dangers originating in the *void* caused by the pope's death. Thus was created an institutional body, the College of Cardinals, that, after constituting part of the reigning pope's body, was called to *be* the church during the vacancy.[11]

A passage from Roger Bacon, in a work he wrote for Pope Clement IV (1265–68), represents the logical extension of these ideas. After speaking of the "approaching" conversion of the Tartars and Saracens, and of the possible return of Byzantium to the bosom of the Catholic Church, Bacon expresses his hope to Clement "that God may preserve your life, so that these things may come about." He permits himself even to advise the pope "not to give yourself over too much to abstinence, nor to excessive vigils," since the exertions of the body *(exercitatio corporis)* accomplish little, whereas faith can do all things. The pope's life was therefore important for the well-being of Christendom. Put so simply, this was a new idea that does not seem to appear in any earlier text. Notably, Bacon argued within the theme of mortality. As a private individual, the pope should think of death. But as an institutional figure *(persona publica),* he "must lead and save others." This amounts to saying that the pope was entitled to a long life, not as a private person *(privata, singularis),* but as an institutional figure *(publica).*[12]

Thus, in the central decades of the thirteenth century, the idea emerged forcefully that the pope's sanctity and a long life were the essential premises of the church's welfare. This is how, in part, we should interpret the extraordinary flowering of sources that speak to us of medicine and doctors at the thirteenth-century papal court, the first in the entire history of the papacy for which it is possible, as we have seen, to draw up a list of the popes' and cardinals' personal physicians.[13] To be sure, we encounter here a new boundary that separated and would eventually oppose institutional discourse (the pope's health advances the prosperity of the church), and individual aspirations for a (too) long life. The theme of the prolongation of life, so prominent was it in the thirteenth century, leads us to the interest of the circles around the papal court in rewriting the Western dream of rejuvenation and the struggle against old age.[14] After all, Roger Bacon himself expounded at length on the *prolongatio vitae* in all the works he wrote for Clement IV.[15] Nor, finally, was it simply by chance that the charge of seeking to prolong his life was among the accusations leveled against Boniface VIII in the process directed against his memory by King Philip the Fair of France.[16]

If the history of the relations between the myth of the prolongation of life and the Roman ecclesiastical elites begins in the thirteenth century with the oldest medieval treaty devoted entirely to problems of old age and its possible postponement,[17] many other texts of this nature emerged in later periods as well. On this point, a still unedited alchemical treatise, written around 1449 by Guglielmo Fabri of Dya, a doctor "of law and medicine" and a member of Pope Felix V's (1439–49) entourage, is not to be overlooked. Before being elected pope at the Council of Basel, while he was still Duke Amadeus VIII of Savoy, Felix had sought an "impossible majesty."[18] As pope, he never truly succeeded in being recognized beyond his home state of Savoy. An aged man, he now suffered in his body as well. Among other things, he was afflicted by a kind of paralysis in a hand and a foot that made him cry out loud, as his conversation with Fabri reveals. Fabri's *Book of the Philosopher's Stone and Potable Gold (Liber de lapide philosophorum et de auro potabili)* is, in effect, a dialogue between the Savoyard pope and the alchemist-doctor, interspersed with short treatises in which the author elaborates on questions the pope has asked him about the possibility of transmuting metals, the therapeutic efficacy of potable gold, and the interpretation of certain occult terms such as *telchem* and *yxir*. At a certain point Felix, "crying out with a certain violence," asks: "Who can say today: I have the true elixir?" It is a safe bet that Boniface VIII might have shown similar anxiety in posing much the same question to his own great doctor and alchemist, Arnald of Villanova!

ABBREVIATIONS

AA SS   *Acta Sanctorum.* 43 vols. Venice, 1734–1770.
COD   *Conciliorum oecumenicorum decreta.* Ed. J. Alberigo et al. 3rd ed. Bologna, 1973.
CSEL   *Corpus scriptorum ecclesiasticorum latinorum.* Vienna, 1866.
DACL   *Dictionnaire d'archéologie chrétienne et de liturgie.* 15 vols. Paris, 1907–1953.
DHGE   *Dictionnaire d'histoire et géographie ecclésiastique.* Paris, 1912–.
JL   *Regesta pontificum Romanorum, ab condita ecclesia ad annum post Christum natum MCXCVIII.* Ed. P. Jaffé, S. Löwenfeld. 2nd ed. 2 vols. Leipzig, 1885–1888.
LC   *Le "Liber Censuum" de l'Eglise Romaine.* Ed., intro. P. Fabre and L. Duchesne, tables by G. Mollat. 3 vols. Paris, 1889–1952.
LP   *Le "Liber pontificalis,"* ed. L. Duchesne. 2 vols. Paris, 1886–1892; vol. 3, ed. C. Vogel. Paris, 1957.
MGH   *Monumenta Germaniae Historiae.*
PL   *Patrologiae cursus completus. Series latina.* Ed. J. P. Migne. 221 vols. Paris, 1841–1864.
RIS   *Rerum Italicarum Scriptores.*

NOTES

Introduction

1. Reconstructing the scientific movement at the Roman curia required specialized studies, which have now been brought together in the volume *Medicina e scienze della natura alla corte dei papi nel Duecento* (Spoleto, 1991).

2. A. Paravicini Bagliani, *I testamenti dei cardinali del Duecento* (Rome, 1980).

3. "Storia della scienza e storia della mentalità: Ruggero Bacone, Bonifacio VIII e la teoria della *prolongatio vitae*," in *Aspetti della letteratura latina nel secolo XIII: Atti del primo convegno internazionale di studi dell' AMUL, Perugia, 3–5 ottobre 1983* (Perugia and Florence, 1986), 243– 280; repub. in *Medicina e scienze della natura*, 281–326.

4. E. A. R. Brown, "Death and the Human Body in the Later Middle Ages: The Legislation of Boniface VIII on the Division of the Corpse," *Viator* 12 (1981): 221–270, and "Authority, the Family, and the Dead in Late Medieval France," *French Historical Studies* 16 (1990): 803–832; F. Santi, "Il cadavere e Bonifacio VIII, tra Stefano Tempier e Avicenna. Intorno ad un saggio di Elizabeth Brown," *Studi Medievali*, ser. 3, 28 (1987): 861–878.

5. R. Elze, "*Sic transit gloria mundi:* la morte del papa nel medioevo," *Annali dell'Istituto storico italo-germanico in Trento* 3 (1977): 23– 41 (German ed. "'Sic transit gloria mundi': Zum Tode des Papstes im Mittelalter," *Deutsches Archiv für Erforschung des Mittelalters* 34 [1978]: 1–18).

6. Ibid., 36.

7. E. Kantorowicz, *The King's Two Bodies* (Princeton, 1957) (French trans. *Les deux corps du roi* [Paris, 1989]).

8. *Roma anno 1300* (Rome, 1983); I. Herklotz, *"Sepulcra" e "monumenta" del Medioevo* (Rome, 1985); J. Gardner, *The Tomb and the Tiara: Curial Tomb Sculpture in Rome and Avignon in the Later Middle Ages* (Oxford, 1992).

9. M. Maccarone, *Vicarius Christi: Storia del titolo papale* (Rome, 1952); *Studi su Innocenzo III* (Padua, 1972); "Die *Cathedra Sancti Petri* im

Hochmittelalter," *Römische Quartalschrift* 75 (1980): 196–197 (repub. as "La *cathedra sancti Petri* nel Medio Evo: da simbolo a reliquia" in *Romana Ecclesia Sancti Petri* [Rome, 1991], 2:1249–1373); *"Ubi est papa, ibi est Roma,"* in *Aus Kirche und Reich. Studien zu Theologie, Politik und Recht im Mittelalter. Festschrift für Friedrich Kempf* (Sigmarigen, 1983), 371–382 (repub. in *Romana Ecclesia Cathedra Petri* [Rome, 1991], 2:1137–1156); and *Romana Ecclesia Cathedra Petri*, 2 vols. (Rome, 1991). G. B. Ladner, *Die Papstbildnisse des Altertums und des Mittelalters*, 3 vols. (Vatican City, 1941–84); "Die Statue Bonifaz' VIII. in der Lateranbasilika und die Entstehung der dreifach gekrönten Tiara," *Römische Quartalschrift* 42 (1934): 35–69; "Der Ursprung und die mittelalterliche Entwicklung der päpstlichen Tiara," in *Tainia. Roland Hampe zum 70: Geburtstag am 2 Dezember 1978 dargebracht* (Mainz am Rhein, 1978), 449–481; "Die Anfänge des Kryptoporträts," in *Von Angesicht zu Angesicht. Porträtstudien: Festschrift für Michael Stettler* (Bern, 1983), 78–97; and *Images and Ideas in the Middle Ages: Selected Studies in History and Art*, 2 vols. (Rome, 1983).

10. P. Niehans, *La sénéscence et le rajeunissement* (Paris, 1937).

11. Dr. Paul Niehans figures among the doctors who lavished attention on Pius XII on December 5 and 11, 1954 (see those issues of the *Osservatore Romano*). On April 6, 1955, the doctor was received in audience with other doctors who had cared for the pope (ibid., April 8). The day before, April 5, the pope had made Niehans a member of the Accademia Pontificia delle Scienze (ibid., April 17, 1955). The *Osservatore Romano* lists Niehans's publications, but says nothing about the theraputic methods that had made him famous. The author of the article was content instead to quote the following declaration by Niehans: "The climax of my long life has been the favor bestowed upon me by Divine Providence of being able to assist His Holiness during his grave illness in 1954." On October 8, 1958, the eve of Pius XII's death, Niehans, who happened to be in Rome, was summoned to the pope's bedside for consultation. See L. D'Orazi, *Pio XII* (Bologna, 1984), 250.

12. B. Schimmelpfennig, *Die Zerermonienbücher der römischen Kurie im Mittelalter* (Tübingen, 1973). M. Dykmans, *Le cérémonial papal de la fin du Moyen Age à la Renaissance*, 4 vols. (Brussels and Rome, 1977–85); and *L'oeuvre de Patrizi Piccolomini ou le cérémonial papal de la première Renaissance*, 2 vols. (Vatican City, 1980–82).

13. The *ordines* were the following, in chronological order: *Ordo XI* of the canon Benedict of Saint Peter's, composed between 1140 and 1143 (*LC* 2:141–174); the *ordines* of Albinus, 1189 (*LC* 2:123–137), and of Cencius, 1192 (*Romanus ordo de consuetudinius et observantiis* = *Liber Censuum* LVII–58:*LC* 1:290–311); the ceremonial of Gregory X, 1272–1273 (ed. Dykmans, *Le ceremonial papal*, 1:155–218); *Ordo XIV*, datable between the thirteenth and fourteenth centuries

(ibid., vol. 3); *Ordo XV* of Pierre Ameil (ibid., 4:69–228); the ceremonial of François de Conzié (ibid., 3:262–335); and the ceremonial of Agostino Patrizi Piccolomini, 1482–92 (ed. Dykmans, *L'oeuvre de Patrizi Piccolomini*, vols. 1–2). On the dating and complex textual histories of these *ordines*, see Schimmelpfennig, *Die Zeremonienbücher*, 1–16 (Benedict, Albinus, and Cencius); 30–35 (Gregory X's ceremonial); 62–100 *(Ordo XIV)*; 107–117 *(Ordo XV)*; and 120–126 (François de Conzié).

Chapter One

1. PL 145:471–480 (as *opusculum vigesimum tertium*, titled *De brevitate vitae Romanorum pontificum, et divina providentia*). The critical edition is *Die Briefe*, 3:188–200 (letter no. 108). The question "Cur papa non diutius vivat?" serves in most manuscripts as the title of the treatise; the phrase "Cur apostolicae Sedis antistes nunquam diutius vivat, sed intra breve temporis spacium diem claudat extremum?" is included in the text. For the date of the work, see Lucchesi, *Per una Vita*, vol. 2, note. 189; and idem, *Clavis Santa Petri Damiani* (Faenza, 1973), 83. *De brevitate* has been examined briefly by Bultot, *La doctrine*, 71–77; Cacciamani, *De brevitate vitae*, 226–242; Colosio, *Riflessioni*, 240–245; and Schmidt, *Alexander II*, 181–182.

2. The tumultuous election of Alexander II in Rome on October 1, 1061, under the influence of Hildebrand, the future Pope Gregory VII (1073–85), was challenged by an angry group of bishops who opposed the reform program of the Roman papacy. A synod held at Basel proceeded to elect another pope, Cadalus, Bishop of Parma, who took the name Honorius II (1061–64).

3. *Die Briefe*, 3:189. On other occasions as well, Alexander II had invited him to write about issues that concerned him: see, e.g., the prologue to the *Vita sancti Rodulphi episcopi Eugubini*, PL, 144:1009, and letter 1, 12 (PL, 144:214); see also Schmidt, *Alexander II*, 181, note 233. Damian in fact wrote nine letters to Alexander (ibid., 180). While he was still Bishop of Lucca, Anselm of Baggio accompanied him on his important legation to Milan in 1059 (ibid., 63). He had played a role in Roman politics from the time of Pope Gregory VI (1045–46), and was one of the inner circle of Leo IX's (1049–54) counselors. Stephen IX (1057–58) raised him at the outset of his pontificate to the much sought after and prestigious post of cardinal bishop of Ostia, thus placing him at the head of the hierarchy of cardinals; see Lucchesi, *Per una Vita*.

4. In his *Disceptatio Synodalis*, Damian asserts that he carefully studied the *Liber pontificalis*: MGH, *Libelli*, 1:79. For the passage concerning Saint Peter, see LP, 1:118: "Petrus ingressus in urbe Roma, Nerone Cesare, ibique sedit cathedram episcopatus ann. XXV m. II d. III." See also the *Catalogo Liberiano* in LP, 1:3: "Petrus ann. XXV mens.

I d. VIII." For the sources, see DACL, 14, 1 (1938), 844−845. The figure of twenty-five years appears in all of the ancient lists of the bishops of Rome: see Klauser, "Die Anfänge," 210−211. Schmidt's thesis in *Studien,* 359, et seq., is considered the most plausible: the legend of Simon Magnus dates Peter's arrival in Rome at the earliest in 42 A.D.; since the lists of Roman bishops assign the beginning of the pontificate of Linus to 67 or 68, we may deduce that there remained exactly twenty-five years for Saint Peter's activity in Rome.

5. A modern analysis of the chronologies contained in the *Liber pontificalis* confirms Damian's conclusions. For the first eight centuries of papal history, from Saint Peter to Adrian I (795), see the chronological tables in LP, 1, cclx−cclxii; for the following period, from 795 to 1458, see ibid., 2, lxxv−lxxviii. Of the ninety popes who held office from Saint Peter to Adrian I, only three ruled longer than twenty-one years: Sylvester I (314−35), Leo I (440−61) and Adrian I (772−95). Just under one-quarter (23.33 percent) of them ruled more than ten but less than twenty years; almost three-quarters (72.22 percent) reigned less than ten years. Fourteen served less than a year, fifteen between one and two, and sixteen between three and six years. For the centuries from the Carolingian Pope Leo III to Alexander's predecessor, Pope Nicholas II, the figures support Damian's thesis even more strongly. Of sixty-three pontificates, fully fifty-eight (92 percent) lasted less than ten years, and only five (8 percent) between eleven and twenty. Indeed, in these three and a half centuries, twenty-two popes (37 percent) served less than a year. None served more than twenty. In the period from Sylvester II (999−1003) to Nicholas II (1058−61), the average length of the pontificates dropped notably. Of the seventeen popes that the *Liber pontificalis* considered legitimate, almost half (eight, 47 percent) ruled less than a year. (The antipopes were not included in the tables for the years 998−1061). No pope ruled more than a dozen years. As we approach the "modern times" *(tempora moderna)* referred to by Damian, the phenomenon of the pontificates' "brevity" comes even more dramatically into view. Of the seven popes who ascended the throne of Saint Peter between 1045 and 1061, only three lived longer than a year, two more than two years, and only one more than five years. In other words, while for the years 998−1044 the average pontificate lasted seventy-seven months (six years and four months), in the following period (1045−61) the average length was no more than twenty-three months. The extremes ran from twenty-four days for Damasus II to Leo IX's five years, two months, and seven days.

6. According to Peter Damian's source, the *Liber pontificalis,* Saint Peter died (the same day as Saint Paul) thirty-eight years after Christ's Passion, corresponding to the year 67. LP, 1:118; see also 119, note 12.

7. *Die Briefe,* 3:189: "Quod considerantibus prodigialis, ut ita lo-

quar, stupor oboritur, quoniam haec breviter vivendi necessitas, quantum ad nostram notitiam, in nulla alia totius orbis aecclesia reperitur."

8. Ibid., 3 : 190.

9. Ibid.

10. Ibid., 3 : 192.

11. Ibid., 3 : 190–191.

12. Ibid.

13. Ibid., 3 : 192–199.

14. Ibid., 3 : 188 and the list of manuscripts.

15. Ibid., 3:199. Biblical translation from H. G. May and B. M. Metzger, eds., *The New Oxford Bible with Apocrypha* (Revised Standard Version; New York, 1973), 637.

16. *Die Briefe,* 3:199. Biblical trans. from *New Oxford Bible,* 21.

17. *Die Briefe,* 3 : 200. For the sources, see Treitinger, *Die oströmische . . . Reichsidee,* 148. According to Rentschler, "Griechische Kultur," 108, Damian's informant was a monk of the Latin monastery of Saint Mary of Constantinople, to whose abbot Damian sent letter no. 131; see also *Die Briefe,* 3 : 200, note 30.

18. *Die Briefe,* 3 : 200.

19. The passage containing the words *universalis episcopus* induced Ryan, *Saint Peter Damiani,* 103–105, note 200, to affirm: "There is in fact no clearer formulation in the contemporary texts reviewed by K. Hofmann, *Der "Dictatus Papae" Gregors VII.,* 1933, 34, et seq. . . . of the renewed consciousness of papal authority, so seriously obscured in the preceding period"; "no one was more conscious of Roman Prerogatives than Damiani, or more articulate in stating them." See also Löwe, "Kaisertum," 529–562.

20. Grauert, *Magister,* 91, verses 669–670: "Papa brevis vox est, sed virtus nominis huius / Perlustrat quicquid arcus uterque tenet."

21. *Die Briefe,* 3 : 192.

22. Even in his letter to the cardinals (of autumn, 1057), Damian argued that the universality of the Lateran Palace, to which flowed various "peoples from every part of the world" (*populi de toto terrarum orbe*) imposed moral obligations on its occupant: "Porro quia ad Lateranense palatium a diversis populis de toto terrarum orbe confluitur, necesse est, ut ibi prae ceteris uspiam locis, recta semper vivendi sit forma, districta teneatur assidue sub honestis moribus disciplina." *Die Briefe,* 2 : 57, no. 48.

23. Ibid., 3 : 192.

24. De Heusch, *Écrits,* 232. On the problem of violent death, see also idem, "The Sacrificial Body," 387–394.

25. LP, 2 : 297.

26. LP, 2 : 323: "Sed nulla potentia longa."

27. Bernardus Claraevallensis, *Epistola* 238 (PL, 182: 430–431); see

also Jacqueline, *Episcopat,* 196. Cancellieri, *Storia,* 54, note 1, affirms: "Sono bellissime le riflessioni di S. Bernardo, *quare nullus excesserit annum 25* scrivendo ad *Eugenio III in lib. 3 de Consol. cap. 2 sect. 5 epist. 104,* che interroga, *quantorum in brevi Rom. Pontificum mortes adspexisti?"* This latter phrase comes from letter 238, for which the text is cited. But it has not been possible to locate the first citation, "because no (pope) has exceeded the twenty-five years (of Peter)," which does not appear in *De consideratione.*

28. Bernardus Claraevallensis, *De consideratione,* bk. 2, ch. 9, 18; trans. Gastaldelli, 817. On the *contemptus mundi,* see Bultot, *La doctrine;* Sot, "Mépris," 6–17.

29. *Johannis Saresberiensis episcopi Carnotensis Policratici sive De nugis cvrialivm et vestigiis philosophorum libri VIII,* ed. C. I. Webb, Oxford, 1909, bk. 8, ch. 23, 814–815.

30. John of Salisbury, *Policraticus. L'uomo di governo nel pensiero medievale,* trans. L. Bianchi and P. Feltrin (Milan, 1984), 297–298. The theme of the burden of the pontifical office finds an unusual development in William Durant's interpretation of the symbolism of the papal pallium. The portion of the pallium placed on the pope's breast symbolized "huius [i.e., the pope's] curas, et solicitudines . . . , quibus et cor et humeri Pontificis sic saepissime gravantur et impediuntur . . ." (Guilellmus Durandus, *Rationale,* bk. 3, ch. 17, no. 4).

31. *Fam.* IX, 5, *Le Familiari,* ed. V. Rossi (Florence, 1933), 229; see also, for the translation: U. Dotti, "Un copricapo più leggero per Boniface VIII," *Belfagor,* 32 (1977), 459–462, who also cites Dario Fo's *Mistero buffo* (1969), in which Boniface VIII does not hesitate to remove his miter temporarily ("oh! se ol è pesante questo!"); picking up a lighter headpiece, he pops it on his head, exclaiming: "eh, questo ol è bon. . . ."

32. Robertus de Torineio, *Chronica,* in MGH, SS, 6:531.

33. This goes for the topos of Peter's twenty-five years, but not for the theme of "brevity" itself, which came up often. Bridget of Sweden claimed to have received orders from Christ to tell Pope Urban V (1362–70): "Tempus tuum breve est; surge et attende, quomodo anime tibi commisse salventur)." *Revelationes Sanctae Birgittae. Reuelaciones extrauagantes,* ch. 44, ed. L. Hollmann (Uppsala, 1956), 160.

34. Magri, *Hierolexicon,* 444, cites a "ceremoniam antiquitus usitatam quod nempe in coronationis actu pontifici haec verba memorabantur: 'Pater sancte non videbis dies Petri' "; see also Sarnelli, *Lettere Ecclesiastiche,* 6:71–73 (Letter XXXVI: *Perchè si dica del Papa: Non videbit dies Petri*). The nonexistence of a rite for which there is no source, either medieval or modern, was challenged by Mezzadri, *Dissertatio,* and by D. Papenbroch, *Conatus chronico-historicus ad catalogum Romanorum pontificum,* AA SS, Maii VIII, 14. Cancellieri, *Storia,* 54, note 1, also rejected the "inveterata opinione, che s'intimasse al nuovo papa, *Non*

videbis dies Petri, per avvisargli, che non sarebbe vissuto più lungamente di 25 anni, che fra le varietà delle opinioni su la durata del Pontificato di s. Pietro è il termine più lungo, che gli è stato assegnato."

35. Antoninus, archepiscopus Florentinus, *Chronicon,* tit. 22, ch. 7, 486: "Benedictus autem Apostaticus relictus ab omnibus in insulam Paniscolae cum paucis se contulit, ubi manens in sua pertinacia transivit annos Petri ad cumulum suae damnationis: nec mirum, quia non in sede Petri, moriensque docuit ex eligendum unum."

36. *Rodorici episcopi Zamorensis . . . Speculum vitae humanae . . . ,* bk. 2, chs. 1–7, 201–257. First edition: Rome, C. Sweynheym and A. Pannartz, 1468 (= Hain and Copinger *13939), fifteen editions in twenty years (1468–88). His meditation on the brevity of the popes' lives fills three entire chapters of the second book, and indeed seems to constitute a treatise in itself, if we may judge from the general title of the work. On the work as a whole, see O'Malley, *Praise,* 179.

37. *Rodorici episcopi Zamorensis . . . Speculum vitae humanae,* 226.

38. Ibid., 226.

39. Ibid.

40. Ibid., 230.

41. Ibid., 250, 251, 256.

42. Ibid., 249.

43. Ibid.: "Romani pontifices qui sibi longam vitam promittunt."

44. In the dedication to the "Orazia" (September 1, 1546), cit. Besso, *Roma,* 201 (English trans. M. Lettieri and M. Ukas, *Trissino's "Sophonisba" and Aretino's "Horatia": Two Renaissance Tragedies* [Lewiston, N.Y.], 1997, 152, verses 147–262).

45. On the various editions of Rangoni's *De vita hominis,* see Marini, *Degli archiatri,* 1:339, note a.

46. Moroni, 86:68: "Leggo in Lodovico Anastasio, *Storia degli Antipapi* (Naples, 1754), 2:264, che raccontasi di avere un famigliare di papa Urbano VIII, mentre questi era vicino di morire, detto con voce sommessa, *non videbis dies Petri,* vale a dire che non poteva oltrepassare i 25 anni vissuti nel Pontificato da s. Pietro; ma il papa avendo udito acutissimo l'intese, onde tosto disse: *Non est de fide.*" See Besso, *Roma,* 200, note 1: "mentre era vicino di morire, un chierico gli avrebbe detto con voce sommessa: 'non vedrai gli anni di Pietro' *(non videbis dies Petri),* vale a dire che non poteva oltrepassare i 25 anni vissuti nel Pontificato da s. Pietro; ma il papa avendo udito acutissimo l'intese, onde tosto disse: *Non est de fide;* trovandosi in fin di vita, udì un suo famigliare mormorare la 'fatale sentenza.'"

47. Burio (Guillaume de Bury), *Romanorum pontificum brevis notitia* (Padua, 1726), 364: "Sint licet assumpti Juvenes ad Pontificatum, Petri annos potuit nemo videre tamen."

48. Simone de Magistris, *Acta martyrum ad Ostia Tiberina* (Rome,

1795), 418, note a: "ut Ecclesiae prodessent diutius Petri Cathedram tenuerunt; idque divinitus renovatum conspicimus in Pio VI . . ."; see also Cancellieri, *Storia,* 54, note 3.

49. Moroni, 54:112: "Septimus ille hic est factus, qui rector in orbe / componet fausto numine cuncta, Pius. / Sextus ut ante Pius Petri superavit et annos, / Sic Sexti superet Septimus ipse dies"; and Besso, *Roma,* 200–201 (2nd ed. [Florence, 1971], 322, et seq.: "Non videbis annos Petri").

50. M. N. Bouillet, *Dictionnaire universel d'histoire et de géographie,* 8th ed. (Paris, 1851), 1343 ("S. Pierre," 34–66). For Robert, "Peter's years" are "the traditional thirty-two" ("les trente-deux ans traditionnels de son pontificat")! See "Années de saint Pierre." I owe this point to Jean-Daniel Morerod of the University of Louvain.

51. L. Huetter, *Iscrizioni della città di Roma dal 1871 al 1920* (Florence, 1959), 2:295: ". . . sacri principavs annos XXV / . . . / in sede Romana / post Petrvm vnvs explevit"; 296: "Pio IX pont. max. / Quod Petri annos / in Romano pontificatv / vnvs aequavit / Clerus Vaticanvs . . ."; 296: "Pio IX admirabili pontificvm maximor. / . . . / ad B. Petri annos divinitvs propagato . . ."; 297: "Pio IX / pontifici maximo / . . . / quo Petri annos in Romana sede / vnvs aeqvavit n. f.," and "Pio IX pontifici maximo / vni post Petrvm in Romana sede / . . . / votis V et XX . . ."; 298: "Pio IX pont. max. / Quem praestantissimo Dei nvmine / vltra Petri annos. . . ."

52. Besso, *Roma,* 200–201; see also Schmidt, *Alexander II,* 183.

53. The entire legend of Gerbert has recently been reviewed by Oldoni, "Gerberto e la sua storia," 629–704; idem, "A fantasia dicitur fantasma," 493–622, and 167–245. On Gerbert, see Riché, *Gerbert d'Aurillac e Gerberto: Scienza, storia e mito.*

54. Guillelmus Godellius, *Chronicon,* in MGH, SS, 26:195 (biographical note at the year 1144).

55. Walter Map, *De nugis curialium,* 182. See also Alberico delle Tre Fontane, in MGH, SS, 23:777.

56. Diacono Giovanni, *Liber de Ecclesia Lateranensi* (Valentini and Zucchetti, *Codice,* 3:348); and Graf, *Miti, leggende e superstizioni,* 2:33–34. The first redaction of the *Descriptio* was drawn up shortly after the pontificate of Alexander II (1061–73); *Codice,* 3:318–325.

57. The abandonment of the Vatican necropolis was an important innovation, particularly because John X was also the first pope to have himself buried within the city walls. In the tenth century, however, the Lateran did not truly have a real papal necropolis. Papal sepulchers continued to be placed in the Vatican or in other Roman basilicas: John XIII (d. 972) was entombed in Saint Paul's outside the Walls, Benedict VII (d. 983) at Santa Croce in Gerusalemme, Damasus II (d. 1048) at Saint Lawrence outside the Walls. See Picard, "Etude sur

l'emplacement des tombes," 725–782; Herklotz, *"Sepulcra,"* 91–92; and Borgolte, *Petrusnachfolge,* 127–137.

58. The *Liber pontificalis* justified Paschal II's decision by asserting that the Lateran basilica was the "the real and true papal residence" (LP, 2:305: "ab ipsis patribus honorifice est deportata in basilicam Salvatoris, in sede propria, in patriarchio, dextro latere templi, in mausoleo purissimi marmoris talapsico opere sculpto . . ."); see Herklotz, *"Sepulcra,"* 97.

59. Ibid., 91–92. See also Borgolte, *Petrusnachfolge,* 354–355; and Stroll, *Symbols,* 185–187.

60. Deér, *Dynastic Porphyry Tombs,* 146–154.

61. Ibid., 152. The fact did not pass unnoted by contemporaries; no less than "quattro autori raccontano che il papa fu sepolto in quel sarcofago del porfido che era già servito come tomba dell'imperatore Adriano.'" Herklotz, *"Sepulcra,"* 97, and note 67. Cardinal Gherard, the future Pope Lucius II, wrote the following to Innocent II in 1137: "Ecclesia te in caesarem totiusque orbis dominatorem et elegit et consecravit," cit. Caspar, *Petrus Diaconus,* 258; and Deér, *Dynastic Porphyry Tombs,* 148, note 112. On the *laudes* emulating imperial models addressed to Innocent II, see LC, 2:173; see also Herklotz, "Der Campus Lateranensis," 13–14; Kantorowicz, *Laudes Regiae,* 129 and 143; and Stroll, *Symbols,* 183.

62. Defeated soldiers are depicted chained to the feet of their mounted conquerors, being forced to march ahead of the cortege with their heads bowed. The representations were inspired by Roman imperial ceremonies; see Herklotz, *"Sepulcra,"* 116 and 124–128.

63. Deér, *Dynastic Porphyry Tombs,* 151.

64. The *Descriptio Lateranensis Ecclesiae* defines the pope as an *imperialis episcopus:* Valentini and Zucchetti, *Codice,* 3:345. On the effort of twelfth-century canonists to justify the concept of the pope as *verus imperator,* see Stickler, "Imperator vicarius papae," 165–212; see also Stroll, *Symbols,* 180–192 ("Innocent II: The Imperial Pope"). The tombs of Eugenius III (1145–53) and Adrian IV (1154–59) at Saint Peter's also contained features recalling the imperial symbolism of porphyry: the first was made of granite, a stone used as a substitute for porphyry; the second was constructed of various kinds of stone, among them definitely porphyry. Later, the character of the stone used in the tomb of Lucius III (d. Nov. 25, 1183) in Verona cathedral, *rosso veronese,* seems to suggest a color symbolism analogous to that of porphyry (Herklotz, *"Sepulcra,"* 114–116 and fig. 24; but Gardner disagrees [*The Tomb,* 30, note 49]). Two angels place the tiara on the pope's head. The deceased pope is thus represented in the act of being crowned by celestial and divine forces. The recourse to an iconographic model drawn from Byzantine imperial art reflected, as has justly been observed, "the

basic assimilation of the papal condition with the imperial" (Herklotz, ibid.). The tradition of building papal tombs of porphyry continued into the thirteenth century: Honorius III (1216–27) was buried in the basilica of Santa Maria Maggiore in a *concha porfyretica: Catalogus pontificum Romanorum Viterbiensis,* in MGH, SS, 22:352; and Deér, *Dynastic Porphyry Tombs,* 152. For the tomb of Innocent V (d. 1276), Charles I of Anjou directed the treasurer of the city of Rome to find a *conca porfidis vel alicuius alterius pulcri lapidis* so that it would match the Lateran sarcophagi (Laurent, *Le bienheureux Innocent V,* 418, no. 14). At Venice, in 1173, Alexander III is said to have received the *proskynesis* from Frederick Barbarossa while standing on the large porphyry *rota* that is still on view in front of San Marco (Deér, *Dynastic Porphyry Tombs,* 155). According to the imperial *Ordo* C, during the *scrutinium* the pope and emperor-elect sat on chairs placed on the large *rota* in Saint Peter's Basilica (ibid., 155). The placement of porphyry *quadrifogli* in the pavement of Roman churches already in the time of Paschal II, during the crucial investiture conflict, is a clear sign of the immitation of imperial motifs: Glass, "Papal Patronage," 386–390.

65. Schramm, *Kaiser, Rom.*

66. Martinus Polonus, *Chronicon pontificum et imperatorum,* in MGH, SS, 22:43. It is well-known that the legend of Sylvester's rumbling bones originated in a misreading of a passage of the inscription that one of Sylvester's successors, Sergius IV (1009–12), had had affixed to the sepulcher of Gerbert d'Aurillac in the Lateran: the second half of the first line alluded to the sounding of the tomb on the day in which "the Lord will arrive" (*venturo Domino conferet ad sonitum:* Valentini and Zucchetti, *Codice,* 3:348, note 5, an edition of the epitaph discovered in 1648, and still in existence: LP, 2:263 note 4). The words *venturus Dominus* referred to the *future pope,* whose advent would be announced by the tomb's sounding. But Martin's version had a great future. In the thirteenth century, it was embraced by the author of the *Flores Temporum* (MGH, SS, 24:245: "Ubi dum celebrearet, ex demonum strepitu mortem timens, publice confessus est; et pedibus ac manibus amputatis, super bigam cum equo domito positus, ad Lateranensem ecclesiam est devectus. Cuius sepulchrum insudat vel strepit, quando papa mortuus est; et hoc est in signum misericordie consecute"; at the beginning of the fourteenth century, for example, it was cited by Leone of Orvieto in his *Chronica summorum pontificum,* carried down to 1312 (Graf, *Miti,* 2:74–75), and by Ricobaldo of Ferrara in his *Historia pontificum Romanorum* (RIS, 9:172–173). Its insertion into the fifteenth-century version of the *Liber pontificalis* (LP, 2:263) perpetuated it.

67. See the article "Résidences pontificales (Moyen Age)" in the *Dictionnaire de la papauté.*

68. The papal chancery used papyrus down to 1057: W. Watten-

bach, *Das Schriftwesen im Mittelalter,* 4th ed. (Graz 1958), 110; and papyrus continued to be available: papyrus plants grew in various regions of southern Italy (including Rome) down to our own times.

69. LC, 2:149, no. 34.

70. The liturgical elements in the *Ordo XI* are difficult to date, and in some cases may date back to as early as the tenth century: Schimmelpfennig, "Die Bedeutung," 58.

71. Sextus Pompeus Festus, *De verborum significatu,* 473, under *struppi:* "Struppi vocantur in pulvinaribus (fasciculi) (de verbenis facti, qui pro de) orum capitibus ponuntur"; and in the epitome of Paulus: "Struppi vocabantur in pulvinaribus fasciculi de verbenis facti, qui pro deorum capitibus ponebantur." See also Cancellieri, *De secretariis,* 971–972: "Quae quidem fortasse cuidam in mentem revocabunt, quae tradit Festus de struppis, sive fasciculis de verbenis, qui pro Deorum capitibus in pulvinaribus ponebantur."

72. Mansi, 20:749 (Council of Benevento); see also F. Cabrol, "Cendres," in DACL, 2, 2, 3041–3042. The first to speak of putting ashes on the head was Regino of Prüm (beginning of the tenth century), but the prescription applied only to penitents: *De ecclesiasticis disciplinis,* bk. 1, ch. 291, PL, 132:245. Rupert of Deutz expressed himself in the same manner: *De divinis officiis,* bk. 4, ch. 10, PL, 170:98. Not surprisingly, therefore, the first ten *Ordines Romani* say nothing of ashes in regard to Ash Wednesday: *Ordo I,* PL, 78:949; *Ordo X,* PL, 78:1017, et seq.

73. LC, 2:149, no. 34. Schimmelpfennig, *Die Zeremonienbücher,* 385, provides a list of sources on the papal rite of ashes.

74. Andrieu, *Le pontifical,* 1:209–210, no. 28.

75. Albinus, LC, 2:129, no. 15; Cencius, 57, no. 15, LC, 1:294.

76. Van Dijk and Walker, *The Ordinal,* 181–183. These prescriptions already figured in the codex containing the "Breviario di Santa Chiara" (= C; 1234–1238); see also ibid., 23–24.

77. Paravicini Bagliani, "La mobilità," 155–278.

78. But only if the cardinal bishops were present; otherwise, the rite was celebrated by the first of the cardinal priests. The annotation probably reflects the ever more frequent absence of the cardinals, who were assigned long and important legations.

79. Van Dijk and Walker, *The Ordinal,* 181: "curia debet et prelati violaceis seu nigris pluvialibus uti, presbiteri vero et diaconi cardinales planetis, capellani superpelliciis."

80. Ibid., 183.

81. Ibid., 371; see also 217.

82. Dykmans, *Le cérémonial,* 3:189, nos. 33–34. See also Cancellieri, *Storia,* 500, note to p. 53 note 3; and Antonelli, *Epistola,* 332.

83. The ashes had to be taken from year-old palms.

84. For the kiss on the mouth (in the liturgical context), and its gradual elimination, see the recent analysis by Carré, *Le baiser sur la bouche,* 221, et seq.

85. It is Bindo of Fiesole's collection that makes no mention of placing ashes on the pope (Schimmelpfennig, *Die Zeremonienbücher,* 259–260, no. 51). It is preserved in the codex *Vat. lat.* 4726; and Florence, Bibl. Riccardiana, MS 471: the note is in the Vatican codex.

86. Dykmans, *Le cérémonial,* 4:105, no. 250. That Ash Wednesday at Perugia not a single cardinal bishop was present. The mass was celebrated by the "Cardinal of Bologna," Cosimo Migliorati, cardinal priest of Santa Croce in Gerusalemme (1389–1404), the future Innocent VII (1404–6). The celebrant and the pope placed ashes on each other respectively without observing the traditional hierarchical order. François de Conzié twice noted the ceremony of the ashes in his *Diario,* but only to recall that Benedict XIII imposed the ashes: ibid., 3:357 and 3:402. Ameil cites an old rubric prescribing that whoever *facit officium coram papa,* whether a cardinal or not, represented the person of the pope, and should therefore be the first to receive the ashes immediately after the first of the cardinal bishops and before all the other cardinals. Pierre Ameil added that this rule should be observed above all in the case of religious (ibid., 4:99, no. 215; see also no. 212).

87. Cancellieri, *Storia,* 239; see also Rocca, *Unde Cineres,* 217. According to Patrizi Piccolomini (1484–92), the senior cardinal penitentiary was required to celebrate the mass on Ash Wednesday (Dykmans, *L'oeuvre,* 2:345, no. 995). This was an innovation.

88. Antonelli, *Epistola,* 338.

89. The tension between mortality and respect for office was also ritualized in the ceremony of the ashes that in modern times was reserved to the cardinals: *Paridis Grassi . . . De caeremoniis cardinalium,* 2, fols. 79r–80v.

90. Sir. 21: 10–11: "stuppa collecta synagoga peccantium et consummatio illorum flamma ignis"; Isa. 1: 31: "et erit fortitudo vestra ut favilla stuppae et opus vestrum quasi scintilla." For the notion of transience, see 1 Cor. 7: 31: "praeterit enim figura huius mundi"; and 1 John 2: 17: "mundus transit et concupiscentia eius"; cit. *Alexander von Roes. Schriften,* ed. Grundmann-Heimpel, 188, note 3.

91. Elze, " '*Sic transit,*' " 40.

92. Peter Damian must have been perfectly up-to-date on Roman practices. The fact that he described the rite of burning flax to Alexander II as though it were unfamiliar is an essential point that enables us to establish a *terminus a quo* for the introduction of the rite in papal circles. Were this not the case, Damian's discussion would make no sense. Likewise, the fact that burning flax was included in the liturgy of

Besançon cathedral reorganized by Archbishop Hugh I (1031–66) also supports the point. Hugh's adoption of the flax rite at Besançon can be traced to his contacts with Damian around 1063–64, precisely on the theme of mortality and humility (see the following note). It is possible, but by no means certain, that the rite was introduced into the papal ceremonial as early as the eleventh century, or in "un tempo in cui sembra che la curia avesse adotato parte del cerimoniale di corte bizantino" (Elze, "'Sic transit,'" 40). Schimmelpfennig also wondered whether the rite of burning flax had not entered the papal liturgy "truly only with the reforming papacy": Schimmelpfennig, "Die Bedeutung," 58; and idem, "Die Krönung," 207–208. The *Opusculum* 23 *(De brevitate),* on which the hypothesis is based, indicates only that Damian wanted to tell his reader about it. The discussion of the antiquity of ritual elements in Benedict's *ordo* should certainly be kept in mind, but regarding the flax it is less useful: the station held at Santa Maria Maggiore on Christmas morning, devoted especially to the flax burning (which Benedict was the first to describe) was, according to Petrus Mallius, introduced under Gregory VII (see below, note 96). In any case, notices of the introduction of the flax rite into the papal coronation ceremony do not appear until the thirteenth century. On this point the evidence furnished by Stephen of Bourbon, until now unnoticed, will permit us to specify the chronology and the motives of its introduction (below, notes 105–108).

93. The *Ordo Canonicorum* of Saint-Jean of Besançon, the principal source on the Byzantine liturgy running back to the episcopate of Hugh I (1031–66), was transmitted in a codex (Besançon, *Bibl. Municipale,* MS 711) copied entirely in a single hand around 1180 from a model predating 1120. The ceremony was celebrated on Christmas (fols. 204v–205r), Saint Stephen's Day (fol. 205v), Easter (fol. 216v), and Pentecost (fol. 222v). On Christmas, after the Kyrie, instead of the words "Reverende pater, sic transit mundus et concupiscentia eius," the archdeacon was supposed to say "Scito te terram esse" (fol. 205r, lines 21–24). The contents of the *ordo* as a whole demonstrate that its redaction goes back to the mid–eleventh century, and that it was not retouched afterwards: B. de Vregille, "Le 'Rituel de saint Prothade' et 'l'Ordo canonicorum' de Saint-Jean de Besançon," *Revue du Moyen Age Latin,* 5 (1949), 97–114; see idem, *Hugues de Salins,* 149–351 and idem, 1:471–473; 2:1153–1156; 3:161*. I owe these notices to the courtesy of P. Bernard de Vregille, whom I thank very kindly.

94. In the thirteenth century, the ceremony of burning flax was also celebrated at Lisieux on Pentecost; see the cathedral ordinale, cit. Cancellieri, *Storia,* 53, note 3; and Moroni, 70:91. The use of the flax rite was undoubtedly more widely diffused than we can document

today: Moroni, ibid., refers to its use also at Lucca ("quando l'arcivescovo intuona il *Gloria in excelsis Deo,* si brucia una quantità di stoppa in mezzo alla cattedrale"), without, however, indicating when.

95. *Die Briefe,* 3:246–258 (no. 111), esp. 248–249.

96. LC, 2:145, nos. 16–17. For reasons unknown, Duchesne chose for his edition of the text the reading *facultatem* in place of *difficultatem,* the word actually contained in the oldest manuscript (Cambrai, 12, et seq.). Petrus Mallius also reports that the station was held in Santa Maria Maggiore, "quoniam via brevis est, et dies parvi sunt" (*Descriptio basilicae Vaticanae,* ed. Valentini and Zucchetti, *Codice,* 3: 439–440). Benedict was the first to indicate the existence of the station at Santa Maria Maggiore, an innovation that Mallius seems to attribute to Gregory VII: "formerly the station was held at Saint Peter's on Christmas morning, until the pontificate of Gregory VII." Benedict's notice provides an important cue for dating the introduction of the flax burning into the realm of Roman liturgy, and by no means contradicts the *terminus a quo* (1064) provided by Damian's *De brevitate.* The fact that Benedict speaks of the station at Saint Peter's as already existing may reflect the existence of a ceremonial tradition predating Gregory VII's pontificate; if so, the detail with which he records the itinerary from Saint Anastasias to Saint Peter's through Rome's antiquities would indicate the existence of a topographical "renewal of Rome" *(renovatio Romae)* that preceded Gregory's reforming papacy (Schimmelpfennig, "Die Bedeutung," 51). In any case, it should be observed that by emphasizing in his account the Roman antiquities that were "touched" by the papal procession, Benedict in effect set up a contrast with the papal flax ceremony that can scarcely have been accidental. The imperial itinerary and the ritual of papal mortality seem to counterbalance each other, and at the same time to justify Benedict's textual emphasis.

97. LC, 2:145, no. 17; see also ibid., nos. 16–19, and 153, no. 47.

98. For the critical problems posed by the antiquity of this itinerary, see above, note 96.

99. For the sake of completeness, it should be borne in mind that Benedict's *ordo* does not report the ceremony for the pope's consecration; but it is equally true that the flax-burning rite is not mentioned in any twelfth-century *ordo coronationis* (the codices of Albinus and Cencius at London and Basel).

100. *Libellus de cerimoniis aule imperialis (Graphia aureae Urbis Romae),* ch. 19, ed. Schramm, *Kaiser,* 3:351. Schramm claimed (*Kaiser, Rom,* 209) that the rite described by the *Graphia aureae Urbis Romae*—for the first and only time—was a borrowing from the Roman church, on the grounds that down to the present flax is burned at the beginning of the papal coronation. But as has been shown, this

interpretation is based on an evolution contrary to the entire rite. Moreover, in the portion concerning the *Mirabilia urbis Romae,* the *Graphia* presents important analogies with the work of the canon Benedict. Bloch, "Der Autor," 55–175, opposes the dating proposed by Schramm (around 1030). The *terminus ante quem* is provided by the reference in chapter 16 to the sarcophagus of Pope Anastasius IV (d. Dec. 3, 1154).

101. Honorius Augustodunensis, *Gemma Ecclesiae,* PL, 172: 611–612. L. Cabrini Chiesa provides an analysis of the work that, though difficult to date, can be assigned to the first decades of the twelfth century; "Temi liturgici in Honorius Augustodunensis," *Ephemerides Liturgicae,* 99 (1985): 443–455. There is no mention at all of the flax rite in Rupert of Deutz (PL, 170: 25–26), a source, moreover, that was directed by Honorius himself.

102. It was now the canons of Santa Maria Maggiore who received the pope at the entrance of the church: Basel, Universitätsbibl., D. 4, 4; ed. Schimmelpfennig, *Die Zeremonienbücher,* 374: "Canonici recipiunt cum processione, ipse dat pacem omnibus. Postea incendit stupam super capita columpnarum, que ibi stant."

103. Lotharius, *De sacro altaris mysterio* (PL, 217: 804–805).

104. Maccarrone, *Lotharii,* 71; see also Lewis, *Lotharius.* The work was written between December 25, 1194, and April 3, 1195.

105. Stephanus de Borbone, *Tractatus de diversis materiis predicalibus,* I, *De dono timoris,* ch. 7, *De memoria mortis,* nos. 98–99, ed. Berlioz and Eichenlaub. I thank J. Berlioz very much for having sent me the proofs of the manuscript of his edition.

106. Ibid., no. 100.

107. Ibid., nos. 101–103. The passage comes from the patriarch's *Vita,* ch. 18 (PL: 73, 354), and figures also in Jacobus de Voragine's *Legenda aurea,* which he composed in the 1260s (ed. Graesse, ch. 27, nos. 7, 130). The paragraphs on the patriarch of Alexandria and the papal flax rite were copied without variations into one of the sermons that medieval manuscripts and fifteenth-century editions attribute to the Dominican Martin of Troppau (d. 1278); but these are in fact simply a collection of *exempla* drawn from Stephen of Bourbon (Martinus Polonus, *Sermones;* see also Käppeli, *Scriptores Ordinis Praedicatorum,* 3 : 115, no. 2972). Diego Moles has recently demonstrated this in a dissertation *(tesi di laurea)* written under my direction at the University of Lausanne (1993).

108. In speaking of the pope, Stephen of Bourbon used the word "consecrated" *(consecratur)* rather than "crowned" *(coronatur),* which he used instead to describe the rite of presenting pieces of marble to the Byzantine emperor. Only with the ceremonial of Gregory X (1273) did the papal coronation become an autonomous constituting element; for this reason, it was not before the end of the thirteenth century that

the term *coronatio* took the place of the traditional *consecratio*. Schimmelpfenig, "Die Krönung," 215, note 100, observes that Martin of Troppau consistently speaks of *consecratio* in his *Chronica imperatorum et pontificum Romanorum,* drawn up around 1270, while Bernard Gui (1281–1328) always uses the word *coronatio* (LP, 2:462, 467, etc.).

109. Despite numerous investigations, it has not been possible to determine whether the words *Sic transit* would already have been pronounced during the flax-burning ceremony at Gregory VII's coronation on Christmas, 1075 (see *Alexander von Roes. Schriften,* 188, note 3, cited by Klewitz, *Zeitschrift der Savigny-Stiftung für Rechtsgeschichte,* kan. Abt., 30, 1931, 97, et seq.). In my view, such a conclusion itself depends on making a deduction from the merely hypothetical possibility that the flax ritual was being practiced at the papal court as early as the eleventh century. On the implausibility of such a hypothesis, which rests on no established facts, see above, note 92. It is well-known that General Charles De Gaulle greeted the news of President John F. Kennedy's assassination with the words *Sic transit.*

110. Cor. 7: 31: "praeterit enim figura huius mundi"; and 1 John 2: 17: "mundus transit et concupiscentia eius"; cit. Alexander von Roes, *Schriften,* 188, note 3; see above, note 90.

111. Ibid. 188, note 3: "Doch dürften, was v. 222 vielleicht andeutet, 224 *(Sic transit)* aber fast gewiss macht, die Verse 215–224 vom Brauchtum bei der päpstlichen Krönungsprozession beherrscht sein; zu ihm gehört dann auch v. 216–218."

112. Dykmans, *Le cérémonial,* 1:180. Even when the pope was elected and crowned outside of Rome, Gregory X's ceremonial required that he hear a Te Deum at Saint Peter's before returning to the Lateran.

113. Eichmann, *Weihe,* 56.

114. Campi, *Dell'historia,* 2:346.

115. LC, 2:19. On the *diadema duplex,* see Ladner, "Der Ursprung," 474.

116. On the imperial and papal "Erstkrönung," see Deér, "Byzanz," 61–62.

117. LC, 2:33.

118. The *Vita Gregorii IX,* whose author may have been Niccolò of Anagni, nephew of the Agnani pope, can be dated between 1254 and 1265: Paravicini Bagliani, "La storiografia pontificia," 52–53. For the date of Stephen of Bourbon's work, see note 105.

119. There is no mention of burning flax in either the *Opus metricum* of Cardinal Jacopo Stefaneschi, an eyewitness of the coronations of Celestine V and Boniface VIII, or in the *ordo* preserved in the manuscript Toulouse 67, which updated the twelfth-century ceremonial with the *ordo* of Gregory X and the *Pontificale,* and which may have

been used for the coronation of Benedict XI at Rome on October 27, 1303: *Opus Metricum,* verses 345–354, ed. Seppelt, 107; for the Toulouse *ordo,* see Dykmans, *Le cérémonial,* 2:272, no. 15.

120. *Ordo* of Gregory X (ibid., 1:212, no. 268). The flax hung from a cord across the threshold of the choir, while according to Benedict's *Ordo XI,* for example, it was suspended from columns at the entrance of the basilica. The same is true of the *Ordo XIV;* the pope continued to play an exclusively active role (ibid., 2:399, no. 18). The source is a Roman sacramentary that we know through the codex *Ottob. lat.* 356 of the Vatican Library: Brinktrine, *Consuetudines,* 37–38 (= Van Dijk and Walker, *The Ordinal,* 32). On this important codex, see below, note 12.

121. *Rationale,* bk. 4, ch. 6, 13.

122. Schrick, *Der Königsspiegel,* 133: "unde sicut vidi, quando dominus papa processionaliter progreditur, manipulo stuppe super columpna in medio chori [= Innocent III] appenso ignis supponitur [= Durant], ne forte qui gloriosus incedit in temporali gloria delectetur [= Innocent]."

123. Turin, Archivio di Stato, *Protocolli rossi,* 2, fols. 79–84, ed. Dykmans, *Le cérémonial,* 3:462–473. See Schimmelpfennig, "Papal Coronations," 184. According to Dykmans, the *ordo* was followed for the coronation of Pope Martin V at Constance (Dec. 21, 1417).

124. Dykmans, *Le cérémonial,* 2:292–293, nos. 10–11, 13–15. It is highly likely that the *ordo* was used for the coronation of Pope Innocent VI (1352) and his successors at Avignon (Schimmelpfennig, "Papal Coronations," 184). With only one exception, all the articles of the first part that concerns us (arts. 1–15) agree with the *ordo* that had been used in 1316 for the consecration of John XXII (1316–34). It was a ceremonial text drawn up for use in papal coronations held *extra Urbem,* that is, outside Rome. The missing article, the penultimate (art. 14), is precisely that which concerns the flax. On Innocent VI, see Guidi, "La coronazione," 571–590.

125. See the texts cited in the preceding note. A wooden *cadestillum* was erected for the coronation of John XXII in 1316 (Dykmans, *Le cérémonial,* 2:299, no. 35, 2. The use of a similar *cadestillum* is attested for the coronations of 1335 and 1342, celebrated in the Dominican church at Avignon (ibid., 2:299, no. 63; and Schimmelpfennig, "Papal Coronations," 189). The sources make no mention of the flax burning ceremony.

126. Trans. Balzani, "La storia," 480; original text in Thompson, ed., *Chronicon,* 87. On the custom of presenting the emperor stones of all kinds for the construction of his tomb, see the analogous text by Martin of Troppau, cit. above, note 108; and Leontios v. Neapolis, *Leben,* ch. 19, 36. On the symbolism of mortality as applied to the

Holy Roman Emperors see, in general, Schramm, *Sphaira,* 86, and notes 6–7.

127. *Leonardi Dathi Epistolae,* 81. On Jacopo Angeli, see Weiss, "Jacopo Angeli," 803–827.

128. A second source for the coronation of Gregory XII is the chronicle compiled by a cleric from Franconia (perhaps Matthias Spengler) around 1415, which contains a description of the death of Innocent VII (Nov. 6, 1406), and of the coronations of Gregory XII (Dec. 19, 1406), Alexander V (July 7, 1409) and John XXIII (May 25, 1410): ed. Finke, "Eine Papstchronik," 361. The author frequently cites the *ordo* contained in the same codex (Eichstätt, Seminary Library, no. 292, ed. Kösters, *Studien,* 93; see also Dykmans, *Le cérémonial,* 3: 143, no. 6. For what interests us here, the Eichstätt *ordo* constitutes a fusion of *Ordo XIV* (ibid., 2:305–306, line 7), concerning coronation ceremonies when the pope is at Rome ("In primis ipse," down to line 15, "tempori congruentis"), and the *Ordo XIV* devoted to coronation ceremonies to be celebrated outside Rome, *extra Urbem* (ibid., 2:290– 305). Although the texts are independent, the author of the Eichstätt codex appears to have adapted the "Avignonese" ceremonial to the requirements of a Roman coronation. He presupposes that the pope will be staying at Saint Peter's, and will go to the Lateran only for the ceremony of taking possession (Kösters, *Studien,* 98). Even in the last decades of the thirteenth century, some popes stayed for lengthy periods at the Vatican (see Paravicini Bagliani, "La mobilità," 240– 245). For this reason, the source of the Eichstätt *ordo* may hark back to a thirteenth-century setting (Schimmelpfennig, *Die Zeremonienbücher,* 119); this would not contradict chronologically Stephen of Bourbon's *exemplum,* cited above. Other facts are needed, however, before it can be concluded that so categorical a reference to the Vatican as "the papal palace" could have been coined at the end of the thirteenth century.

129. *Acta Concilii Pisani,* ed. D'Achery, *Spicilegium,* 6:334: "Et illa die fuerunt multa solemnia, ut puta, de stupibus combustis dicendo: 'Sic transit.'" On Alexander V, see also the preceding note.

130. Two fragments of the *Ordo XIV* derive from it, and represent updates that can themselves be dated to around 1400 (*Barb. lat.* 570 and codex F. IV. 14 of the Biblioteca Nazionale of Turin; see Schimmelpfennig, *Die Zeremonienbücher,* 120 and 411; for the edition, see 377). As in the Eichstätt *ordo,* the setting was adapted to Rome (ibid., 376–377, no. 1). Like the "Avignonese" *ordo,* it contains a notice relating that "some believe it would be better if such a rite were held in front of the portals of the church, before the multitude, and in an elevated setting, *so that everyone can see* that earthly glory lasts but a brief time" (ibid., 377, no. 2). In the Turin codex, Francesco Giacomo (Piendebene) of

Montepulciano is again called *secretarius;* later he was bishop of Arezzo (1413 – 1433). The source of this fragment therefore predates 1413.

131. Ulrich von Richental, *Chronik,* ed. Buck, 126; idem, *Das Konzil,* ed. Feger, 2, fol. 102; see also Schimmelpfennig, *Die Zeremonienbücher,* 377, note 2.

132. Ibid., 258, no. 8. For the identification of places, see Schimmelpfennig, "Die Krönung," 207–208.

133. The cycle can be dated between 1505 and 1507: P. Misciatelli, *The Piccolomini Library in the Cathedral of Siena* (Siena 1924); A. Schmarsow, *Raphael und Pinturicchio in Siena* (Stuttgart 1880). See also *Le Vite di Pio II,* ed. Zimolo, 105, note 3. At Innocent VIII's coronation in 1484, Burchard was given the task of presenting the flax to the pope just before he was crowned, and of pronouncing the words of the rite (*Liber notarum,* ed. Celani, 1 : 75).

134. Dykmans, *L'oeuvre,* 1 : 70, no. 122.

135. For notices down to the late eighteenth century: Moroni, 70 : 92–93; for the twentieth century, see Bernhart, *Der Vatikan,* 349 (1951, 364).

136. Elze, " 'Sic transit,' " 41: "Ma penso che nessuno di questi vari gesti cerimoniali simbolizzi con altrettanta incisività le transitorietà e caducità umane quanto l'accensione dei fascetti di stoppa, che dal Quattrocento è testimoniata regolarmente solo nel cerimoniale della coronazione del papa e non altrettanto regolarmente per altri sovrani. E ciò mi sembra anche con piena giustificazione. Solo per il papa infatti un tale gesto simbolico assume il suo peino significato." The rite was performed in 1414 at Sigismund's coronation as king of Germany (Nuremberg, Sept. 25): *Deutsche Reichstagsakten,* 7 : 215 ("post cujus conclusionem dominus plebanus incendebat stupam sive linum et alte dicebat: 'serenissime rex, Sic transit' "); *Städtechroniken,* 3 : 344 and 363; 11 : 515 (see also F. X. Haimerl, *Das Prozessionswesen des Bistums Bamberg im Mittelalter* [Munich 1937], 97).

137. For a general treatment of the problem, see Eichmann, *Weihe;* Schimmelpfennig, "Ein bisher unbekannter Text," 43–70; idem, "Ein Fragment," 323–331; idem, *Die Zeremonienbücher,* 381 (a complete list of the sources on ceremonies pertaining to the pope's taking possession of the Lateran); Maccarrone, "Die Cathedra," 196–197; Boureau, *La papesse,* 108, et seq.; and Herklotz, "Der mittelalterliche Fassadenportikus," 46–48.

138. LP, 2:296. The text is identical in the Tortosa codex, published by C. Vogel in the new edition of the LP, 3 : 144.

139. LP, 2:297; see also Maccarrone, "La 'cathedra,' " 1312, note 192.

140. LP, 2:328, note 8.

141. LP, 2:327 (see also LP, 3:171).

142. *Bernardi vita prima,* bk. 2, ch. 7 (PL, 185: 268–269). In denouncing Anacletus II, the cardinals who elected Pope Innocent II accused him of having treated the papal seats "with contempt": "Sedes pontificum contrivit" (*Codex Uldarici,* ed. Jaffé, 248). The verb *contero* here suggests disrespect rather than actual destruction, and it is therefore useless to speculate whether the "ruined" chairs were made of wood, while the two marble seats located at the entrance to the inner basilica of Saint Sylvester would have remained undamaged, as Maccarrone points out in "La 'cathedra,'" 1314, note 194.

143. Albinus, LC, 2:123–125, no. 3; Cencius, ibid., 1:311–313 (48.77). The Basel *ordo* has been published by Schimmelpfennig, "Ein bisher unbekannter Text," 43–70; that of London in idem, "Ein Fragment," 323–333.

144. Deér, *Dynastic Porphyry Tombs,* 136–146.

145. *Descriptio Lateranensis Basilicae,* ed. Valentini and Zucchetti, *Codice,* 3:338; see also Schimmelpfennig, "Ein bisher unbekannter Text," 63, no. 28.

146. On the not very convincing proposal to interpret the position *inter* in the sense of the German locution "zwischen zwei Stühlen sitzen," which suggests indeterminancy and cannot apply to a rite of enthronement, see Maccarrone, "La 'cathedra,'" 1318, note 198.

147. Biblical translation from *New Oxford Bible,* 1405.

148. The presbytery is a gift of money that the pope traditionally distributed on solemn occasions.

149. Albinus, LC, 2:123–124, no. 3; Cencius, ibid., 1:311 b.

150. Ps. 112: 7–8; and 1 Sam. 2: 8 (biblical trans. from *New Oxford Bible,* 332): Albinus writes *stercorata* or *stercoraria;* Cencius and the Basel and London codices instead give the reading *stercorata.* Pius IV was the last pope to use the seat in 1540: afterward it was moved (along with the two porphyry chairs) to the Lateran cloister, where they can be seen today, arranged among other pieces that derive, however, from a different period. See D'Onofrio, *La papessa Giovanna,* 148–149, figs. 94–95.

151. *Liber diurnus Romanorum pontificum,* ed. von Sickel, 104: "neque enim hoc mea merita, karissimi [the speaker is the pope], quae nulla sunt, sed vestrae Christianitatis vota apud altissimum promeruerunt quod in me indigno desuper cernitis exultantes, ut nimirum omnipotens *de terra inopem et de stercore pauperem sublimaret,* prerogativam sacerdotii concederet dispensatoremque suae constitueret familiae"; see also Maccarrone, "La 'cathedra,'" 1315, note 196.

152. Guilellmus Neubrigensis, *Historia Anglicana,* in MGH, SS, 27:228: "De quo dicendum est, quomodo tamquam de pulvere elevatus sit, ut sederet in medio principum et apostolice teneret solium

glorie." On the rhetoric of humility in *De Consideratione,* see above, note 28.

153. A. Blaise [*Dictionnaire latin-français des auteurs chrétiens* (Strasbourg 1954), 775], translates the words *"de stercore"* in the biblical verse (Ps. 112: 7) as "fumier, excréments."

154. In the *Vita* of Pope Joan, B. Platina defines the *sedes stercorata* as follows: "questa sedia è stata così preparata affinchè colui che è investito di un si grande potere sappia che egli non è Dio, ma un uomo; che egli è così sottomesso alle necessità della natura e che deve defecare. Per questo motivo questa sedia viene giustamente definita stercoraria (escremenziale)." For the Latin text, see G. Gayda, *Vitae pontificum Romanorum* (Rome, 1932), 151–152; see also Boureau, *La papesse,* 29.

155. On this aspect, see ibid., 104.

156. Ps. 90: 13: "Super aspidem et basiliscum ambulabis et conculcabis leonem et draconem"; see Maccarrone, "La 'cathedra,'" 1311, note 190.

157. Schimmelpfennig, "Ein bisher unbekannter Text," 62, no. 26: "Hee quidem due sedes et illa, que dicitur stercorata, non fuerunt patriarchales, sed imperiales."

158. The fact that Albinus and Cencius spoke of the cardinals collectively reflects the influence of the conciliar decree of 1179, which no longer distinguished between the various orders of cardinals. For the decree of 1059, see the *Corpus iuris canonici,* ed. Friedberg, 1:77–79 (D. 23 c. 1); see also Jasper, *Das Papstwahldekret.* For the conciliar decree of 1179, see the *Corpus iuris canonici,* 2:51 (10 1.6.6) and *Conciliorum oecumenicorum decreta,* 211; see also Maleczek, "Abstimmungsarten," 103, et seq.

159. Albinus and Cencius were the first to prescribe an active role for the cardinals, who accompanied the pope on horseback right up to the throne. The youngest cardinal priest blessed the ashes; the first of the most important order—that of the bishops—placed them on the pope and pronounced to him out loud the words meant to remind him of death and the dust of the tomb. The youngest of the cardinal deacons initiated the procession to the church of Santa Sabina. For all of these problems, see above, 27–28.

160. Isidore, *Etymologiae,* 16:5, 5: "Porphyretes in Aegypto est rubeus, candidis intervenientibus punctis. Nominis eius causa quod rubeat ut purpura."

161. Until the time of Napoleon the two marble seats were kept in the Lateran palace: see E. Visconti, *Descrizione.* By the Treaty of Tolentino, Napoleon had one of them taken to Paris, where it remains today (in the Louvre). (F. de Clarac, *Musée de sculpture antique et moderne ou description . . . du Louvre,* II [Paris, 1841], 993, note 631; Lauer, *Le palais,* 158, fig. 61). The other is in the Vatican Museum (Deér, *Dynastic*

Porphyry Tombs, 142–146). See also Maccarrone, "La 'cathedra,'" 1312, note 191; and the excellent illustrations in D'Onofrio, *La papessa Giovanna,* figs. 85–91.

162. This hypothesis, already advanced by Montfaucon, was confirmed by the further investigations of Deér, *Dynastic Porphyry Tombs,* 142–146. For a full historiographical discussion, see Maccarrone, "La 'cathedra,'" 1319, note 200. The use of the letter *sigma* to designate bathers' seats located in the cooling room *(frigidarium)* is confirmed, for example, by a passage in Sidonius Apollinaris (c. 480/490). He added that for the public baths crimson marble was imported from Ethiopia, which matches exactly the marble *(rosso antico)* of the two Lateran chairs: Sidonius Apollinaris, *Lettres,* II, ed. A. Loyen, Paris 1970, bk. 2, 2, 46; see also Maccarrone, "La 'cathedra,'" 1319, note 200.

163. Constantinus Porphyrogenitus imperator, *De Caerimoniis aulae Byzantinae,* 2:1, 15, ed. Reiskij, 521 and 587; Treitinger, *Die oströmische . . . Reichsidee,* 32, note 1; Deér, *Dynastic Poprhyry Tombs,* 145; and Maccarrone, "La 'cathedra,'" 1322, note 208.

164. *Vita Honorii II, LP,* 2:327; see above, note 39.

165. Gandolfo, "Reimpiego," 203–207. See now also Deér, *Dynastic Porphyry Tombs,* 140–141, Maccarrone, "La 'cathedra,'" 1325, note 215; and Stroll, *Symbols,* 1–15.

166. Liutprandus, *Historia Ottonis,* c. 22, in MGH, *Scriptores rer. Germanic.,* 175; Maccarrone, "La 'cathedra,'" 1323, note 212. The *ferula* is "der gerade Stab des römischen Bischofs" (Servatius, *Paschalis II,* 39, note 23). According to Eichmann, *Weihe,* 32, et seq., the *ferula* derived from the imperial sceptre; but Deér, *Dynastic Poprhyry Tombs,* 14, note 86, disagrees. The *ferula* was a symbol used for the "Belehnungen innerhalb des Kirchenstaates," and was therefore a symbol of temporal power (Deér, *Papsttum,* 16, et seq.; so also Ladner, *Die Papstbildnisse,* 3:309: "vielmehr war und blieb die Ferula, wie die Schlüssel, ein Symbol der Herrschaft, einschliesslich der 'Korrektion' d.h. aber von Strafe und Busse"); according to Salmon, *Mitra,* 67–73, the *ferula* instead represented both temporal and spiritual power. Rather significantly, the Dominican liturgist William Durant submitted this symbol of power to an interpretation that emphasized its representation of humility: *Rationale,* bk. 3, ch. 15: "Aliquando in ferula scribitur homo: ut Pontifex se hominem memoretur, et de potestate collata non elevetur. . . ."

167. *LP,* 2:296. The text is identical to that of the Tortosa codex, pub. by C. Vogel in the new edition of *LP,* 3:144.

168. See also Maccarrone, "La 'cathedra,'" 1316–1317.

169. Vogel and Elze, *Le pontifical,* 1:292–306 *(Ordines LXXXI–LXXXIII);* Schimmelpfennig, "Ein bisher unbekannter Text, 62 n., cites Epifanius of Salamis, *De XII gemmis,* ed. Guenther, 743–773, no. 244. In his sermon on Gregory the Great, Pope Innocent III devoted consider-

able attention to the symbolism of the precious stones in the liturgical vestments of the "pontifex" (PL, 217: 519–522).

170. Biblical trans. from *New Oxford Bible*, 1399.

171. Albinus (LC, 2:124) and Cencius (LC, 1:311, 48, no. 79) write: "Muscus includitur ad percipiendum odorem, ut ait apostolus: 'Cristi bonus odor sumus Deo'"; to *odorem*, the London ordo adds: "quod significat bonam conversationem" (Schimmelpfennig, "Ein Fragment," 328, no. 16); see also Eichmann, *Weihe*, 50.

172. Albinus (LC, 2:123, no. 3). The texts of Cencius (LC, 1:312, 48, no. 79) and of the ceremonial conserved in the London codex (Schimmelpfennig, "Ein Fragment," 328, no. 14) are identical. The Basel codex (idem, "Ein bisher unbekannter Text," 62, no. 21) instead contains an insignificant variant: "In illis autem sedibus sic sedere oportet electum ac si videatur inter duos lectos iacere, id est ut accumbat inter Petri primatum et Pauli assiduam operationis praedicationem."

173. The pope must sit as though lying. Both positions must be kept in mind also because, on the seat to the left, the pope must "pause for a bit of time": "In qua dum aliquantula mora pausat" (Albinus and Cencius); "Post aliquantula mora pausaverit" (London ordo, ed. Schimmelpfennig, "Ein Fragment," 328, no. z13).

174. Poncelet, "Vie," 290; see also Boureau, *La papesse*, 350, note 42. For the reading of this and other texts, I wish to extend my heartfelt thanks to my colleague at the University of Lausanne, Jean-Daniel Morerod.

175. Maccarrone, *Lotharii*, 3, 4, 80: "Qui modo sedebat gloriosus in throno, modo iacet despectus in tumulo; qui modo fulgebat ornatus in aula, modo sordet nudus in tumba; qui modo vescebatur deliciis in cenaculo, modo consumitur a vermibus in sepulcro."

176. Under Benedict III (855–58), the pope's name had begun to be written on chancery bulls. Two centuries later, under Victor II (1055–57), Saint Peter was portrayed on the front *(recto)* receiving the keys extended to him from heaven by the hand of Christ; on the back *(verso)*, the figure of Rome *(Aurea Roma)* was circumscribed by the pope's name, written in the genetive: *Victoris papae II.* P. Rabikauskas, *Diplomatica pontificia*, Rome 1964, 122. A brief interruption in this centuries-long development took place under Pope Paul II (1464–71), who substituted for his name on the back an image of the pope enthroned, adorned with the symbols of his power, flanked by a cardinal on each side and several kneeling personages; Miglio, *"Vidi thiaram,"* 276.

177. See above, 39–40.

178. Valentini and Zucchetti, *Codice*, 3:384: "Sic inclusit corpus beati Petri et Pauli." The *Liber pontificalis* refers only to *Petri.* According to it (LP, 1:312), Gregory the Great had ordered the celebration of masses "super corpus beati Petri . . . item et in ecclesiam beati Pauli

apostoli eadem fecit." Two manuscripts that may date back as far as the eleventh century or the early decades of the twelfth (*Vat. lat.* 3764 = E1 and *Vat. lat.* 3761 = G; see also LP, 1 : 195 and 200) add *et Pauli* at precisely the point at which the *Liber pontificalis,* in its purest manuscript versions, had only *beati Petri* (LP, 1 : 312; see Dykmans, *Le cérémonial,* 1 : 38, note 60). The legend makes no further reference, however, to the presence of the bodies of Peter and Paul in the Altar of Confession.

179. LP, 1 : 150.

180. Bibl. Vat., *Vat. lat.* 3627, fol. 16v; see also ibid., 1 : 38, note 61. In the edition of Valentini and Zucchetti, *Codice,* 3 : 421, the difference between the two authors is not indicated: "De altare Petri et Pauli. Ante aditum, qui vadit in confessionem beati Petri, est altare apostolorum Petri et Pauli, *ubi eorum ossa pretiosa, ut dicitur, ponderata fuerunt.*" The final phrase is an addition by the canon Romanus. The legend was picked up by the *ordo* of Gregory X (1272–73): "at the altar (of Peter and Paul) were weighed the remains of the blessed apostles Peter and Paul" (Dykmans, *Le cérémonial,* 1 : 196, no. 157). But even earlier, Bartolomeus of Trent, O.P., had inserted the new version of the legend into his hagiographic compilation dating from the years 1245–51: in the time of Pope Cornelius, the Greeks reputedly threw the bodies of the two apostoles into a cavern of the catacombes; the bones "were then taken out and divided in halves between Saint Peter and Saint Paul; with the utmost diligence they were then reassembled and venerated" (Bibl. Vat., *Barb. lat.* 2300, fol. 17v, cit. ibid., 1 : 38, note 61). In 1265 the English liturgist John Beleth, author of the *Explicatio divinorum officiorum,* reported that after Emperor Constantine's conversion to Christianity it was decided to build a church for each of the two apostles, whose bodies had long been buried together: "since it was unclear which bones were Saint Peter's and which Saint Paul's, prayers and fasts were held, and a voice from heaven replied: 'The bigger bones are those of the Preacher, the smaller those of the Fisherman.' The bones of the two saints, having separated themselves spontaneously, were carried into the churches that had been consecrated to them" (*Summa de ecclesiasticis officiis,* ed. Douteil, 271). But this version of the legend favored one of the two apostoles (Paul, the Preacher!), and therefore could not be universally accepted. In his *Legenda aurea,* Jacobus de Voragine repeats Beleth's version and adds: "But other authors assert that Pope Sylvester had the largest and smallest bones weighed in equal measures on a scale, and gave each church exactly half of the two bodies" (Jacobi a Voragine, *Legenda Aurea,* 378; thus also Guilellmus Durandus, *Rationale,* bk. 7, ch. 15, fol. 292).

181. Though the use of porphyry reflects a conscious embrace of the *imitatio imperii* ("imitation of empire") from the eighth century

onward, in ecclesiastical contexts porphyry had initially been used only for the tombs of saints. The decision of twelfth-century popes to begin constructing porphyry monuments thus also amounted to an appropriation of a privilege that in earlier centuries had been reserved exclusively to the cult of saints and martyrs. The use of porphyry for imperial tombs had already ceased by the fifth century, although the marble sarcophagus containing the remains of Otto II (d. 983) had a porphyry cover; see Herklotz, 'Sepulcra,' " 110–113, who quite rightly cites two famous articles of the *Dictatus papae:* "only the pope may use the imperial insignia" (8: *Quod solus possit uti imperialibus insigniis*), and "the Roman pontiff, if canonically ordained, is undoubtedly sanctified by the merits of Blessed Peter" (23: *Quod Romanus pontifex, si canonice fuerit ordinatus, meritis beati Petri indubitanter efficitur sanctus*); see *Gregorii VII Registrum*, 2:55a, ed. Caspar, *Das Register*, 1:202 and 207.

182. Jackson, *Vive le roi!*, 133. Charles V's *ordo* was the first to describe the king assuming such a reclining position on a bed at the moment in which two bishops arrived to lead him to the coronation ceremony. Even according to Saint Louis's *ordo,* datable to around 1250 (Godefroy, *Le cérémonial français*, 1:13–25 (lat.: *exeunte autem rege de thalamo*), 26–30 (a thirteenth-century French translation), at the beginning of the ceremony the king got out of the *"thalamus,"* a word which in this context could be taken to refer to a bed: Le Goff, "A Coronation Program," 46–71. Moreover, the prescription of Louis's *ordo* dates back literally to the Romano-Germanic pontifical of Mainz (961): Schramm, "Die Krönung," 310–311; see also Jackson, *Vive le roi!*, 255, note 11: "Primum, exeunte illo [the king] thalamum. . . ."

183. Le Goff, "A Coronation Program," 52. According to Saint-Simon, *Mémoire,* 221, the prince "entièrement couché et trouvé comme dormant sur son lict entre ses rideaux fermés" is "comme nud puisqu'il n'a qu'une camisole de satin sur sa chemise, comme déchaussé puisqu'il ny bottines ny esperons . . . tout cela ne peut marquer qu'un homme qui ne pense à rien, qui est enseveli dans le sommeil assés profondément puisqu'il n'a point ouï ce qui se vient de passer, quoy qu'assés long à sa porte, qui se laisse lever par qui le prend, et conduire encore assoupi et mal éveillé où on le veut mener."

184. For this affirmation see, as always, Elze, " 'Sic transit,' " passim.

185. The relics were believed to have been a gift from the Emperor Constantine to Pope Sylvester: Schimmelpfennig, "Ein bisher unbekannter Text," 63, no. 28. The earlier versions of the *Descriptio Lateranensis Ecclesiae* (eleventh–twelfth centuries) affirm that at that altar "only the pope or a cardinal bishop" could celebrate mass. On the altar was a "wooden table, on which were painted the images of

Peter and Paul," whom Constantine admitted to Pope Sylvester having first seen in a dream before he was baptized: Valentini and Zucchetti, *Codice,* 3 : 338.

186. Ibid., 3 : 356 (description of the church of Saint Lawrence). According to the editor, in the oldest codex, "A," dating slightly after 1073, the words *umbilicus* and *praeputium* have disappeared. In the chapter "De Arca et Sanctis Sanctorum, quae sunt in Basilica Salvatoris," the words "Et circumcisio Domini" appear only in the codex containing the oldest version of the *Descriptio,* that of John the Deacon (written for Alexander III). They appear as a marginal addition written in the hand of the same copiest, or of a contemporary; ibid., 337.

187. Jacopo Caetani Stefaneschi, *Opus Metricum,* lines 345–354, ed. Seppelt, 107.

188. The sources are Gregory X's *ordo* (see Van Dijk and Walker, *The Ordinal,* 546–547) and the thirteenth-century pontifical of the Roman curia (13 B): Andrieu, *Le pontifical,* 2 : 378, nos. 48–49. The *ordo* discovered by Dykmans may reflect the Avignonese situation; however, it does not report the ceremony of possession: Dykmans, *Le cérémonial,* 3 : 462–473. Nor does Pierre Ameil provide an *ordo coronationis.* The *ordo* of Francesco of Conzié cites, for the coronation and the "possession," Gregory X's thirteenth-century pontifical and ceremonial (ibid., 298, no. 175). The author of a chronicle on the death of Gregory XII simply refers to the existence of an *ordo* (Finke, "Eine Papstchronik," 361: "et fuit ordo in equitando, ut in proximis precedentibus foliis continetur").

189. Dykmans, *L'oeuvre,* 1 : 82, no. 157; similarly, later on, in the modern *Caeremoniale Romanum:* Catalani, *Pontificale,* 1 : 138, ch. 24. The confusion is already evident in the B. Platina's *Vitae pontificum Romanorum* (1474). In the *Vita* of Pope Joan, the perforated chair is explicitly identified with the *sedes stercorata:* ed. Gayda, *Vitae pontificum Romanorum,* 151–152; see Boureau, *La papesse,* 29.

190. Giovanni Burcardo, *Alla corte,* 90.

191. That is, not only to contest the legend of Saint Joan (Cancellieri, *Storia,* 60–112; and Boureau, *La papesse,* 31, 56, 114). It is beyond the chronological scope of the present work to analyze the ritual during which there was displayed to the pope while he sat before the Lateran basilica "a bronze rooster mounted atop a porphyry column by the door of the basilica to remind him that he must excuse the shortcomings of others just as Christ had pardoned Peter, the first pope, for his failures in having denied him three times"; see Cancellieri, *Storia,* 54, note 3. The rooster is reputed to have been moved into the basilica, and then the cloister, by Pope Alexander VII, ibid. See also Moroni, 70 : 91–92.

192. Turner, *The ritual process*, 166–203, ch. 5: "Humility and Hierarchy: The Liminality of Status Elevation and Reversal."

193. The anecdotes are obviously more numerous for the modern period. Moroni, 70:93 recounts that "in 1585 Sixtus V was crowned in the presence of the ambassadors from Japan. While the flax was being burned, four times the verse was recited 'Holy Father, thus passes the glory of this world.' But Sixtus, always ready with a sharp reply, unlike the custom of other popes who remained silent during the rite, with a hearty soul replied out loud: 'Our glory will never pass away, for we have no other glory than to render good justice.' And then, turning to the Japanese ambassadors, he added: 'Tell our sons, your princes, the substance of this noble ceremony.'" In 1769 Clement XIV "seeing that in the ceremony of burning the flax it failed to catch fire, perhaps because it was damp, showed great pleasure, taking it as a good omen that his pontificate would last a long time . . ." (ibid.).

194. At Byzantium, the ablution of the emperor's hands could have a humbling significance; but it is nevertheless true that on Ash Wednesday the emperor symbolically washed his hands in "Pilate's inkwell": see Treitinger, *Die oströmische . . . Reichsidee*, 231, note 104; and Kantorowicz, *Les deux corps du roi*, 380, note 24.

195. *Annales Genuenses*, RIS, 17:1019 B. I owe this point to the generosity of the late Jean Coste.

Chapter Two

1. Pier Damiani, *Disceptatio synodalis*, in MGH, *Libelli*, 1:93; cit. Kantorowicz, *Les deux corps du roi*, 544, note 402.

2. Ibid., 316.

3. Epistola 46, *Die Briefe*, 2:41. In his treatise "On the Celibacy of Priests," dedicated to Nicholas II (1059–61), Damian added that the pope "acts in place of Christ" (PL, 145: 386; cit. Maccarrone, *Vicarius Christi*, 86).

4. In a letter he addressed to Clement II in April 1047, the pope is "Vicar of God" (epist. 26, *Die Briefe*, 1:241).

5. Bernardus Claraevallensis, *De consideratione*, bk. 2, ch. 8, 16, ed. Leclercq and Rochais, *Sancti Bernardi Opera*, 3:424.

6. Ibid., bk. 2, ch. 8, 15; 3:423.

7. Ibid.; trans. Gastaldelli, 813.

8. Ibid., bk. 3, ch. 4, 17; trans. Gastaldelli, 853.

9. *Sancti Bernardi Opera*, ed. Leclercq and Rochais, 8, Epistola 1: 313 (= epistola 126, PL, 182: 275). The model is biblical: see Gen. 2: 23: "dixitque Adam hoc nunc os ex ossibus meis et caro de carne tua"; Gen. 29: 14: "os meum es et caro mea"; 2 Sam. 19, 13: "nonne os meum es et caro mea"; 1 Chron. 11: 1: "os tuum sumus et caro tua."

The passage from Paul, Eph. 5: 30 — "quia membra sumus corporis eius de carne eius et de ossibus eius"—refers to all Christians.

10. In a letter of April 10, 1153, addressed to the dean and canons of Saint Peter's in the Vatican, Eugenius III declared that the pope took the place of Christ: epistola 575 (PL, 180: 1589 = JL, 9714); cit. Maccarrone, *Vicarius Christi*, 100. Among the first Roman sources to use the title should be noted John the Deacon's description of the Lateran Basilica (in the version dating from the mid–twelfth century); see Herklotz, "Der mittelalterliche Fassadenportikus," 93, note 271.

11. Maccarrone, *Vicarius Christi*, 106.

12. PL, 217: 519 (*Sermo XIII* on the feast day of Saint Gregory the Great). In the *Summa Reginensis,* composed in 1192 by one of Huguccio's followers, the word bishop *(episcopus)* is glossed with the explanation that it was he who "holds the person of Christ *(personam habet Christi),"* cit. Maccarrone, *Vicarius Christi*, 107, notes 89 and 91.

13. Reg. 1 : 354 (*Die Register,* 1 : 515).

14. Ibid., 1 : 515. For the legates, see Reg. 1 : 526 (ibid., 1 : 759); Reg. 2 : 114 (2 : 239); Reg. 2 : 193 (2 : 367); for the vicars, see Reg. 2 : 204 (2 : 399).

15. Reg. 1 : 445 (ibid., 1 : 668); Reg. 1 : 495 (1 : 724).

16. The formula dates back to Leo I (440 – 61): "Vices enim nostras ita tuae credidimus charitati, ut in partem sis vocatus sollicitudinis, non in plenitudinem potestatis," epist. 14, PL, 54: 671; see also Rivière, " '*In partem sollicitudinis,' "* 210–31; and W. Ullmann, "Leo I and the Theme of Papal Primacy," *Journal of Theological Studies* 11 (1960): 25 – 51. Gratian included Leo's declaration in the *Decretum* (C. 3 q. 6 c. 8) and used the term *plenitudo potestatis* in a *dictum* (Dict. pr. C. 9 q. 3), thus definitively favoring the diffusion of the concept, especially because he inserted into his *Concordantia discordantium canonum* two analogous texts, a false letter of Pope Gregory IV (C. 2 q. 6 c. 11) and a pseudo-Isidoran text (C. 2 q. 6 c. 12). In Gratian's time, however, the term was not yet reserved exclusively to the papal office. The twelfth-century decretists in fact hesitated to use a formula that could still be applied to the plenipotentiary powers of ambassadors and bishops (Tierney, *Foundations,* 143). The popularity of the formula was assured by the enthusiasm with which Bernard of Clairvaux embraced it (*De consideratione,* 2, 8, 16; 3, 4, 14; epist. 131 and 132) and by Huguccio's classic definition: "full power exists when it contains an order *[praeceptum],* general validity, and necessity: these three elements are found united in the pope, while a bishop possesses only the first and the third" (*Glossa Palatina, ad Dist.* 11 c. 2, cit. ibid., 146). The papacy used the formula only in the last decades of the twelfth century. Thus, it shows up incidentally already in one of Lucius III's letters: PL, 201 : 1288; see Zerbi, *Papato,* 170–173. By the first year of Innocent III's pontificate (1198) it had entered the

language of the papal chancery. The references to it in Innocent's decretals have been assembled by Watt, "The Term," 175–177. The canonists immediately adopted it: indeed, the term appears in all the collections of decretals of this period, the so-called *Quinque Compilationes Antiquae:* ibid., 165. At the very outset of his pontificate Innocent wrote: "Although our Lord Jesus Christ, when he instituted his church, gave the same power of binding and loosing the faithful to all of his disciples, he willed that in this church one of them, the Blessed Apostle Peter, should have preeminence. He thus in fact declared: Thou art Peter, and upon this rock I will build my church. He therefore instructed all the faithful that, in the same way that between God and mankind there was only one mediator, Christ made man, he who, reestablishing peace between heaven and earth . . . reestablished unity among them; so also, within his church, there was only one head, common to all, who received from him his power and exercised it for him. . . . And it is precisely in virtue of this power, given to the Blessed Peter by the Lord himself, that the Holy Roman Church, instituted and founded by our Lord Jesus Christ through the Blessed Peter, received authority over all the other churches, in order that the decisions of his providence should be received definitively everywhere": Reg. 1:316, *Die Register,* 1:448.

17. Innocent III, sermon for the feast of Saints Peter and Paul (PL, 217:551); see also PL, 217:656.

18. Innocent III, sermon for the feast of Saint Gregory the Great (PL, 217:517); see Bougerol, "La papauté," 266.

19. PL, 217:665; and below, chap. 3.

20. Kempf, *Regestum,* 6.

21. J. Leclercq, *L'idée de la royauté du Christ au Moyen Age* (Paris, 1959), 59.

22. Maccarrone, " 'Ubi est papa,' " 371–382.

23. *Decretum Gratiani,* D. 93 c. 4, ed. Friedberg, 1:321.

24. J. F. von Schulte, *Die Summa,* 160. The *Summa magistri Rolandi* (ed. Thaner, *Summa,* 11), composed more or less contemporaneously (R. Weigand, "Magister Rolandus und Papst Alexander III," *Archiv für katholisches Kirchenrecht,* 149 [1980], 3–44), again repeated Gratian's *dictum* citing the *limina apostolorum.*

25. *Summa Stephani,* ed. J. F. von Schulte, 112–113.

26. *The Summa Parisiensis,* ed. McLaughlin, 71.

27. Maccarrone, " 'Ubi est papa,' " 377.

28. "Idem intelligo si curie Romane, ubicumque sit"; M. Maccarrone's transcription of the Vatican codices *Pal. lat.* 626, fol. 89rv; and *Barb. lat.* 272, fol. 53v: idem, ibid., 376, note 29.

29. Kempf, *Regestum,* 48, note 18. And further: "The pope is the plenipotentiary of Him who rules over kings and governs princes and

gives kingdoms to whom he finds suitable" (sermon for the feast of Gregory the Great: PL, 217:517); "The pope is the vicar of Him whose kingdom has no limits" (PL, 216:1044); see also PL, 217:552, 778– 779. For a general view of this issue, see Bougerol, "La papauté," 266. The concept of the royalty of Christ is at the center of the pictorial program of the chapel of Saint Sylvester in Tivoli, and was probably inspired by Innocent III. The frescoes, datable to around 1210–55, are believed to have been executed by an artist close to the "Master of the Translations" of the cathedral crypt of Anagni: Lanz, *Die romanischen Wandmalereien.*

30. MGH, SS, 24:737: "Viterbium tandem deveni et ibidem Romam inveni"; see Maccarrone, *Studi,* 60–61.

31. Pagnotti, "Niccolò," 91.

32. Sinibaldo Fieschi, *Apparatus,* fol. 117a, gloss on 10, 2, 24 *ad verbum Apostolorum;* see Maccarrone, " 'Ubi est papa,' " 377, note 35.

33. Commenting on the same canonistic text (10, 2, 24, 4), Hostiensis declared, concerning the words *Limina apostolorum,* "et dic Apostolorum, scilicet Petri et Pauli, id est Curiam Romanam: nam ubi papa, ibi Roma. Et ex hoc patet, quod ubi papa sit, ibi et Apostoli esse intelliguntur." Full text in ibid., 378. See also Hostiensis, *In quintum decretalium librum commentaria,* fol. 60va, comment on X, 5, 20, 4. The idea that Rome is wherever the pope is found expression also in the *Siete Partidas, partida* 1, tit. 10, ley 4.

34. "Quia non ubi Roma est, ibi papa est, sed econverso."

35. Hostiensis, *Summa aurea,* fol. 30r, *ad* X, 1, 8, 4, line *De corpore B. Petri sumptum.*

36. *Decretum Gratiani,* D. 40 c. 12 *(Multi sacerdotes):* "locus enim non sanctificat hominem, sed homo locum"; for the comments of the decretists (from Ruffinus to Johannes Teutonicus), see Lindner, "Die sogenannte Erbheiligkeit," 15–26.

37. Cit. McCready, "The Papal Sovereign," 183, note 28.

38. Jung, *Alvaro Pelayo,* 150, note 2: "Corpus Christi mysticum ibi est, ubi est caput, scilicet papa." Kantorowicz, *Les deux corps du roi,* 453, note 33, observes that the passage from Ignatius, *Ad Smyrn.,* 8:2, cannot be translated as "Where there is the bishop, there is the church," but as "Where there is Christ, there is the church.' " This indicates even further the significance of the equation Christ = pope that was established in the twelfth and thirteenth centuries.

39. Alvarus Pelagius, *Collirium,* ed. Scholz, *Unbekannte,* 2: 506–507.

40. Baldus, c. 4 X 2, 24, line 11, fol. 249, cit. Kantorowicz, *Les deux corps du roi,* 454, note 35.

41. Bernardus Claraevallensis, *De consideratione,* 4, 4, 9 (PL, 182: 778; ed. Leclercq and Rochais, *Sancti Bernardi Opera,* 3:455).

42. Johannes Sarisberiensis, *Historia pontificalis* 21, 51, 9; see Miczka, *Das Bild,* 138 note 177.

43. Millor and Brooke, *The Letters,* 2:432, no. 234: ". . . audivit et vidit Ecclesiae Romanae, cuius membrum est"; see Miczka, *Das Bild,* 139, note 176. Lucius III declared Archbishop William of Reims, cardinal priest of Santa Sabina, to be a *magnum Ecclesiae membrum* (JL, 14799, June 2, 1182); see Sägmüller, *Die Thätigkeit,* 225. During his pontificate, the head-members *(caput-membra)* relationship was incorporated into the language of the canonists. In the *Summa 'Et est sciendum'* (c. 1185), "the term Roman church is taken 'for the pope alone' *[pro solo papa],* sometimes 'for head and members' *[pro capite et membris],* or else for the pope and the college of cardinals"; see Gillmann, "Die Dekretglossen," 224. According to Leclerc, " *'Pars corporis papae,' "* 2: 185, between this step and its subsequent (thirteenth-century) development there would be only "plus de précision." In the *Summa 'Et est sciendum,'* the cardinals are "members (of the church)" *(membra [Ecclesiae]);* in the thirteenth century, instead, they are "part of the pope's body" *(pars corporis papae).* This reflects not merely greater precision, but a fundamental distinction: see also Imkamp, *Das Kirchenbild,* 286.

44. *Ottonis et Rahewini Gesta,* 86–87; see Miczka, *Das Bild,* 138, note 176.

45. Boso, *Vita Alexandri III,* LP, 2:417.

46. Letter 345 of the first year of his pontificate, *Die Register,* 1: 515, et seq. (PL, 214:319–320); see also Watt, "The Constitutional Law," 152, et seq.; and Maleczek, *Papst,* 283. In a letter of November 15, 1202, devoted to the problem of the election of the new archbishop of Amalfi, Innocent III again cites the tradition, describing one of the candidates, Peter, Cardinal of Santa Marcello, as "a great member of the Roman church" *(membrum magnum Ecclesiae Romanae).* Innocent refused to confirm Peter's election to the bishopric: "tum quia nolebamus eodem cardinale, utpote tam magno membro Ecclesiae Romanae, carere . . ." (Potthast 1761). In another letter of late 1201, Innocent refers to a cardinal as "a member of the head" *(membrum capitis)* (Potthast 1546; see Maleczek, *Papst,* 284, note 207). The formula was not the pope's, but came from the arguments of the canons of Ravenna who favored the election of Soffredus, cardinal priest of Saint Praxedes, to the archbishopric: "etsi talis conditio fuisset adiecta, poterat tamen de Romane sedis collegio propter ipsius privilegium prefata postulari persona [i.e. Soffredus], cum membra capitis a membra corporis censeri non debeant aliena." In one of Pope Clement IV's letters, as well, cardinals and pope are defined as being members *(membra)* of a single church subject to a single head *(caput),* Christ (Potthast 20201, letter to Henry of Castile, Dec. 30, 1267): "Parce igitur persequi cardinalem praedictum, quem tamquam specialem Ecclesiae filium, immo nobile

membrum eius non potes tangere, nobis et aliis fratribus nostris intactis, cum in Domino corpus unum et invicem singula membra simus"; cit. Sägmüller, *Die Thätigkeit,* 226.

47. Paul, Eph. 5: 30: "quia membra sumus corporis eius de carne eius et de ossibus eius"; see above, 59.

48. Leclerc, *"'Pars corporis papae,'"* 185.

49. For the relevant texts, see ibid., 186; and Tierney, *Foundations,* 211, note 2.

50. *Cod. Iust.* 9, 8, 5: "virorum illustrium qui consiliis et consistorio nostro intersunt, senatorum etiam, nam et ipsi pars corporis nostri sunt"; Kantorowicz, *Les deux corps du roi,* 455, note 42; see also *Cod. Iust.* 12, 1, 8. Frederick II, too, in 1244 at Verona, designated the imperial electors as "princes of the empire, noble members . . . of our body" *(imperii principes nobilia membra . . . corporis nostri)* (MGH, *Constitutiones,* 2:333 no. 244). In Innocent III's ecclesiology, the bond between pope and cardinals was intimate and privileged, but not exclusive: he called upon the *katholikos* Gregory and his supporters to acknowledge that they were "part of our body" *(pars nostri corporis), Die Register,* 2:407: ". . . confiteris et te ac fratres et coepiscopos tuos partem nostri corporis recognoscis . . ."; see Imkamp, *Das Kirchenbild,* 287.

51. Hostiensis, *Lectura,* at c. 23 X v, 33, tit. IV, 86, V°; see Leclerc, *"'Pars corporis papae,'"* 185–186.

52. In his testament, dictated at Viterbo on October 29, 1271, Cardinal Henry of Susa (Hostiensis) calls without hesitation for the dismemberment of his corpse to facilitate its transport for burial (Paravicini Bagliani, *I testamenti,* 134, no. 2).

53. Hostiensis, ch. *Ecclesia vestra,* cit. Perez, *Pentateuchum fidei,* bk. 2, *dubium* 3, *caput* 8, 20 (= Rocaberti, *Bibliotheca,* 4:705 D); see Magri, *Hierolexicon,* 126: "quia cardinales cum papa incorporantur. . . ."

54. Hostiensis, *Apparatus* 3.5.19, *episcopi Prenestinensis;* cit. Watt, "The Constitutional Law," 153.

55. Denifle, "Die Denkschriften der Colonna gegen Bonifaz VIII. und der Cardinäle gegen die Colonna," *Archiv für Litteratur- und Kirchengeschichte des Mittelalters* 5 (1989): 509–524.

56. Their political motives were quite obvious, but this was certainly not the first time that the terms themselves were used. It is therefore not possible to accept the view of Wilks, *The Problem,* 458, note 3: "From now on they are to be *coniudicatores et coadiutores* with the pope." These are terms that we find already being applied to the cardinals in the writings of Bernard of Clairvaux.

57. The letter *Non mediocri* (1439), *Codicis iuris canonici fontes,* 1 (Vatican City, 1932), no. 50; see also L. Thomassin, *Ancienne et nouvelle discipline de l'Église,* 2 (Paris, 1864), 425–426; Leclerc, *"'Pars corporis pape,'"* 188.

58. LP, 2:446.

59. Jacopo Caetani Stefaneschi, *Opus metricum*, ed. Seppelt, 100: "Post ipsam (crucem) quadratus equus . . . cigneus ad dextram vehitur." Matthew of Acquasparta, one of the cardinals closest to Boniface VIII, emphasized the theme of the crucifixion in his seal: Gardner, "Some Cardinals' Seals," 95.

60. Rocca, *De sacrosancto Christi corpore*, 37–73.

61. Rocca, *Thesaurus*, 2:374–378; see also Alexander a Turre Cremensis, *De fulgendo radio*, radius 22 (in Rocaberti, *Bibliotheca*, 2:55–57); and Jean Papire Masson, *Libri sex de episcopis Urbis, qui Romanam Ecclesiam rexerunt* (Paris, 1586), 286–287v.

62. Amalricus Augerii, in RIS, 3:2, c. 9. See also Acts 17, 3: "Hic est Jesus Christus, quem ego annuntio vobis."

63. Dante, *Purg*. 20, 86–87: "veggio in Alagna entrar lo fiordaliso / e nel vicario suo Cristo esser catto."

64. Alvarus Pelagius, *De statu et planctu*, bk. 1, ch. 13, fol. 4r.

65. Ibid., fol. 4r.

66. Antonius de Butrio, *Super prima primi decretalium commentarii*, *glossa ad* 2, X, I, 7, fol. 154ra, cit. Maccarrone, *Vicarius Christi*, 237, note 9.

67. The bust of Christ in the apse of Saint John Lateran, considerably restored, is of paleo-Christian origin and was conserved, as its inscription states, by Torriti at the express order of Pope Nicholas IV (Y. Christe, "A propos du décor absidal de Saint-Jean du Latran à Rome," *Cahiers archéologiques* 20 (1970): 197–206; see also Herklotz, "Der mittelalterliche Fassadenportikus," 93). As has recently been noted, the archaism cannot be imputed to the artist Torriti alone, but was due to the commissioning pope's own decision, recorded in the inscription. The iconographic conservatism had some basis in a legend, not of great antiquity but documentable from the twelfth century onward, according to which Christ's image had appeared to the faithful on the day of the basilica's solemn consecration. The inscription insisted, morever, upon the bust's physical verisimilitude to Christ's face (Christe, "A propos," 199: "Facies hec integra . . ."). In the confessional of the Lateran Basilica, a fourteenth-century fresco depicted the appearance of the Savior at the ceremony of Pope Sylvester I's consecration (in the presence of Emperor Constantine); see Herklotz, "Der mittelalterliche Fassadenportikus," 93, note 269.

68. Innocent III, *De sacro altaris mysterio libri sex*, bk. 6, ch. 9, PL, 217:911.

69. Guilellmus Durandus, *Rationale*, bk. 4, ch. 54; cf. 4, 52. Bonaventura, *Expositio in Psalterium* (Ps. 21:26), *Opera omnia*, 9, Paris 1867, p. 182, summarized the debate a few years earlier by declaring: "Christus in communi, et omnibus videntibus, passus est; unde Papa, quando

sumit corpus Christi in Missa, sumit omnibus videntibus, nam sedens in cathedra convertit se ad populum." Nicholas III (1277–80) gave the chapter of Saint Peter's in the Vatican a "cannulam argenteam ad observandum corpus Christi a summo pont.": Egidi, *Necrologi*, 1:289.

70. Kantorowicz, *Les deux corps du roi*, 585–586, ad indicem.

71. Pellens, *Die Texte*, 130; Kantorowicz, *Les deux corps du roi*, 383, note 8.

72. Pellens, *Die Texte*, 135; Kantorowicz, *Les deux corps du roi*, 384, note 13.

73. Pellens, *Die Texte*, 144–145; Kantorowicz, *Les deux corps du roi*, 387, note 25.

74. Pellens, *Die Texte*, 134; see Kantorowicz, *Les deux corps du roi*, 388, note 30.

75. Pellens, *Die Texte*, 6.

76. See the *Dictatus papae* (*Registro di Gregorio VII*, 2:55a, no. 19), ed. Caspar, *Das Register*, 1:206: "Quod a nemine ipse iudicari debeat."

77. Pellens, *Die Texte*, 6. On the author, see Baer, *Studien*.

78. Pellens, *Die Texte*, 226–227.

79. T. Haluscynski, *Acta Innocentii pp. III, 1198–1216* (Vatican City, 1944), 189, cit. in D. L. d'Avray, "A Letter of Innocent III and the Idea of Infallibility," *Catholic Historical Review* 66 (1980): 419, note 13. *Summa, ad Dist.* 21 *ante* c. 1, cit. in Tierney, *Origins*, 34, note 1. On this question, see also the observations of K. Pennington in *Speculum* (1995), 441.

80. Pembroke Coll., MS 72, fol. 129vb, cit. Tierney, *Origins*, 34, note 4.

81. For this term see ibid., passim.

82. Oliger, "Epistola," 366–373.

83. M. Maccarrone, "Una questione inedita dell'Olivi sull'infallibilità del papa," *Rivista di storia della Chiesa in Italia* 3 (1949): 328; see also Tierney, *Origins*, 93, et seq.

84. See above, note 74.

85. Innocent III, *Sermo XXI in festo SS. Petri et Pauli*, PL, 217:551: "Duas autem confitetur in Christo naturas, et unam personam . . ."; 552: ". . . dignitas haec in duobus attenditur, quia scilicet beatissimus Petrus et fundamentum est et caput Ecclesiae . . ."; 554: "quae uni Petro duas claves commisit, propter illam excellentissimam fidem, quae in uno Christo duas naturas veraciter recognovit."

86. Augustinus Triumphus, *Summa*, 1:6: "In papa est duplex potestas, una respectu corporis Christi veri, et ista vocatur potestas ordinis . . . alia respectu corporis Christi mystici, et ista vocatur potestas iurisdictionis vel administrationis"; cit. Wilks, *"Papa,"* 81; see also McCready, "The Papal Sovereign," 196.

87. Jacobus de Viterbio, *De regimine christiano*, bk. 2, ch. 5, ed. Ar-

quillière, *Le plus ancien traité,* 106; cit. Maccarrone, *Vicarius Christi,* 158.

88. Alvarus Pelagius, *De statu et planctu,* I, art. 37, par. P, no. 8, fol. 8v. 1; cit. Jung, *Alvaro Pelayo,* 92.

89. Honorius Augustodunensis, *Expositio in Cantica Canticorum,* PL, 172:414. On these themes, see above all Arduini, *"Rerum mutabilitas,"* 365–373.

90. Lotharius, *De sacro altaris mysterio* (PL, 217:910; the theme was taken up by William Durant in his *Rationale,* bk. 4, ch. 53, 13. See also Restaurus Castaldus, *Tractatus,* fol. 58, no. 7: "Papa in VII partes corporis recipit osculum."

91. Innocent III, *Sermo XIII in festo d. Gregorii papae,* PL, 217:513–522. The symbolic transformation wrought by Innocent is discussed in the next chapter.

92. Reg. IX, no. 113 (PL, 215:949); Imkamp, *Das Kirchenbild,* 195; see also Struve, *Die Entwicklung,* 34–35.

93. Sermon on the first anniversary: PL, 217:663; see Munk, *A Study,* 2:9–12.

94. Ruysschaert, "Le tableau Mariotti de la mosaïque absidale de l'ancien Santa Pierre," *Rendiconti della Pontificia Accademia di Archeologia* 40 (1967–1968): 295–317; Ladner, *Die Papstbildnisse,* 2:56–68. According to Honorius III, "as the body is joined to the head by the neck, so the church is joined to Christ by Peter," *Sermo XI* on the See of Saint Peter, ed. Horoy, *Honorii III opera omnia,* 2.

95. Aegidius Romanus, *De ecclesiastica potestate,* 3, ch. 12, ed. Scholz: "summus pontifex, qui tenet apicem Ecclesie et qui potest dici Ecclesia"; see idem, *Die Publizistik,* 60; and Kantorowicz, *Les deux corps du roi,* 453, note 31.

96. Salomon, *Opicinus,* II, plate 24.

97. Ibid., plate 17.

98. Ibid., plate 47.

99. On the distinction between person and office, see Peter Damian's play on the words *dominus* and *domnus* in *carmen* CXLIX that he sent to Hildebrand, the future Gregory VII: "Vivere vis Romae, clara depromito voce: Plus *Domino* papae quam *domno* pareo papae" (PL, 145:961).

100. Honorius III, *Sermo XI,* ed. Horoy, *Honorii III opera omnia,* 2.

101. Letter of Honorius III of July 25, 1216, Potthast 5317–5318; ed. Horoy, *Honorii III opera omnia,* 2:8–9. See also Phil. 1:8: "quomodo cupiam omnes vos in visceribus Christi Iesu"; Phil. 1:21: "nihi enim vivere Christus est et mori lucrum"; and Phil. 1:23: "desiderium habens dissolvi et cum Christo esse."

102. *Les Registres de Nicolas III,* no. 1 (Jan. 15, 1278).

103. Augustinus Triumphus, *Summa, quest.* 8. 3, cit. McCready, "The Papal Sovereign," 184, note 33.

104. Alvarus Pelagius, *De planctu Ecclesiae,* bk. 1, ch. 18, ed. Rocaberti, *Bibliotheca,* 3:165: "Item Christi vicarius agit non excellenter ut Christus, sed ministerialiter."

105. Ibid., 3:166.

106. In his *Collirium* Alvarus, returning to the concept of the pope's two natures, argues that Pilate judged Christ not as a *persona publica aut dignitate preeminens,* but *tanquam persona privata.* Christ did not, therefore, before Pilate "tenebat personam pape, sed simplicis hominis coram suo iudice accusati. Unde nec in hoc papa Christo succedit, non in persona, non in accusatione . . . ," ed. Scholz, *Unbekannte,* 2:513.

107. Alvarus Pelagius, *De statu et planctu Ecclesiae,* 2:13, fol. 44r.

Chapter Three

1. The pages devoted by Bertelli, *Il corpo del re,* 117–127, to the rite of the *agnus dei* constitute the only modern treatment of the problem.

2. John 13:27 (biblical translation from *New Oxford Bible,* 1308).

3. LC, 2:153, no. 48.

4. Basel, Universitätsbibl., Cod. D.IV. 4, ed. Schimmelpfennig, *Die Zeremonienbücher,* 373–374. The passage concerning the *agape* is slightly abbreviated compared to the *Ordo XI* (ibid., 374 = Anhang 1, no. 20).

5. LC, 2:151, no. 43. In the Basel codex, the description of the ceremony of Holy Saturday and of Saturday *in albis* is practically identical to Benedict's text (Schimmelpfennig, *Die Zeremonienbücher,* 373 = Anhang 1, note 15).

6. PL, 78:960; trans. Bertelli, *Il corpo del re,* 121.

7. LC, 2:154, no. 53.

8. Albinus's *ordo* does not describe the ceremony of the wax lambs.

9. LC, 1:307, no. 52, 62.

10. Bertelli, *Il corpo del re,* 122.

11. Ibid., 125 and 127.

12. Bibl. Vat., *Ottob. lat.* 356; and Avignon, Bibl. du Musée Calvet, MS 100. This is a rubricated sacramentary of Roman origin deriving not from the papal chapel, but from the liturgy of one of the Roman churches, presided over by a person of high ecclesiastical rank in close contact with the Franciscan order. According to Van Dijk, he can be identified as Cardinal Gian Gaetano Orsini, the future Nicholas III (1277–80), believed to have carried out a reform of the liturgy in Rome beginning in 1253/54. The Ottobonian codex dates to the period 1267–1270/79, while that of Avignon, a copy, was produced a bit later; see Van Dijk and Walker, *The Ordinal,* 298–299; Schimmelpfennig, *Die*

Zeremonienbücher, 393; Dykmans, *Le cérémonial,* 2:143 and 254; and Voci, *Nord o Sud,* 82.

13. "Isti sunt agni novelli qui annuntiaverunt alleluia. Modo veniunt ad fontes. Repleti sunt claritate, alleluia"; see also note 24.

14. "Domine, domine, isti sunt agni."

15. So far as the ceremony of the lambs is concerned, it is impossible to know the age of the sources of the Roman missal preserved in the Ottobonian codex. Nor is it possible to say how the ceremony was described in the original codex of Innocent III's ordinal. No source is given by the modern editors (Van Dijk and Walker, *The Ordinal,* 298–299). The passage concerning the third phase, the recitation of the words of the rite, is contained only in the Avignon codex. This version was repeated in the *Ordo XIV,* whose composition goes back to the pontificate of Clement VI and his immediate successors (see Schimmelpfennig, *Die Zeremonienbücher,* 78; and Dykmans, *Le cérémonial,* 2:405). The oldest surviving codex of Innocent III's ordinal (1365) contains a few (minor) liturgical details lacking in the Ottobonian codex (Van Dijk and Walker, *The Ordinal,* 298–299, initial O).

16. An *agnus Dei* is designed on the boss of the cope that dresses the body of Adrian V (d. 1276), lying in the church of San Francesco alla Rocca of Viterbo (Ladner, *Die Papstbildnisse,* 2, plate 39). This is the only case noted to date: see Gardner, *The Tomb,* 72.

17. Stephen of Bordeau does not specify how many times the words of the rite had to be addressed to the pope; the triple recitation of the words *Sic transit* is attested for the first time in 1404 (see above, chap. 1).

18. The search for an equilibrium between the Vatican and the Lateran was an essential feature of the liturgical collection transcribed in the Roman missal of 1215: Van Dijk, "The Urban and Papal Rites," 411, et seq.

19. Van Dijk and Walker, *The Ordinal,* 298–299: "imprimunt illa sigilla in formulis propter hoc adinventis." On Paride de Grassi's description of the arms and year of coronation, see the following paragraph.

20. Dykmans, *Le cérémonial,* 4:182, no. 729; see also no. 730.

21. On the upturned miters, see the description of the ceremony under Gregory XVI (Moroni, 1:130): "Dopo aver ricevuto dai Cardinali il bacio della mano, del ginocchio e degli stessi *Agnus Dei,* [the pope] ne pose loro nella mitra. I patriarchi, gli arcivescovi e vescovi baciarono il ginocchio e gli Agnus Dei, posti egualmente nella mitra, in cui pure l'ebbero gli abbati mitrati, dopo il bacio di quelli e del piede: indi i penitenzieri di Santa Pietro, con pianete bianche, facendo altrettanto, li riceverono nelle berrette. Finalmente tutti quelli che

hanno luogo in cappella, ed i nobili forestieri, con quella gradazione che si pratica nel ricevere le candele, le ceneri e le palme, baciando il piede al papa e gli Agnus Dei, li ricevettero anch'essi dal Pontefice." See also Gattico, *Acta,* 1 : 382–385.

22. Dykmans, *Le cérémonial,* 4 : 183, no. 742: "Primo namque cera munda et albissima fuit posita supra altare beati Petri apostoli"; ibid., 3 : 340, no. 13: "Quare omnes volentes habere Agnus Dei deferant bona hora ceram albam, et mundam ac pulcram, nec cum alia intermixtam . . ." (addition of April 3, 1395, pontificate of Benedict XIII). Ceremonial annotations datable to the pontificate of Benedict XIII read (ibid., 3 : 339): "Rogamus ergo clementiam tuam ut hos agnos immaculatos benedicere, sanctificare et consecrare digneris, quos de cera virginea in tui honorem formavimus . . . quam absque contagione ac propagine humana . . . sic eos deferentes tuearis. . . ."

23. Ibid., 2 : 182, no. 731.

24. Ibid., 2 : 182, no. 732.

25. Ibid., 2 : 185, no. 745.

26. Thompson, *Chronicon Adae de Usk,* 93. The acolytes and papal familiars in charge of making the wax lambs had to abstain from eating meat; Dykmans, *Le cérémonial,* 3 : 337. Did the number twenty-five have a symbolic character, tied to the topos of Peter's twenty-five years?

27. Ibid., 3 : 236, no. 240.

28. This is recounted in a rubric added to the Avignon "long ceremonial" during the pontificate of Benedict XIII (April 7, 1395), ibid., 3 : 341, no. 16.

29. Ibid., 3 : 341, no. 16. These verses circulated widely; see ibid., 3 : 77; and Moroni, 1 : 131.

30. The papal letter is preserved in one of the principal chancery collections of the second half of the thirteenth century, known by the name of the notary of the papal chancery, Marino Filomarini (Bibl. Vat., *Vat. lat.* 3976, fols. 58v–59r = Schillmann, *Die Formularsammlung,* 102, no. 201). Urban V is identified as the author in a marginal note of one of the codices of the Marino collection: Bibl. Vat., *Archivio di Santa Pietro,* C 117, fol. 36v; see also ibid., 102, note 3.

31. Dykmans, *Le cérémonial,* 3 : 339; Guilelmus Durandus, *Rationale,* bk. 1, ch. 7, 34.

32. Interesting, on this point, is the view of Stefano Borgia (c. 1750): "Questi *Agnus Dei* sono di cera vergine, e si vogliono di tal materia per dimostrare l'umana natura di Cristo, assunta nel purissimo ventre di Maria Santissima senza alcuna macchia di colpa. Hanno la figura impressa di un agnello, come simbolo di quell'Agnello immacolato, che per la salute del genere umano si sagrificò sulla croce, e s'immergono nell'acqua benedetta, essendo questo un elemento, del quale servissi Dio nell'antica e nuova legge per operare molti prodigi.

Vi si mescola *il balsamo per significare il buon odore di Cristo,* di cui i redenti debbono spargere se stessi. Il crisma, che vi s'infonde, adombra la carità . . . ," cit. Moroni, 1:129.

33. Trans. Bertelli, *Il corpo del re,* 123–124.

34. Bull of Dec. 7, 1447 (Moroni, 1:131), March 21, 1470 (ibid.) and May 25, 1572 (*Bullarum,* 8:10–11).

35. LC, 2:150, no. 36. On the golden rose see, above all, Cornides, *Rose;* C. Burns, *Golden Rose;* and Dykmans, *Le cérémonial,* 1:35–38. The earliest notice comes from the first year of Leo IX's pontificate (1049–54). The monastery of Heiligenkreuz near Woffenheim, in Alsace, founded by the pope's parents, was exempted from the jurisdiction of the local bishop and put under the special protection of Saint Peter. In return, the abbess vowed to send the Apostolic See every year a fine golden rose or an equivalent sum of money. The rose was to weigh two ounces, and to be presented eight days before the fourth Sunday of Lent, when the pope carried it during the procession (LC, 1:180, note 1; see also PL, 143:635). Thus, by 1049 the golden rose already seems to have been a part of the tradition of the Roman church. The first notice of the gift of a golden rose by a pope is in 1097. During his sojourn at Tours, Urban II offered it to Count Fulk of Anjou (*Chronicon Santa Martini Turonensis,* in MGH, SS, 26:461: "Mihi florem aureum quem manu gerebat donavit"). Thus, the pope even carried the golden rose outside of Rome.

36. LC, 2:294, 8, no. 17.

37. PL, 180:1346, letter to Alfonse of Castile (1148).

38. *Recueil des historiens des Gaules,* 15, Paris 1878, 794. Though he does not talk specifically about the golden rose, the papal biographer Boso highlights the fact that the Romans, seeing Alexander III enter Rome on the Sunday of *Letare Jerusalem* (1177), "stared at his [the pope's] face like the face of Christ, of whom he takes the place on earth" (biblical trans. from *New Oxford Bible,* 816): see above, chap. 2.

39. PL, 217:393–398; 395; see also Eichmann, *Weihe,* 50; and Cornides, *Rose,* 29.

40. The sermons of Honorius III have been edited by G. Bottino, based on MS *Sess.* 51 of the Bibl. Vittorio Emanuele, in Horoy, *Honorii III opera omnia,* 1–2. For the two sermons *de laetare,* see 1:787–805.

41. Ibid., 1:802–804.

42. Interesting on this point is the digression of Rocca, *Thesaurus,* 1:208, who interprets the balsam of the golden rose as an elixir of youth.

43. See Innocent III's second sermon on the golden rose, PL, 217:395.

44. Dykmans, *Le cérémonial,* 1:159.

45. Ibid., 1:174–176.

46. Ibid., 1:160, no. 7.

47. Ibid., 1:172, nos. 44–48. The text is practically identical in the *Ordo XIII B* (ed. Andrieu, *Le pontifical romain,* 2:370–380), that Dykmans suggests dating around 1275–1300 (Dykmans, *Le cérémonial,* 1:167, note 10); see also the *Ordo XIV,* ibid., 2:281. The cavalcade reemerges in the ceremonial that, according to Dykmans, served for the consecration of Martin V at Constance on Dec. 21, 1417 (ibid., 3: 469–479; but for the dating of this ceremonial, see chap. 1, note 123). See also the ceremonial of Patrizi, Dykmans, *L'oeuvre,* 1:68, no. 118 (for the white vestments), and 143–154 (for the cavalcade to the Lateran).

48. Gregory X's ceremonial was therefore copied verbatim by Stefaneschi: Dykmans, *Le cérémonial,* 2:267–269.

49. Schimmelpfennig, *Die Zeremonienbücher,* 30, et seq.

50. LC, 2:123 no. 3; see also LC, 1:311 no. 58, 77. Referring to the cavalcade from Saint Peter's to the Lateran, Albinus records the decoration of the pope's horse without mentioning its color (LC, 2: 124: Albinus); see the London codex, ed. Schimmelpfennig, "Ein Fragment zur Wahl," 330, no. 33. The Basel codex contains an explanatory variant: ". . . et ubi archidiaconus recipit regnum, quod alio vocabulo frigium dicitur, de manu marascalci maioris, de quo dominum papam coronat," ed. Schimmelpfennig, "Ein bisher unbekannter Text," 65, nos. 20–21. Cencius is even more succinct (LC, 1:312: "Missa autem celebrata, revertitur ad palatium coronatus . . ."). Of the clothes the pope was supposed to put on before going to table (after taking possession of the Lateran), neither Albinus nor Cencius says a word, LC, 2:124: "Dato presbiterio dominus papa intrat ad mensam preparatam . . . Omnes tamen sedent mitrati. . . ."

51. See, for example, *Germania Pontificia,* 3:201, no. 7 (May 1, 1020): the bishop of Bamberg promises to send the pope every indiction (fifteen years), ". . . equum unum album sibi suisque successoribus . . . cum sella conveniente Romano pontifici"; JL 5960 (1099–1104). The abbey of Remiremont offered a similar gift: "infra trium annorum spatium cum auscolino pallio equum candidum Lateranensi palatio persolvant" (see also LC, 1:175). On this problem see, among others, Schramm, *Herrschaftszeichen,* 3:711–713. The legates of Pope Leo IX brought to Rome, as a gift from the Byzantine emperor Constantine IX Monomachos, an "equina sella auro mirifice culta." But the notice was passed on only in a fourteenth-century chronicle: Johannes de Bayone, ed. H. Belhomme, Strassbourg 1724–1733, 250 (see also Schramm, *Herrschaftszeichen,* 3:714–715). The color of the raiment is absent also in Abbot Suger of Saint Denis's famous passage on the adornment of the Roman popes: Suger, *Vie de Louis le Gros,* 58. Albinus records only

that, after celebrating mass, the newly elected pope descended to the place "where the papal horse is decorated," LC, 2:124: "Celebrata missa descendit ad locum ubi est equus papalis ornatus. . . ." The same is true of the *ordo* contained in the Basel codex: Schimmelpfennig, "Ein bisher unbekannter Text," 65, no. 20. While indicating that during the return procession the pope wore a tiara, Cencius makes no mention of the horse, LC, 1:313, 48, no. 77.

52. Dykmans, Le cérémonial, 1:172, no. 48.

53. *Constitutum Constantini*, 14: ". . . clamidem purpuream atque tunicam coccineam," ed. Fuhrmann, *Das Constitutum Constantini*, 87, ch. 14.

54. MGH, SS, 3:672 lib. 49, et seq.: "sublimo solio residentem veste purpurea et aurea radiantem"; see Schramm, *Herrschaftszeichen*, 1:57. Eichmann, *Weihe*, 33, observes that the red imperial mantle with which Otto III was dressed after his coronation (998: MGH, SS, 4:620) had become, in the papal context, the pope's *cappa rubea* or *clamys*, at the latest in the first half of the eleventh century. In this regard, the imperial *ordo* used by Otto III (996–1002) very likely exercised a considerable influence. At the beginning of the coronation mass (996), the emperor removed his cope to put on "his proper mantle" (Eichmann, *Die Kaiserkrönung*, 1:139).

55. *Die Briefe des Petrus Damiani*, 3:189.

56. LP, 2:361: "indutus rubea chlamide sicut moris est"; see Eichmann, *Weihe*, 34.

57. Urban II was dressed in the *cappa rubea* in 1088 (MGH, SS, VII, 760); Calistus II "vix cappa rubea amiciri sustinuit" (LP, 2:322); according to tradition, Honorius II at first refused the "mitram et mantum" (LP, 2:379); Innocent II's electors wrote to King Lothar in 1130, reporting that they had awarded the newly elect "omnia insignia pontificalia" (Ebers, *Devolutionsrecht*, 171); the antipope Anacletus "cappam rubeam indecenter induit fictitiaque pontificatus insignia arripuit" (ibid.); in 1160, the chapter of Saint Peter's wrote to Barbarossa on the recent election of the antipope Octavian (Victor IV): "electus est et manto indutus ac in sede beati Petri positus" (Watterich, 2:475). Regarding Alexander III's election, the *Liber pontificalis* noted that "electum . . . papali manto induerunt" (LP, 2:397); Alexander himself complained in September 1159 that Octavian had violently taken his "mantum quo nos . . . iuxta morem ecclesiae prior diaconorum induerat" (PL, 200: 69 = JL, 10584); for all of these points, see Eichmann, *Weihe*, 33–34.

58. Bruno di Segni, *Tractatus*, PL, 165:1108, cit. Klewitz, "Die Krönung," 106, note 33.

59. Albinus (LC, 2:123); Cencius (ibid., 1:311).

60. Zoepffel, *Die Papstwahlen*, 168, et seq.; Braun, *Die liturgische Gewandung*, 351, et seq.; Klewitz, "Die Krönung," 120; Wasner, "De consecratione," 249–281.

61. *Libellus de cerimoniis aule imperialis*, ch. 19, ed. Schramm, *Kaiser*, 3:344. The *terminus ante quem* is provided by the mention in ch. 16 of Pope Anastasius IV's sarcophagus (d. Dec. 3, 1154); see chap. 1, note 100.

62. Delbrueck, "Der spätantike Kaiserornat," 7–15. Treitinger, *Die oströmische Kaiser- und Reichsidee*, 9: "Im Palast Heleniani wechselt er die Kleider, zieht die purpurnen Kaiserschuhe, ein weisses goldgestreiftes Dibetison und eine Purpurchlamys an."

63. In the description of Isidore, *Etymologiae*, 16:55, the porphyry is "rubeus, candidis intervenientibus punctis." Thus, also, Anna Comnena, *Alexiade*, 7:2, 4, ed. Leib, 2:90; see Deér, *Dynastic Porphyry Tombs*, 144, note 90.

64. For the white horse see Träger, *Der reitende Papst;* and the review by E. Garms-Cornides, *Art Bulletin* (1973), 451–456. Bernard of Clairvaux, *De consideratione*, 4:3, 6, reminded Eugenius III that Peter had never "been carried on a white horse": "Petrus hic est, qui nescitur processione aliquando vel gemmis ornatus vel sericis, non tectus auro, non vectus equo albo. . . ."

65. *Vita Gregorii IX*, LC, 2:19: "insignibus papalibus precedentibus, equo in faleris pretiosis evectus. . . ."

66. LC, 2:33. More or less contemporaneously, a commentator on the apocalypse paused, in a codex conserved at Prague, to discuss the symbolism of the emperor's white horse (Träger, *Der reitende Papst*, 13, note 41).

67. PL, 217:517–521.

68. COD, 243, c. 16, ceremonial of the cardinal bishop Latino Malabranca, ch. 53, ed. Dykmans, *Le cérémonial*, 1:228, no. 5. On the rochet generally, see Moroni, 58:70–78; and Braun, *Die liturgische Gewandung*, 130.

69. Innocent III, *Sermo III in consecratione pontificis*, PL, 217:665; see also *Sermo II in consecratione pontificis*, PL, 217:654. See Moroni, 58:70: "Il rocchetto è un abito giurisdizionale, insegna vescovile principalmente."

70. PL, 217:481: "Sacerdos, non solum magnus, sed maximus, pontificali et regali potestate sublimis."

71. This is one of the central arguments astutely defended by Ladner, who has brought his studies on the tiara together in *Der Ursprung*, 449–481; and *Die Papstbildnisse*, 3:270–307.

72. Rupertus abbas Tuitiensis, *In Cantica Canticorum*, 5, 10 (PL, 168:920): "candidus sanctitate, rubicundus passione."

73. Adamannus, *De locis sanctis* 1, 3 (CSEL 39:232); see Beda, *De*

locis sanctis, c. 2 (CSEL 39:305); Haupt, *Die Farbensymbolik,* 97; and Hermann, "Farbe," 432.

74. Hieronimus, *Epistola 64 ad Fabiolam,* CSEL 54:586–615, c. 3.

75. Ambrosius, *De mysteriis,* 29–30, 34–35, 37, 42, ed. Botte, 117–121.

76. PL, 172:415.

77. G. Bing, "The Apocalypse Block—Books and Their Manuscript Models," *Journal of the Warburg Institute* 5 (1942): 154, note 1.

78. S. Löwenfeld, "Der *Dictatus papae* Gregors VII. und eine Überarbeitung desselben im XII. Jahrhundert," *Neues Archiv* 16 (1891): 200, note 9: "[papa] solus utitur rubra cappa in signum imperii vel martirii."

79. Matt. 27: 28: "et exuentes eum clamydem coccineam circumdederunt ei . . . ," and John 19: 2: "et veste purpurea circumdederunt eum."

80. Sicardus, *Mitrale,* 1, 12; PL, 213:40; see also Hermann, "Farbe," 432.

81. Ladner, *Die Papstbildnisse,* 3:301.

82. Van Heck, ed., *Pii II Commentarii,* 106: "Nec plura locutus priora exuit indumenta et albam Christi tunicam accepit."

83. Moroni, 96:238.

84. See again Innocent III, the *Sermo VI* delivered at the Fourth Lateran Council, in PL, 217:676–677: the pope is a "Vir ergo vestitus lineis . . . quoniam summus pontifex, qui super domum Israel constitutus est speculator, transire debet per universam Ecclesiam, quae est civitas regni magni, civitas posita supra montem, investigando et inquirendo merita singulorum: ne dicant bonum malum, vel malum bonum. . . ."

85. Pastoureau, "L'Eglise," 219.

86. Galbreath, *Papal Heraldry,* 3, et seq.; and Erdmann, "Kaiserliche und päpstliche Fahnen," 46.

87. Guilellmus Durandus, *Rationale,* bk. 3, ch. 19, 18: "Hinc est quod summus pontifex capa rubea exterius semper apparet indutus, cum interius sit indutus candida veste: quia etiam interius candere debet per innocentiam et charitatem: et exterius rubere per compassionem, ut videlicet ostendat se semper paratam ponere animam pro ovibus suis: quia personam gerit illius, qui pro nobis universis rubrum fecit indumentum suum."

88. Urban V, *De curia,* ch. 31, cit. Moroni, 58:74. Boniface VIII's corpse was dressed in a rochet girded with a belt of red silk (see chap. 5, 137).

89. Boniface VIII seems to be wearing a mozzetta in the statue of the Museo Civico of Bologna: Ladner, *Die Papstbildnisse,* 2:296–302. In the fresco by Melozzo of Forlì, done to commemorate the founding of the Vatican Library (1477), Sixtus IV wears a mozzetta, a rochet, and

a white soutane. The rochet is shortened to below the knee; the belt, no longer necessary, has been eliminated (Braun, *Die liturgische Gewandung*, 130).

90. Sermon delivered on the feast of Saint Sylvester, Horoy, *Honorii III opera omnia*, 2:101.

91. Bonaventura, *Expositio in Psalterium*, 207. If all of the prelates constitute the *ordo perfectivus,* the pope "has to be the most perfect of all": Bonaventura, *Illuminationes Ecclesiae in Hexameron, Sermo XXII*, 141–142. See also Bonaventure's, *Apologiae pauperum responsionis primae caput* 3:429, 430. In a passage from his *Sermo IV* on the third Sunday after Pentecost (*Sermones de tempore*, 342–343), Bonaventure recounts that "quidem s. Papa, cum confitebatur, nolebat sedere ad latus sui capellani, qui eum audiebat, sed pedibus ejus provolutus, quousque confessione completa, morabatur; dicebat enim: Modo non teneo locum Papae, sed peccatoris; et ideo cum recogito omnes defectus meos, necesse habeo humiliari."

92. In the ceremony of the lambs described by Pierre Ameil, the pope was covered by a cloth of very fine silk; see above, note 24.

93. Guilellmus Durandus, *Rationale*, bk. 1, ch. 8, notes 22 and 23.

94. Campi, *Dell'historia ecclesiastica di Piacenza*, 2:349. For the dating of the *Vita Gregorii X* there is only a *terminus ante quem:* the canonization of King Louis IX of France (1297); ibid., 3:342.

95. Tholomeus Lucensis, *Historia ecclesiastica*, in RIS, 11:1161: "carnes diu non comedit; asperrimo lecto est usus, nec vestibus lineis ad carnem utebatur; et sic sanctissimam vitam duxit."

96. Grauert, *Magister*, 147. On Adrian V's gisant, see chap. 5, 136. The theme was still relevant in the fifteenth century: Martin V "indulged in little sleep, rest, or food" (LP, 2:515); Nicholas V "retained the color *subcandido* from birth right up to his pontificate"; in the first four years of his pontificate he was so burdened by the duties of his office that "he ate little and slept even less." Sickened by gout and the pains of arthritus, the pope lost his *subcandido* complexion and took on a coloration *croceum subcinericiumque* (RIS, 3, 2: 918–919).

97. Hostiensis, *Summa*, cit. Moroni, 96:219. And again: "Cardinales debent esse, quoad mores, et vitae munditiam, candidiores nivis: imo etiam sanctos"; cit. ibid., 58:70.

98. Rogerius Bacon, *Opus Tertium*, 86 and 402. On the angelic pope in general, see McGinn, "Angel Pope," 155–173. In the twenty-third article of his *Dictatus papae* (ed. Caspar, *Das Register*, 1:201–208), Gregory VII declares: "Quod Romanus Pontifex, si canonice fuerit ordinatus, meritis beati Petri indubitanter efficitur sanctus testante sancto Ennodio Papiensi episcopo eis multis sanctis patribus faventibus, sicut in decretis beati Symachi pape continetur." The twelfth-century canonists wrote lengthy commentaries on the problem of the pope's

hereditas innocentiae (Lindner, "Die sogenannte Erbheiligkeit," 15–26), following for the most part Gratian's position, according to which *Non loca sed vita et mores sanctum faciunt sacerdotem* (comment on Dist. 40): it was the pope's personal sanctity that made him saintly, not the office he filled. The pope had to make Peter's innocence his own, as though it were an inheritance (Rufinus, ibid., 20, note 22: "cum ipsa innocentia, quam propriam velut hereditatem debet apostolicus possidere"). See also Fuhrmann, "Über die Heiligkeit," 28–43.

99. Delisle, *Notices et extraits des manuscrits de la Bibliothèque Nationale*, 38, 2 (Paris 1906), 739–740; see Baethgen, *Der Engelpapst*, 14–17.

100. Salimbene, *Chronica*, in MGH, SS, 33:493: "En circa mille bis centum septuaginta / Tetraque: tunc ille, velut annorum quadraginta, / Sanctus parebit et Christi scita tenebit, / Angelice vite, vobis pavor, o Giezite!" These verses contain the oldest reference to the *angelica vita* of the future pope; McGinn, "Angel Pope," 161.

101. Gieben, "Robert Grosseteste," 362–363, no. 26; see also nos. 22 and 25.

102. Ibid., 354.

103. Southern, *Robert Grosseteste*, 278.

104. Melloni, *Innocenzo IV.*

105. Dykmans, *Le cérémonial*, 1:205, no. 224.

106. Ibid., 2:473, no. 114.

107. Ibid., 2:473; see also 239–240.

108. Dykmans, *L'oeuvre*, 2:434; an identical situation is described by Burchard for November 2, 1484 (Johannes Burckardus, *Liber notarum*, ed. Celani, 1:122). The vestments found in the chambers of Calixtus III (d. 1458) and Pius II (d. 1464) after their deaths were of only two colors: white and red: ed. Müntz, *Les arts*, 213–219, 323–326.

109. Dykmans, *L'oeuvre*, 2:443, no. 1362. It is true that at the funeral of Emperor Charles IV (Rome, Feb. 2, 1379), the pope did not say the mass, but assisted in it dressed in a closed wool cloak and a white miter (Dykmans, *Le ceremonial*, 4:194; this accords with ceremonial prescriptions: see Schimmelpfennig, *Die Zeremonienbücher*, 288).

110. Rocca, *De rebus praecipuis*, 67: "In exequiis pro omnibus S.R.E. Cardinalibus defunctis Missam cantavit Illustrissimus, ac Reverendissimus D. Cardinalis Paravicinus, praesente S.R.E. Cardinalium Collegio, absente Papa, qui eis interesse non solet."

111. Dykmans, *L'oeuvre*, 2:343.

112. Dykmans, *Le cérémonial*, 4:95: "Verumtamen modernis temporibus Romana ecclesia istis tribus utitur quasi uno colore [that is, black, violet, *indii coloris*], sed hac die papa utitur violaceis paramentis vel indii coloris"; see also the "long" ceremonial, ibid., 3:188 no. 30).

113. "Long ceremonial" of Avignon (ibid., 3:214); ceremonial of Pierre Ameil (ibid., 4:147); ceremonial of Patrizi Piccolomini (idem,

L'oeuvre, 2:382, no. 1130, and 391, no. 1169). On Good Friday, 1288, Nicholas IV celebrated in black liturgical dress: A. Baumstark, "Die österliche Papstliturgie des Jahres 1288 nach dem Bericht eines syrischen Augenzeugen," *Ephemerides liturgicae* 62 (1948): 188.

114. Dykmans, *L'oeuvre,* 2:502, no. 1593. For the white Easter mantle, see above. The problem "An Pontifex Maximus exequiis funeralibus, et exequialibus interesse soleat," was treated by Paride de Grassi in his treatise on funerals (on which see Herklotz, "Paris de Grassi," 217–248); Paride himself alluded to it in his *Diarium Curiae Romanae,* ed. Hoffmann, 466. At Byzantium, as well, the emperor did not dress for mourning: Treitinger, *Die oströmische Kaiser- und Reichsidee,* 156, no. 57; Kantorowicz, *Les deux corps du roi,* 541, no. 376.

115. Richerius, *Gesta Senoniensis Ecclesiae,* in MGH, SS, 25:297.

116. Alexander a Turre Cremensis, *De fulgendo radio hierarchiae ecclesiae militantis,* Rocaberti, *Bibliotheca,* 2:41–63, published thirteen of the *radii* from book 4 and the first part of book 5.

117. Book 5, *radius* 19: "De singulari ornatu summi Romani pontificis" (ibid., 2:44–47); *radius* 22: "De calceis atque sandalis aurea Cruce obsignatis" (ibid., 2:55–57); *radius* 24: "De pontificio pluviali; ubi longitudo, latitudo, sublimitas, atque profundum pontificiae auctoritatis enucleatur" (ibid., 2:59–63). Book 5, *radius* 21: "De candidis, atque purpureis summi Romani praesulis indumentis" (ibid., 2:53–55).

118. Ibid., 2:53; see also Luca 23, 11; ibid., 2:53.

119. Ibid., 2:54.

120. Ibid., 2:54. Torquemada cites Livy (bk. 5), Vegetius, Virgil, and refers to Pithagoras, etc.

121. See again Moroni, 96:219: "Ecco pertanto i Papi vestiti di bianco, ad indicare la purità sacerdotale, e di ostro o porpora, *insieme* a presentare nell'abito stesso una perpetua professione, un voto *eterno* di spargere il sangue per la propria sposa la Chiesa universale"; on p. 235, the list of garments "che si dovevano preparare pel nuovo papa in tempo della Sede Apostolica" (MS of the pontifical sacristan Landucci, 1655), contains only two colors: white and red.

122. Rocca, *An Summmo pontifici,* 78.

123. Ibid., 75, 78–79. See also Eccles. (9: 8). The concept (inherent in the first part of the verse) is already in *Sermo VI,* delivered by Innocent III to the Fourth Lateran Council: PL, 217:676.

124. See above, 89.

Chapter Four

1. Petrus Damiani, *Die Briefe,* 1:336–339, no. 35 (JL, 4210); 337.

2. Ibid., 1:338.

3. Poncelet, "Vie et miracles," 290; see also the *Vita Leonis IX,*

ed. S. Borgia, *Memorie istoriche della pontificia Città di Benevento* (Rome 1764), 2:327.

4. Poncelet, "Vie et miracles," 290.

5. Ibid.

6. Ibid.

7. Mansi, 7:390, no. 22. The entire chapter 22 was dedicated to disciplining the clergy.

8. Ibid., 8:836, no. 6.

9. Ibid., 8:614–615, no. 16.

10. Ibid., 10:541–542, no. 10.

11. Ibid., 10:1191, no. 7.

12. Ibid., 11:28–29.

13. It is true, however, that the Council of Toledo of 655 inveighed against "the many persons guilty of theft."

14. Obviously, an exception has to be made for the prescriptions of the Council of Rome of 595, which concern not the spoliation of the "palace," but the custom of the faithful of dividing among themselves the dalmatics that covered the pope's body, "which henceforth should not be covered," MGH, *Epistolae,* 1:364: "Ex amore quippe fidelium huius sedis rectoribus mos ultra meritum erupit, ut, cum eorum corpora humi mandanda deferuntur, haec dalmaticis contengant easdemque dalmaticas pro sanctitatis reverentia sibimet partiendas populus scindat: et cum adsint multa a sacris corporibus apostolorum martyrumque velamina, a peccatorum corpore sumitur, quod pro magna reverentia reservetur. De qua re praesenti decreto constituo, ut feretrum quo Romani pontificis corpus ad sepeliendum ducitur, nullo tegmine veletur. Quam decreti mei curam gerere sedis huius presbiteros ac diaconos censemus." Clearly the thrust of this conciliar decree is quite different from that of the conciliar prescriptions noted above: the 595 Council of Rome wanted above all to prohibit the use of those *multa velamina* belonging to the *sacris corporibus apostolorum martyrumque,* which traditionally were used to cover the pope's corpse. The justification was the following: those *velamina,* reserved "for the highest respect," if carried away by the people, would be brought into contact with "the body of sinners" *(a peccatorum corpore sumitur).* The decree was not so much concerned, therefore, with the spoliation of papal goods as it was with the inappropriate use (in a certain sense, "sacrilege") of *velamina* considered as relics. On this text, see Braun, *Die liturgische Gewandung,* 254; and chap. 5, note 1. It should further be noted that, as has been demonstrated by E. Caspar, *Geschichte,* 528, what took place at the death of Pope Severinus (640) was not the result of pillage by the people, but amounted to a real sequestration of goods. The episode, narrated in the *Liber pontificalis (Vita Severini),* should therefore be taken

off the list of "ritual" pillages connected to the deaths of Roman popes (LP, 1:328–329).

15. *Vita Stephani VI, LP,* 2:192.

16. Ibid.

17. Ibid.

18. Mansi, 18:225.

19. Ibid., 225–226.

20. F. Lesne, *Histoire de la propriété ecclésiastique en France* (Lille, 1920) 2:49, note 1.

21. For Stephen V, see Flodoardus, *Historia Remensis Ecclesiae,* 4:1, MGH, SS, 13:557–558; and for Formosus, 4:2, ibid., 559.

22. Flodoardus, *Historia,* 4:5, MGH, SS, 13:49, note 3.

23. Mansi, 18:302–303; see also Lesne, *Histoire,* 2:49, note 4.

24. A. Boretius, *Capitularia regum Francorum,* 1:323; see also Lesne, *Histoire,* 2:49, note 1. Several years later, in 832, Lothar promulgated an analogous Italian capitulary; there, the practice of pillaging is described as a recent development *(moderno tempore);* see Boretius, *Capitularia,* 2:64; and ibid., 2:49, note 1.

25. Matthaei Parisiensis, *Historia Anglorum, ad annum* 1227, 294: "De quo Honorio decima die ante mortem eius, cum mortuus crederetur, nec erat, et exhaustus et semivivus populo Romano in res papales debacanti, quod viveret, per altam fenestram monstraretur, ait quidam versificator: O pater Honori, multorum nate dolori, / Est tibi decori vivere, vade mori."

26. Victor II died at Arezzo (July 28, 1056), Stephen X in Florence (March 29, 1058), Nicholas II in Florence (July 17, 1061), Gregory VII at Salerno (May 25, 1085), Victor III at Montecassino (Sept. 16, 1087), Gelasius II at Cluny (Jan. 29, 1119), Eugenius III at Tivoli (July 8, 1153), Adrian IV at Anagni (Sept. 1, 1159), Alexander III at Città di Castello (Aug. 30, 1181), Lucius III at Verona (Nov. 25, 1185), Urban III at Ferrara (Oct. 20, 1186), Gregory VIII at Pisa (Dec. 17, 1188), and Innocent III at Perugia (July 16, 1216).

27. Versnel, "Destruction," 618, uses the term "folkloric desperation."

28. The *Liber provincialis,* the official collection of formulas of the thirteenth-century papal chancery, contains a formula for papal condemnation of pillage but, notably, refers only to cases occurring on the death of a bishop. The entire formula X, moreover, is aimed at problems related to episcopal, rather than specifically papal, successions. See Tangl, *Die päpstlichen Kanzlei-Ordnungen,* 261, no. 9.

29. Innocent IV died in Naples (Dec. 7, 1254), Urban IV in Perugia (Oct. 2, 1264), Clement IV in Viterbo (Nov. 29, 1268), Gregory X at Arezzo (Jan. 10, 1276), Adrian V at Viterbo (Aug. 16, 1276), Nicholas III at Soriano (Aug. 22, 1278), Martin IV at Perugia

(March 28, 1285), and Benedict XI at Perugia (July 7, 1305). Gregory IX (Aug. 22, 1241), the ephemeral Celestine IV (Oct. 10, 1241), the Dominican Innocent V (June 22, 1276), Honorius IV (April 3, 1286), the Franciscan Nicholas IV (April 4, 1292), and Boniface VIII (Oct. 11, 1303) all died in Rome.

30. Burning and looting are mentioned after the death of Clement V at Carpentras on April 20, 1314. But it should quickly be pointed out that the notices that have survived (Baluze and Mollat, *Vitae*, 3: 234, 316, and 4:175) agree in demonstrating that the disorders did not break out at the time of the pope's death, and were not directed against "the pontifical goods," but were tied instead to the Gascons' desire to impose an election favorable to themselves, and thus to prevent the election of an Italian. The plundering took place during the conclave; the victims were the inhabitants of the city, the merchants *Curiam sequentes,* as well as several cardinals (also Italians).

31. See below, note 121.

32. Borgolte, *Petrusnachfolge,* 357 and 358.

33. No sackings of the Apostolic Palace are mentioned by Nussdorfer, "The Vacant See," 173–189.

34. On the disorders of 1484, see Stefano Infessura, *Diario della Città di Roma,* 161 (see also Bertelli, *Il corpo del re,* 48); Gaspare Pontani (*Il diario romano di Gaspare Pontani,* ed. D. Toni, in RIS, 2nd ed., 3:2 [Bologna, 1907–1908], 37–38); and a letter by Guidantonio Vespucci (in Johannes Burcardus, *Diarium,* 3, appendix, 498: "e perchè non si dubitava che rubbassero li signori di casa Ursina, dalle dette sbarre in su verso Santo Pietro non erano sbarre, perchè il signor Paolo Orsino diceva che non ci fussero sbarre, per potere bisognando mandarce in aiuto sua gente di arme a cavallo et a piedi"). On the death of Sixtus IV, see also the notices in Antonio de Vascho, *Il diario della Città di Roma dall'anno 1480 all'anno 1492 di Antonio de Vascho,* ed. G. Chiesa, in RIS, 2nd ed., 23, 3 (Bologna, 1904–1911), 513: "Ricordo come a dì 12 di agosto 1484 papa Sisto morì ad hore quattro di notte, venendo il venerdì. Ricordo in questo sopradetto dì come in Roma si cominciò a fare cose strane, cioè rubbare, ferire et altre simili." For the death of Innocent VIII, see Pastor, *Storia dei papi,* 3:278: "Durante la lunga infermità d'Innocenzo VIII erano accaduti in Roma brutti disordini; con preoccupazione pensavasi al periodo della Sede vacante. Questo però, grazie alle energiche misure prese dai cardinali e dalle autorità di Roma, trascorse da principio abbastanza tranquillo. . . . La situazione continuò però ad essere tale, che i cardinali credettero bene di affrettare le esequie pel defunto pontefice." The dispatch of Brognolus (ambassador of the Gonzaga), dated Aug. 7, 1492, is important (ibid.): "Vero è che l'è stato amazato qualche persona e feriti alcuni altri maxime in quello tempo che'l papa era in quello extremo; poi le cose tuta via sono asetate

meglio." Antonio de Vascho (*Il diario della Città di Roma*, 545, note 12) expressed himself thus: "Ricordo come papa Innocentio si ammalò di maggio e poi il mese di luglio morì, et in Roma furono fatti molti homicidii e molti feriti e latrocinii, e dopo li cardinali entrarono in conclave. . . ."

35. P. Nores, "Storia della guerra di Paolo IV sommo pontefice contro gli Spagnoli," *Archivio Storico Italiano*, ser. 1, 12 (1847), doc. 41, 452–453; see also Ginzburg, "Saccheggi," 615–636; and Bertelli, *Il corpo del re*, 4.

36. C. Bromato, *Storia di Paolo IV pontefice massimo* (Ravenna, 1753), 2:577–582; see also Bertelli, *Il corpo del re*, 49.

37. Dykmans, *L'oeuvre*, 233, no. 687.

38. *Die Briefe*, ed. Reindel, 1:338; and above, note 2.

39. Otto IV (1198 and 1209), Philip of Swabia (1203), and Frederick II (1213, 1216, 1219 and 1220); see R. Eisenberg, *Das Spolienrecht*, Marburg 1896, with the critical comments of Tangl, "Die Vita Bennonis," 77–94; d'Aussac, *Le droit de dépouille;* Forchielli, "Il diritto di spoglio," 13–55; Sheehan, *The Will*, 241–253; H.-J. Becker, "Spolienrecht," in *Handwörterbuch zur deutschen Rechtsgeschichte*, 31, Lieferung (Berlin, 1989), 1779–1780; Meyer, "Das päpstliche Spolienrecht," 399–405. The right of spoils claimed by the *potentiores* tended to disappear over the course of the eleventh and twelfth centuries in a typically Gregorian climate. In 1120, a papal legate and King Louis VI of France obtained restitution from the royal seneschal of goods he had seized at the death of the Bishop of Senlis (*Gallia christiana*, X, *preuves*, 209). Already, in 1084, Raymond of Saint-Gilles had solemnly renounced his right to take possession of the goods of the bishop of Béziers when he died (Lesne, *Histoire*, 2:50, note 5). In the kingdom of France, the bishops managed to liberate themselves under Louis VII (1137–80): F. Senn, *L'institution des vidamies en France*, Paris 1907, 150–151; D. Lohrmann, *Kirchengut im nördlichen Frankreich. Besitz, Verfassung und Wirtschaft im Spiegel der Papstprivilegien des 11.–12. Jahrhunderts* (Bonn, 1983), 125–126; O. Guyotjeannin, *'Episcopus et comes': Affirmation et déclin de la seigneurie épiscopale au nord du royaume de France (Beauvais-Noyon, Xe-début XIIIe siécle)* (Geneva, 1987), 77, note 50. For a useful general survey of episcopal documents, see D. Loades, "The Death of the Bishop in the Early Middle Ages," in *The End of Strife: Papers Selected from the Proceedings of the Colloquium of the Commission Internationale d'Histoire Ecclésiastique Comparée Held at the University of Durham 2 to 9 September 1981* (Edinburgh, 1984), 32–43.

40. Elze, " 'Sic transit,' " 38. By the second half of the thirteenth century the papacy had managed to reverse the situation completely: on November 18, 1262, Urban IV decreed that the goods of deceased ecclesiastics who had drawn up their wills *apud Sedem Apostolicam*

should devolve to the Roman Church. To avoid the confiscation of their personal property, prelates had to acquire a papal *licentia testandi:* see my *I testamenti,* xlii–lxv and, in general, F. Prochnow, *Das Spolienrecht und die Testierfähigkeit der Geistlichen im Abendland bis zum 13. Jahrhundert* (Berlin, 1919).

41. Paravicini Bagliani, *I testamenti,* 155–158.

42. See above, note 8. When Pope Stephen VIII died (Florence, Oct., 942), Abbot Hugh of Cluny, who had assisted the pope during his final days, undertook personally the washing, dressing, and burying of the corpse, all of which seems to confirm the absence of precise pontifical funeral rites: PL, 159:896.

43. LP, 2:305: ". . . Corpus eius balsamo infectum et, ut ordo habet, sacris indutum vestibus . . ."; see Herklotz, "Sepulcra," 209, note 168.

44. LP, 2:294. A passage from the *Vita* of Pope Benedict III (855–58) would seem at first to constitute an exception. But apart from the fact that, chronologically, this comes nearly three centuries before the pontificates of Paschal II and Honorius II, the exception is itself only partially valid, since the pope's effort to regulate the funerel ceremony is here set in the broader context of ecclesiastical burial.

45. Watterich, 2:189: "ut eum (scil. Honorium), sicuti mos est, antiquam iuxta Romani ordinis normam honorifice sepelirent."

46. *Liber pontificalis nella recensione di Pietro Guglielmo e del card. Pandolfo,* 2:756: "nec vestitum in antiquo, praeter bracas solummodo et cum camisia—heu, quantum misere!—in feretro nudis certe sindonibus, quod dolendo dicimus, hinc vel inde relatum." See also the *Historia Compostellana,* ed. Watterich, 2:188; and below, note 55.

47. In his glosses on Pietro Guglielmo's *Liber pontificalis,* Pieter Bohier noted, concerning the word *gleba:* "Id est terra, hoc est terrenum corpus" (*Liber pontificalis nella recensione di Pietro Guglielmo e del card. Pandolfo,* 3:550). For the definition of *gleba* as cadaver, see the medieval Latin dictionaries (Ducange, Latham, etc.); these confirm the exactness of Bohier's gloss.

48. The problem of funeral monuments has been the subject of a series of important art historical studies and studies of monuments. The most recent treatment (Herklotz, *"Sepulcra"*) has laid out the problem in all of its complexity across a broad chronological framework; but see also Montini, *Le tombe;* Picard, "Etude," 725–782; and Ladner, *Die Papstbildnisse.*

49. On Boso, see Engels, "Kardinal Boso," 147–168.

50. *Vita* of Leo IX, LP, 2:356: "Eo autem in eadem ecclesia digno cum honore sepulto. . . ." (Boso's source, the *Liber ad amicum* of Bonizone of Sutri, ed. Dümmler, MGH, *Libelli,* 1:589, said analogously: "Cuius corpus in eadem ecclesia cum honore magno humatum est");

Vita of Gregory VII, LP, 2:368: "honorifice tumulatum"; *Vita* of Paschal II, LP, 2:376: "cum honore maximo tumulatus"; *Vita* of Gelasius II, LP, 2:376: "honorifice tumulatus"; *Vita* of Calixtus II, LP, 2:378: "honorifice tumulatus"; *Vita* of Honorius II, LP, 2:379: "digno cum honore sepultus"; *Vita* of Innocent II, LP, 2:385: "honorifice tumulatus"; *Vita* of Lucius II, LP, 2:386: "digno cum honore sepultus"; *Vita* of Eugenius III, LP, 2:387: "cum totius fere cleri et populi Romani frequentissima turba, maximo luctu et communi atque inmensa tristitia deportatus est, et in ipsa beati Petri ecclesia coram maiori altari tumulatus"; *Vita* of Alexander III, LP, 2:397: "honorifice tumulatus."

51. Erlande-Brandenburg, *Le roi est mort,* 14.

52. Ibid., 16, cites a note by Roger of Howden on this point.

53. Schmale, *Quellen,* 478 (decrees of the Synod of Brixen); Wido, Bishop of Ferrara, *De scismate Hildebrandi,* in MGH, *Libelli,* 1:534: "Nam, ut a viris religiosissimis didici et fama ferente recognovi, *beatae memoriae Alexandro defuncto necdum humato,* clero et populo, omni senatu pariter collecto. . . ."

54. Bonizo, *Liber ad amicum,* beginning of book 7, in MGH, *Libelli,* 1:601: "Eodem itaque die prefati pontificis corpore in ecclesia sancti Salvatoris humato, *cum circa sepulturam eius venerabilis Ildebrandus esset occupatus,* factus est derepente concursus clericorum, virorum ac mulierum clamantium: 'Ildebrandus episcopus.'"

55. *Historia Compostellana,* ed. Watterich, 2:188.

56. Ibid., 2:186.

57. *Liber pontificalis nella recensione di Pietro Guglielmo e del card. Pandolfo,* 2:181 (LP, 1:316; Mansi, 10:503); see Zoepffel, *Die Papstwahlen,* 18.

58. Ibid., 17.

59. Beno, *Gesta Romanae Aecclesiae contra Hildebrandum,* 1:2 (MGH, *Libelli,* 2:370); see also Zoepffel, *Die Papstwahlen,* 18. The Bonifacian text was repeated in various collections of canons, such as the *Deusdedit* of Anselm of Lucca, ibid., 16.

60. *Gesta Innocentii III,* c. 5, PL, 217:19: "Ipse cum quibusdam aliis apud basilicam Constantinianam voluit decessoris exequiis interesse."

61. On the conclave of 1241 see Zoepffel, *Die Papstwahlen;* Schimmelpfennig, "Papst- und Bischofswahlen," 178.

62. Hampe, "Ein ungedruckter Bericht," 30 (Anagni, after Nov. 19, 1241): "nec vestrum aliqui prepotentes in Urbe ac nobiles ausi fuerint ad summi pontificis funus accedere, debiti honoris celebraturi exequias iuxta morem. . . ."

63. Gutmann, *Die Wahlanzeigen.*

64. PL, 143:869 (JL, 4372): "Promotioni nostrae, sicut nobis scripsisti, non ambigimus te gratulari. . . ." The letter is undated.

65. PL 144:348 (JL, 4469). The letter bears no date: Alexander II was elected pope on October 1, 1061.

66. JL, 4771–4774 (April 22–26, 1073).

67. Caspar, *Das Register Gregors VII.* (Rome, April 24, 1073; JL, 4772).

68. Paschal II took an additional step. In his letter of election (Sept. 10, 1099), addressed to the abbot of Cluny, the pope indicates *the date of death* of his predecessor, and states that his election took place *the day after the death of his predecessor* (PL, 163: 31; JL, 5807).

69. JL, 6682 (to Adalbert, archbishop of Magonza); JL, 8370 (Feb. 24, 1130, to the archbishops, bishops, abbots, provosts, clergy, and laity of Germany and Saxony).

70. D'Achery, *Spicilegium,* 6:461; Eugenius III's letter of March 2, 1145, to the prior of the church of San Frediano in Lucca (PL, 180: 1014–1015; JL, 8714).

71. PL, 200:70 (JL, 10584).

72. JL, 14426. See also Watterich, 2:460–461: "Felicis memoriae papa Adriano praedecessore nostro viam universae carnis ingresso (et) in beati Petri basilica tumulato." There are no discernible innovations in the only two papal letters of election that have reached us from the last decades of the twelfth century: on December 3, 1185 (JL, 15475), Urban III announced the death of Lucius III and his own election to the Emperor Frederick I. On October 27, 1187 (JL, 16014), Gregory VIII announced the death "in bona confessione" of Urban III to the archbishops, bishops, abbots, and prelates of *Theutonia;* the cardinals met *the day after the burial* to carry out his election (Watterich, 2:587).

73. *Die Register,* 1:4, no. 1.

74. *Regesta Honorii papae III,* I, no. 1: "et sequenti die, celebratis exequiis ac cum honore debito collocato ipsius corpore in sepulcro." Interesting in this regard is a passage from a sermon delivered by the same pope on July 25, 1216, that is, only a week after the death of Innocent III. The pope's body is described as *venerabile,* and the participation of the cardinals is attributed to a *celebre* custom (Horoy, *Honorii III opera omnia,* 2:8–9).

75. Gregory IX, Alexander IV, Urban IV, Clement IV, Gregory X, John XXI, Nicholas III, Martin IV.

76. *Les Registres de Nicolas IV,* no. 1.

77. *Les Registres de Benoît XI,* no. 1. Boniface VIII's letter of election (*Les Registres de Boniface VIII,* no. 1) does not concern us in this context, since Boniface was not elected after the death of his predecessor.

78. Significantly, John XXII (Sept. 5, 1316; *Lettres secrètes et curiales de Jean XXII,* 1, no. 2) again notes these points explicitly. For the most

part, it can be observed that the emphasis on institutional continuity, under the impetus of which the notification of the burial of the deceased pope had emerged as a basic constitutive element, as we have seen, in the course of the eleventh to the fifteenth centuries, was once more underlined in the letters of election of Benedict XII (Jan. 8, 1335) and Clement VI (May 21, 1342). At their enthronement, the rites of benediction and coronation were celebrated "juxta morem in personis felicis memorie Romanorum pontificum predecessorum nostrorum hactenus observatum": *Benoît XII: Lettres closes,* 3–4, no. 2 (letter of election sent to Philip IV, king of France, Jan. 9, 1335); *Lettres de Clément VI se rapportant à la France,* 1:3–4, no. 4 (letter of election sent to the king of France, May 21, 1342).

79. LP, 2:387: ". . . maximo luctu et communi atque immensa tristitia deportatus est. . . ."

80. Paravicini Bagliani, "La storiografia," 53, note 25.

81. *Vita Gregorii IX,* LC, 2:19: "Demum vero Romanis exultantibus, populis ac clero jubilante pre gaudio, irruentibus etiam catervatim utriusque sexus hominibus, pontificali decoratus infula in Lateranensi palatio magnifice cathedratur. Tunc lugubres vestes mutavit Ecclesia et urbis semiruta menia pristinum ex parte receperunt fulgorem."

82. Campi, *Dell'Historia,* 2:343: "sicque ipsa Ecclesia lugubria viduitatis indumenta deponens. . . ."

83. The ceremonial inserted into Cencius's *Liber Censuum* (c. 1180) explained only that during the vacancy the cardinals were accustomed to meet three times: *mortuo Romano pontifice et sepulto;* the following day, to sing the *missa mortuorum;* and on the day after that, to handle the election after having celebrated the mass of the Holy Spirit (LC, 1: 311, 48, no. 77).

84. The recent critical edition is Dykmans, *Le cérémonial,* 4:69–288. The passage on the pope's death is contained also in MS *Vat. lat.* 5944, fols. 230r–234r; see Herklotz, "Paris de Grassi," 228, note 45. A *socius* of the papal sacristan under Urban V (1362–70), Ameil was the official confessor of popes Gregory XI (1370–78) and Urban VI (1378–89). He remained loyal to Urban during the schism, who named him bishop of Sinigaglia (1386), then patriarch of Grado (1387). In 1400 Boniface IX trasferred him to the patriarchate of Alexandria; a year later he died in Rome: Dykmans, *Le cérémonial,* 4:13–24.

85. Dykmans, *Le cérémonial,* 4:221, no. 990.

86. Ibid., 4:218, no. 967.

87. Ibid., 4:220, no. 984.

88. Ibid., 4:221, no. 989.

89. Ibid., 4:222, no. 998.

90. Ibid., 4:224–225, nos. 1021–1027.

91. The fanon is a white silk ornament worn only by the pope;

round, made of two strips of cloth with parallel red and gold stripes, with a hole in the middle to pass over the head, he wears it over his alb.

92. Dykmans, *Le cérémonial,* 4:219, no. 976: "pallio de corpore Petri sumpto."

93. Ibid., 4:217, no. 953.

94. Ibid., 4:217, nos. 954 and 955.

95. Ibid., 4:217, nos. 957, 958, and 960.

96. Ibid., 4:217, no. 959.

97. Ibid., 4:223, no. 992.

98. Ibid., 4:222, no. 999: "Neque alii cardinales per totam novenam dictis coloribus debent uti" (i.e., black, red, green). Should he die in Rome, not even the senator of the city dressed in black, "propter officium," "unless he wishes to do so out of love of the pope," that is, as a private person (ibid., 4:219, no. 1029: "Senator urbis propter officium non utitur nec vestitur, nisi vellet facere per se amore pape").

99. Ibid., 4:223, no. 1011.

100. Ibid., 4:222, no. 1001.

101. Ibid., 4:219, no. 1039.

102. Ibid., 4:219, no. 976: "Tunc quasi sedendo erigant eum dicti penitentiarii, et induant ipsum . . . pallio de corpore Petri sumpto . . ."; 223, no. 978 (see also no. 1003); 223, no. 979.

103. Ibid., 4:227, no. 1042: "Item sciendum quod barbitonsor pape non retiret cassam cum rasoribus et cum hiis que intra sunt; item de bacili argenteo. Postea novus papa facit sibi dare X vel XII florenos. Verumtamen bacile semper in camera pape cum rasoriis et tobaliolis remanet."

104. Ibid., 4:218, no. 970: "Et interim cum illis fratribus de bulla, si fuerint, vel de Pignota, cum aqua calida cum bonis herbis, quam cubicularii parare debent, lavent corpus bene, et barbitonsor radat sibi caput et barbam."

105. Ibid., 4:227, no. 1043: "Item si paneterii et buticularii petunt tobaleas vel bottas, nihil detur eis, quia habent gagia sua. Quod si non darentur eis, rationem haberent petendi in tobaleis in quibus papa ultimo comedit, et in bottis de quibus tunc ultimo bibebat vinum." These dispositions appear to conflict with what can still be read in a book composed to assemble the rights and duties of the members of the papal *familia,* datable between 1261 and 1294: it recognizes the right of the papal *servientes* to receive "capas vetustas alterius pape, creato successore"; the wage-earners who prepared and dressed the pope's corpse had the right, by custom, to receive the bed in which he had died: Frutaz, "La famiglia pontificia," 301 and 308; on this document, see also below, chap. 5, note 53.

106. On the pope's death, see Dykmans, *Le cérémonial,* 4:216–227, nos. 949–1044; on the conclave: ibid., 228–231, nos. 1045–1076.

107. LP, 2:305.

108. LP, 2:318: "subita passione correptus quam a costa Greci pleuresyn appellari iusserunt, suis ac multis fratris undique convocatis, facta confessione ac corpore cum sanguine Redemptoris acceptis. . . ."

109. LP, 2:323: "Nec mora, confessus et ordinatus, omnibus ululantibus, obdormivit in Domino.'"

110. LP, 2:458: "In Suriano castro prope Viterbium, ubi cardinales et curiales in Viterbio morantes ad suum conspectum evocabant. . . ."

111. Schimmelpfennig, *Die Zeremonienbücher*, 44.

112. The scene described in the *Liber pontificalis* (LP, 2:511), of the death of Alexander V, obviously served to legitimate the election of a pope by a council (Pisa).

113. On the testaments of cardinals, see Paravicini Bagliani, *I testamenti*, 43, et seq. The pontifical testaments for which we have notices from the thirteenth to the fifteenth centuries are rare. Concerning Martin IV, Salimbene de Adam, *Chronica*, 823, reports that the pope nominated Cardinal Giacomo Savelli to be his executor; see also Wadding, *Annales Minorum*, V, 154. Martin's testament, however, has not survived. For Giacomo Savelli, the future Honorius IV, we have his testament as a cardinal: ed. Paravicini Bagliani, *I testamenti*, 197–206; on the "testament" or, better, the *donatio causa mortis* of Clement V, see Ehrle, "Der Nachlass," 104–149; Gregory XI's testament has been published by D'Achery, *Spicilegium*, VI, 675–690); that of Nicholas V by Muratori, RIS, 3:2, 945–958.

114. Dykmans, *Le cérémonial*, 4:216, no. 951.

115. Editions: Gattico, *Acta*, 1:231–255, chs. 1–41; Dykmans, *Le cérémonial*, 3:262–335 (on the death of the pope: 262–270, nos. 1–30); for dating and the textual tradition, see Schimmelpfennig, *Die Zeremonienbücher*, 120–126; and Dykmans, *Le cérémonial*, 3:47–73.

116. Ibid., 3:264–265, nos. 8–11.

117. At the trial of the nephews of Clement V (1305–14), Cardinal Raymond of Santa Maria Nuova claimed to know "quod lapides pretiosi dicti domini mei una cum sigillo piscatoris fuerunt traditi collegio dominorum meorum cardinalium apud Carpentoratum, in loco ubi omnes conveniebamus, et per aliquos de dictis dominis meis cofinus, in quo erant, fuit sigillatus": ed. Ehrle, "Der Nachlass," 40. For a description of the custom of breaking the fisherman's ring, which was observed on the deaths of Pius IV, Gregory XIII, Urban VII and others; see Cancellieri, *Notizie*, 1–11.

118. Dykmans, *Le cérémonial*, 3:266, no. 16.

119. Ibid., 3:268, no. 23; see Schimmelpfennig, *Die Zeremonienbücher*, 120–125.

120. Dykmans, *Le céréronial*, 3:264, no. 7: "Item debet ordinare quod statim claudantur omnes porte palatii, una tantum excepta, que

videbitur aptior et magis opportuna pro introitu et exitu illorum qui ibi (aliquid) fuerint facturi."

121. Ibid., 3:266–267, nos. 17–18.

122. Vielleville, *Mémoires*, Paris 1836–1839, 63; cit. Kantorowicz, *Les deux corps du roi*, 536, no. 343. See, for the papal context, J. Aymon, *Tableau de la cour de Rome*, La Haye 1707, 384: "(At the pope's death) La Rote et tous les Tribunaux cessent de rendre la justice."

123. Kantorowicz, *Les deux corps du roi*, 535, nos. 336, 337, 338, 340; Giesey, *Le roi ne meurt jamais*, 340, no. 344.

Chapter Five

1. Jacques de Vitry, *Lettres*, 73: "Post hoc veni in civitatem quandam que Perusium nuncupatur in qua papam Innocentium inveni mortuum, sed nundum sepultum, quem de nocte quidam furtive vestimentis preciosis, cum quibus scilicet sepeliendus erat, spoliaverunt; corpus autem eius fere nudum et fetidum in ecclesia relinquerunt. Ego autem ecclesiam intravi et oculata fide cognovi quam brevis sit et vana huius seculi fallax gloria." Jacques then speaks of Honorius III (1216–27) in words hinting at mild criticism of Innocent III. The new pope "is a good old man, religious, very simple and benevolent, ready to give all he has to the poor." On the Roman curia's stay at Perugia, see Paravicini Bagliani, "La mobilità," 228–231. Already, the Roman synod of 595 cited the Romans' custom of appropriating the pontifical vestments that covered the pope's body. The canon prohibited covering the coffin in which the deceased pope would be carried to the tomb with a funeral or other sheet. Before then, the popes' corpses had been covered with precious liturgical garments, the *dalmaticae*, a "custom exceeding merit" *(mos ultra meritum)*; the people used to tear them away and divide them among themselves, "out of reverence for holiness" *(pro sanctitatis reverentia)*, that is, to venerate the dignity of the deceased: MGH, *Epistolae*, 1:364. Apart from the fact that the conciliar decree of 595 makes no allusion whatsoever to the topos (which came much later) of *Sic transit*, this text cannot be associated with the episode recounted by Jacques de Vitry. And the decree's aim was quite different: to prevent the people from appropriating the veils (*velamina*, pertaining to the relics of apostles or martyrs) and sacred vestments (see above, chap. 4, note 14). Even Elze, " '*Sic transit*,' " 26, admits "che l'uso non è attribuito all'avidità o alla cupidigia del popolo, sebbene al suo desiderio di procurarsi delle reliquie."

2. Editions of Lothar's *De miseria*: Maccarrone, *Lotharii cardinalis* (x–xx: a list of 435 MSS); Lewis, *Lothario* (236–53: a list of 672 MSS). Lothar: "qui modo fulgebat ornatus in aula, modo sordet *nudus tumba*" = Jacques de Vitry: "nudum in ecclesia"; Lothar: "quid ergo prosunt divitie? Quid epule? Quid honores?" = Jacques de Vitry:

"cognovi quam brevis sit et vana huius seculi fallax gloria"; Lothar: "mortuus producet putredinem et fetorem . . . quid ergo fetidius humano cadavere? . . . quod horribilius mortuo homine? . . . nudus egreditur, et nudus regreditur" = Jacques de Vitry: "corpus autem eius fere nudum et fetidum." See Petrocchi, "L'ultimo destino," 202–207. It was the *De miseria conditionis humanae* that made Lothar's name as a writer. He wrote it between Dec. 25, 1194, and April 13, 1195. Introductions to the work are R. Bultot, "Mépris," 442; Moore, "Innocent's '*De Miseria*'"; Sot, "Mépris."

3. Blanc, *Les usages du paraître.* Also, for Louis of Saint-Simon, *Mémoire succint sur les formalités,* in *Ecrits inédits de Saint-Simon,* ed. M. P. Faugère, 2, *Mélanges* I (Paris, 1880), 221, the prince is nude because he is dressed only in a shirt: "Le Prince entièrement couché et trouvé comme dormant sur son lict entre ses rideaux fermés, comme nud puisqu'il n'a qu'une camisole de satin sur sa chemis. . . ."

4. Gregorovius, *Die Grabdenkmäler,* 56; see also Elze, " 'Sic transit,' " 23. The "cupe parole" are Petrocchi's: "L'ultimo destino," 206–207.

5. The episode recounted by Jacques de Vitry is not unlike another one related by the English monk and chronicler Matthew Paris. The victim was the archbishop of Canterbury, Richard Le Grant, who died three days' distant from Rome on Aug. 3, 1231. He had traveled to the curia to discuss King Henry III's ecclesiastical politics with Pope Gregory IX (1227–41). The archbishop's corpse was dressed "in preparation for the sepulcher in pontifical vestments, as is traditional." But some of the people of the region opened the tomb at night, "hoping to steal the ring and other episcopal insignia; but they were unable to do so, either by force or with tools." Jacques was an eyewitness; Matthew Paris was generally a well-informed chronicler of the ecclesiastical events, English as well as curial, of his time. There were thus numerous perils that could still befall the corpses of high prelates in the late Middle Ages (Matthaei Parisiensis, *Chronica maiora,* 3 : 206). See, for example, the fifth *novella* of the second day of Boccaccio's *Decameron* (the spoliation of the corpse of archbishop of Naples, already entombed).

6. An anonymous contemporary account of Innocent III's sojourn and death in Perugia: Perugia, Archivio Capitolare, MS 41, Petrocchi, "L'ultimo destino," 206–207.

7. Salimbene, *Chronica,* 608: ". . . et remansit super paleas nudus et derelictus ab omnibus, sicut mos est Romanorum pontificum, quando ultimum diem claudunt."

8. Pagnotti, "Niccolò," 119: ". . . Fratres Minores, Predicatores et alii religiosi quam plurimi nec non et clerici seculares circa ipsius patris feretrum pernoctantes ac divinis etiam laudibus et orationibus assistentes."

9. Elze, " 'Sic transit,' " 28.

10. Paravicini Bagliani, "La storiografia," 52, note 20.

11. It is curious that Salimbene uses the plural form of the word *palea* (straws).

12. Thomas of Eccleston, *De adventu,* 67. Because Adam of Marisco (d. 1258) is cited as deceased, this passage must have been written during the reign of Henry III (d. 1272): ibid., 72–73.

13. Ibid., 66.

14. Ibid.

15. Ibid.

16. Ibid., 67: "Dixit autem dictus Frater Mansuetus quod nullus mendicus, ne dicam nullus homo, miserabilius et vilius moritur quam papa quicunque."

17. Ibid.

18. Thomas of Eccleston is the only writer who mentions Saint Francis's presence at Innocent III's funeral. His testimony "è non diretta, tarda e non suffragata da altre fonti": Petrocchi, "L'ultimo destino," 206; the problem is also seen in these terms by Huygens, *Lettres de Jacques de Vitry,* 73, no. 62. One strain of Franciscan historiography is more sympathetic, but short on proof: see, for example, P. Gemelli, "Giacomo da Vitry e le origini del movimento francescano," *Aevum* 39 (1965): 485–486.

19. According to Wadding, *Annales,* 5:154, Martin IV expressed the desire to be buried dressed as a Franciscan. It should be noted that Thomas of Eccleston included Niccolò of Calvi in his list of Friars Minor whose lives should serve as models. Curiously, he cast Niccolò's role as Innocent's confessor in a favorable light (Thomas de Eccleston, *De adventu,* 61). In certain respects, Niccolò's description of the much attended nocturnal vigil around the corpse of Innocent IV, which might at first glance seem strained, takes on special value as evidence (he may have been writing Innocent's biography while his nephew, Cardinal Guglielmo Fieschi, was still living: see Paravicini Bagliani, "La storiografia," 52, note 20). Niccolò's emphasis may be an indication of innovations, or at least of funeral practices that were being revived. From this viewpoint as well, and lacking other facts, Salimbene cannot be preferred to Niccolò of Calvi.

20. L. Oliger, "Liber exemplorum Fratrum Minorum s. XIII," *Antonianum* 2 (1927): 247, no. 88, and note 2. For a detailed discussion of these *exempla,* see Paravicini Bagliani, "Die Polemik," 355–362.

21. M. Dufeil, *Guillaume de Saint-Amour et la polémique universitaire parisienne 1250–1259* (Paris, 1972), 146, note 247.

22. Thomas Cantimpratanus, *De Apibus,* Duaci 1627, bk. 2, ch. 11, no. 37; see also Wadding, *Annales,* 3:370, et seq.

23. Döllinger, *Beiträge,* 3:428–429.

24. Ibid., 428; see Elze, " 'Sic transit,' " 39.

25. The text continues as follows (Giovanni Burcardo, *Alla corte*, 44–45): "Ciò malgrado ne avessi fatto più volte richiesta al cardinale di Parma, a Pietro di Mantova, ad Accursio, a Giorgio e Bartolomeo della Rovere, allo spazzino particolare, al barbiere Andrea, che erano stati tutti ciambellani e domestici del defunto Papa, il quale molto li aveva favoriti. Alla fine il cuoco mi ha dato un vaso di rame, usato abitualmente per scaldare l'acqua per lavare i piatti, con un pò d'acqua calda; e il barbiere Andrea mi ha fatto portare dalla sua bottega un unguento. Così il Pontefice è stato lavato. Ma non essendoci panni per asciugarlo, ho fatto tagliare in due la sua camicia, la stessa che aveva addosso nei morire, e l'ho fatto asciugare; e non essendoci altri calzoni oltre a quelli che aveva addosso nel morire, non ho potuto cambiarglieli, dopo lavato. . . . "

26. Johannes Burckardus, *Liber notarum*, 1 : 352; Burcardo, *Alla corte*, 404–406.

27. Johannes Burckardus, *Liber notarum*, 1 : 355; Burcardo, *Alla corte*, 406–407.

28. Johannes Burckardus, *Liber notarum*, 2 : 394; Burcardo, *Alla corte*, 430.

29. Johannes Burckardus, *Liber notarum*, 1 : 15–16: "In hoc erravi: debebat enim in habitu sancti Francisci, cujus ordinem professus erat, sepeliri, desuper in vestibus sacris pontificalibus sibi impositis."

30. Burcardo, *Alla corte*, 47; see also Johannes Burckardus, *Liber notarum*, 1 : 16: ". . . et ratio est, quia in eo, quod homo est, moritur et desinit esse major hominum, ideo, ut homo ante apostolatum, sepeliri debet." The problem presented itself twice in the fifteenth century with the election of the Franciscans Alexander V (1409–10) and Sixtus IV (1471–84).

31. Paride de Grassi, *Tractatus de funeribus et exequiis* (*Vat. lat.* 5986, fol. 127v): cit. Herklotz, "Paris," 229, no. 52. Dykmans, "Paris de Grassi," 436, no. 122, paused to consider the argument in his comment on Patrizi Piccolomini's ceremonial (1484–92). Piccolomini emphasized that the deceased pope must be dressed in the vestments he had worn before becoming pope, above all if he came from a religious order (Dykmans, *L'oeuvre*, 1 : 247). It is scarcely coincidental that the problem was presented in identical terms in prescriptions by the fifteenth-century papal penitentiary; see below, note 53.

32. Dykmans, *L'oeuvre*, 1 : 231, no. 679.

33. Ibid., 1 : 247: "Ubi etiam privatim nudus supra aliquam tabulam nudam positus ab eisdem plumbatoribus lavatur et extergitur."

34. Elze, " 'Sic transit,' " 24, et seq., and 36. The passage "ipse papa moritur" comes from Augustinus Triumphus, cit. Spinelli, *La vacanza*, 97 and 164 (see also below, chap. 6, note 36). Elze, " 'Sic transit,' " 36,

juxtaposed these maxims in a historiographical survey. The famous maxim "Le roi ne meurt jamais" was first noticed by Giesey in Bodin, *Les Six Livres de la République*, 1, 8, ad finem (ed. Paris 1583, 160): "Car il est certain que le Roy ne meurt jamais, comme l'on dit, ainssi tost que l'un est decedé, le plus proche masle de son estoc est saisi du Royaume, et en possession d'iceluy auparavant qu'il soit couronné"; see Giesey, *Le roi ne meurt jamais*, 268.

35. On pillaging in regard to the kings of France, see Erlande-Brandenburg, *Le roi est mort*, 17. The stripping of the corpse of William the Conqueror (1087), recorded by Ordericus Vitalis, *Historia ecclesiastica*, 7, 16, ed. M. Chibnall, 4 (Oxford, 1973), 100–108, was not, therefore, the "unica spoliazione sicura che (si) conosca d'un re del medioevo" (Elze, "'Sic transit,'" 36, note 47).

36. See chap. 6, 148.

37. Aymon, *Tableau de la Cour de Rome*, 382, declares that "Quand le pape est à l'extrémité, ses neveux, ou autres domestiques emportent de son palais tous les meubles qu'ils y trouvent; et aussi-tôt qu'il a rendu l'Esprit les Officiers de la Chambre Apostolique viennent dans l'appartement où il est décédé pour se saisir de sa dépouille, mais les parens du défunt y mettent si bon ordre, qu'il n'y reste que les autres murailles . . ."; see W. Jones, *Crowns and Coronations: A History of Regalia* (London, 1883), 401; Bertelli, *Il corpo del re*, 49.

38. Herklotz, "'Sepulcra,'" 194.

39. Andrieu, *Le pontifical romain*, 2:501–504.

40. LP, 2:387.

41. Herklotz, "'Sepulcra,'" 194 (fig. 85); idem, "Paris," 230, and fig. 1.

42. Herklotz, "'Sepulcra,'" 194; idem, "Paris," 230, and illustration C.

43. Herklotz, "'Sepulcra,'" 194.

44. Ibid., 199.

45. Dykmans, *Le cérémonial*, 4:219, no. 978. Pope Clement VI's coffin was covered with a black silk cloth embroidered with gold, with the papal arms at the bottom done in red silk: Déprez, "Les funérailles," 238. On the cushions, see Dykmans, *Le cérémonial*, 4:220, no. 979.

46. Herklotz, "Paris," 230–231.

47. Davidsohn, *Geschichte von Florenz*, 4:3, 371, et seq. The documents discovered by Davidsohn are learnedly summarized by Herklotz, "Sepulcra," 224–225.

48. Constantin VII Porphyrogénète, *Le livre des cérémonies*, 2 (Paris 1939), 1:69 (60).

49. Erlande-Brandenburg, *Le roi est mort*, 19.

50. See chap. 4, note 43.

51. Von Rudloff, *Über das Konservieren*, 20.

52. Dykmans, *Le cérémonial*, 4:219, no. 969; trans. Moroni, 6: 201–202.

53. In a book meant to summarize the rights and duties of the members of the pontifical *familia,* drawn up between 1261 and 1294, and containing customs prevailing under Boniface VIII, Benedict XI, and Clement V (1294–1314), the rubric on the almoners begins with a description of their duties in the event of the pope's death. They were entrusted with the responsibility of preparing the pope's corpse and dressing it, according to custom, in pontifical vestments, before turning it over to the penitentiaries. In return, the almoners received the bed in which the pope had died. It should be noted that the passage that concerns us is found only in the codex at Naples, Bibl. Nazionale, ix, D. 15: "Ipsi vero fratres elemosinarii presentes in obitu summi pontificis debent preparare dominum, lavare mundare et vestire in vestibus pontificalibus, sicud consuetum est, postea presentare in manibus penitenciarii; et dicti fratres debent habere lectum, in quo moritur dominus noster papa": ed. J. Haller, "Zwei Aufzeichnungen," 20; and not in the more complete version (conserved in a codex in the Archivio Storico of the Bishopric of Aosta), discovered by Frutaz, "La famiglia pontificia," 301. Another, more elaborate redaction, predating 1328, is conserved in MS 1706 of the Bibl. Municipale of Avignone; several excerpts have been published by G. Mollat, "Miscellanea Avignonensia. I. Notes sur trois fonctionnaires de la cour pontificale au début du XIVe siécle," *Mélanges d'archéologie et d'histoire* 44 (1927): 1–5; see also Schimmelpfennig, *Die Zeremonienbücher,* 46. This is the only passage in the entire document that deals with the entombment of the pope. The only other reference to problems of entombment is contained in the paragraph concerning the rights and obligations of the Antoniani of Vienne, but this concerns the burial of curialists and people who died *apud Sedem Apostolicam,* not popes or cardinals. The tasks of the penitentiaries, *cubiculari,* and almoners are again described, with a few variations, in a fifteenth-century formulary of the penitentiary: Göller, *Die päpstliche Pönitentiarie,* 1 : 145; see von Rudloff, *Über das Konservieren,* 20, note 1.

54. Guido de Cauliaco, *Cyrurgia magna,* tract. 6, doct. 1, ch. 8; see von Rudloff, *Über das Konservieren,* 37.

55. Guido de Cauliaco, *Cyrurgia magna,* tract. 1, doct. 1, ch. 8, 274.

56. Ibid., tract. 6, doct. 1, ch. 8: ". . . ut dicebat Jacobus pharmacopoeus [in other editions: apothecarius], qui multos Romanos pontifices praeparaverat." The presence at the papal court of Avignon in the years 1321–1360 of a certain *Jacobus* (or *Jaquetus*), *Melioris, apothecarius (hypothecarius) Curiae Romanae,* is attested by numerous documents of the camera (Schäfer, *Die Ausgaben . . . unter Johann XXII.,* 859, *ad indicem;* idem, *Die Ausgaben . . . unter Benedikt XII.,* 874 ad indicem); see von Rudloff, *Über das Konservieren,* 21.

57. The notices provided by Chauliac postdate the promulgation of Boniface VIII's famous decretal *Detestande feritatis,* which prohibited the dismemberment and evisceration of the corpse. For the text of Boniface's bull of Sept. 27, 1299, see *Les Registres de Boniface VIII,* no. 3409 (Potthast, 24881). It was inserted into the *Liber Sextus* with the date of Feb. 18, 1300 (*Corpus iuris canonici,* ed. Friedberg, 2:1272–1273 [Potthast, 24914]). For a full examination, see Brown, "Death," 221–270. Herklotz, "Paris," 245, no. 127, seems to draw from the existence of the Bonifacian decretal *Detestande feritatis,* studied by Brown, the conclusion that "die Ausweidung des Leichnams am pèpstlichen Hof nie zum festen Brauch geworden (ist)." His view is partially refuted by the sources on "internal" embalming assembled here. Apart from the fact that, already, Clement V did not hesitate to grant dispensations from Boniface's decretal, it should be noted that embalming—even internal—did not require using the procedures prohibited by Boniface VIII, that is, dismemberment and boiling the corpse.

58. Guido de Cauliaco, *Cyrurgia magna,* tract. 6, doct. 1, ch. 8: "De facie tenenda detecta, usque ad octo dies, in quibus corpora consueverunt alterari et putrefieri . . ."; see von Rudloff, *Über das Konservieren,* 37.

59. Pietro Argellata, *Cirurgia,* bk. 5, tract. 12, ch. 3, fol. 109r: "Demum fuit indutus ut summus pontifex (that is, with pontifical liturgical vestments) et stetit per dies octo sine aliquo fetore mundi"; see von Rudloff, *Über das Konservieren,* 39. The notice is not contradicted by an independent source, edited by D'Achery, *Spicilegium,* 6:254–256, according to which the body of Alexander V was buried after the novena, in which numerous cardinals and bishops had taken part, *secundum morem.* On exposing the hands, feet, and face: Pietro Argellata, *Cirurgia,* bk. 5, tract. 12, ch. 3, fol. 108v: "Et ego dico quod iste modus non debet fieri in summo pontifice quia manus et pedes debent videri et similiter facies"; see von Rudloff, *Über das Konservieren,* 37–39. For Argellata's biography: M. Crespi, "Argellata, Pietro," in *Dizionario Biografico degli Italiani* (Rome, 1962), 4:114.

60. Pagel, *Die Chirurgie,* tract. 3, doct. 1, ch. 7, 390 et seq.: "Et istorum corporum praeparandorum tres sunt modi, quorum quaedam pauca aut nulla praeparatione corruptionis praeservativa indigent sicut pauperum et quorundam divitum, in infra tres dies in aestate aut infra quattuor in hieme debeant sepeliri. Alia sunt quae praeparatione indigent, sicut homines mediocris status, ut milites et barones, alia facie discooperta, sicut reges et reginae, summi pontifices et praelati"; see von Rudloff, *Über das Konservieren,* 29. On this learned surgeon see, in general, Pouchelle, *Corps.*

61. When the tomb of Gregory VII was opened in 1578, it was discovered that on his face had been "sovrapposto un velo," which has

been taken (by Herklotz, 'Sepulcra,' 210, note 185) as an "indizio che potrebbe parlare a sfavore di una esposizione nella bara." But this indicates only the way in which he was laid in his sepulcher, not the manner of his exposition, which took place "with the face uncovered." The notarial document is transcribed in A. Capone, *Il Duomo di Salerno* (Salerno, 1927), 1:125.

62. Iazeolla, "Il monumento," 143–152.

63. See above, 115–16.

64. See Brown, "Death," 268; on the uncovered faces of the dead, see Alexandre-Bidon, "Le corps," 203–205.

65. The Salerno document was edited by Capone, *Il Duomo di Salerno*, 1:124–125. Canon Grimaldi's report on the opening of Boniface VIII's tomb has been published by Strnad, "Giacomo," 145–202 (ed.: 188–202). Moroni, 6:205, records that at the opening of Adrian IV's sepulcher (d. Sept. 1, 1159) in 1607, he "si trovò incorrotto, e adorno de' pontificali arredi di color nero."

66. Moroni, 6:205. On the death of Clement VI, the Apostolic Camera acquired some fine white cloth from Rheims to dress the pope's corpse: Déprez, "Les funérailles," 238.

67. Strnad, "Giacomo," 193. It should be emphasized that Grimaldi does not follow the text of a ceremonial book, but scrupulously describes the contents of the tomb.

68. Herklotz, "'Sepulcra,'" 194; idem, "Paris," 230–231. See also Gardner, *The Tomb*, 181, ad indicem.

69. Dykmans, *Le cérémonial*, 4:219, no. 977.

70. Aymon, *Tableau*, 385–386: "Derriére le Lit de parade sur lequel est le corps du pape, on voit son Maistre d'étable sur un Cheval noir, sans oreilles, qui n'a pour tout harnois que des bandes de toile, un Drap satin blanc, et une aigrette à trois rangs de filet de verre, et de clinquant doré sur la tête. On voit passer ensuite vingt quatre autres Palefreniers conduisant des Mules noires, avec des couvertes blanches, et une dozaine d'Estasiers avec des haquenèes blanches, couvertes de velours noir." Benedict VIII (1012–1024) was represented after his death riding a black horse, but this feature refers to a *damnatio memoriae*, and has nothing to do with this aspect of the funeral ceremony (RIS, 3:2, 339).

71. Capone, *Il Duomo di Salerno*, 1:124–125.

72. This undermines the argument of Herklotz, "Sepulcra," 210, note 185, according to which the covered face in the report on Gregory VII would be an "indizio che potrebbe parlare a sfavore di una esposizione nella bara."

73. LP, 1:293.

74. LP, 1:338.

75. Manegold's *Liber ab Gebehardum,* MGH, *Libelli,* 1:326: ". . . ad-

huc locuntur miracula. . . ." The notice is repeated in the version of the *Liber pontificalis* redacted by Boso, LP, 2:356. Boso used a very similar formula in describing the burial of Gregory VII (LP, 2:368).

76. Pietro Mallio, *Descriptio,* in Valentini and Zucchetti, *Codice topografico,* 3:387, 395; see Maccarrone, "Il sepolcro," 755, note 16.

77. MGH, SS, 22:352: "Tumulum autem eius reverenter habetur."

78. Pagnotti, "Niccolò," 119: "Et eo ibidem sepulto in spetiosa et celebri sepultura, obsessi . . . liberantur et omnes, qui ibidem puro corde implorant auxilium, salubrem sue petitionis (consequuntur) effectum."

79. Chronicle of the Dominican convent of Santa Maria in Gradi in Viterbo, composed in 1615 by the Dominican Giacinto de Nobili. The chronicler may have had access to older sources (AA SS, Propyl. Maii, 2:54*, et seq.): "Clemens Papa IV . . . in ecclesia Gradensi corpus suum sepeliri mandavit. Die XXIX . . . mensis Novembris miraculis coruscare coepit: Indeque populi ejus sanctitate ac miraculis moti ad ejus sacrum cadaver visendum tangendum et deosculandum confluere," cit. Ladner, *Die Papstbildnisse,* 2:155. Not wanting to let a similar treasure slip away, the canons decided to bury him, against the wishes of the Dominicans, in the cathedral (Saint Lawrence). Gregory X (1271–76) threatened them with excommunication (Potthast 20876, 20924, 20935, 21914; for the texts of the principal documents, see Ladner, *Die Papstbildnisse,* 2:155, et seq.; see also Garms, "Gräber," 96). In 1885, the convent of Santa Maria in Gradi having been turned into a prison, the tomb of Clement IV was transferred to the church of Santa Francesco alla Rocca in Viterbo, where it still stands; see Bertelli, "Traversie," 53–63.

80. Campi, *Dell'historia,* 2:347–349. On the cult of Gregory X, see the documentation collected by Vauchez, *La sainteté,* 366, note 160.

81. Ladner, *Die Papstbildnisse,* 2:174.

82. Mann, *The Lives of the Popes,* 16:354.

83. *Continuatio Romana della Chronica pontificum et imperatorum* by Martinus Polonius, MGH, SS, 22:481: "et qui scripsit hec, vidit ea"; see also LP, 2:465. Like John XXI, Martin IV had also died, at least so it was said, of an accident, this time of an alimentary nature (Dante, *Divina Commedia,* Purg. 24:20–24). In both cases, there was perhaps a desire to authenticate the pope's death by means of a prolonged public display of the corpse.

84. Edition of the letter: Wadding, *Annales,* 5:168; see also 154 and 167. The pope, moreover, would have expected to be buried in the Franciscan habit (ibid., 166). Honorius IV himself affirms that he was named Martin IV's testamentary executor: ibid., 168. Possible traces of the pope's testament appear in several Franciscan obituaries (the

Cluniac priory of Saint-Martin-des-Champs in Paris, Sens cathedral, the abbeys of Sainte-Geneviève in Paris and of Saint-Denis; see Paravicini Bagliani, *I testamenti*, 37.

85. Wadding, *Annales*, 5:167: "ne sancto privarentur corpore . . . varias interposuerunt appellationes . . . obiitque Honorus, neque fuit qui amplius translationem urgeret."

86. Statutes of the city of Perugia, no. 437. Later, a new sepulcher for Martin IV was constructed in the cathedral of Perugia. Boniface VIII conceded a two years' indulgence to the faithful who took part in the solemn translation of the pope's *venerabile corpus*. The letter (Feb. 28, 1296) is conserved in the Archivio Capitolare of Perugia (perg. C, 29). It is "la bolla piombata di Bonifatio Ottavo" cited by C. Crispolti, *Perugia Augusta* (Perugia 1648), 68, that Ladner, *Die Papstbildnisse*, 2: 228, had unsuccessfully sought in the Archivio di Stato of Perugia.

87. Bernardus Guidonis, *Catalogus*, LP, 2:472.

88. Steinmann, *"Die Zerstörung,"* 145–171 (esp. 154); and Schmidt, "Typen," 52. Testimonials of miracles taking place at the death of an Avignonese pope appear only with Urban V (*Vita V*, Baluze and Mollat, 1:404). Popular devotion had assumed forms not witnessed for any other pope of the thirteenth and fourteenth centuries: "an infinite number of wax statuettes *[imagines ceree]* were hung before the sepulcher and in almost the entire church of the aforesaid monastery [Saint Victor of Marseille]; they had been brought there by people saved from dangers and sickness who had invoked his name." These statuettes depicted the pope. The *Vita II* of Urban V in fact ends the story by declaring emphatically: "There is not a church in the world in holy places in which there is not a wax statute of the pope painted and honored with vigils and oblations" (Baluze and Mollat, 2:393). For his contemporaries, Urban V was a candidate for the honor of the altars. The popular devotion that erupted around his corpse and at his sepulcher was akin to that reserved for a saint; see Albanès, *Abrégé;* and Vauchez, *La sainteté*, 368–372.

89. LP, 2:143–157.

90. In the epitaph of Urban IV (1261–64), the contrast between "high and low" is explicit: the inscription plays on the pope's name to underline that he had been *ab Urbe monarcha;* but the following verse recalls that he is *nunc cinis* (Ladner, *Die Papstbildnisse*, 2:130): ". . . nvnc cinis exigvi tvmvli conclvdor in archa. . . ."

91. Monferini, "Pietro di Oderisio," 39, et seq., was the first to call attention to the possible connections between the sepulcher of Clement IV and the Preachers at Viterbo. The hypothesis that the realism of the gisant served the Dominican iconography of death accords perfectly with the rhetoric of *Sic transit,* then so intense. Thomas Aquinas's presence at Viterbo further supports the thesis, which has the

virtue of connecting funeral monuments to a cultural context. The problem was then taken up by Claussen, "Pietro di Oderisio," 173 – 200. In precisely these years, in curial circles, the mendicants showed themselves capable of presenting models for the preparation for death. Cardinal Vicedomino Vicedomini (d. 1276) ordered a sepulcher similar to those existing in the church of the Dominicans at Lyons; other cardinals ordered suffragan masses in the same manner in which they were prescribed by the mendicants (Paravicini Bagliani, *I testamenti,* 157, et seq.; on this issue, see also the views of Rigon, "Orientamenti").

92. An old tradition attributes Urban IV's epitaph (see above, note 91) to the pen of Thomas Aquinas; see Ladner, *Die Papstbildnisse,* 2:157.

93. *Vita Gregorii X,* in Campi, *Dell'historia,* 2:347.

94. Dykmans, *Le cérémonial,* 2:205–207, and 411–412. The role listing members of the papal *familia,* whose redaction dates back to the last decades of the thirteenth century, records Alexander IV's decision to aid the two hundred poor (Haller, "Zwei Aufzeichnungen," 30; Frutaz, "La famiglia pontificia," 316). We know, in addition, that consistory was not held that day (see the *Ordo XIV,* ed. Dykmans, *Le cérémonial,* 2:419). Sermons have come down to us from Cardinal Odo of Châteauroux that were delivered on the feast instituted by Alexander IV (the Arras MS 137 contains a sermon on the anniversary of Pope Innocent IV [fols 158ra–159va] and of the popes and cardinals [fols. 156va–158ra]). The clergy of the church of Saint Urban, which Cardinal Ancher Pantaléon had erected in Troyes in memory of his uncle Urban IV (1261–64), were required by statute to celebrate a mass every day in honor of Urban, and at least one mass a week "pro Romanis pontificibus defunctis" (Borgolte, *Petrusnachfolge,* 205). In his testament (1296), the mathematician Campano of Novara, who was a papal chaplain for thirty years, from Urban V to Boniface VIII, ordered that an *officium defunctorum* be celebrated daily in memory of Cardinal Gerardo of Parma, and of the popes *a quibus bonum habuit* (Paravicini Bagliani, *Medicina,* 112–113).

95. Egidi, *Necrologi,* 1:passim. On the anniversaries established by the popes at Saint Peter's, see Borgolte, *Petrusnachfolge,* 179–232. For the kings of France, it is difficult to establish the date on which the celebration of the anniversary (of all the kings) was instituted. The oldest sources go back only to the fourteenth century: see A. Wilmart, "Les anniversaires célébrés à Saint-Denis au milieu du XIVe siècle," in *Revue Mabillon* (1924), 22–31; and Erlande-Brandenburg, *Le roi est mort,* 103. But already, in 1211, Bishop Peter of Paris had founded a chaplaincy in memory of Louis VII, Adèle, their parents, and "all of their ancestors" (ibid., 100).

96. Tillmann, *Papst Innozenz III,* 9, note 59.

97. Horoy, *Honorii III opera omnia,* 352–363, no. 31.

98. Ryccardus de Sancto Germano, *Chronica,* RIS, 7, 2, 151. In 1241 the cardinals, meeting in "conclave," wrote to an abbot (Walter of Peterborough?) in the diocese of Lincoln, asking him to grant an ecclesiastical benefice to a cleric named John of the deceased Cardinal Robert of Somercotes. The cardinals justified their request by declaring that the deceased *nobis vivit post funera* (Hampe, "Ein ungedruckter Bericht," 31).

99. The text, unedited, can be reconstructed using the manuscripts cited by Schillmann, 212.

100. Moroni, 55:62. Concerning the vital organs, Pietro Argellata, assigned to embalm Alexander V's (d. May 3, 1410) cadaver, noted succinctly: "The intestines and other members were buried immediately," but he does not say where (*Cirurgia,* bk. 5, tract. 12, ch. 3, fols. 108v–109r). When Pius II died at Ancona, the *praecordia*—a term that later entered the language of the curia to define the vital organs of the deceased pope—were buried in that city, his biographer informs us, "in the Temple of San Ciriaco" (Campano, *Le vite di Pio II,* RIS 3:2, 87). On the "papal precordia" see Moroni, 55:62–63.

101. *Diario di Roma,* 1757, no. 6186; see also Moroni, 60:62; and Bradford, *Heart Burial,* 53–54.

Chapter Six

1. Zoepffel, *Die Papstwahlen,* 18–19.

2. Ibid., 24.

3. *Regesta Honorii papae III,* no. 1. The letter (July 25, 1216) agrees, in substance, with the norms that still prevailed in this first stretch of the century: the official funeral was held the day after death, burial took place the same day as the funeral, and electoral negotiations began on the third day after the death. The eyewitness account is edited by Petrocchi, "L'ultimo destino," 206–207.

4. *Les Registres de Grégoire IX,* no. 1; see also Potthast, 2:677.

5. Hampe, "Ein ungedruckter Bericht," 26. The testimony of Niccolò of Calvi concerning Innocent IV can be accepted, particularly because his chronology agrees with Alexander IV's letter of election (Pagnotti, "Niccolò," 119). For Alexander IV's letter, see *Les Registres d'Alexandre IV,* no. 119 (Dec. 22, 1254).

6. Jean Papire Masson, *Libri sex de episcopis Urbis, qui Romanam Ecclesiam rexerunt* (Paris, 1586), fol. 251v: "Sepultusque Idibus Maij [May 13] millesimo ducentesimo septuagesimo septimo at post ruinam sexto die. . . . Hoc autem exemplo monemur, ne Romanos quidem Pontifices humanis casibus exceptos esse: quia ut sint Pontifices, homines tamen esse non desinunt." The date given by Masson is incorrect, because John XXI died on May 20. It is impossible to determine

Masson's source, and it is difficult to say whether such a long period should be attributed to the accidental nature of the pope's death. Masson's notice is not repeated by either Riccobaldo of Ferrara or Francesco Pipino, *Chronicon*, RIS, 9, col. 723, or by Siegfried of Balnhuisin, *Compendium historiarum*, MGH, SS, 25:708. In his letter of election, Nicholas III, though remaining vague about the chronology of events, emphasizes the solemnity of his predecessor's funeral and explicitly recalls the presence of his corpse, a detail that had not been part of the traditional chancery formula before that time: *Les Registres de Nicolas III*, no. 1.

7. It may further be noted that in his donation to the canons of Saint Peter's, Pope Nicholas III emphasized what Alexander IV had prescribed in his *ordinatio* of 1259, namely, that the *novem lectiones* be celebrated on his anniversary: Egidi, *Necrologi* 1:244–245, at Aug. 23. On Nicholas III's donation to Saint Peter's, see Borgolte, *Petrusnachfolge*, 212–218.

8. April 1: Johannes de Eversden, *Chronicon*, 2:235; April 2: *Annales Mantuani*, MGH, SS, 19:29; see also Potthast, 2:1794. The chronology suggested by the chroniclers is confirmed by Honorius IV's letter of election (to the archbishop of Milan), which, modifying the customary formula, gives the date of both Martin IV's death (March 28) and the beginning of negotiations for the election of his successor (April 1); see *Les Registres d'Honorius IV*, no. 472.

9. See chap. 5, 139–40.

10. *Conciliorum oecumenicorum decreta*, 314–318; on the bull *Ubi periculum maius*, see Spinelli, *La vacanza*, 103, et seq.; and Petrucci, "Il problema," 69–96.

11. *Conciliorum oecumenicorum decreta*, 314–315: "Sacro concilio approbante, statuimus ut, si eumdem pontificem in civitate, in qua cum sua curia residebat, diem claudere contingat extremum, cardinales qui fuerint in civitate ipsa praesentes, absentes expectare decem diebus tantummodo teneantur."

12. Johannes Monachus, *Commentario al Liber Sextus*, at *concilio*, cit. Dykmans, "Les pouvoirs," 128, note 9.

13. Adrian, who died (Aug. 18) only a few days after his election (July 11), did not have time to have his decision formally written down. John XXI, elected pope on September 2, 1276, published his decree of suspension on September 30: *Bullarum*, 4:37–38. See also Dykmans, "Les pouvoirs," 128.

14. *Quia in futurorum* (Potthast, 23980). Just before abdicating, Celestine V confirmed the validity of *Ubi periculum* in cases in which the pope resigned his office.

15. Jacopus Caietanus de Stefaneschis, *Opus metricum*, bk. 2, verses 24–31, ed. Seppelt, 87: ". . . Regis, et excusso bis quino lumine Phebi. . . ." In 1298 Boniface VIII had *Ubi periculum* incorporated into

his *Liber Sextus,* 10, 1, 6, 3, ed. Friedberg, 2:946–949. Although Gregory X's constitution was not applied between 1276 and 1294, it was considered important that the election be held in the same place where the preceding pope had died. Martin IV, in his letter of election (el. Feb. 22, 1281) emphasized that while the corpse of his predecessor Nicholas III was being buried in Rome, the cardinals, "ancxii de vacatione ipsius Ecclesie," had remained in Viterbo, "ubi tunc Romana residebat curia" (*Les Registres de Martin IV,* no. 1). Similarly, Nicholas IV recorded explicitly (Feb. 23, 1288) that the cardinals had met in the palace of Santa Sabina, "in quo predecessor ipse resederat" (*Les Registres de Nicolas IV,* no. 1). Benedict XI (October 31, 1303) expressed himself even more precisely, using the very words of Gregory's constitution: the cardinals met "in palatio sancti Petri de Urbe, in quo decesserat predecessor ipse" (*Les Registres de Benoît XI,* no. 1).

16. Cipolla, *Le opere,* 1:159 et seq.: ". . . consumatis exequiis, in Vaticano, basilice Sancti Petri de more vetusto telluri obrute mandavere, marmore superiecto."

17. Tholemeus Lucensis, *Historia ecclesiastica,* RIS, 11:1223: "Minori reverentia sepelitur, quam pontificalis status requireret"; see also Cipolla, *Le opere,* 1:164, note 1. The burial of Benedict XI took place the day immediately following his death, but we do not know which funeral ritual was observed: B. Guidonis, *Libellus,* cit. Potthast, 2:2038.

18. Baluze and Mollat, 1:272, 288; and 1:329–330, 342. On the novena held at the death of Innocent VI, see Déprez, "Les funérailles," 238, 241.

19. See, e.g., the *Vita IV Urbani V,* Baluze and Mollat, 1:398: "Peractis exequiis domini Innocentii more solito IX diebus, die decima, cardinales viginti intraverunt conclave." This can be confirmed in the accounts of the Apostolic Camera: the corpse of Innocent VI was displayed for two days (Sept. 12–14, 1362) in the great chapel of the Apostolic Palace and given an honor guard; during the day, some priests celebrated mass for the repose of the soul of the deceased (Déprez, "Les funérailles," 241); black dress was acquired for the papal officials whose offices ended with the pope's death (242).

20. Baluze and Mollat, 1:442–443. The chronicle of Garoscus, ed. Ehrle, "Die Chronik," 331, provides an exact calendar: the pope died on Saturday, March 27; on Monday, the corpse was displayed in the choir of Saint Peter's in the Vatican. The formal exposition took place in Santa Maria Nuova, to which the body was transferred on March 30. There were entire decades in which no papal funerals took place in Rome. Rather significantly, Urban VI, perhaps in pursuit of legitimacy, again held funeral services for his predecessor four days after he had been elected: Vanel, *Histoire des conclaves,* 16.

21. See chap. 4.

22. In imperial Rome, the *funus duplex* was not widespread, as Bickermann has tried to argue: "Die römische Kaiserapotheose," 1–34; idem, "Le culte," 7–37. But it appears to be confirmed in the cases of Pertinax and of Septimius Severus: Hohl, "Die angebliche Doppelbestattung," 169–185; see Kantorowicz, *Les deux corps du roi,* 565, note 6; and Dupont, "Corps des dieux." The *novemdiale* (a lunch held in honor of the deceased, which ended the time of mourning) practiced among the Romans was fought against by Saint Augustine (see Freistedt, *Altchristiliche Totengedächtnisstage,* 119–126). Sources and bibliography in Herklotz, "Paris," 247, notes 134–136. For the most recent bibliography on the history of the novena, see ibid., 247–248, note 138.

23. Treitinger, *Die oströmische Kaiser- und Reichsidee,* 156, note 57 (based on the fourteenth-century testimony of the pseudo-Kodinos).

24. *Nicephori Gregorae byzantina historia IX,* 4, ed. L. Schopen (Bonn 1829), 1 : 463.

25. Dykmans, *Le cérémonial,* 1 : 158: "Quia 'omnis potentatus vita brevis,' idcirco sepe contingit quod Romani pontifices, qui in subcelesti ierarchia primatum obtinent, infra breve temporis spatium vitam finiunt et, carnis ergastulo derelicto, ad libertatem transeunt patrie supernorum. . . ."

26. Watt, "The Constitutional Law," 156.

27. The basic works are Spinelli, *La vacanza,* 156, et seq.; Dykmans, "Les pouvoirs," 119–145.

28. Matthaei Parisiensis, *Chronica majora,* ed. Luard, 6 : 250.

29. Hostiensis, *Lectura,* fols. 104v–105, *De poenis,* 14: *Cum ex eo,* notes 24–28; see Dykmans, "Les pouvoirs," 133.

30. Hostiensis, *Apparatus* 5, 38, 14, under *plenitudinem potestatis,* cit. Watt, "The Constitutional Law," 156.

31. Johannes Monachus, *Glossa in Sextum* (Venice 1586), fols. 365v–366; see also Dykmans, "Les pouvoirs," 135.

32. Rocaberti, *Bibliotheca,* 2, c. 24, 59: "Dicebant quidam, quod Ecclesia nunquam moritur. Ideo sede vacante remanet potestas papalis in Ecclesia vel collegio cardinalium"; cit. Sägmüller, *Die Thätigkeit,* 228, note 3.

33. Oliger, "Epistola," 369–370: "Et certe, mortuo papa et necdum altero substituto, residet apud eos precipua auctoritas totius Ecclesie gubernande"; see Jeiler, "Ein unedierter Brief," 656; and Sägmüller, *Die Thätigkeit,* 228, note 3.

34. Oliger, "Petri Iohannis Olivi," 353–354: ". . . sed solum collegium cardinalium, qui proprie et anthonomastice sunt ipsa sedes Ecclesie Romane"; thus also in the passage cited in the preceding note; and see also Petrus Iohannis Olivi, *Expositio,* 3, fol. 107vb: c. 1: ". . . et his, qui, mortuo papa, tenent locum eius."

35. "Potestas et auctoritas Romani pontificis, sede vacante, apud collegium cardinalium sancte Romane Ecclesie remanet" (letter of July 21, 1304, ed. Dykmans, "Les pouvoirs," 131). After Clement V's death (April 20, 1314), the cardinals issued absolutions from sentences of excommunication: Schimmelpfennig, *Die Zeremonienbücher*, 189.

36. Augustinus Triumphus, *De potestate collegii mortuo papa*, ed. Scholz, *Die Publizistik*, 501–508 (from MS *Vat. lat.* 4046, fol. 32): Because the "potestas papae [. . . cannot be] perpetuari in papa, quia ipse moritur, sicut et alii homines, oportet quod perpetuetur in Collegio. . . . Sed capud Ecclesie simpliciter est immortale quia Christus, qui est capud Ecclesie simpliciter, est pontifex sanctus in eternum secundum ordinem Melchisedech, uti dicitur ad Hebreos, et per consequens potestas papae est perpetua, simpliciter loquendo, quia remaneat semper in collegio vel in Ecclesia, que est simpliciter ipsius Christi capitis incorruptibilis et permanentis." See Spinelli, *La vacanza*, 163–165; and Elze, *"Sic transit,"* 36.

37. Augustinus Triumphus, *Summa*, quest. 3, 8, cit. McCready, "The Papal Sovereign," 300, note 97.

38. Alvarus Pelagius, *De statu*, 2:68, fol. 94r: "Immo vacante Ecclesia per mortem pape: non est dicendum quod remaneat sine capite: quia hoc dictum non esset remotum ab heresi que tunc corpus cardinalium et tota Ecclesia habet caput Ecclesie generale et verum et proprium Christum scilicet viventem."

39. Clem., bk. 1, tit. 3, *de elect.*, ch. 2, *Corpus iuris canonici*, ed. Friedberg, 2:1135–1136; see Göller, *Die päpstliche Pönitentiarie*, 1: 99–100.

40. This development came to maturity around 1300, and has continued down to modern times; see, for example, Aymon, *Tableau*, 384: "La Rote et tous les Tribunaux cessent de rendre la justice; il n'y a plus que le Cardinal Camerlingue et le Cardinal Grand Pénitencier qui continuent les fonctions de leurs charges."

41. Göller, *Die päpstliche Pönitentiarie*, 1:145, note 2.

42. Rusch, *Die Behörden*, 22. Urban IV distinguished the *camera praedecessoris nostri* from the *camera nostra: Les Registres d'Urbain* IV, Reg. Cam. no. 138.

43. Iohannes de Deo, *Summa de poenitentiis*, codex *Vat. reg.* 177, fol. 31, cit. Göller, *Die päpstliche Pönitentiarie*, 1:98. A fifteenth-century papal *ordo* shows that the office of the papal penitentiaries expired at the pope's death, and that they had to present themselves, along with the cardinal penitentiary, before the cardinals to receive authorization to exercise their office *sede vacante*: Göller, *Die päpstliche Pönitentiarie*, 1: 145, note 2.

44. The nomination and deposition of the provincial rectors and collectors in the papal state had to be taken *de consilio cardinalium;* the

requirement of their *consensus* is implicit; see *Les Registres de Nicolas IV,* nos. 7059–7064, 7074–7075; Baumgarten, *Untersuchungen;* and J. Lul-vès, "Die Machtbestrebungen," 85, et seq.

45. Johannes Andreae, *Novella,* c. 6, 1, 3, note 5: "tenens papatum vel dignitatem est corruptibilis, papatus tamen, dignitas vel imperium semper est"; cit. Kantorowicz, *Les deux corps du roi,* 524, note 239.

46. Baldus, *Super decretalibus, glossa ad* 2, 10, 1, 7; Venice 1580, fol. 93ra, note 4; cit. Maccarrone, *Vicarius Christi,* 237.

47. Baldus, *Consilium* 159, 3 (Frankfurt 1589), fol. 41r: "Imperator in persona mori potest: sed ipsa dignitas, seu imperium immortalis est, sicut et summus Pontifex moritur, sed summus Pontificatus non mor-itur; et immo que procedunt a persona, et nova sede, personalia sunt, si a successiva voluntate dependent. . . . Si autem statim transferunt secum in plenum, tunc mors collatoris non impedit beneficium."

48. Baldus, *Consilium* 159, 3, fol. 41v: "Porro duo concurrunt in Rege: persona, et significatio, et ipsa significatio, quae est quoddam intellectuale, semper est perseverans enigmatice: licet non corporaliter: nam licet Rex deficiat, quid ad rumbum, nempe loco duarum person-arum Rex fingitur."

49. In these formulations, Kantorowicz, *Les deux corps du roi,* 289, and 531, note 295, discerns the clearest medieval anticipations of the Tudor jurists' famous declarations on "the king's two bodies."

50. Dykmans, *Le cérémonial,* 2:471. The passage is contained in two codexes, the oldest going back to 1350.

51. Ibid., 3:264, no. 7.

52. Ibid., 3:266–267, nos. 17–18.

53. Baluze and Mollat, 1:446. Belvederi, "Cerimonie," 172, ad-vanced the hypothesis that the assault on the residence of the neo-elect cardinal should be linked to the ritual of destroying the baldacchin (of a bishop or pope) in the ceremony that followed their election; see Ginzburg, "Saccheggi rituali," 632, note 10; and S. Bertelli, "All'Istituto Italiano per gli studi Storici," *Belfagor* 22 (1967): 318–319 (concerning the seminar of D. Cantimori). The rite of destroying the baldacchin seems to be attested by later sources (Leo X promised the Conservators and Roman *Caporioni,* who claimed the right to do so, that he would cede them the baldacchin; see Gnoli, *La Roma,* 81). And this certainly does not run counter to the chronology of the rite of sacking property, which shows up in the sources only from 1378 onwards.

54. Valois, *La France,* 1:51 (full citations of the documents). The Orsini *casus* has been published by Döllinger, *Beiträge,* 359; see also Val-ois, *La France,* 55: "Le cardinal de Bretagne n'y parvint qu'à la nuit . . . il avait cherché un premier refuge dans sa maison, située, comme on l'a vu, en train de la piller. . . ."

55. Trans. Balzani, *La storia,* 478–479; orig. ed.: *Chronicon Adae de Usk,* ed. Thompson, 86.

56. Leonardi Dathi Epistolae 32:79: "Privata interea quondam domus sua publice, aperteque diripitur. . . ."

57. Mansi, 27:1170.

58. Eneas Silvus Piccolomini, *Oratio de morte Eugenii pp. IV creationeque et coronatione Nicolai V,* in RIS, 3:2, 894.

59. *Pii II Commentarii,* 1:106–107: "Tum qui erant in conclaui ministri cardinalium cellulam eius spoliauere atque argentum, quamuis erat modicum, et libros et uestes turpi more diripuere, et domum eius in Vrbe uilissima plebs atque infamis non expilauit tantum, sed disrupit etiam marmoribus asportatis"; see Eneas Silvius Piccolomini, *I commentari,* trans. L. Totaro (Milan 1984), 2:223.

60. *Pii II Commentarii,* 1:106–107: ". . . et Genuensis pro Senensi auditus partem substantie amisit"; see *I commentarii,* 2:223.

61. Delicati and Armellini, *Il Diario,* 43: "erat de non invadendis aedibus cardinalis illius qui esset electus in Papam, sicut est mos Romanorum, qui etiam saepe simulant hunc vel illum electum esse papam, ut hac occasione diripiant domum et suppellectilem ejus, et placuit omnibus indifferenter."

62. *Bullarum,* 5:649.

63. Ginzburg, "Saccheggi rituali," 621–624.

64. Cortesi, *De cardinalatu,* ch. *De domo,* cit. Bertelli, *Il corpo del re,* 52.

65. This according to what Giovanni Carga wrote the bishop of Feltre (May 18, 1555), Bibl. Vat., *Chigi* R. II. 54, fol. 233v, cit. Bertelli, *Il corpo del re,* 51.

66. Ginzburg, "Saccheggi rituali," 621.

67. See chap. 4, 103.

68. Ginzburg, "Saccheggi rituali," 625, et seq.

69. Boureau, *La papesse Jeanne,* 113.

70. Dykmans, *L'oeuvre,* 1:233, no. 686.

71. Ibid., 1:221, no. 637 *(summos viros),* 33, 93, 157, 196, 213 *(senatus).*

72. Ibid., 1:236, no. 705; see also 1:248; 1:233, no. 687.

73. Ibid., 1:250.

74. Ibid., 1:251.

75. Ibid.

76. Dykmans, *Le cérémonial,* 4:222, no. 1000, et seq.

77. Ibid., 4:224, no. 1011; see Herklotz, "Paris," 245, note 127.

78. Between the Avignon period and the late fifteenth century, from Ameil to Burchard, the ritual of burying the Roman popes was in large part overturned. These changes were not brought about formally. Analysis of the ceremonials of the fourteenth and fifteenth centuries

reveals a different general attitude regarding the times, spaces, and protagonists of the papal funeral ceremony. Ameil discusses ceremonial
problems concerning the pope's death over an arc of time running from
the last instants of the dying pope's life to the conclave for electing his
successor. He devotes a separate appendix to the burial of the cardinals.
In Patrizi Piccolomini's ceremonial, compiled by order of Innocent
VIII (1484–92), *Titulus XV* instead opens with the articles concerning
the death and funerals of the cardinals, designated as *summi viri,* then
proceeds to present the ceremonial pertaining to the popes, devotes
considerable space to the most strictly liturgical aspects, but ends with
the rituals that begin the period of the vacancy of the Apostolic See
(Dykmans, *L'oeuvre,* 1:248–252; comment: 156*–162*). An autograph
manuscript of part of Johann Burchard's *Titulus XV* has survived (ibid.,
1:248–252; these additions are cited based on the autograph MS *Vat.
lat.* 5633, fols. 60–62v). Burchard begins with the pontiff's death—
leaving aside, that is, the ceremonial prescriptions concerning the dying
pope's illness and his preparation for death.

79. Dykmans, *L'oeuvre,* 1:249: "Maneatque ibidem defunctus
usque ad noctem. Solebat tamen antiquitus ibidem tribus diebus per-
manere." By Burchard's own account (394), the body of Pius III was
displayed at Saint Peter's from Tuesday, October 17 (6–7 P.M.), to Friday, October 19, 1503 (3 A.M.).

80. A contemporary chronicle, edited by Finke, "Eine Papstchronik," 362, records that the body of Alexander V (d. May 3, 1410)
"et die dominico ponebatur in sala magna in palacio suo indutus
pontificaliter et custodiebatur a gentibus armorum et quilibet poterat
osculari pedes eius."

81. Aeneas Sylvius Piccolomini, *De morte Eugenii IV,* in RIS, 3:2,
894: "Corpus eius balsamo conditum per integrum diem populo patuit,
atque inde sepultus est apud S. Petrum in Vaticano juxta Eugenium III."

82. *Il diario romano di Jacopo Gherardi,* RIS, 23:3 (Bologna, 1904–
1911), 136–137.

83. Burcardo, *Alla corte,* 45–46.

84. Ibid., 404. See also 394, at the death of Pius III.

85. Ibid., 406.

86. The chronology may be summarized as follows: Saturday,
Nov. 6, death of Pope Innocent VII; the same day ("immediata-
mente"), transport from the chamber to the hall; Sunday, Nov. 7,
transport to the chapel (vespers); Wednesday, Nov. 10, transport to
Saint Peter's; Nov. 10–18, novena, Nov. 18–22, conclave. The sources
are Stefano Infessura, *Diario,* 14; and an anonymous contemporary
chronicle that provides even more precise details (Finke, "Eine Papstchronik," 359).

87. Toni, *Il Diario Romano di Gaspare Pontani,* RIS, 3:2, 39–41; see

also Infessura, *Diario,* 155–170; and Johannes Burckardus, *Liber notarum,* 1:12, et seq.

88. Infessura, *Diario,* 278–279.

89. We do not know how long the "rite of the fly-shooing fans" lasted.

90. The passage is cited in Giesey, *Le roi ne meurt jamais,* 228–229. See also Eccles. 10: 1: "muscae morientes perdunt suavitatem unguenti."

91. Wolkan, *Der Briefwechsel,* 2:255–256: "concedendum est aliquid consuetudini."

92. Ibid., 2:226, no. 655.

93. For a full recent treatment of the problem of cardinals' funerals, see Herklotz, "Paris," 217–248; and now also Gardner, *The Tomb,* 12, et seq.

94. In his *Opus Metricum,* Cardinal Iacopo Caetani Stefaneschi devotes particular attention to the death of the cardinals Latino Malabranca (Aug. 11, 1294) and Matteo Rosso Orsini (Sept. 4, 1305). The cardinal-poet records the funerals of both; in Orsini's he has the entire College of Cardinals participate (*Opus metricum,* verse 200: "Decubuit moriens, toto presente senatu / Exequiis, laus digna viro").

95. Dykmans, *Le cérémonial,* 4:247–251.

96. Duchesne, *Histoire,* 2:281: ". . . et aliae exequiae solemniter celebrentur, et etiam postea usque ad nonam diem, prout est de aliis cardinalibus fieri solitum." Twice in his testament Cardinal Guglielmo Teste expressed his wish that the burial ceremonial used by the cardinals be observed: first regarding the obsequies to be observed in the church of the Friars Minor at Avignon, then at the entombment itself: "altre esequie si celebrino solennemente, et fino al nono giorno, come è solito farsi per agli altri cardinali." For the Avignon cardinals, the novena was generally prescribed outside of Avignon (in Perugia, Toulouse, etc.). Two cardinals specified that it should be performed in the city *in qua moriar* (G. Francon) or *super locum sepolture* (P. Blau). Even when it was to be celebrated at Avignon, it took place at the sepulcher. Such ceremonies were the object of detailed instructions: the celebration of three hundred masses during the novena (G. di Chanac), solemn masses *cum nota* (P. di Saint-Martial), or twelve masses a day (P. Girard); the distribution of alms (G. Francon); a precise amount of wax to be used (P. di Saint-Martial); and the type of cloth—a black drape with a cross—to be placed during the entire novena *super locum sepulture* (Pierre Blau). Three cardinals (P. di Saint-Martial, G. di Malesec, and P. Girard; respectively 1397, 1407, 1410) called for special liturgical celebrations on the last day of the novena.

97. Testaments of cardinals: Philippe Cabassole, ibid., 2:424; Jean de Dormans, ed. Carolus-Barré, "Le cardinal," 353–354; Guil-

laume de Chanac, ed. Baluze and Mollat, 4:277; Pierre de Saint-Martial, ibid., 4:370; Jean de La Grange, ed. Duchesne, *Histoire*, 2:472; Guy de Malesec, ibid., 2:458; Pierre Blau, ed. Labande, "Pierre Blau," 168–169 and 170; Pierre Girard, ibid., 2:552; and Jean Francon, ibid., 2:515–516.

98. Dykmans, *Le cérémonial*, 4:250–251.

99. The *domus fustea cum candelis accensis desuper,* ordered by Guillaume de Chanac in his testament of 1384, concerns the celebration of a solemn *officium exequiarum,* for which he prescribed other traditional ceremonial elements, such as the lighting of no more than one hundred *intorticia* weighing no more than five pounds of wax each, and the presence of all his *socii et familiares* dressed in black. Pierre Blau's desire not to set up a *capella ardens* was formulated in his 1407 testament in relationship to the *missa sepulture,* but not the novena, for which he prescribed instead that a drape of black oilcloth be placed *super locum sepulture* (Labande, "Pierre Blau," 170). The long articles of his testament on the ritual features of the burial constitute a real *vademecum* of a ceremonial nature; they demonstrate that the *capella ardens* had been in use for some time. Even Pierre Ameil prescribed the preparation of a *castrum doloris* for the cardinals (Dykmans, *Le cérémonial*, 4:248–249, no. 1190); not, certainly, because there was a novena for the cardinals, which in the fourteenth century was celebrated at the place of burial, but, obviously, for cardinals who had been buried on the same day as their death, with only a very brief public display, and before the curial funeral. Pierre Bertrand specified in his testament (1361) that he wanted no *pannus aureus* on his catafalque (Duchesne, *Histoire*, 2:365; see also Herklotz, "Paris," 230, no. 55). This indicates the existence of a tradition, confirmed as well by other late fourteenth-century testators (Guillaume de Chanac, Guy de Malesec, Pierre Blau). In 1407, Cardinal Blau stipulated in his testament that his burial should take place either on the night of his death, or two or three days afterwards, obviously to avoid the burdensome display of the cadaver; the cloths used to cover the bier were to be decorated with his cardinals' arms.

100. The master of ceremony's comment was no longer (as it had been a century before) the object of a simple note, but occupies the first forty-one articles of *Titulus XV* of the ceremonial, which are followed, without any specific intermediate title, by the twenty-seven articles concerning the papal funeral ceremonies. In an appendix to the ceremonial of Pope Nicholas V (1447–55), we find described the funeral of the corrector of apostolic letters, John of Rieti, who died on Jan. 25, 1452. The author of the note explains that "nel caso di morte di non cardinali, non è consueto fare la novena" (Dykmans, "Le cérémonial de Nicolas V," 796; see Schimmelpfennig, *Die Zeremonienbücher,* 136 and note 844). The oldest description of novenas for the cardinals

is offered by Burchard (the burial of the Franciscan Cardinal Gabriele of the title of Saints Sergius and Bacchus, 1486: *Liber notarum,* 1:161–165). The date must be seen in relation to an article of Patrizi Piccolomini's funeral ceremonial (1484–92) for the cardinals, in which he declares that "prima del pontificato di Sisto IV, i cardinali non avevano l'abitudine di recarsi nella dimora del cardinale defunto, a meno che non fossero esecutori testamentari; vi inviavano però i loro familiari. Da quei tempi quasi tutti sono presenti alle vigilie, ma non accompagnano il feretro" (Dykmans, *L'oeuvre,* 2:222, no. 641). At the vigil for Cardinal John of Aragon (Oct. 14, 1485), Burchard notes the participation of the familiars, but not of the cardinals (*Liber notarum,* ed. Celani, 1:120; see Herklotz, "Paris," 232, note 61).

101. Herklotz, " 'Sepulcra,' " 244.

102. Johannes Burckardus, *Liber notarum,* 2:359 (Aug. 24, 1503): ". . . habuit tamen hoc singulare quod per totam congregationem habuit super rochetum, manteletum violatium tangentem terram. Cardinalibus hoc redarguentibus dixit hoc facere propter frigus." The cardinal wore the same mantle in all the other meetings of the congregation: Friday, Aug. 25 (360); Saturday, Aug. 26 (360); Monday, Aug. 28 (361); Friday, Sept. 1 (363); and Sunday, Sept. 3 (364).

103. Ibid., 2:368 (Sept. 9, 1503, after the death of Alexander VI): ". . . extra Castrum fuerunt tracti multi scopeti et clamatum: Ecclesia! Ecclesia! Collegio! Collegio! et per viam . . . a multis acclamatum: San Georgio! San Georgio!"

104. On the twelfth-century birth of the maxim *Dignitas non moritur,* see Kantorowicz, *Les deux corps du roi,* 278, et seq. For the history of the maxims *Le roi est mort! . . . Vive le roi!* and *Le roi ne meurt jamais,* attested respectively for the first time in 1515 (at the funeral of Louis XII) and 1576 (Bodin, *Les six livres de la république,* 1, ch. 8), see Kantorowicz, *Les deux corps du roi,* 296–302. On exclamations at the funerals of French kings, see Giesey, *Le roi ne meurt jamais,* passim.

105. The bibliography on the notion of sanctity regarding the pope is abundant but not always helpful. See now above all Fuhrmann, "Über die Heiligkeit des Papstes," 28–43.

106. If it is true that "l'embaumement est donc une pratique ancienne qui tend à rapprocher le corps mort du fidèle de celui du Christ" (Alexandre and Bidon, "Le corps," 187), this should be even more the case for the pope.

Chapter Seven

1. Absences from Rome: Innocent III (62 months; 27.89 percent of his entire pontificate); Honorius III (40.3 months; 31.48 percent); Gregory IX (109.5 months; 53.29 percent); Innocent IV (122.3 months; 89.27 percent); Alexander IV (59.4 months; 77.14 percent); Urban IV

(37 months; 100 percent); Clement IV (46 months; 100 percent); Gregory X (48.6 months; 93.46 percent); Innocent V (1 month; 20 percent); Adrian V (1 month; 100 percent); John XXI (8.3 months; 100 percent); Nicholas III (12 months; 36.36 percent); Martin IV (49 months; 100 percent); Honorius IV (8 months; 33.33 percent); Nicholas IV (27.2 months; 55.51); Celestine V (5.27 months; 100 percent); Boniface VIII (46.3 months; 43.88 percent), Benedict XI (2.8 months; 33.73 percent).

2. Paravicini Bagliani, "La mobilità," 155–278.

3. Segni (3), Ferentino (3), Viterbo (3), Anagni (1), Subiaco (1), Perugia (1).

4. Paravicini Bagliani, "La mobilità," 248.

5. *Vita Pauli I*, LP, 2:465. This account, along with some of the others cited in the following notes, was already collected by S. Borgia, *Memorie istoriche della pontificia Città di Benevento* (Rome, 1769), 3:198–204, note 1; see also Cancellieri, *Lettera*, 19–22; and idem, *Notizie*.

6. The cause was the fever contracted in Rome, not poison, as claimed by Cardinal Benno, *Gesta Romanae Aecclesiae contra Hildebrandum*, 9, in MGH, *Libelli de lite*, 2:379; see also Celli, "La malaria," 19.

7. JL, *ante* 4376—*post* 4384.

8. *Die Briefe*, 2:344.

9. JL, 4874, 4961, and 5002; see Celli, "La malaria," 20.

10. LP, 2:303. It left Rome on April 8 and returned there in May, at Trastevere and at Castel Sant'Angelo (JL, *ante* 6522–6523), but in June it headed to Sezze (JL, *ante* 6528). It returned to Trastevere again in the autumn (JL, 6530–6534).

11. LP, 2:305 (JL, 6559–6560).

12. JL, 6982–6991.

13. LP, 2:387; the approximate date of the construction of the summer palace at Segni is confirmed by a document in the Archivio Capitolare of Veroli (Aug. 28, 1152), cit. Toubert, *Les structures*, 1052, note 2.

14. Ibid., 1052, note 1.

15. Watterich, 2:331; and LP, 2:393; see also Celli, "La malaria," 23.

16. LP, 2:395.

17. Toubert, *Les structures*, 1052, note 2.

18. For what follows, see Paravicini Bagliani, "La mobilità," 155–278.

19. Herklotz, "'Sepulcra,'" 139, note 195, rightly observed that the reference to the *palatium hiemale* contitutes a clear *terminus a quo* for the difficult dating of the *De Mirabilibus Urbis Romae;* see also J. Osborne, *Master Gregorius: The Marvels of Rome* (Toronto, 1987), 11.

20. Potthast, 7857. For the text, see Cancellieri, *Lettera*, 19–22: "propter intemperiem aeris."

21. Cancellieri, *Lettera,* 19–22: "cum nos propter aestivos calores et fratrum nostrorum absentiam procuratorers licentiaverimus universos."

22. R. B. C. Huygens, *Magister Gregorius (XXIIe ou XIIIe siècle): Narracio de Mirabilibus Urbis Romae* (Leiden 1970), 30: ". . . in porticu etiam ante hiemale palatium domini pape"; see also Osborne, *Master Gregorius,* 96–97. The author, who should perhaps be identified with the homonymous chaplain of the Piedmontese Cardinal Ottone of Tonengo (1227–1251), shows that he had some familiarity with other protagonists of the curial scene, because he often reports the opinions of cardinals and curialists on certain Roman monuments. See now C. Nardella, *Il fascino di Roma: Le 'Meraviglie di Roma' di maestro Gregorio* (Rome 1997).

23. Periods of papal residence in the thirteenth century in localities of the papal state: Innocent III (62 months, 27.89 percent of his entire pontificate); Honorius III (40 months; 31.48 percent) Gregory IX (102 months; 58.95 percent); Innocent IV (33 months; 24.14 percent); Alexander IV (54 months; 70.12 percent); Urban IV (37 months; 100 percent); Clement IV (46 months; 100 percent); Gregory X (17.77 months; 34.17 percent); Innocent V (0.5 months; 100 percent); Adrian V (1 month; 100 percent); John XXI (8.3 months; 100 percent); Nicholas III (12 months; 36.36 percent); Martin IV (49 months; 100 percent); Honorius IV (8 months; 33.33 percent); Nicholas IV (27.2 months; 55.51 percent); Celestine V (1.4 months; 26.56 percent); Boniface VIII (46.3 months; 43.88 percent); Benedict XI (2.8 months; 33.73 percent).

24. For an examination of the problem, see Paravicini Bagliani, "La mobilità," 166–216.

25. Schmidt, *Libri rationum,* nos. 993, 1239, 2703, and 2237.

26. Paravicini Bagliani, "La mobilità," 212–215.

27. Toubert, *Les structures,* 1051–1053.

28. LP, 2:423: ". . . tanquam dominus per XXVI menses resedit."

29. R. Ambrosi de Magistris, "Il viaggio di Innocenzo III nel Lazio e il primo ospedale di Anagni," *Studi e documenti di storia del diritto* (1898), 365–378; see also Maccarrone, *Studi,* 181, et seq.

30. Finke, *Aus den Tagen,* 14.

31. Finke, *Acta Aragonensia,* 1:65 and 71.

32. At Rome, the celebration of the feast of Easter (in Saint John Lateran) accorded with tradition. Only two of the thirteen transfers of the curia ordered by Innocent III preceded the feast of the Ascension (in 1203 and 1216). In the years 1206–09, the pope always left Rome in May, after the Ascension, twice on Ascension Day itself (1207 and 1208), a point that was explicitly recorded by two chroniclers: the author of the *Gesta Innocentii III* and the *Chronicon Fossae Novae.* The

Roman departures of Innocent's successor, Honorius III, also took place—except one (1225)—after the Ascension. All of Nicholas IV's moves took place in May; only one came before the feast of the Ascension (1289). Boniface VIII's last five transfers of the court to Anagni instead came after the feast.

33. Innocent III: Ascension (1207–08), Holy Trinity (1209); Honorius III: Pentecost (1217) and Jubilee (1225); Gregory IX: Holy Trinity (1227 and 1238), Pentecost (1231), and Holy Trinity (1238); Alexander IV: Low Sunday (1257); Nicholas III: Vigil of Corpus Christi (1278) and Vigil of Pentecost (1280); Honorius IV: Low Sunday (1285); Nicholas IV: Holy Trinity (1290); Boniface VIII: Vigil of Pentecost (1297). The *Ordo XIV* notes almost as exceptional the fact that on the feast of Saints Peter and Paul (29 May) vespers were celebrated inside the Vatican Basilica (Dykmans, *Le cérémonial,* 3 : 418).

34. Of nineteen thirteenth-century popes, only six were elected in Rome (Innocent III, Gregory IX, Celestine IV, Adrian V, Nicholas IV, and Benedict XI). The elections of Innocent III, Gregory IX, and Benedict XI took place, respectively, in winter, spring, and autumn. On thirteenth-century conclaves, see in general Herde, "Election"; Schimmelpfennig, "Papst- und Bischofswahlen," 173–196.

35. Hampe, "Ein ungedruckter Bericht."

36. Tholemeus Lucensis, *Historia Ecclesiastica,* bk. 24, ch. 19, RIS, 8, 1168; see also Herde, "Election," 423–424.

37. Jacopus Caietanus de Stefaneschis, *Opus metricum,* 36–37; see also Finke, *Aus den Tagen,* 28.

38. PL, 217: 393: "Scitis enim, charissimi, quod corruptibile corpus inter anxietates continuas non potest subsistere, nisi quandoque recreationis remedium intercedat."

39. *Chronica Andrensis,* MGH, SS, 24 : 732: ". . . propter estivum tempus corpori suo contrario. . . ."

40. Ordinary of Innocent III (Paris, Bibl. Nat., MS *Lat.* 4162A, fol. 164va), ed. Van Dijk and Walker, *The Origins,* 462: ". . . cum eramus apud illam aridam Signiam . . ."; see also p. 97; and Maccarrone, *Studi,* 59.

41. Letter of Vice Chancellor Thomas of Capua, E. Heller, "Der kuriale Geschäftsgang in den Briefen des Thomas von Capua," *Archiv für Urkundenforschung* 13 (1935): 258, note 3; see also Celli-Fraentzel, "Quellen," 383; and Tillmann, *Papst,* 253, note 8.

42. Hugo (Ugo, or Ugolino, as he is called in numerous contemporary sources) belonged to the family of the counts of Segni, proprietors in the region of Anagni, where around 1170 he was born and educated. The declaration of the English chronicler Matthew Paris (*Chronica Majora,* ed. Luard, 4 : 162), that Gregory IX died "fere centenarius," should not be taken literally. The *Vita Gregorii IX* says he was

related to Innocent III "tertio gradu consanguinitatis," which means that they had a great-great-grandfather in common.

43. Hampe, "Eine Schilderung," 531. The codex is conserved in Paris, Bibl. Nat., MS *Lat.* 11867. Notably, in the *De misera conditionis humanae,* Lothar of Segni (Innocent III) inveighs against the practice of *pingere cameras* (Maccarrone, *Lotharii,* 71, bk. 2, ch. 40)!

44. Hampe, "Eine Schilderung," 531.

45. Ibid., 531: "A quarto latere, quod calentem solem plenius intuetur, sanctissimi Habrahe patris nostri parvum tabernaculum est defixum, de quo sepe ab eodem videri possumus, dum dormimus, cum predicti nostri hospicii sala communis nonnichil distet a nostris cameris picturatis."

46. The *Gesta Innocenti III* (PL, 217:clxxxvii) indicates that the pope moved from Anagni to Ferentino at the end of September 1203, "cum fere totam aestatem demoratus fuisset" (Potthast, *post* 1999). Riccardo of San Germano noted in correspondence of June 1212: "mense iunii Innocentius papa urbem exiens venit Signiam, ubi per aestatem moram faciens, mense Septembri remeavit ad Urbem" (RIS, 8:984; see also Potthast *post* 4547).

47. *Vita Gregorii IX,* LC, 2:24: ". . . mense augusti Anagniam civitatem ingressus, ibi majori parte yemis feliciter consumata."

48. Ibid., 19.

49. Ibid., 22.

50. Ibid., 23.

51. Ibid., 26–27.

52. Ibid., 29.

53. Höfler, *Albert von Beham,* 63 and 77: "quem ibidem conclusum nimii ardoris cauma (?) peremit . . . eo quod salubriori aere foveri consueverit in aestate."

54. Pagnotti, "Niccolò da Calvi," 82.

55. Ibid.

56. Sambin, *Un certame,* 24, 28–29.

57. Teodorico da Vaucouleurs, fol. 233v, ed Campi, *Dell'historia,* 2:410; see Signorelli, *Viterbo,* 2:240.

58. RIS, 3:605.

59. Finke, *Aus den Tagen,* xiv.

60. Potthast, 24879.

61. Lothar of Segni uses phrases such as the following (Maccarrone, *Lotharii,* 80, bk. 3, 4): "mortuus, producit putredinem et fetorem. Vivus, hominem unicum inpinguat; mortuus, vermes plurimos inpinguabit. Quid ergo fetitius humano cadavere? . . . Non liberabunt a morte, non defendent a verme, non eripient a fetore . . ."; "Conceptus in pruritu carnis, in fervore libidinis, in fetore luxurie: . . . agit vana et turpia quibus polluit famam, polluit personam, polluit conscien-

ciam . . . massa putredinis qui semper fetet et sordet horribilis." They can be compared to several passages from the *Quaestiones Salernitanae,* ed. Lawn, *The Prose Salernitan Questions,* 25, no. 54: "Ad fetidum odorem tria occurrunt, aut extranei caloris habundantia, aut naturalis debilitas, aut humiditatis excessus. Verbi gratia, . . . corruptione generata, odorem faciunt fetidum ut in stercore hominis; aut ex habundantia humoris ut in cicuta, unde sequitur corruptio et odor fetidus; aut ex intensione caloris innaturalis corpus corrumpentis, unde sequitur corruptio vel corruptus odor ut in fetido cadavere apparet"; ibid., 231, no. 66: "Quare vultures percipiunt remota cadavera? Quoniam in eis spiritus animalis subtilis est, qui veniens ad fantasticam cellulam facile immutatur secundum aerem qui est infectus a fumo qui est resolutus a cadaveribus, et ideo longe posita facile percipiunt."

62. Lawn, *The Prose Salernitan Questions,* 346.

63. Books 5and 6 of Aristotle's *Historia animalium* are devoted to reproduction.

64. Hampe, "Eine Schilderung," 533.

65. F. von Raumer, *Geschichte der Hohenstaufen und ihrer Zeit* (Leipzig, 1825), 4:22; see Celli, "La malaria," 31.

66. *Vita Gregorii IX, LC,* 2:22.

67. Arnaldus de Villanova, *Breviarium,* in *Opera omnia,* ed. Basil 1585, bk. 2, 30.

68. *Vita Gregorii IX, LC,* 2:22.

69. Ibid., 27.

70. Ibid., 23.

71. Hampe, "Eine Schilderung," 27 and 29.

72. Haskins, "Latin Literature," 141.

73. The problems of contagion are treated by Avicenna in *Canone,* bk. 4, fen 1, tract. 2, ch. 1, and tract. 4, chs. 1–5 (ed. Venice 1507, fols 398r, 416r–v); see also Winslow, *The Conquest.*

74. *De retardatione,* 8: "Mundo senescente senescunt homines, non propter mundi senectutem, sed propter multiplicationem viventium inficientium ipsum aerem, qui nos circumdat."

75. P. Diepgen, "Studien zu Arnaldus von Villanova," *Archiv für Geschichte der Medizin* 5 (1912): 95.

76. Michael Scot, *Liber particularis,* Oxford, Bodleian Library, MS *Canon. Misc.* 555, fol. 41r: "Et ista corruptio aeris non contigit ubique sed transfertur de regione in regionem latenter et manet."

77. F. Hönger, *Ärztliche Verhaltungsmassregeln auf dem Heerzug ins Heilige Land für Kaiser Friedrich II., geschrieben von Adam v. Cremona (ca. 1227),* Diss. (Born-Leipzig, 1912), 39–43; see also J. F. Powell, "Greco-Arabic Influences on the Public Health Legislation in the Constitutions of Melfi," *Archivio Storico Pugliese* 31 (1978): 89–90. See as well the Constitutions of Melfi, bk. 3, tit. 48 ("De conservatione

aerie"), ed. H. Dilcher, *Die Konstitutionen Friedrichs II. von Hohenstaufen für sein Königreich Sizilien* (Köln-Vienna, 1973), 309.

78. Paravicini Bagliani, *Medicina*, 76. According to Albertus Magnus, "the conjunction between Jove and Mars in the sign of Gemini causes pestilential winds, and the air's corruption provokes unforseen epidemics among men and beasts"; see also Winslow, *The Conquest*, 96. The epidemics brought about by changes of temperature and the condition of the air created a poison in the body: *De animalius*, 7.2, 1–2.

79. *Les Registres d'Urbain IV,* nos. 1000–1001. On John of Toledo, see chap. 9.

80. Paravicini Bagliani, "La mobilità," 202–203.

81. J. Bale, *Scriptorum illustrium maioris Brytanniae, quam nunc Angliam et Scotiam vocant, Catalogus,* Basel 1557–1559. For a critical discussion of the sources, see Paravicini Bagliani, *Medicina*, 393–408.

82. Hampe, "Ein Schilderung," 529.

83. Ibid., 530: "Hec [the water] a tercio Salomone diligitur, cum in eadem manus sacras apponat liberter et de ipsa frigido gargarismo utatur. . . ."

84. J. S. Brewer, *Giraldi Cambrensis opera* (London, 1863), 3:252–253 *(De jure et statu Menevensis Ecclesiae).*

85. LP, 2:416–417: "Set propitiante Domino in die tertia visus est prandere cum sociis ad radicem montis Circhegi, ad fontem qui ex tunc Papalis est appellatus."

86. *Gesta Innocentii III,* PL, 214: xxv–xxvi.

87. Ibid., clxxxviii: "Cumque apud Ferentinam per totam aetatem demoratus fuisset, ubi fieri fecit optimum et pulcherrimum fontem."

88. I. Ciampi, *Cronache e statuti della città di Viterbo* (Florence, 1872), 14.

89. On the baths at Viterbo, see G. Durante, *Trattato di dodici bagni singolari della illustre città di Viterbo* (Perugia, 1595), ch. 6. For the identification of Bagno dello Scoppio, see Burchardt, *Witelo*, 53, note 168. Giles of Viterbo extolled the virtues of the baths of Viterbo in a treatise *(De balneis Viterbiensibus),* still unedited, dedicated to Pope Innocent VI (1352–62). Interest in water was a basic feature of the Norman and Swabian royal courts: on this point, see Calò Mariani, "Utilità," 343–372.

90. MGH, SS, 28:1674: "Fuit papa calculosus et valde senex et caruit balneis, quibus solebat Viterbii confoveri."

91. Witelo, *Opticae libri decem,* 10:67: "Invenimus et nos diebus estivis circa horam vespertinam vel modicum ante circa Viterbium in quodam precipitio apud Balneum, quod dicitur Scopuli, aquam vehementer precipitari, descendentesque ad videndum quod in ipsa posset accidere soli sibi opposito, vidimus iridem perpetuam sole circa aspectum illi debitum existente, et multas ex proprietatibus iridis notavimus."

92. *Les Registres de Boniface VIII,* no. 1648. In his testament, Campano left one of his servants the usufruct of a field, a vineyard, and his house at Viterbo, with all the appurtenances. His Viterban possessions were valued at 12,000 florins by the king of Aragon's ambassador to the papal court.

93. Belonging to this latter category are the stays of Innocent IV (1245 to 1250) and Gregory X (1274–75) at Lyons, the city in which two ecumenical councils were held.

94. Le Goff, "La perception," 11–16.

95. Tholemeus Lucensis, *Historia ecclesiastica,* RIS, 11:1180: "Viridarium de diversis consitum arboribus, et magnae amplitudinis." On the concept of *amoenitas* in the Norman and Swabian contexts, see now Calò Mariani, "Utilità," 361, et seq.

96. Geographical map by Fra Paolino of Venice (1323), Bibl. Vaticana, *Vat. lat.* 1960, fol. 270v, pub. Krautheimer, *Rome,* 208, fig. 165). In the zoo of the papal palace at Avignon and in the castle of Pont-de-Sorgues there were even, among other things, peacocks; see Schäfer, *Die Ausgaben . . . unter Benedikt XII,* 15.

Chapter Eight

1. On the spelling of Giovanni's name—*Castellomata, Castellionate,* etc.—see Paravicini Bagliani, *Medicina,* 217. The first person to bear the title of *medicus pape* is the *magister* Filippo, whom Pope Alexander is supposed to have sent as his ambassador to Prester John: Zarncke, *Der Priester Johannes,* 941–42.

2. See chap. 9, 201.

3. Kamp, *Kirche,* 1:1, 475–476.

4. Aegidius Corboliensis, *De laudibus,* 52–53, bk. 1, 20, 131–44, ed. L. Choulant, Aegidius Corboliensis, *Carmina Medica,* Leipzig 1826.

5. Archbishop Romuald says himself that he was "in arte medicinae valde peritus": *Chronicon,* in RIS, 7:171; Ugo Falcando, *Liber de Regno Siciliae,* 362, calls him "vir in physica probatissimus." See De Renzi, *Collectio Salernitana,* 4:568–576.

6. This evidence, of great importance for demonstrating the Salerno school's influence on the circles around the papal court in the last decades of the thirteenth century, does not, however, prove that Romuald himself lived at the Roman curia, or that he was the personal physician of a pope; De Renzi, ibid., criticized Marini, *Degli archiatri,* 1:10, for having included Romuald among the "archiatri pontificij."

7. Paravicini Bagliani, *Medicina,* 9, 11–12, 72–79.

8. Hampe, "Eine Schilderung," 535.

9. Ibid.

10. PL, 217:688: "arte enim medicinae contraria contrariis curantur."

11. Hampe, "Eine Schilderung," 535.

12. Hugenholtz, "The Anagni Frescoes," 139–172.

13. *Gesta Innocentii III*, PL, 217.

14. Rusch, *Die Behörden*, 69.

15. Reg. 1:456, *Die Register*, 1:681; Reg. 2:198; *Die Register*, 2: 377; *Regestum*, 177. On the limits of the human condition: PL, 217:656.

16. Tillmann, *Papst*, 239.

17. PL, 217:582, 680, 1121.

18. PL 217:333: "Caro quippe lebrosi alicubi est plana et alicubi inflata, alicubi rubicunda, alicubi est nigra, et alicubi corrosa"; 387: "Sciendum est autem, quod quaedam febris simplex, quaedam duplex, quaedam continua, et quaedam interpolata"; 388: "Quidam patiuntur dolores, quidam tumores, quidam calores, et quidam furores. . . ."

19. PL, 217:673, et seq.

20. PL 217:65; PL 216:161.

21. O'Neill, "Innocent III," 429–431.

22. On June 6, 1206, Innocent III granted the cleric R., nephew of the *magister* David, a papal chaplain, the part of the prebend held by David in the collegiate church of Dinant in the diocese of Liège (Potthast 2790).

23. Théry, *Autour*, 9, et seq.; Kurdzialek, "David von Dinant," 181–192; idem, "L'idée," 311–322.

24. Kurdzialek, *Davidis de Dinanto*, 38. The passages concerning anatomy and embriology that can be found in his works, which have reached us only in fragmentary form (Gand, MS 5, fols. 158v–182v; Paris, Bibl. Nat., MS Lat. 15433, fol. 215rv; and Vienna, Nationalbibl., *Cod. lat.* 4753, fols. 141r–143v), have been published by Kurdzialek, "Anatomische . . . Äusserungen," 1–22. For the relevant passages, see Gand, MS 5, fol. 179v and fol. 182r; cit. ibid., 3, note 3. Quite important is the testimony of Albertus Magnus, according to whom "quidam Davit" translated from Greek into Latin a treatise titled *De problematibus* (which in turn became the *Problemata* by the same David of Dinant) for a certain Emperor Frederick: Alberto Magno, *Politica*, bk. 2, ch. 7, ed. Borgnet, 8:163; see also Kurdzialek, *Davidis de Dinanto*, 20.

25. Sudhoff, "Richard der Engländer," *Janus* 28 (1924): 397–403; and Paravicini Bagliani, *Medicina*, 17, 19–20.

26. In the chapter on fistulas in his *Trattato di Chirurgia*, Tederico Borgogni speaks of the nephew "domini pape Innocentii quarti qui paciebatur fistulam in . . . [a laceration in the parchment] profundum penetrabat inter duas costas": cit. Giacosa, *Magistri Salernitani*, 440, ed. Tabanelli, *La chirurgia*, 1:211–213. Tederico remained faithful to him and in his old age dedicated to him the final version of his *Cyrurgia*.

27. Henri de Mondeville, *Chirurgie*.

28. Seidler, "Die Medizin," 51.

29. *Les Registres de Grégoire IX*, no. 4875.

30. *Les Registres d'Innocent IV*, no. 2199.

31. Benjamin and Toomer, *Campanus of Novara;* see also C. Burnett, "Catalogue," in *Adelard of Bath: An English Scientist and Arabist of the Early Twelfth Century* (London, 1987), 170–171.

32. Sources and bibliography in Paravicini Bagliani, *Medicina,* 88–115.

33. Equally significant phrases, even if expressed in stereotypical phrases and chancery formulas, were used about Campano by Urban IV (*Les Registres d'Urbain IV,* no. 1692).

34. Baethgen, "Quellen," 195, 201, 203, and 204. The title *phisicus* appears only at p. 195; on Giovanni di Luca, see Marini, 1:26–27.

35. Arnaldus de Villanova, *Breviarium,* in *Opera omnia,* col. 1070: "Pillulis, sine quibus esse nolo, utebatur magister Campanus quotidie, omni die sumendo duas vel tres in modo cicerum." This is not the place to reopen the delicate and complicated problem of the authorship of the *Breviarium praticae,* which would require a fuller analysis of the textual tradition than that attempted by Verdier, *Études*.

36. Simon Januensis, *Clavis sanationis,* Venice 1507, fol. iir.

37. Paravicini Bagliani, *Medicina,* 191–198.

38. Ibid., 193, 249.

39. Simon Januensis, *Clavis,* fol. xlii v: "Et ego vidi Rome in gazofilatiis antiquorum monasteriorum libros et privilegia ex hac materia scripta ex litteris apud nos non intelligibilibus."

40. Ibid., fol. iir.

41. See, e.g., Paravicini Bagliani, *I testamenti,* 338.

42. Ibid., 130.

43. Ibid., 227 and 335.

44. Ibid., 338.

45. *Les Registres de Clément IV,* no. 1608; see also Stapper, *Papst,* 28.

46. Marburg, Universitätsbibl., MS 9, fol. 107: "Pillule mirabilis operationis quas composuit frater Theotonichus pro papa Gregorio"; see Burnett, "An Apocryphal Letter," 162; Todi, Bibl. Comunale, MS 85, fol. 77v.

47. *Liber de sanitate a magistro Johanne de Toleto compositus,* contained in codex *Clm.* 480 of the Bayer. Staatsbibl. of Munich, fol. 26v. He speaks about it again on fol. 33v: "Nota quod istud est electuarium experti iuvamenti, quod fecit Innocentius papa ad opus S. Pauli Rome, qui amiserat visum, qui licet esset centenarius, optime recuperavit visum," cit. Grauert, "Meister," 138. In cod. viii. G. 100 of the Bibl. Naz. of Naples, some prescriptions follow Accanamusali's treatise on

eye diseases (fols. 68r–115r: Giacosa, *Magistri Salernitani,* 468), the first of which in fact begins: "Innocentius papa quartus hoc electuarium composuit." A similar prescription, but administered to Innocent III, is described in Sarti and Fattorini, *De claris,* 1:387, no. 1; another one, for John XXII, is in Marini, 1:11, note a.

48. Arnaldus de Villanova (?), *Breviarium,* in *Opera omnia,* bk. 1, ch. 21, 1110; bk. 2, ch. 3, add., 1190; bk. 3, ch. 22, add., 1364. The *Breviarium* moreover describes an *experimentum* conducted against the tertian fever by a papal doctor identifiable only as Franc. V. (ibid., bk. 4, ch. 17, 1416) and the electuary of another papal doctor indicated by the initials "F.B.," perhaps the same as the preceding: the medicine is described as "useful against the stone and colic" (bk. 2, ch. 32, add., 1266: "utile contra vitium lapidis, et contra cholicam . . ."); bk. 2, ch. 44, add., 1291 and bk. 2, ch. 45, add., ibid., 1298 (Thorndike, *Michael Scot,* 74). See Salins, Bibl. Comm., MS 45, 15–16, fol. 63v: "Pillule gloriose regis Cicilie, quibus utebatur qualibet die papa Alexander." The medical experience of the "white cardinal" *(cardinalis albus),* the Cistercian John of Toledo, is confirmed by independent sources. The codex in the Vatican Library contains verses "composed by the white cardinal for Pope Urban, who died of pleurisy" (*Barb. lat.* 171, fol. 155v: "quos fecit cardinalis albus ad papam Urbanum mortuum de pleuresi"; incipit *Urbanus per se nescit pretium scabiose;* Walther 19692; see also Basel, Universitätsbibl., MS 2 13, fol. 103; Paris, Bibl. Nat., MS *Lat.* 3267, fol. 54v; Troyes, Bibl. Munic., MS 1840, fol. 55). In MS 85 of the Bibl. Com. of Todi, numerous medical prescriptions are attributed to members of the papal court including, in fact, the "white cardinal" and John of Procida (fol. 77r): fully two times there appears the prescription of an "electuarium magistri Iohannis de Procida maximi contra reuma." One prescription was drawn up for Gregory IX (fol. 77r).

49. Henri de Mondeville, *Chirurgie,* xxxvii, 790; see *La Grande Chirurgie de Guy de Chauliac,* 44:256, 263, 617, 624, 660; tract. 7, doctr. 1, ch. 6. See also the codex in Florence, Bibl. Riccard., MS 1066, part 3, fol. 37r. Codex 977 (1885) of the Bibl. Univ. of Bologna (fol. 95r) contains the prescription for an electuary "that was given to Pope Boniface VIII": "Confectio electuarii quod datum fuit Bonifacio VIII": see Thorndike and Kibre, *A Catalogue of Incipits,* 1332; incipit *Recipe piperis albi quod reperitur.* On Henri de Mondeville, see Pouchelle, *Corps.*

50. Prosopographic data in Paravicini Bagliani, *Medicina,* 3–51.

51. In studies of the diffusion and knowledge of Avicenna's work in the West, his *De retardatione* is not taken into consideration: Corner, *Anatomical Texts;* Schipperges, *Die Assimilation;* McVaugh, "The 'Humidum Radicale' "; Jacquart, "La réception"; Siraisi, *Avicenna.*

52. Grauert, *Magister,* 97, verses 814–824.

53. *Gesta Innocentii III,* PL, 214: chs. 137, 188; see also the *Regestum,* 91, 96.

54. Burchard of Ursberg, MGH, *Scriptores rerum Germanicarum,* 1916, 101.

55. Davidsohn, *Forschungen,* 2:203, no. 1468; see also Laurent, *Beatus,* 458, no. 184: "qui dicebatur esse infirmus."

56. Ibid., 459, no. 189.

57. Matthaei Parisiensis, *Chronica Majora,* 5:430: "Nec potuit ei cardinalis albi phisica suffragari."

58. Martinus Polonus, *Continuatio Romana,* MGH, SS, 22:481; these assertions were repeated by Francesco Pipino, RIS, 9:726.

59. The clinical symptoms of Cardinal Stephan of Hungary's death were described by an eyewitness in a codex of the Bibl. Nat. of Paris, which contains, in a plate below the binding, a note also on the chronology of Clement IV's death: Paravicini Bagliani, "Un frammento," 173; ibid., note 16.

60. Matthaei Parisiensis, *Chronica majora,* 5:299. Another famous thirteenth-century papal doctor—Arnald of Villanova—received the gift of a gold cross from the pope: see the inventory of his library and personal goods, no. 236: "Item crux argenti cum pede quam dedit dominus Papa," ed. R. Chabas, "Inventario de los libros, ropas y demàs efectos de Arnaldo de Villanueve," *Revista de Archivos, Bibliotecas y Museos* 9 (1903): 198.

61. Paravicini Bagliani, *I testamenti,* 338.

62. Ed. Dykmans, "Les pouvoirs," 131 (see above, note 35); see also Schimmelpfennig, *Die Zeremonienbücher,* 191, et seq.

63. Petrocchi, "L'ultimo destino," 207: "lingua expeditissimus, vox eius sonora et si supresse proferebatur, audiebatur ab omnibus et intelligebatur."

64. Ibid., 207: "Aspectus eius reverebatur ab universis plurimum et timebatur." On these problems in general, see Schmidinger, "Das Papstbild," 106–129.

65. Jean Papire Masson, *Libri sex de episcopis Urbis, qui Romanam Ecclesiam rexerunt,* Paris 1586, 223 et seq.; see also Schmidinger, "Das Papstbild," 33.

66. *Continuatio Romana brevis,* MGH, SS, 30:712: "decorus facie, nobilitatem et pulchritutidem moribus et prospicuitate decorans, statura procerus. . . ." For Gardner, "Patterns," 440, this was perhaps "a *collage* of conventional phrases."

67. Tholemeus Lucensis, *Historia ecclesiastica,* RIS, 11:1179: "Hic fuit multum compositus homo in moribus: unde et apud multos el composto appellabatur, et erat de pulchrioribus clericis mundi."

68. Francesco Pipino, *Chronicon,* RIS, 9:724: "Corpus et exterius

tibi quid sors blanda negavit? . . . / Corporis egregio decus ejecere decori / Mira pudicitia, graviumque decentia morum"; see also Ladner, *Die Papstbildnisse*, 2:21.

69. Herklotz, *"Sepulcra,"* 199. Already in his *Carmen de statu Curie Romane,* the poet Henry of Würzburg (c. 1261–65) had expressed his desire to put his muse at the service of the *fame* of Cardinal *Gaietanus* (ed. Grauert, *Magister,* 94, verses 749–752; and 140–145). Even after the cardinal's death, the poet was able to assure him perpetuity.

70. Ibid., verses 949–950 and 957–958; cf. 250.

71. Gardner, "Arnolfo di Cambio," 430.

72. Tholemeus Lucensis, *Historia ecclesiastica,* in RIS, 11:1191; see also *Willelmi Rishanger . . . Chronica et Annales,* 109.

73. Tholemeus Lucensis, 1176. The theme reappears markedly in the fifteenth century: Filelfo based himself on Aristotle in declaring that "regem oportet ab aliis differre *vestitu,* oratione, honoratione," and that the Vicar of Christ on earth "et cui ipsius coeli potestas data est" and he "must have nothing in common with the multitude," cit. Miglio, "Vidi thiaram," 275.

74. *Secretum secretorum,* 171: "Ille vero homo est optime memorie bene compositus in natura, qui habet carnes molles, humidas, mediocres inter asperitatem et lenitatem. . . ." The word *compositus* figures also in the humanist Giovanni Antonio Campano's polemic against Pope Paul II (1464–71): "Es compositus et splendidus, quae res et si est pontifice summo dignissima . . . ," cit. Miglio, "Vidi thiaram," 292–293.

75. *Secretum secretorum,* 146: "Sicut ergo oportet te esse virum spiritualem pulcri aspectus et ornatum."

76. Brams, "Mensch," 545–548.

77. See now J. Agrimi, "Fisiognomica e Scolastica," *Micrologus. Nature, Sciences and Medieval Societies* 1 (1993): 235–271.

78. *Secretum secretorum,* 49; on poisons, see ibid., 59. Campano of Novara, one of the most talented astronomers and mathematicians of the thirteenth century, brought into the papal chapel by Pope Urban IV (1261–64), played the role of professional astronomer at the papal court (ibid., 60).

79. Although, at the beginning of the century, the sources speak only of a single *medicus pape,* in the second half of the thirteenth century the popes generally had two available at the same time: Frutaz, "La famiglia," 310.

80. This identification was first proposed by Haskins, *Studies,* 137–140; doubts, largely unfounded, have been expressed by Grignaschi, "La diffusion"; the problem has been reopened by Paravicini Bagliani, *Medicina,* 203–216; and by Williams, "The Early Circulation."

81. *Les Registres de Grégoire IX,* no. 118. Philip told the recipient of

his translation, Bishop Guido de Vere of Valencia, that he had found the Arab original in Antioch (ed. Förster, *De Aristotelis*, 38). He accompanied his uncle Ranier, patriarch of Antioch has well as vice chancellor of the curia under Honorius III, to his new patriarchal see (1219–25). The curialist Philip was therefore a cleric very well informed on medical issues.

82. Burnett, "An Apocryphal Letter," 157.

83. The *Secretum secretorum* declares that the celestial bodies exercise their influence on terrestrial events by means of light, the real mediator between the celestial and sublunar worlds. Brams, "Mensch," 545–548; see also Grignaschi, "La diffusion," 19, note 35.

84. Tea, "Witelo," 22, et seq.

85. Simi Varanelli, "Dal Maestro d'Isacco," 129.

86. Brams, "Mensch," 556.

87. See chap. 7, note 91.

88. Lindberg, "Lines," 66–83; and Paravicini Bagliani, *Medicina*, 119–140.

89. Ibid., 132.

90. Ed.: Berger, *Die Ophtalmologie*. Peter of Spain dedicated his *Thesaurus pauperum* to Gregory X, "qui pater pauperum nuncupatur." Note also his play on words in the incipit of *De oculo:* "In nomine summi pontificis vel opificis, a quo omnes cause procedunt casualiter suum esse et originem extraverunt"; see Stapper, *Papst Johannes XXI.*, 24. Before being elected as Pope John XXI (1276), Peter of Spain lived for at least fifteen years at the Roman curia. Between 1261 and 1264, he was part of the entourage of Cardinal Ottobono Fieschi. We first come upon him, in fact, at the papal court in Viterbo on December 31, 1261, as witness to a sentence issued by Cardinal Ottobono Fieschi (*Les Registres d'Urbain IV*, no. 49). He appears for the first time in the registers of papal letters in the early months of 1260 (*Les Registres d'Alexandre IV*, nos. 3182 (March 14, 1260) and 3183 (Jan. 1).

91. Romanini, "Gli occhi di Isacco," 1, et seq.

Chapter Nine

1. Zarncke, *Der Priester Johannes*, 837–843; 845–846. Otto of Freising tells us, moreover, that on November 18, 1145, he met the bishop of Dsjebel (to the south of Laodicea) at Viterbo while he was leaving an audience with the pope. The bishop told him about a certain John, a Nestorian king and priest, who lived in the Far East beyond Persia and Armenia. Attempting to come to the aid of the church in Jerusalem, he had nonetheless been unable to cross the Tigris River and had had to turn back.

2. Trans. Pacaut, *Alexandre III*, 191.

3. See note 1 above.

4. Maccarrone, *Lotharii,* 16.

5. Ibid., 15–16. According to the *Gesta Innocentii III* (PL, 217: xviii), Lothar was twenty-nine when he was promoted to the cardinal-ate (1190) and thirty-seven when he was elected pope (1198), which enables us to put his date of birth around 1160. The *De miseria* was written between December 25, 1194, and April 13, 1195. Biblical translation from *New Oxford Bible,* 727.

6. Grmek, *On Aging,* 56–57.

7. See chap. 8, 186.

8. See chap. 8, 187.

9. *De retardatione,* 39.

10. See chap. 8, 186.

11. The author of *De retardatione* mentions having spent time in France, 38. The documents on Chancellor Philip's stay in Italy have been published in Denifle and Châtelain, *Chartularium,* 1. Summoned to Rome in 1219, Philip presented himself before Pope Honorius III (93, doc. no. 33, Nov. 20, 1219); he was summoned again by Gregory IX on May 10, 1230 (134, doc. no. 75), but we do not know whether he actually went.

12. Paris, Bibl. Nat., MS *Lat.* 6978, fol. 36r; see also *De retardatione,* 89: "Explicit epistola de accidentibus senectutis s'. d'. q domini castri gret, et missa ad Innocencium quartum summum pontificem."

13. Paris, Bibl. Nat., MS *Lat.* 10938, fol. 93vb: "Item epistola domini castri dicti goet de accidentibus senectutis missa ad fredericum imperatorem." The presence of that *epistola* in Abbot Ivo of Cluny's catalog of books had already been indicated by Haskins, "Latin Litera-ture under Frederick II," 135–36; see also Kantorowicz, *Friederich II., Ergänzungsband,* 154, who had not, however, noticed the similarity to the *De retardatione.* This book catalog was copied twice in the Paris MS (fols. 84vb–85rb and 93va–b). Delisle, *Le Cabinet,* 2:484–485, pub-lished the text of fols. 93va–b, which give the better reading. On fol. 85rb, the word *domini* is missing: *Item epistola castri dicti goet de acci-dentibus senectutis missa ad Fredericum imperatorem.* Ivo's rule as abbot would have lasted from 1256 to 1273 according to Delisle, from 1257 to 1275 according to the DHGE (Paris 1956), 13:87. It is difficult to say which text should be preferred. The Goet version (in Ivo's catalog) may be preferable to that of Gret (in the explicit of MS Lat. 6978 in Paris), because in the latter manuscript the "r" has been added to "Get."

14. The title *Domine mundi* was also used by Michael Scot to ad-dress Frederick II in the prologue to his translation of Avicenna's *De animalibus (Frederice Romanorum imperator, domine mundi;* see Thorndike and Kibre, *A catalogue of Incipits,* 57).

15. Melloni, *Innocenzo IV,* 23–26.

16. On the whole question, see now Paravicini Bagliani, *Medicina,* 55–84.

17. *De retardatione,* ed. Little and Withington, xxi–xxiii.

18. Clark, "Roger Bacon," 230–232.

19. *De retardatione,* 1. This is proved not only by the author's declarations, but by the existence of two versions of the work, a long and a short one; the author's contacts with the chancellor Philip, Giovanni Castellomata, Frederick II, and Innocent IV; his numerous travels in France and Italy, which enabled him to make observations (the miraculous plants) and to gather information; and above all, by his exact knowledge of a good dozen works that had not yet been completely assimilated in the European West, and which the *dominus castri Goet* was one of the first to use. Such was the case with Avicanna's "Canone" (one hundred citations), the pseudo-Aristotelian *Secretum secretorum* (25), Rhazi (15), Haly Regalis (15), Haly super Tegni (15), Isaac (12), Ahmed ben al-Gezzar (12) and J. Damascenus (9).

20. Ibid., 2

21. Ibid.

22. Ibid.; Augustinus, *De civitate Dei,* bk. 15, 10–15.

23. *De retardatione,* 2.

24. The part of *De retardatione* concerning theories of aging is based on a very attentive and meticulous reading of Avicenna's theory of old age. It is even possible to assert that *De retardatione* may be the first Western treatise to have assimilated with care and a certain fullness Avicenna's theories on aging. For these see, for example, McVaugh, "The *Humidum Radicale.*"

25. *De retardatione,* 45, 16.

26. Ibid., 15–16.

27. See chap. 1, note 45.

28. *De retardatione,* 15: "Quarum una latet in visceribus terre"; "Altera natat in mari"; "Tertia repit super terram"; "Quarta vegetatur in aere"; "Quinta assimilatur medicine que egreditur de minera nobilis animalis"; "Sexta egreditur de animali longe vite" ("lapis quadratus nobilis animalis"); "Septima est medicina sive res cuius minera est planta Indie."

29. Ibid., 43–44.

30. Grignaschi, "La diffusion," 19.

31. See chap. 8, 195.

32. Rogerius Bacon, *The 'Opus Maius,'* 2:204–213; *Opus Minus,* 373–374; *Opus Tertium,* 45–54; see also the letter Bacon sent accompanying his three principal works to Clement IV (Bettoni, *Ruggero Bacone,* 147–148); the *Epistola de Secretis operibus,* ch. 7, 538–542; the *Liber sex scientiarum,* perhaps a fragment of his projected *Scriptum Principale* or *Compendium Philosophiae,* 181–186 ("Appendix 1," of MS *Bodley* 438,

fols. 28–29). Two articles of Bacon's *De erroribus medicorum* are also devoted to gold (no. 56) and to vipers (no. 64) as tools of rejuvenation;
see Welborn, "The Errors," 52–53.

33. E. Massa, *Ruggero Bacone. Etica e poetia nella storia dell' 'Opus
Majus'* (Rome, 1955).

34. Gruman, "A History," 62–67; and Needham, *Science,* 5, 2:
10–15, 71, 74, 282; 5, 4:491–496; see also Paravicini Bagliani, *Medicina,* 329–361.

35. On the concept of constitution, see Jacquart, "De *krasis* à
complexio."

36. Needham, "The Elixir," 167–192.

37. See the works cited in note 34.

38. Brehm, "Roger Bacon's Place," 53–58.

39. Thorndike, *A History of Magic,* 2:499: London, British Library, Royal MS 13-A-7, 15, fols. 149r–153v.

40. Schipperges, "Makrobiotik," 129–155.

41. Berger, *Die Ophtalmologie,* 45–47. On medicinal waters, see
now Wilson, "Philosophers," 101–210.

42. Guillelmus de Nangiaco, *Chronicon,* MGH, SS, 26, cit. by Potthast, 2:1718.

43. Roger Bacon, *Liber sex scientiarum,* in *De Retardatione,* 185. On
the hermetic intertwining of scientific-sacred knowledge and power,
see Crisciani, "Labiriniti," 140, and note 2, which explores suggestions
of a nexus between the three *arcana,* developed elsewhere by Ginzburg,
"High and Low," 28–41. Among the texts cited by Crisciani it is worth
recalling here Roger Bacon's *De secretis nature* and a passage from the
letter John Dastin sent to Pope John XXII, ed. Josten, p. 43: "Hoc
ergo magisterium pertinet ad reges et huius mundi altiores, quia qui
habet ipsum indeficientem habet thesaurum!" On Dastin, see chap. 11,
note 18.

44. Paravicini Bagliani, *Medicina,* 53–84.

45. John XXI died after the ceiling collapsed in one of the rooms
of the papal palace he had had constructed at Viterbo. See, for example,
Sifridus de Balnhusin, *Compendium historiarum,* MGH, SS, 25:708:
"Quid fiet de libello meo? Quis complebit libellum meum?" "Hic dum
quendam librum, ut dicebatur, hereticum et perversum dictaret, subito
domus in qua sedebat super eum corruit in tantumque concussit, ut
infra spacium quinque dierum miserabiliter moreretur."

Chapter Ten

1. January 24, 1295, is the date of his episcopal consecration and
papal coronation. The *Liber benefactorum* of the chapter of Saint Peter's
notes on May 6 the "dedicatio altaris sancti Bonifatii, quod est in
navi basilicae principis apostolorum": Egidi, *Necrologi,* 1:210. Churches

were usually consecrated on Sundays; May 6 fell on a Sunday only in 1296: see Maccarrone, "Il sepolcro," 756, note 25. In a thirteenth-century Roman calendar (Van Dijk and Walker, *The Ordinal*, 7), the "Dedicacio capelle s. Bonifacii in ecclesia b. Petri" took place in 1296. Since the pope's nephew, Cardinal Benedetto Caetani (d. Dec. 14, 1296), was buried "ante altare Sancti Bonifatii," the altar must already have been consecrated. On September 29, 1297, Boniface speaks of his chapel having already been constructed, and of the preparations already made for his own burial in Saint Peter's (Potthast 24758). The word *mausoleo* is in Giovanni di Vitring, *Liber certarum historiarum,* cit. Maccarrone, "Il sepolcro," 762, note 59.

2. We have only Tasselli's reproduction in the album of the Archivio del Capitolo of Saint Peter's, reprinted by G. Grimaldi, *Descrizione della Basilica antica di Santa Pietro in Vaticano, codice Barberini latino 2733,* ed. and notes by R. Niggl (Vatican City, 1972), 37.

3. Ladner, *Die Papstbildnisse,* 2: table 70.

4. Maccarrone, "Il sepolcro," 758.

5. *Collectionis bullarum sacrosanctae basilicae Vaticanae,* 1:198–201; see also the letter of September 17, 1279 (Maccarrone, "Il sepolcro," 754).

6. Picard, "Étude," 763–764.

7. Letter of April 27, 1300, addressed to the Chapter of Saint Peter's (*Collectionis bullarum sacrosanctae basilicae Vaticanae,* 1:226a, and 230a). According to Guido of Baisio, instead, Boniface was a martyr and not a pope (Mansi, 25:418).

8. Maccarrone, "Il sepolcro," 755; see also Jounel, *Le culte,* 177 and 238–239.

9. Sigfridus de Balnhusin, *Compendium,* 712: "Ipse edificavit altare in basilica sancti Petri super sepulchrum sancti Bonifatii pape, qui templum Pantheon a Foca cesare quondam impetraverat, et super altare illud subimet tumbam eminentem et preciosam de candidissimo marmore sculptam et auro [desuper] ornatam fieri statuit, et ciborium desuper quatuor columnis suffultum, similiter de marmore auroque preciosum, et iuxta tumbam in pariete simulachrum suum sculptum atque auro ornatum."

10. "Brachium s. Bonifatii IIII pape": Forcella, *Iscrizioni,* 4:305, note 742.

11. Deér, *Dynastic Porphyry Tombs,* 140–141; see also chap. 1, note 164.

12. Picard, "Étude," 763, et seq.

13. Forcella, *Iscrizioni,* 8:390, note 718.

14. Hugenholtz, "The Anagni Frescoes."

15. Letter of April 27, 1300, cit. Maccarrone, "Il sepolcro," 756, note 22.

16. *Les Registres de Boniface VIII*, no. 3416; see also Schmidt, *Libri rationum*, 72.

17. Ladner, *Die Papstbildnisse*, 2:308.

18. Claussen, "Pietro di Oderisio," 186–187.

19. Romanini, "Ipotesi," 113.

20. See chap. 5, 141.

21. Bernardus Guidonis, *De secta illorum*, 22–23: "qui fecit sibi fieri monumentum et imaginem supra petram sicut esset viva."

22. The pope himself wanted the sepulcher *sibi vivens* (Bernardus Guidonis, *Continuatio*, LP, 2:471: "Sequenti vero die fuit in tumulo, quem sibi vivens praeparari fecerat, tumulatus in ecclesia sancti Petri"). It made a certain sense that Boniface should not have consecrated his own chapel, as Nicholas III had done his. How could he consecrate a chapel containing a gisant in his likeness? The pope instead had it consecrated by Cardinal Matteo of Acquasparta, a cardinal closely tied to him (and who, as bishop of Porto, exercised episcopal jurisdiction over the Vatican Basilica; see Maccarrone, "Il sepolcro," 756). Matteo's sepulcher is the first—after Boniface's—with effigies (Gardner, "Arnolfo di Cambio," 420–439). His interest in physiognomic and visual problems is evident in an important sermon he delivered on Saint Francis (idem, "Some Cardinals' Seals," 72–96). On the verisimilitude of the portraits of Boniface, see now the conclusive judgement of Gardner, *The Tomb*, 174–175.

23. Erlande and Brandenburg, *Le roi est mort*.

24. A new edition of the verses concerning the sepulcher is based on a rereading of *Vat. lat.* 2854, fols. 22v–23r. Maccarrone, "Il sepolcro," 759: "Jam te funus habe, iam te mirare cadaver / Exequias iam cerne tuas, te vermibus escam . . . Ecce pater patrum divini pastor ovilis, / Puppis apostolice remex, vigil arbiter orbis / Nec non terrenus eterne claviger aule / . . . insompnesque minus ledat vel tempora tardet."

25. PL, 217:658: "constitutus inter Deum et hominem medius."

26. Galfridus de Vinosalvo, *Poetria nova*, 261: "Non Deus es nec homo: quasi neuter es inter utrumque" (verses 2068–2069); 197 (verse 20): "Trans homines totus."

27. Rocaberti, *Bibliotheca*, 4:57.

28. Maccarrone, "Il sepolcro," 757.

29. Romanini, "Ipotesi," 127. Archeological analysis of the monument confirms the view of Grimaldi (*Descrizione*, 37) that the altar faced the sarcophagus and was so close to it "ut dum sacerdos Missae sacrum perageret tumulum ipsius Bonifacii conspiciebat."

30. Gardner, "Boniface VIII," 520.

31. Paschal II brought together under a single altar the bodies of Leo I and his homonymous successors Leo II, III, and IV; see Maccarrone, "Il sepolcro," 754, note 11.

32. On the visibility of the figure of the pope in relation to the celebration of the eucharist, see above, 194–96.

33. The gisant wears only the tiara.

34. The reference to the bones in Boniface IV's epitaph (today conserved in the Vatican Grottos, Chapel of the Madonna delle Parturienti) is in the last two verses that Boniface VIII had added: "Octavus titulo hoc Bonifatius ossa reperta / hac locat erecta Bonifatii nominis ara": Ladner, *Die Papstbildnisse*, 2:310.

35. Thus also Maccarrone, "Il sepolcro," 758.

36. Ibid.; see also Herde, *Cölestin V.,* 154–155.

37. November, 1295, and July 23, 1296; Maccarrone, "L'indulgenza," 741.

38. See chap. 6.

39. Boyle, "An Ambry," 343–344.

40. Unless one is willing to accept the identification of the Knight of Bamburgh with Frederick II (Ladner, "Die Anfänge," 84–88).

41. Ibid., 88. In the San Clemente tympanum, the pope is wearing a circular tiara; at the top there seems to be discernible a "knot," which reveals the ruby of Boniface VIII's tiara, subsequently lost at Clement V's coronation; Boyle, "An Ambry," 329–350.

42. Maddalo, "Bonifacio VIII," 148; idem, "Alcune considerazioni," 621–628.

43. According to Stefaneschi, Boniface proclaimed the Jubilee from a pulpit at Saint Peter's adorned with silk and gold, to pilgrims who had come to the tomb of the apostle. The date of the beginning of the Jubilee year (Feb. 22) coincides with the feast of the see of Saint Peter. The bull of proclamation was promulgated from the Lateran, but was mistakenly dated from Saint Peter's in the Vatican; the bull of indulgence for pilgrims (thirty days) had been conceded for the basilicas of Saints Peter and Paul. The hypothesis of Maddalo, "Bonifacio VIII," 136, is entirely justified: "Il Laterano, quindi, per lo meno nelle prescrizioni ufficiali, rimane fuori dai percorsi giubilari."

44. In the drawing at the Ambrosian Library, and in a miniature representing the coronation at the Vatican (*Vat. lat.* 4933), the person on the pope's right has been identified as Cardinal Matteo Rosso Orsini.

45. Maddalo, "Bonifacio VIII," 145.

46. Even the oldest miniature of a papal coronation, contained in *Vat. lat.* 4933, fol. 7v (Jacopo Stefaneschi, *Opus metricum*) concerns Boniface VIII.

47. Maddalo, "Bonifacio VIII," 145, et seq.

48. Mitchell, "The Lateran Fresco," 1–6.

49. Poggi, "Arnolfo di Cambio," 193–94.

50. See above, note 9.

51. N. Rash, "Boniface VIII and Honorific Portraiture: Observations on the Half-Length Image in the Vatican," *Gesta* 21, 1 (1987): 47–58.

52. There are important analogies to the statues of Boniface VIII at Orvieto, in which the pope is seated on a throne giving a benediction: ibid., 48. But their poor state of conservation makes it impossible to say whether the pope is holding the keys in his left hand. Boniface VIII is the first pope for whom it is possible to document the depiction of the keys of Saint Peter on the papal arms (Galbreath, *Papal Heraldry,* 52).

53. Romanini, "Nuovi dati," 33, et seq., demonstrates that the bust of Boniface VIII is almost identical to the Vatican bronze of Saint Peter, which confirms the paternity of Arnolfo.

54. Jacopo Caetani Stefaneschi, *Opus metricum,* 98: "imposuit capiti spere cubitique figuram"; see Ladner, "Die Statue," 59, note 102.

55. P. E. Schramm, "Zur Geschichte der püpstlichen Tiara," *Historische Zeitschrift* 152 (1935): 307 et seq.

56. *Les Registres de Boniface VIII,* no. 59: "Una nemque fuit diluvii tempore archa Noe unam Ecclesiam prefigurans, que in uno cubito consumata unum Noe videlicet gubernatorem habuit et rectorem."

57. Ibid., no. 3410: "parati solemniter . . . portabimus in capite nostro diadema seu coronam, quod regnum vulgariter appellatur, per quod potest unitas sancte Ecclesie designari, quam ipsi in Ecclesia dei immisso scismate scindere fuerant ante moliti."

58. Ladner, "Die Statue," 58.

59. Rash, "Boniface VIII," 49.

60. Sommer, *Die Anklage,* 21, et seq., 36; idem, "Papst Bonifaz VIII.," 75–107.

61. December 4, 1290 (Varin, *Archives administratives,* 1, 2:1049). On the document, see now the meticulous analysis by Schmidt, "Papst Bonifaz VIII.," 91.

62. *Cessatio a divinis* imposed by the bishop.

63. *Les Registres de Boniface VIII,* no. 4299.

64. On the same day, Boniface wrote the abbot of Compiègne, informing him of his decisions and ordering him to have the statuettes constructed.

65. The maxim "The pope bears the whole law *[iura omnia]* in his bosom" became official thanks to Boniface VIII (*Liber Sextus,* C. 1, 6, 1, 2, ed. Friedberg, *Corpus iuris canonici,* 2:937; see Gillmann, "Romanus pontifex," 156–174; and Kantorowicz, *Les deux corps du roi,* 378–379, note 15).

66. See chap. 2.

67. See chap. 2.

68. The papacy's incessant struggle against the *cessatio a divinis* had

important ecclesiological implications. The Fourth Lateran Council had already decreed (in the canon *Irrefragabili*) that a bishop need not respect an unjustified *cessatio a divinis* and should intervene with appropriate sanctions. The Second Council of Lyons (*Liber sextus,* ed. Friedberg, 2:986) tried to check the practice of *cessatio a divinis* by requiring the parties to document their reasons exactly. Gregory X condemned the custom of placing "crosses and statues of the Virgin and other saints" on the ground as a means of reinforcing the *cessatio a divinis.* Boniface VIII decreed on April 4, 1296, that a *cessatio* could be imposed only by a majority vote of the chapter; the two parties had to present themselves before the Apostolic See. On March 3, 1298, the pope dropped the clause on the majority vote, but increased the penalties for failure to obey the Lyons decree (ibid., 2:988; and see Potthast 24310).

69. Coste, *Boniface VIII en procès.*

70. In this sense, one of the charges in the process against Boniface is not without foundation. Boniface is said to have declared that "in truth, every new pope should immediately have a statue erected in his name, that great and small alike can revere, and to which all the princes of the world may bow in reverence and humility," ibid., 331: "In veritate quicunque papa creatur de novo, statim deberet erigi statua nomine illius, quod creatus est, quam omnes magni et parvi revererentur et cui omnes mundi principes cum omni humilitate et reverentia inclinarent"; see Ladner, *Die Papstbildnisse,* 2:301.

Chapter Eleven

1. Paravicini Bagliani, "La mobilità," 155–278.

2. The prosopographic documentation is collected in idem, *Medicina,* 38–51.

3. Ibid., 40.

4. *Les Registres de Boniface VIII,* no. 3123.

5. Finke, *Aus den Tagen,* xxx, xxxi, xxxiv.

6. Holtzmann, *Wilhelm von Nogaret,* 234, et seq.; and Finke, *Aus den Tagen,* 203, note 1.

7. Finke, *Aus den Tagen,* xxx. He was probably referring to the *Pratica summaria* (Arnaldus de Villanova, *Opera omnia,* 1439–1452), of which at least one codex (Munich, Bayerische Staatsbibl., clm. 2848) bears a dedication to Boniface VIII. Arnald mentions his stay at La Scurcola in his letter to Benedict XI: Finke, *Aus den Tagen,* clxxix–clxxx.

8. Ibid., xxx: ". . . magister Arnaldus modo mense Julii preterito, dum sol esset in signo Leonis, fecit quendam denarium et quoddam bracale pape, que cum portaret, malum lapidis amodo non sentiret. . . ." See also the text cited in the following note. The *bracale,* mentioned in other of Arnald's works, was a kind of bandage that

served to compress the kidneys; it makes medical sense: ibid., 205. For a description of the seal, see also Arnald's *De sigillis* in *Opera omnia*, 2037–2042. See also Finke, *Aus den Tagen*, xxxiv and xxxv.

9. Petrus de Abano, *Conciliator*, 9, 4; ibid., 48, 3; cit. E. Paschetto, *Pietro d'Abano medico e filosofo*, Florence, 1984, 29, note 34.

10. Ibid, 25–26.

11. Petrus de Abano, *Tractatus de venenis*, "Prologus": "Sanctissimo in Christo patri et domino . . . divina providentia summo pontifici Petrus de Abano minimus medicorum"; see Paravicini Bagliani, *Medicina*, 38.

12. Ibid., ch. 4: ". . . et Avenzoar hoc invenit, ut in libro translato papae Bonifacio scriptum est." According to Thorndike, *A History of Magic*, 3 : 937, in a Viennese manuscript the translation of Avenzoar's treatise on the effectiveness of an emerald as an antidote to poisons is addressed to Pope Boniface VIII.

13. Paravicini Bagliani, *Medicina*, 200–201.

14. On the papal documentation, see Pogatscher, "Von Schlangenhörnern," 162–215; K. Eubel, "Vom Zaubereiunwesen anfangs des 14. Jahrhunderts," *Historisches Jahrbuch* 18 (1897): 609–631; and Paravicini Bagliani, *La vita quotidiana*, passim. The inventory of Boniface's treasury is in Molinier, "Inventaire," 20–22, sec. 15, nos. 273–287. The "tasting" was one of the duties of the papal *supracoci:* Frutaz, "La famiglia pontificia," 2 : 294.

15. Paravicini Bagliani, *Medicina*, 258–259.

16. Thorndike and Kibre, *A Catalogue of Incipits*, 266.

17. R. Manselli, "La religiosità di Arnaldo da Villanova," *Bullettino dell'Istituto Storico Italiano per il Medio Evo* 63 (1951), 18–19: "Nam qui debuit, uti vir evangelicus, dicere: 'Palam etiam confitebatur, quod non zelus Christi vel salutis animarum, set corporum regnabat in eo, cum ob commodum corporum et non spirituum ministro communi sponderet honorem.'"

18. Paris, Bibl. Nat., MS *Lat.* 7817, fol. 54r: ". . . aurum potabile . . . est maximum decretum [secretum?] in medicinis naturalibus; ita iurabat et affirmabat *dominus Hugo.* . . . *Et scias quod dominus cardinalis de Toleto et omnes cardinales fuerunt usi in cibariis quam diu vixerunt in cardinalatu et habuerunt pro maiori et meliori secreto quod scirent vel haberent*" (ed. and trans.: Calvet, "Le *De vita philosophorum,*" 73); see Paravicini Bagliani, *Medicina*, 263–264. The definition of the elixir in the *Rosarium philosophorum* is very close to that of the *De vita*: Pereira, "Un tesoro inestimabile," 161–187.

19. Grauert, "Meister Johann von Toledo."

20. In the *Liber de sanitate conservanda a Johanne de Toleto compositus* (Florence, Bibl. Riccard., Cod. 1246, fol. 32v) an *aqua balsami* is praised: according to the author and *dominus Ugo cardianalis,* a few drops were

enough to cure "omnes infirmitates aurium." The Munich Bayerische Staatsbibl., Cod. 405, contains an alchemic-medical treatise on the *aqua gloriosa benedicta et laudabilis* discovered by the cardinal *magister* Johannes de Toledo. The treatise was purportedly translated in Greece (fol. 102) by the *magister* Glodiane Constantino at the request of the *magistri* John of Toledo and *Ugo cardinale Ostiense* (!); see Grauert, "Meister Johann," 139, note 140. The *cardinalis de Toleto* could also, however, be identified as Gonsalvo Gudiel, cardinal bishop of Tusculum from 1298 to 1299, who possessed Michael Scot's autographs and William of Moerbeke's translations, as well as the works of Campano of Novara, among them even the "Parvo Almagesto": see Paravicini Bagliani, *Medicina*, 229, et seq. Gudiel had Avicenna's *Liber secundus* and *Liber quartus* translated (Bibl. Vat., *Urb. lat.,* 186); see Santi, "Il cadavere," 875.

21. Arnaldus de Villanova, *Opera omnia,* col. 591: "Multi modernorum de nobilioribus, et *maxime de prelatis* faciunt bullire petias auri cum cibis, alii accipiunt cum cibis, vel cum electuariis, alii in limatura sicut in confectione, que dicitur diacameron, quam ingreditur utraque, auri scilicet et argenti limatura. . . ."

22. Ed. Ehrle, "Der Nachlass," 65–66: "et limam ipsorum florenorum et lapides iuxta ordinationem medicorum in cibariis, que parantur pro ipso domino Clementi."

23. Paravicini Bagliani, *Medicina*, 263–264.

24. E. Föster, *Roger Bacon's "De retardandis senectutis accidentibus et de sensibus conservandi" und Arnaldo von Villanova's "De conservanda iuventute et retardanda senectute,"* Leipzig, Diss., 1912.

25. Arnaldus de Villanova, *Opera omnia,* 1566–1580. In chapter 5 he advises using an *electuarium benedictum* when the sun enters the sign of Leo, as for the gold seal that he had given Boniface VIII (see note 8 above).

26. Finke, *Aus den Tagen,* xxxi: "Papa enim non curat nisi de tribus et circa hoc totalis sua versatur intentio, ut diu vivat et ut adquirat pecuniam, tercium ut suos ditet, magnificet et exaltet. De aliqua autem spiritualitate non curat."

27. Coste, *Boniface VIII en procès,* 267, H 19: "Frequentissime etiam dicebat: Dicunt iste asine de Urbe, loquens de devotis dominabus Urbis: Dio ti dia vita eterna, id est: Deus det tibi vitam eternam. Longe plus placet mihi audire: Deus det tibi longam vitam; sed adhuc plus placet audire: Deus det tibi longam et bonam vitam."

28. Jacopone da Todi, *Le satire,* 319.

29. On the word *augurio* see Brambilla Ageno, "Sull'invettiva," 388–391. On Boniface VIII and alchemy, see Finke, *Aus den Tagen,* 207–209.

30. In Vienna, Öesterr. Nationalbibl., MS 5230, fol. 171, is

recorded a *"recepta, qua operabat Bonifacius papa antequam ipse esset papa et multum fuit lucratus cum ista recepta";* in Bologna, Bibl. Univ., Cod. 168 (180) is preserved the *Liber de pratica aquarum roris madii datum pape Bonifatio VIII a domino Iohanne filio sororis carnalis dicti domini pape* (Thorndike, *A History of Magic,* 3 : 53, note 6). The English alchemist John Dastin wrote alchemeic works for Cardinal Napoleone Orsini (d. 1342) and sent Pope John XXII (1316-34) a letter on potable gold, which is also interesting for what it reveals of the history of the *De retardatione* and of Bacon's theory; see now Josten, "The Text of John Dastin's Letters," 34-51; Theisen, "John Dastin's Letter," 76-87; and idem, "John Dastin," 73-78.

31. Johannes Andreae, *Additamenta ad Speculat. tit. de crim. falsi:* "Plus nostris diebus habuimus magistrum Arnaldum de Villanova in Curia Romana summum medicum et theologum de quo scripsi de observatone jeju. consilium qui est magnus alchemista virgulas auri quas faciebat consentiebat omni probationi submitti," cit Thorndike, *A History of Magic,* 3 : 50.

32. Santi, "Il cadavere," 878.

33. On Chinese alchemy, see Needham, *Science,* 5, 2 : 10-15, 71, 74, 282; 5, 4 : 491-96. On relations with the West, see idem, "The Elixir," 167-192.

34. G. Petti Balbi, "Arte di governo e crociata. Il 'Liber sancti passagii' di Galvano da Levanto," in *Studi e ricerche dell'Istituto di civiltà classica medievale* 7 (1986): 131-168.

35. Paris, Bibl. Nat., MS *Lat.,* 3181, fol. 39r: ". . . Andromachus grece, vir bellicosus latine, ab Andreas qui est vir, et machi bellum, cupiens humano generi esse utilis et vivere post mortem in memoria hominis ex diversitate rerum—aromatum, . . . balsamo, opio et carnibus serentis comperiit. . . ."

36. Tenenti, *Il senso della morte.*

37. Ibid., 21-47 and 83-91.

38. Ehrle, *Historia,* 1 : 31 (= Per. 53); see also Pelzer, *Addenda,* 88.

39. *Detestande* was promulgated twice: September 27, 1299 (*Les Registres de Boniface VIII,* no. 3409), and February 18, 1300 (*Extrav. Comm.,* bk. 3, tit. 6, *De sepulturis,* ch. 1, in *Corpus iuris canonici,* ed. Friedberg, 2 : 1271-73); see Brown, "Death," 221-270; see also idem, "Authority," 803-832.

40. Santi, "Il cadavere," 878.

41. *Extrav. Comm.,* bk. 3, tit. 6, ch. 1: "quia corpus humanum, cuius facies ad similitudinem caelestis pulchritudinis est figurata, nec maculari nec defigurari debet."

42. Oliger, "Epistola," 367: "Ex hiis autem concludunt, quod papatus est aliquid indelebile et inseparabile a substantia humanitatis eius, qui assumitur ad papatum, ut sicut in hostia consecrata, manentibus

accidentibus, manet semper Christus, sic, manente humanitate, manet semper in eo sacramentaliter Christus seu Christi papatus."

43. Ibid, 368: "Quod vero dicunt, quod papa est ymago Christi eterni et immutabilis, ergo papa debet esse eternus et immutabilis; si bene arguunt, sequitur etiam, quod post mortem pape non possit substitui alius papa, quia constat, quod post mortem Christi non potuit substitui alius Christus. Unde autem sequitur, quod, quia papa vel episcopus est quoad aliquid Christi ymago, ergo quoad omnia est Christi ymago? Dicant ergo, quod est increatus et immensus et impeccabilis et infallibilis et omnium prescius, sicut Christus, quod nullus dicet vel sapiet, nisi demens." According to Charles I of Anjou, Cardinal Guglielmo of San Marco *ironically* used to call Giovanni Gaetano Orsini, the future Pope Nicholas III, "Veronica" (Baethgen, *Ein Pamphlet,* 19).

44. Boureau, *La papesse,* 16–51. Not by chance, the legend according to which, while the pope was seated on the porphyry chairs, a check was made as to whether "the pope is a man," was confirmed for the first time by Robert of Uzès, ed. Bignami Odier, "Les Visions," 274, in a collection of texts that deplore, in sorrow and affliction, the decadence of the Roman church: Boureau, *La papesse,* 41–43.

45. Concerning this passage from Augustinus Triumphus, see chap. 6, note 36.

46. Elze, " 'Sic transit,' " 23–41; and the introduction, xv.

47. On the pope's nudity, see chap. 5; and see now also Paravicini Bagliani, "Rileggendo i testi sulla 'nudità' del papa,' " 103–125.

48. See chap. 6, note 36.

Epilogue

1. I take this opportunity to express my most sincere thanks to my friends Gilmo Arnaldi, Jacques Dalarun, Mauro Ronzani, and Francesco Santi for all of the suggestions and comments that I have been able to incorporate into this epilogue.

2. See above, 122–32.

3. This sermon has been published by P. Cole, D. L. d'Avray, and J. Riley-Smith, "Application of Theology to Current Affairs: Memorial Sermons on the Dead of Mansurah and on Innocent IV," in N. Bériou and D. L. d'Avray, *Modern Questions about Medieval Sermons. Essays on Marriage, Death, History and Sanctity* (Spoleto, 1994), 239, note 99. See A. Paravicini Bagliani, "Rileggendo i testi sulla 'nudità del papa,' " in *Re nudi. Congiure, assassini, tracolli ed altri imprevisti nella storia del potere. Atti del Convegno di studio della Fondazione Ezio Franceschini. Certosa del Galluzzo, 19 novembre 1994,* Spoleto, 1996, 103–125. I thank M. Alexis Charansonnet for sending me his transcription of Eudes of Châteauroux's sermon, as well as those of the two other sermons to which I refer further on. The critical edition of these sermons will appear in his

thesis, *L'Université, l'Eglise, l'Etat dans les sermons du cardinal Eudes de Châteauroux (1190?–1273)*.

4. See above, 122.

5. Cole, d'Avray, Riley-Smith, "Application," 239, notes 100, 101.

6. *Sermo in anniversario summorum pontificum et cardinalium instituto a domino papa Alexandro;* see Charansonnet, *L'Université*.

7. *In electione pontificis;* see Charansonnet, *L'Université*.

8. Idem.

9. See above, 89.

10. See above, 95.

11. See above, 147.

12. Roger Bacon, *Opus tertium*, ch. 24, ed. J. S. Brewer, Rogerius Bacon, *Opus Tertium, Opus Minus, Compendium philosophiae* (London, 1859), 86–87. In his *Eruditio regum et principum*, written for Saint Louis, Guibert of Tournai also says that the king has a right to a long life; see J. Le Goff, *Saint Louis* (Paris, 1996), 413.

13. See above, 186–92.

14. See above, 199–204.

15. See above, 205–9.

16. It is now possible to consult the splendid work by J. Coste, *Boniface VIII en procès. Articles d'accusation et dépositions des témoins (1303–1311)* (Rome, 1995).

17. On this text, see G. Carbonelli, *Sulle fonti storiche della chimica e dell'alchimia in Italia* (Rome, 1925), 84–93. For a critical study, see now C. Crisciani, "From the Laboratory to the Library: Alchemy According to Guglielmo Fabri," in *Renaissance Natural Philosophy and the Disciplines* (Cambridge, Mass., forthcoming). I thank Chiara Crisciani for letting me consult the text of her study. The critical edition she is preparing will appear soon in the *Cahiers lausannois d'histoire médévale*.

18. J. Chiffoleau, "Amédée VIII ou la Majesté impossible?" in *Amédée VIII—Felix V premier duc de Savoie et pape (1383–1451)* (Lausanne, 1992), 19–49.

BIBLIOGRAPHY

Primary Sources

Aegidius Romanus. *De ecclesiastica potestate.* Ed. R. Scholz. Weimar, 1929.

Albanès, J.-H. *Abrégé de la vie et des miracles du bienheureux Urbain V.* Paris, 1872.

Albertus de Bezanis. *Chronica pontificum et imperatorum.* In MGH, *Scriptores rerum Germananicarum,* vol. 3. Hannover, 1980.

Albertus Magnus. *De animalibus.* Vol. 11 of *Opera omnia,* ed. A. Borgnet. Paris, 1891.

————. *Politica.* Vol. 8. of *Opera omnia,* ed. A. Borgnet. Paris, 1890.

Albinus. *Eglogarum digesta liber XI (ordo).* In LC, vol. 2, 123–137.

Alexander a Turre Cremensis. *De fulgendo radio hierarchiae ecclesiae militantis.* Venice, 1604.

Alexander von Roes. *Schriften.* Ed. H. Grundmann and H. Heimpel. Stuttgart, 1958 (MGH, Staatsschriften I, 1).

Alvarus Pelagius. *Collirium adversus haereses novas.* Ed. R. Scholz. *Unbekannte kirchenpolitische Streitschriften aus der Zeit Ludwigs des Bayern (1327–1354).* 2 vols. Rome, 1911–1914.

————. *De statu et planctu.* Venice, 1560 (= Rocaberti, *Bibliotheca,* vol. 3, 23–266).

Andreas de Barbatia. *De praestantia cardinalis.* In *Tractatus juris universi,* vol. 14. Lyons, 1546.

Andrieu, M. *Le pontifical romain.* 4 vols. Vatican City, 1938.

Anna Comnena, Porphyrogenita. *Alexiade.* Ed. B. Leib. 4 vols. Paris, 1945–1976.

Antoninus, Archiepiscopus Florentinus. *Chronicon.* Lyons, 1586.

Antonius de Butrio. *Super prima primi decretalium commentarii.* Venice, 1578.

Argellata, Pietro. *Chirurgia.* Venice, 1513.

Arnaldus de Villanova. *Opera omnia.* Basel, 1585.

Arquillière, H. X. *Le plus ancien traité de l'Eglise. Jacques de Viterbe: De regimine christiano (1301–1302).* Paris, 1926.

Augustinus Triumphus. *De potestate collegii mortuo papa.* In *Die Publizistik zur Zeit Philipps des Schönen und Bonifaz VIII.,* ed. R. Scholz. Stuttgart, 1903, 501–508.

Avicenna. *Canon.* Venice, 1507.

Baluze, E., and G. Mollat. *Vitae paparum Avenionensium.* 4 vols. Paris, 1914–1922.

Balzani, U. "La storia di Roma nella Cronica di Adamo da Usk." *Archivio della Reale Società Romana di storia patria* 3 (1880): 473–488.

Beda. *De locis sanctis.* Ed. P. Geyer. In CSEL, vol. 39, 301–324. Vienna, 1898.

Benedictus. *Liber politicus.* In LC, vol. 2, 141–174.

Benjamin, F. S., and G. J. Toomer. *Campanus of Novara and Medieval Planetary Theory: Theorica planetarum.* Madison, Wis., 1971.

Benoît XII (1334–1342). *Lettres closes, patentes et curiales se rapportant à la France.* Ed. G. Daumet. Paris, 1920.

Bernardus Claraevallensis. *De consideratione.* In *S. Bernardi Opera,* ed. J. Leclercq and H. M. Rochais, vol. 3, 394–493. Rome, 1963.

———. *De consideratione.* In *Opere di San Bernardo,* ed., trans. F. Gastaldelli, vol. 1, *Trattati,* 761–939. Milan, 1984.

Bettoni, E. *Ruggero Bacone: Lettera a Clemente IV.* Milan, 1964.

Bonaventura. *Apologia pauperum.* In *Opera omnia,* vol. 14, 410–520. Paris, 1868.

———. *Expositio in Psalterium.* In *Opera omnia,* vol. 9, 154–578. Paris, 1867.

———. *Illuminationes Ecclesiae in Hexamaeron.* Sermo XXII. In *Opera omnia,* vol. 9, 17–153. Paris, 1867.

———. *Sermones de tempore.* In *Opera omnia,* vol. 13, 1–492. Paris, 1868.

Boretius, A. *Capitularia regum Francorum.* Hannover, 1881.

Bullarum, diplomatum et privilegiorum sanctorum Romanorum pontificum . . . Vols 4–5, Augustae Taurinorum, 1859–1860; vol. 8, Naples, 1863.

Caspar, E. *Das Register Gregors VII.* Vol. 1. Berlin, 1920; repr. Munich, 1978.

Catalani, G. *Pontificale Romanum.* 3 vols. Paris, 1850–1853.

Cencius. *Romanus ordo de consuetudinibus et observantiis* (= *Liber Censuum* 57–58). In LC, vol. 1, 290–311.

Chartularium Universitatis Parisiensis. Ed. H. Denifle and E. Chatelain. Vol. 1. Paris, 1894.

Cipolla, C. *Le opere di Ferreto de' Ferreti Vicentino.* Vol. 1. Rome, 1908.

Codicis iuris canonici fontes. 9 vols. Vatican City, 1932–1951.

Collectio Avellana. Ed. O. Günther. In CSEL, vol. 35. Vienna, 1895.

Collectio bullarum sacrosanctae basilicae Vaticanae. 3 vols. Rome, 1747–1752.

Constantinus Porphyrogenitus Imperator. *De Caerimoniis aulae Byzantinae*. Ed. J. J. Reiskij. Bonn, 1829–1830.

"Constitutum Constantini." ed. H. Fuhrmann. *Das Constitutum Constantini (Konstantinische Schenkung)*. Text, MGH. Hannover, 1968.

Corpus iuris canonici. Ed. E. Friedberg. 2 vols. Leipzig, 1879–1881.

Cortesi, P. *De cardinalatu*. In castro Cortesio, 1511.

D'Achery, Luc. *Veterum aliquot scriptorum Spicilegium*. Vol. 6. Paris, 1664.

De retardatione accidentium senectutis. Ed. A. G. Little, E. Withington. Oxford, 1928.

Decretum Gratiani. Ed. E. Friedberg. *Corpus Iuris Canonici*. Vol. 1. Leipzig, 1892.

Del Re, G. *Cronisti e scrittori sincroni Napolitani*. Vol. 1. Naples, 1845.

Delicati, P., and M. Armellini. *Il Diario di Leone X di Paride de Grassi*. Rome, 1884.

Denifle, H., and E. Châtelain. *Chartularium Universitatis Parisiensis*. Vol. 1. Paris, 1894.

Die Briefe des Petrus Damiani. Ed. K. Reindel. 3 vols. Munich, 1983–1989.

Die Register Innocenz' III. Vol. 1, ed. O. Hageneder and A. Haidacher, Graz-Köln, 1964; vol. 2, ed. O. Hageneder, W. Maleczek, and A. A. Strnad, Rome and Vienna, 1979.

Dykmans, M. *L'oeuvre de Patrizi Piccolomini ou le cérémonial papal de la première Renaissance*. 2 vols. Vatican City, 1980–1982.

———. *Le cérémonial papal de la fin du Moyen Age à la Renaissance*. 4 vols. Brussels and Rome, 1977–1985.

Egidi, P. *Necrologi e libri affini della Provincia romana*. 2 vols. Rome, 1908.

Egidius Corboliensis. *Viaticus*. Ed. V. Rose. Leipzig, 1907.

Ehrle, F. *Historia bibliothecae Romanorum pontificum tum Bonifatianae tum Avenionensis*. Vol. 1. Rome, 1890.

Epifanius de Salamis. *De XII gemmis*. Ed. O. Günther. Vienna, 1895, 743–773.

Finke, H. *Acta Aragonensia: Quellen zur deutschen, italienischen, französischen, spanischen, zur Kirchen- und Kulturgeschichte aus der diplomatischen Korrespondenz Jaymes II. (1291–1327)*. 3 vols. Berlin, 1908–1922.

Galfridus de Vinosalvo. *Poetria nova*. Ed. E. Faral. *Les arts poétiques du XIIe et du XIIIe siècle*. Paris, 1924, 197–262.

Gattico, G. B. *Acta selecta caeremonialia Sanctae Romanae Ecclesiae*. Vol. 1. Rome, 1753.

Gesta Innocentii pape III. In PL 214, xvii–ccxxviii.

Giovanni Burcardo. *Alla corte di cinque papi: Diario 1483–1506*. Ed. L. Bianchi. Milan, 1988.

Guido de Cauliaco. *Cyrurgia magna*. Lyons, 1585.

Guilellmus Durandus. *Rationale divinorum officiorum*. Venice, 1568.

Guy de Chauliac. *La Grande Chirurgie . . . composée en l'an 1363*. Ed. E. Nicaise. Paris, 1890.

Hampe, K. "Eine Schilderung des Sommeraufenthaltes der römischen Kurie unter Innozenz III." *Historische Vierteljahsschrift* 8 (1905): 509—535.

Henri de Mondeville. *Chirurgie . . . composée de 1306 à 1320*. Ed. E. Nicaise. Paris, 1893.

Höfler, C. *Albert von Beham und Regesten Papst Innocenz' IV.* Stuttgart, 1847.

Horoy, C. *Honorii III opera omnia*. In *Medii aevi Bibliotheca Patristica ab anno 1217 usque ad Concilii Tridentini tempora*. 4 vols. Paris, 1879— 1883.

Hostiensis. *In quintum decretalium librum commentaria*. Venice, 1581.

————. *Lectura in quinque Decretalium libros*. Venice, 1581.

————. *Summa aurea*. Lyons, 1588.

Infessura, Stefano. *Diario della città di Roma* . Ed. O. Tommasini. Rome, 1890.

Jacobus a Voragine. *Legenda aurea*. Ed. T. Graesse. 3rd ed. Vratislavia, 1890.

Jacopone da Todi. *Le satire*. Ed. B. Brugnoli. Florence, 1914.

Jacopus Caietanus de Stefaneschis. *Opus Metricum*. In *Monumenta Coelestiniana: Quellen zur Geschichte des Papstes Coelestin V.*, ed. F. X. Seppelt, 1—145. Paderborn, 1921.

Jacques de Vitry. *Lettres*. Ed. R. B. C. Huygens. Leiden, 1960.

Johannes Beleth. *Svmma de ecclesiasticis officiis*. Ed. H. Douteil. 2 vols. Tvrnholti, 1976.

Johannes Burcardus. *Diarium*. Ed. L. Thuasne. 3 vols. Paris, 1883— 1885.

————. *Liber notarum ab anno MCCCCLXXXIII usque ad annum MDVI*. Ed. E. Celani. In RIS (2nd ed.), vol. 32, 1. Bologna, 1907— 1942.

Johannes Diaconus. *Descriptio Lateranensis Ecclesiae*. Ed. R. Valentini and G. Zucchetti, *Codice topografico della città di Roma*. Vol. 3. Rome, 1946, 326—373.

Kurdzialek, M. *Davidis de Dinanto Quaternulorum fragmenta*. Warsaw, 1963.

Lawn, B. *The Prose Salernitan Questions edited from a Bodleian Manuscript (Auct. F. 3. 10)*. London, 1979.

Le Vite di Pio II e di G. A. Campano e Bartolomeo Platina. Ed. G. C. Zimolo. In RIS (2nd ed.), vol. 3, 3. Bologna, 1964.

Leonardi Dathi Epistolae XXXII, recensente Laurentio Mehus . . . accessit elegantissima Jacobi Angeli Epistola ad Emmanuelem Chrisoloram addita ejusdem vita. Florence, 1743.

Leontios von Neapolis. *Leben des Heiligen Johannes des Barmherzigen*. c. 19. Ed. H. Gelzer. Freiburg and Leipzig, 1893.

Les Registres d'Alexandre IV (1254–1261). Ed. C. Bourel de La Roncière, J. de Loye, P. Hellouin de Cenival, and A. Coulon. Paris, 1895– 1959.

Les Registres d'Honorius IV (1285–1287). Ed. M. Prou. Paris, 1886–1888.

Les Registres d'Innocent IV (1243–1254). Ed. E. Berger. Paris, 1884–1921.

Les Registres d'Urbain IV (1261–1264). Ed. J. Guiraud, S. Clémencet. Paris, 1892–1958.

Les Registres de Benoît XI (1303–1304). Ed. C. Grandjean. Paris, 1905.

Les Registres de Boniface VIII (1294–1303). Ed. A. Thomas, M. Faucon, G. Digard, and R. Fawtier. Paris, 1884–1939.

Les Registres de Clément IV (1265–1268). Ed. E. Jordan. Paris, 1893– 1945.

Les Registres de Grégoire IX (1227–1241). Ed. L. Auvray, S. Clémencet, and L. Carolus-Barré. Paris, 1890–1955.

Les Registres de Martin IV (1281–1283). Ed. F. Olivier-Martin. Paris, 1901–1935.

Les Registres de Nicolas III (1277–1280). Ed. J. Gay. Paris, 1898–1938.

Les Registres de Nicolas IV (1288–1292). Ed. E. Langlois. Paris, 1886.

Lettres de Clément VI se rapportant à la France. Ed. E. Déprez, J. Glénisson. Vol. 1. Paris, 1901–1925.

Lettres secrètes et curiales de Jean XXII. Ed. A. Coulon and S. Clémencet. Paris, 1906–1972.

Lewis, R.E. *Lotario di Segni (Pope Innocent III): De miseria condicionis humanae*. Athens, GA, 1978.

Libellus de cerimoniis aulae imperatoris (Graphia aureae Urbis Romae). In *Kaiser, Könige und Päpste,*ed. P. E. Schramm. Vol. 3, 319–353. Stuttgart, 1960.

Liber Pontificalis nella recensione di Pietro Guglielmo e del card: Pandolfo. Ed. U. Prérovsky. 3 vols. Rome, 1978.

Maccarrone, M. *Lotharii cardinalis (Innocentii III): De miseria humanae conditionis.* Lucca, 1955.

Mansi, G. D. *Sacrorum conciliorum nova et amplissima collectio*. Ed. altera. 53 vols. Paris, 1901–1927.

Martène, E. *De antiquis Ecclesiae ritibus libri IV.* 3 vols. Rouen, 1700– 1702.

Martinus Polonus. *Sermones, Exempla de morte*. Strasbourg, 1480, 1484, 1486, 1488.

Matthaei Parisiensis. *Chronica maiora*. Ed. H. R. Luard. ser. Rerum Britannicarum Medii Aevi Scriptores, 57. 7 vols. London, 1872– 1883.

———. *Historia Anglorum*. Ed. F. Madden. ser. Rerum Britannicarum Medii Aevi Scriptores, 44. London, 1886–1869.

May, H. G., and B. M. Metzger, eds. *The New Oxford Bible with Apocrypha* (Revised Standard Version). New York, 1973.

Mezzadri B. *Dissertatio critica-historica de vigintiquinque annis Romanae Petri Cathedrae adversus utrumque Pagium.* Rome, 1750.

MGH. *Constitutiones et acta publica imperatorum et regum* . . . . Vol. 2. Hannover, 1896.

————. *Libelli de lite imperatorum et pontificum saec: XI et XII conscripti.* 3 vols. Hannover, 1891–1897.

Molinier, E. "Inventaire du trésor du Saint Siège sous Boniface VIII (1295)." *Bibliothèque de l'Ecole des Chartes,* 43 (1882): 19–310, 626–646; 45 (1884): 31–57; 46 (1885): 16–44; 47 (1886): 646–667; 49 (1888): 226–237.

Munk, C. M. *A Study of Pope Innocent III's Treatise: De quadripartita specie nuptiarum.* Diss., Univ. of Kansas, Lawrence, 1976.

Müntz, E. *Les arts à la cour des papes pendant le XVe et le XVIe siècle. Recueil de documents inédits tirés des archives et des bibliothèques romaines.* Paris, 1878.

Nabuco, J., and F. Tamburini. *Le cérémonial apostolique avant Innocent VIII.* Rome, 1966.

Oliger, P. L. "Epistola ad Conradum de Offida." *Archivum Franciscanum Historicum* 11 (1918): 366–373.

————. "Petri Iohannis Olivi de renuntiatione papae Coelestini V quaestio et epistola." *Archivum Franciscanum Historicum* 11 (1918): 309–366.

Ostermuth, H. J. *"Flores Diaetarum": Eine salernitanische Nahrungsmitteldiätetik aus dem XII. Jahrhundert, verfasst vermutlich von Johannes de Sancto Paulo.* Diss., Leipzig, 1919.

Pagel, J. L. *Die Chirurgie des Heinrich von Mondeville.* Berlin, 1892.

Pagnotti, F. "Niccolò da Calvi e la sua Vita d'Innocenzo IV con una breve introduzione sulla istoriografia pontificia dei secoli XIII e XIV." *Archivio della Reale Società Romana di storia patria* 21 (1898): 6–120.

Paridis de Crassis Diarium Curiae Romanae. Ed. G. Hoffmann. In *Nova scriptorum ac monumentorum . . . Collectio.* Leipzig, 1731.

Paridis Grassi Bononiensis olim Apostolicarum Caeremoniarum magistri ac episcopi Pisauren: De caeremoniis cardinalium et episcoporum in eorum dioecesibus libri duo. 2 vols. Venice, 1582.

Pellens, K. *Die Texte des Normannischen Anonymus.* Wiesbaden, 1966.

Pelzer, A. *Addenda et emendanda ad Francisci Ehrle Historiae Bibliothecae Romanorum pontificum tum Bonifatianae tum Avenionensis.* Vol. 1. Vatican City, 1947.

Petrus de Abano. *Tractatus de venenis.* Mantua, 1472.

Petrus Iohannis Olivi. *Expositio Regulae Fratrum Minorum.* Venice, 1513.

Petrus Mallius. *Descriptio basilicae Vaticanae.* In *Codice topografico della città di Roma,* ed. R. Valentini and G. Zucchetti, vol. 3, 319–441. Rome, 1946.

Pii II Commentarii rerum memorabilivm qve temporibvs svis contigervnt. Ed. A. Van Heck. 2 vols. Vatican City, 1984.

Poncelet S. "Vie et miracles du pape S. Léon IX." *Analecta Bollandiana* 25 (1906): 258–297.

Pontificale Romanum-Germanicum. Ed. C. Vogel and R. Elze. *Le pontifical romano-germanique du dixième siècle.* 3 vols. Vatican City, 1963–1972.

Potthast, A. *Regesta pontificum Romanorum inde ab a. post Christum natum MCXVIII ad a. MCCCIV.* 2 vols. Berlin, 1875.

Regesta Honorii papae III. Ed. P. Pressutti. 2 vols. Rome, 1888–1895.

Regestum Innocentii papae III super negotio Romani imperii. Ed. F. Kempf. Rome, 1947.

Restaurus Castaldus. *Tractatus de imperatore.* In *Tractatus universi iuris,* vol. 12. Lyons, 1549.

Rocaberti, J. T. *Bibliotheca Maxima Pontificia.* 21 vols. Rome, 1698–1699.

Rodorici episcopi Zamorensis, Speculum vitae humanae . . . Intermixto de brevitate vitae pontificum Romanorum. Frankfurt, 1689.

Rogerius Bacon. *Opus Tertium, Opus Minus, Compendium philosophiae.* Ed. J. S. Brewer. London, 1859.

———. *The "Opus Maius."* ed. J. H. Bridges. 3 vols. London, 1897–1900.

Ryccardus de Sancto Germano. *Chronica.* Ed. C. A. Garufi. RIS (2nd ed.). Vol. 7, 2. Bologna, 1938.

Salimbene de Adam. *Chronica.* Ed. G. Scalia. 2 vols. Bari, 1966.

Sambin, P. *Un certame dettatorio tra due notai pontifici (1260): Lettere inedite di Giordano da Terracina e di Giovanni da Capua.* Rome, 1955.

Schäfer, K. H. *Die Ausgaben der Apostolischen Kammer unter Benedikt XII., Klemens VI. und Innozenz VI. (1335–1362).* Paderborn, 1914.

———. *Die Ausgaben der Apostolischen Kammer unter den Päpsten Urban V. und Gregor XI.* Paderborn, 1937.

———. *Die Ausgaben der Apostolischen Kammer unter Johann XXII.* Paderborn, 1911.

Schillmann, F. *Die Formularsammlung des Marinus von Eboli.* Vol. 1, *Entstehung und Inhalt.* Rome, 1929.

Schmidt, T. *Libri rationum Camerae Bonifatii papae VIII (Archivum Secretum Vaticanum, collect. 446 necnon Intr. et ex. 5).* Vatican City, 1984.

Scholz, R. *Unbekannte kirchenpolitische Streitschriften aus der Zeit Ludwigs des Bayern (1327–1354).* 2 vols. Rome, 1911–1914.

Schrick, G. *Der Königsspiegel des Alvaro Pelayo (Speculum regum).* Diss., Bonn, 1953.

Secretum secretorum cum glossis et notulis: Tractatus brevis et utilis ad declar-

andum quedam obscure dicta Fratris Rogeri. Ed. R. Steele. Oxford, 1920.

Sextus Pompeus Festus. *De verborum significatu quae supersunt cum Pauli epitome*. Ed. W. M. Lindsay. Leipzig, 1913.

Sidonius Apollinaris. *Lettres*. 2 vols. Ed. A. Loyen. Paris, 1970.

Sinibaldus de Flisco. *Apparatus in quinque libros decretalium*. Venice, 1578.

Stephanus de Borbone. *Tractatus de diversis materiis predicalibus*. Vol. 1, *De dono timoris*. Ed. J. Berlioz, J.-L. Eichenlaub. Turnhout, 1994.

Tabanelli, M. *La chirurgia italiana nell'Alto Medio Evo*. 2 vols. Florence, 1965.

Tangl, M. *Die päpstlichen Kanzlei-Ordnungen von 1200–1500*. Innsbruck, 1894.

Thaner, F. *Summa magistri Rolandi*. Innsbruck, 1874.

Thomas de Eccleston. *De adventu fratrum Minorum in Angliam*. In *Monumenta Franciscana* (Rerum Britannicarum Medii Aevi Scriptores 4), ed. J. S. Brewer, 5–72. London, 1858.

Thompson, E. M. *Chronicon Adae de Usk: A.D. 1377–1404*. London, 1876.

Töply, R. V. *Anatomia Richardi Anglici*. Vienna, 1902.

Ulrich von Reichental. *Das Konzil zu Konstanz*. 2 vols. Ed. O. Feger. Constance, 1962–1964.

Ulrich von Richental. *Chronik des Constanzer Concils*. Ed. M. R. Buck. Tübingen, 1882.

Valentini, R., and G. Zucchetti. *Codice topografico della Città di Roma*. 3 vols. ser. Fonti per la Storia d'Italia 81, 88, 90–91. Rome, 1940–1953.

Van Dijk, S. J. P., and J. H. Walker. *The Ordinal of the Papal Court from Innocent III to Boniface VIII and Related Documents*. Fribourg: 1975.

Varin, P. *Archives administratives de la ville de Reims*. 3 vols. Paris, 1839–1848.

Vita Gregorii IX. In LC, vol. 2, 18–36.

Wadding, L. de. *Annales Minorum*. Ad Claras Aquas. 1931–.

Walter Map. *De nugis curialium*. Ed. M. R. James. Oxford, 1983.

Watterich, J. M. *Pontificum Romanorum qui fuerunt Vitae*. 2 vols. Leipzig, 1862.

Witelo. *Opticae libri decem instaurati*. Ed. F. Risner. Basel, 1572.

Wolkan, R. *Der Briefwechsel des Eneas Silvius Piccolimini*. 4 vols. ser. Fontes rerum Austriacarum, 61, 62, 67, 68. Vienna, 1909–1918.

Secondary Sources

Albert, J.-P. *Odeurs de sainteté: La Mythologie chrétienne des aromates*. Paris, 1990.

Alessio, F. *Mito e scienza in Ruggero Bacone*. Milan, 1957.

Alexandre-Bidon, D. "Le corps et son linceul." In *A réveiller les morts: La mort au quotidien dans l'Occident médiéval*, 183–206. Paris, 1993.

Antonelli, N. *Epistola de ritu inspergendi Sacri Cineris super Caput Romanorum Pontificum*. In E. de Azevedo, SJ, *Vetus Missale Romanum Monasticum Lateranense*. Rome, 1754.

Arduini, M. L. " 'Rerum mutabilitas.' Mondo, tempo, immagine dell'uomo e 'Corpus Ecclesiae-Christianitatis' in Onorio di Ratisbona (Augustodunensis). Per la comprensione di un razionalismo politico nel secolo XII." In *L'homme et son univers au Moyen Age*, vol. 1, 365–373. Louvain-la-Neuve, 1986.

Aussac, F. d'. *Le droit de dépouille (jus spolii)*. Strasbourg and Paris, 1930.

Aymon, J. *Tableau de la cour de Rome*. The Hague, 1707.

Baer, W. *Studien zum sogenannten Anonymus von York*. Diss., Munich, 1966.

Baethgen, F. *Der Engelpapst: Idee und Erscheinung*. Leipzig, 1943.

Baethgen, F. *Ein Pamphlet Karls I von Anjou zur Wahl Papst Nikolaus III.* In "Sitz.-Ber. d. bayer. Akad. d. Wissen." Phil.-hist., Klasse, 1960.

——. "Quellen und Untersuchungen zur Geschichte der päpstlichen Hof- und Finanzverwaltung unter Bonifaz VIII." *Quellen und Forschungen aus italienischen Archiven und Bibliotheken* 20 (1928–1929): 114–237.

Ballestreri, L. G. "Arnaldus de Vilanova (c. 1240–1311) y la reforma de los estudios medicos en Mentpellier (1309): El Hipocrates latino y la introducion del nuevo Galeno.'" *Dynamis* 2 (1982): 27–158.

Baumgarten, P. M. *Untersuchungen und Urkunden über die Camera collegii cardinalium*. Leipzig, 1898.

Berger, A. M. *Der von Michel Angelo Buonarotti eigenhändig geschriebene Augentraktat*. Munich, 1897.

Berger, A. M. *Die Ophtalmologie (liber de oculo) des Petrus Hispanus (Petrus von Lissabon, später Papst Johannes XXI)*. Munich, 1899.

Bernhart, J. *Der Vatikan als Thron der Welt*. Leipzig, 1930.

Bertelli, C. "Traversie della tomba di Clemente IV." *Paragone* (1969): 53–63.

Bertelli, S. *Il corpo del re*. Florence, 1990.

Besso, M. *Roma e il Papa nei proverbi e nei modi di dire*. Rome, 1904. 2nd ed. Florence, 1971.

Bibliotheca Sanctorum. 12 vols. Rome, 1961–1970.

Bignami Odier, J. "Les Visions de Robert d'Uzès." *Archivum Fratrum Praedicatorum* 25 (1955): 258–320.

Bloch, H. "Der Autor der *Graphia aureae urbis Romae*." *Deutsches Archiv für Erforschung des Mittelalters* 4 (1984): 55–175.

Bodin, J. *Les Six Livres de la République*. Paris, 1576 (Paris, 1583).

Bonanni, F. *La gerarchia ecclesiastica*. Rome, 1720.

Borgolte, M. *Petrusnachfolge und Kaiserimitation: Die Grablegen der Päpste, ihre Genese und Traditionsbildung.* Göttingen, 1989.

Bougerol, J. G. "La papauté dans les sermons médiévaux français et italiens." In *The Religious Roles of the Papacy: Ideals and Realities, 1150–1300,* 247–275. Toronto, 1989.

Boureau, A. *La papesse Jeanne.* Paris, 1988.

Boyle, L. E. "An Ambry of 1299 at San Clemente, Rome." *Mediaeval Studies* 26 (1964): 329–350.

Bradford, C. A. *Heart Burial.* London, 1933.

Brambilla Ageno, F. "Sull'invettiva di Iacopone da Todi contro Bonifacio VIII." *Lettere italiane* 16 (1964): 373–414.

Brams, J. "Mensch und Natur in der Übersetzungsarbeit Wilhelms von Moerbeke." In *Mensch und Natur im Mittelalter,* 545–548. Berlin and New York, 1992.

Braun, J. *Die liturgische Gewandung im Occident und Orient nach Ursprung und Entwicklung, Verwendung und Symbolik.* Freiburg im Breisgau, 1907.

Brehm, E. "Roger Bacon's Place in the History of Alchemy." *Ambix* 23 (1976): 53–58.

Brown, E. A. R. "Authority, the Family, and the Dead in Late Medieval France." *French Historical Studies* 16 (1990): 803–832.

———. "Death and Human Body in the Later Middle Ages: The Legislation of Boniface VIII on the Division of the Corpse." *Viator* 12 (1981): 221–270.

Bultot, R. *La doctrine du mépris du monde 4, Le XIe siècle.* Vol. 1, *Pierre Damien.* Louvain, 1963.

———. "Mépris du monde, misère de l'homme dans la pensée d'Innocent III." *Cahiers de civilisation médiévale* 4 (1962): 441–456.

Burchardt, J. *Witelo, filosofo della natura del XIII sec. Una biografia.* Warsaw, 1984.

Burnett, C. "An Apocryphal Letter from the Arabic Philosopher Al-Kindi to Theodore, Frederick II's Astrologer, Concerning Gog and Magog, the Enclosed Nations, and the Scourge of the Mongols." *Viator* 15 (1984): 151–167.

Burns, C. *Golden Rose and Blessed Sword.* Glasgow, 1970.

Butzek, M. *Die kommunalen Repräsentationsstatuen der Päpste des 16. Jahrhunderts in Bologna Perugia und Rom.* Diss. phil., Berlin, Bad Honnef, 1978.

Cacciamani, G. "De brevitate vitae pontificum Romanorum, et divina providentia." *Vita monastica* 26 (1972): 226–242.

Calò Mariani, M. S. "Utilità e diletto. L'acqua e le residenze regie dell'Italia meridionale fra XII e XIII secolo." *Mélanges de l'Ecole Française de Rome. Moyen Age et Temps Modernes* 104 (1992): 343–372.

Calvet, A. "Le *De vita philosophorum* du pseudo-Arnaud de Villeneuve. Texte du manuscrit B.N. lat. 7817 édité et traduit." *Chrysopoeia* 4 (1990–1991): 35–79.

Campi, P. M. *Dell'Historia ecclesiastica di Piacenza, con mentione di famiglie, huomini illustri, registro de' privilegi, ecc.* 3 vols. Rome, 1651–1662.

Cancellieri, F. *De secretariis basilicae Vaticanae veteris ac novae libri II.* 4 vols. Rome, 1786.

——. *Lettera sopra il tarantismo, l'aria di Roma e della sua Campagna.* Roma, 1817.

——. *Notizie istoriche delle stagioni e dei siti diversi in cui sono tenuti i conclavi nella città di Roma.* Rome, 1823.

——. *Storia de' solenni possessi dei sommi pontefici detti anticamente processi o processioni dopo loro coronazione dalla basilica Vaticana alla Lateranense.* Rome, 1802.

Carolus-Barré, L. "Le cardinal de Dormans, chancelier de France 'principal conseiller' de Charles V d'aprés son testament et les Archives du Vatican." *Mélanges d'archéologie et d'histoire* 52 (1935): 353–354.

Carré, Y. *Le baiser sur la bouche au Moyen Age. Rites, symboles, mentalités, XIe–XVe siècles.* Paris, 1992.

Caspar, E. *Die älteste römische Bischofsliste. Kritische Studien zum Formproblem des euseb. Kanons sowie zur Geschichte der ältesten Bischofslisten und ihrer Entstehung aus apostolischen Sukzessionsreihen.* Berlin, 1926.

——. *Geschichte des Papsttums von den Anfängen bis zur Höhe der Weltherrschaft.* 2 vols. Tübingen, 1930–1933.

——. *Petrus Diaconus und die Monte Cassineser Fälschungen.* Berlin, 1909.

Celli, R. "La malaria nella storia medievale di Roma." *Archivio della Reale Società Romana di storia patria* 47 (1924): 5–44.

Celli-Fraentzel, A. "Quellen zur Geschichte der Malaria in Italien und ihrer Bedeutung für die deutschen Kaiserzüge des Mittelalters." *Quellen und Studien zur Geschichte der Naturwissenschaften und der Medizin* 4 (1935).

Chodorow, S. *Christian Political Theory and Church Politics in the Mid-Twelfth Century: The Ecclesiology of Gratian's Decretum.* Berkeley, 1972.

Clark, J. R. "Roger Bacon and the Composition of Marsilio Ficino's *De Vita Longa* (*De Vita*, Book II)." *The Journal of the Warburg and Courtauld Institutes* 49 (1986): 230–232.

Claussen, P. C. "Pietro di Oderisio und die Neuformulierung des italienischen Grabmals zwischen Opus romanum und Opus Francigenum." In *Skulptur und Grabmal*, 173–200.

Colosio, I. "Riflessioni di S. Pier Damiani sulla morte dei papi." *Rivista di ascetica e mistica* 3 (1978): 240–245.

Corner, G. W. *Anatomical Texts of the Earlier Middle Ages.* Washington, 1927.

Cornides, E. *Rose und Schwert im päpstlichen Zeremoniell.* Vienna, 1967.

Coste, J. *Boniface VIII en procès. Articles d'accusation et dépositions des témoins (1303–1311).* Rome, 1995.

Crisciani, C. "Labirinti dell'oro. Specificité e mimesi nell'alchimia latina." *Aut Aut,* n.s. 184–185 (1981): 127–151.

Crowley, T. *Roger Bacon. The Problem of the Soul in his Philosophical Commentaries.* Dublin, 1950.

D'Onofrio, C. *La papessa Giovanna. Roma e papato tra storia e leggenda.* Rome, 1979.

Davidsohn, R. *Geschichte von Florenz.* 4 vols. Berlin, 1896–1927.

Deér, J. "Byzanz und die Herrschaftszeichen des Abendlandes." In *Byzanz und das abendländische Herrschertum. Ausgewählte Aufsätze,* 42–69. Sigmaringen, 1977.

———. *The Dynastic Porphyry Tombs of the Norman Period in Sicily.* Cambridge, Mass., 1959.

Delbrueck, R. "Der spätantike Kaiserornat." *Die Antike* 8 (1932): 7–15.

Delisle, L. *Le Cabinet des manuscrits de la Bibliothéque Nationale.* 4 vols. Paris, 1868–1881.

Déprez, E. "Les funérailles de Clément VI et d'Innocent VI d'après les comptes de la cour pontificale." *Mélanges d'archéologie et d'histoire* 20 (1900): 235–250.

Dictionnaire historique de la papauté. Paris, 1994.

Digard, G. *Philippe le Bel et le Saint-Siège de 1285 à 1304.* Vol. 2. Paris, 1936.

Döllinger, J. J. J. von. *Beiträge zur politischen, kirchlichen und Cultur-Geschichte der sechs letzten Jahrhunderte.* 3 vols. Vienna, 1862–1882.

Duchesne, F. *Histoire de tous les cardinaux françois.* 2 vols. Paris, 1660.

Dupuy, P. *Histoire du différend d'entre le pape Boniface VIII et Philippes le Bels, roy de France.* Paris, 1655.

Dykmans, M. "Le cérémonial de Nicolas V." *Revue d'histoire ecclésiastique* 63 (1968): 365–825.

———. "Les pouvoirs des cardinaux pendant la vacance du Saint Siège d'après un nouveau manuscrit de Jacques Stefaneschi." *Archivio della Società Romana di storia patria* 104 (1981): 119–145.

———. "Paris de Grassi." *Ephemerides liturgicae* 96 (1982): 407–482.

Easton, S. C. *Roger Bacon and His Search for a Universal Science. A Reconsideration of the Life and Work of Roger Bacon in the Light of His Own Stated Purposes.* New York, 1952.

Ehrle, F. "Der Nachlass Clemens V und der in Betreff desselben von Johann XXII (1318–1321) geführte Process." *Archiv für Litteratur- und Kirchengeschichte des Mittelalters* 5 (1889): 1–158.

Eichmann, E. *Die Kaiserkrönung im Abendland*. 2 vols. Würzburg, 1942.

Eichmann, E. *Weihe und Krönung des Papstes im Mittelalter*. Munich, 1951.

Elze, R. " 'Sic transit gloria mundi': la morte del papa nel medioevo." *Annali dell'Istituto storico italo-germanico in Trento* 3 (1977): 23–41.

Engels, O. "Kardinal Boso als Geschichtsschreiber." In *Konzil und Papst. Historische Beiträge zur Frage der höchsten Gewaltin der Kirche. Festgabe für H. Tüchle*, 147–168. Munich, 1975.

Erdmann, C. "Kaiserliche und päpstliche Fahnen im hohen Mittelalter." *Quellen und Forschungen aus italienischen Archiven und Bibliotheken* 25 (1933–1934): 1–48.

Erlande-Brandenburg, A. *Le roi est mort. Etude sur les funérailles, les sépultures et les tombeaux des rois de France jusqu'à la fin du XIIIe siècle.* Geneva and Paris, 1975.

Finke, H. *Aus den Tagen Bonifaz VIII. Funde und Forschungen*. Munich, 1902.

———. "Eine Papstchronik des XV. Jahrhunderts." *Römische Quartalschrift* 4 (1890): 340–362.

Forcella, V. *Iscrizioni delle chiese e di altri edifici di Roma dal secolo XI fino ai giorni nostri.* 14 vols. Rome, 1869–1884.

Forchielli G. "Il diritto di spoglio e il diritto di regalia in Germania nel medioevo." In *Für Kirche und Recht. Festschrift für J. Heckel*, 13–55. 1959.

Förster, E. *De Aristotelis quae feruntur Secretis secretorvm commentatio.* Kiliae, 1888.

Frutaz, A. M. "La famiglia pontificia in un documento dell'inizio del sec. XIV." In *Palaeographica Diplomatica et Archivistica. Studi in onore di Giulio Battelli*, vol. 2, 277–323. Rome, 1979.

Fuhrmann, H. " 'Il vero imperatore è il papa.' Il potere temporale nel medioevo." *Bullettino dell'Istituto storico italiano e Archivio Muratoriano* 92 (1985–1986): 367–379.

———. "Über die Heiligkeit des Papstes." *Jahrbuch der Akademie der Wissenschaften in Göttingen* (1981): 28–43.

Galbreath, D. L. *Papal Heraldry*. Cambridge, 1930.

Gandolfo, F. "Reimpiego di sculture antiche nei troni papali del XII secolo." *Rendiconti della Pontificia Accademia Romana di Archeologia.* ser. III, 47 (1974–1975): 203–207.

Gardner, J. "Arnolfo di Cambio and Roman Tomb Design." *Burlington Magazine* 115 (1973): 420–439.

———. "Boniface VIII as a Patron of Sculpture." In *Roma anno 1300*, 513–520.

———. "Patterns of Papal Patronage circa 1260–circa 1300." In *The Religious Roles of the Papacy: Ideals and Realities, 1150–1300*, 439–456. Toronto, 1989.

————. "Some Cardinals' Seals of the Thirteenth Century." *The Journal of the Warburg and Courtauld Institutes* 38 (1975): 72–96.

————. *The Tomb and the Tiara. Curial Tomb Sculpture in Rome and Avignon in the Later Middle Ages.* Oxford, 1992.

Garms, J. "Gräber von Heiligen und Seiligen." In *Skulptur und Grabmal,* 83–105.

Gay, V., and H. Stein. "Embaumement." In *Glossaire archéologique du Moyen Age et de la Renaissance,* 625 ss. Paris, 1887–1928.

Gerberto. Scienza, storia e mito. Bobbio, 1985.

Getz, F. "To Prolong Life and to Promote Health: Baconian Alchemy and Pharmacy in the English Learned Tradition." In *Health, Disease and Healing in Medical Culture.* New York, 1991.

Gieben, S. "Robert Grosseteste at the Papal Curia, Lyons 1250. Edition of the Documents." *Collectanea Franciscana* 41 (1971): 340–393.

Giesey, R. E. *Le roi ne meurt jamais.* Paris, 1987.

Gillmann, F. " 'Romanus pontifex iura omnia in scrinio pectoris sui censetur habere' (c. 1 in VIto de Const. I, 2)." *Archiv für katholisches Kirchenrecht* 92 (1912): 1–17; 106 (1926): 156–174.

Ginzburg, C. "High and Low. The Theme of Forbidden Knowledge in the Sixteenth and Seventeenth Centuries." *Past and Present* 73 (1976): 28–41.

Ginzburg, C. "Saccheggi rituali. Premesse a una ricerca in corso." *Quaderni storici* 22 (1987): 615–636.

Glass, D. "Papal Patronage in the Early Twelfth Century. Notes on the Iconography of Cosmatesque Pavement." *The Journal of the Warburg and Courtauld Institutes* 32 (1969): 386–390.

Godefroy, T., and D. Godefroy. *Le cérémonial français.* 2 vols. Paris, 1649.

Göller, E. *Die päpstliche Pönitentiarie.* 2 vols. Rome, 1907–1911.

Göring, H. *Die Beamten der Kurie unter Bonifaz VIII.* Königsberg, 1934.

Graf, A. *Miti, leggende e superstizioni del Medio Evo.* 2 vols. Turin, 1892–1893.

Grauert, H. *Magister Heinrich der Poet von Würzburg und die römische Kurie.* Munich, 1912.

————. "Meister Johann von Toledo." *Sizungsberichte der bayerischen Akademie der Wissenschaften* (1901).

Gregorovius, F. *Die Grabdenkmäler der Päpste.* 3rd ed. Leipzig, 1911.

Grignaschi, M. "La diffusion du *Secretum secretorum* (Sirr-al-'Asrar) dans l'Europe occidentale." *Archives d'histoire doctrinale et littéraire du Moyen Age* 47 (1980): 7–70.

Grmek, M. D. *On Aging and Old Age: Basic Problems and Historic Aspects of Gerontology and Geriatrics.* The Hague, 1958.

Gruman, G. J. "A History of Ideas about the Prolongation of Life. The Evolution of Prolongevity Hypotheses to 1800." *Transactions of the American Philosophical Society.* n.s. 56, pt. 9 (1966).

Guidi, P. "La coronazione d'Innocenzo VI." In *Papsttum und Kaisertum. Forschungen . . . Paul Kehr . . . dargebracht,* 571–590. Munich, 1926.

Gutmann, F. *Die Wahlanzeigen der Päpste bis zum Ende der avignonesischen Zeit.* Marburg, 1931.

Haller, J. "Zwei Aufzeichnungen über die Beamten der Curie." *Quellen und Forschungen aus italienischen Bibliotheken und Archiven* 1 (1898): 1–31.

Haskins C. H. "Latin Literature under Frederick II." *Speculum* 3 (1928): 129–151.

―――. *Studies in the History of Mediaeval Science.* Cambridge, 1924.

Haupt, G. *Die Farbensymbolik in der sakralen Kunst des abendländischen Mittelalters.* Diss., Leipzig 1941.

Herde, P. *Célestin V. 1294 (Peter vom Morrone). Der Engelpapst.* Stuttgart, 1981.

―――. "Election and Abdication of the Pope: Practice and Doctrine in the Thirteenth Century." In *Proceedings of the Sixth International Congress of Medieval Canon Law,* 411–436. Vatican City, 1985.

Herklotz, I. "Der Campus Lateranensis im Mittelalter." *Römisches Jahrbuch für Kunstgeschichte* 22 (1985): 1–43.

―――. "Der mittelalterliche Fassadenportikus der Lateranbasilika und seine Mosaiken. Kunst und Propaganda am Ende des 12 Jahrhunderts." *Römisches Jahrbuch für Kunstgeschichte* 25 (1989): 27–95.

―――. "Die Beratungsräume Calixtus' II im Lateranpalast und ihre Fresken, Kunst und Propaganda am Ende des Investiturstreits." *Zeitschrift für Kunstgeschichte* 52 (1989): 145–214.

―――. "Grabmalstiftungen und städtische öffentlichkeit im spätmittelalterlichen Italien." In *Materielle Kultur und religiöse Stiftung im Spätmittelalter,* 233–271. Vienna, 1990.

―――. "Paris de Grassi *Tractatus de funeribus et exequiis* und die Bestattungsfeiern von Päpsten und Kardinälen in Spätmittelalter und Renaissance." In *Skulptur und Grabmal,* 217–248.

―――. *"Sepulcra" e "monumenta" del Medioevo.* Rome, 1985.

Hermann, A. "Farbe." In *Reallexikon für Antike und Christentum,* vol. 7, 358–447. Stuttgart, 1969.

Heusch, L. de. *Ecrits sur la royauté sacrée.* Brussels, 1987.

―――. "The Sacrificial Body of the King." In *Fragments for a History of the Human Body,* vol. 3, 387–394. New York, 1989.

Hugenholtz, F. W. N. "The Anagni Frescoes—A Manifesto." *Mededelingen van het Nederlands Instituut te Rome* 6 (1979): 139–172.

Iazeolla, T. "Il monumento funebre di Adriano V in S. Francesco alla Rocca a Viterbo." In *Skulptur und Grabmal,* 143–152.

Imkamp, W. *Das Kirchenbild Innocenz' III. (1198–1216).* Stuttgart, 1983.

Jackson, R. A. *Vive le roi! A History of the French Coronation from Charles V to Charles X.* Chapel Hill and London, 1984.

Jacquart, D. "De *krasis* à *complexio*. Note sur le vocabulaire du tempérament en Latin médiéval." In *Mémoires*, vol. 5, *Textes Médicaux Latins Antiques*. Centre Jean Palerne, St. Etienne, 1984.

———. "La réception du 'Canon' d'Avicenne. Comparaison entre Montpellier et Paris au XIIIe et XIVe siècles." In *Actes du 110e Congrès national des sociétés savantes*, 69–77. Paris, 1985.

Jacqueline, B. *Episcopat et papauté chez saint Bernard de Clairvaux*. Sainte-Marguerite-d'Elle, 1975.

Jasper, D. *Das Papstwahldekret von 1059. Ueberlieferung und Textgestalt*. Sigmaringen, 1986.

Jeiler, J. "Ein unedierter Brief des P. Olivi (d. 1297)." *Historisches Jahrbuch* 3 (1882): 648–659.

Jones, W. *Crowns and Coronations. A History of Regalia*. London, 1883.

Jung, N. *Alvaro Pelayo*. Paris, 1931.

Kamp, N. *Kirche und Monarchie im Staufischen Königreich Sizilien*. Vol. 1. *Prosopographische Grundlegung: Bistümer und Bischöfe des Königreichs 1194–1266*. 3 vols. Munich, 1972–1975.

Kantorowicz, E. *Kaiser Friedrich II*. Berlin, 1927; *Ergänzungsband*. Berlin, 1931.

———. *Laudes Regiae: A study in Liturgical Acclamations and Mediaeval Ruler Worship*. Berkeley, 1946.

———. *The King's Two Bodies*. Princeton, 1957 (Fr. trans. *Les deux corps du roi*, Paris, 1989).

Keller, H. "Büste." In *Reallexikon der Deutschn Kunstgeschichte*, vol. 3, 257–274. Stuttgart, 1954.

———. "Der Bildhauer Arnolfo di Cambio und seine Werkstatt." *Jahrbuch der preussischen Kunstsammlungen* 55 (1934): 205–228; II, 56 (1935): 22–43.

Klauser, Th. "Die Anfänge der römischen Bischofsliste." *Bonner Zeitschrift für Theologie und Seelsorge* 8 (1931): 210–211.

Klewitz, H.-W. "Das Ende des Reformpapsttums." *Deutsches Archiv für Erforschung des Mittelalters* (1939): 371–412.

———. "Die Krönung des Papstes." *Zeitschrift der Savigny-Stiftung für Rechtsgeschichte. Kanonistische Abteilung* 3 (1941): 96–130.

———. *Reformpapsttum und Kardinalkolleg*. Darmstadt, 1957.

Kösters, J. *Studien zu Mabillons Römischen Ordines*. Diss., Freiburg/Br. Munich, 1905, Beilage 3.

Krautheimer, R. *Rome. Profile of a City, 312–1308*. Princeton, 1980.

Kroos, R., and F. Kobler. "Farbe, liturgisch (kath.)." In *Reallexikon der deutschen Kunstgeschichte*, vol. 7, 54–122. Munich, 1981.

Kurdzialek, M. "Anatomische und embryologische Äusserungen Davids von Dinant." *Sudhoffs Archiv* 45 (1961): 1–22.

———. "David von Dinant als Ausleger der aristotelischen Naturphilosophie." *Miscellanea Mediaevalia* 10 (1976): 181–192.

——. "L'idée de l'homme chez David de Dinant." *Symbolae*, ser. A, 1 (1976): 311–322.

Kuttner, S. "Die Konstitutionen des ersten allgemeinen Konzils von Lyon." *Studia et documenta historiae et iuris* 6 (1940): 70–123.

——. *Mediaeval Councils, Decretals and Collections of Canon Law.* London, 1980.

Ladner, G. B. "Der Ursprung und die mittelalterliche Entwicklung der päpstlichen Tiara." In *Tainia. Roland Hampe . . . dargebracht*, 449–481. Mainz-am-Rhein, 1978.

——. "Die Anfänge des Kryptoporträts." in *Von Angesicht zu Angesicht. Porträtstudien. Festschrift für Michael Stettler*, 78–97. Bern, 1983.

——. *Die Papstbildnisse des Altertums und des Mittelalters.* 3 vols. Vatican City, 1941–1984.

——. "Die Statue Bonifaz' VIII. in der Lateranbasilika und die Entstehung der dreifach gekrönten Tiara." *Römische Quartalschrift* 42 (1934): 35–69.

——. *Images and Ideas in the Middle Ages. Selected Studies in History and Art.* 2 vols. Rome, 1983.

Lauer, P. *Le palais du Latran.* Paris, 1911.

Laurent, J. "La perception de l'espace de la chrétienté par la curie romaine et l'organisation d'un concile oecuménique en 1274." In *Histoire comparée de l'administration (IVe–XVIIIe siècles)*, 11–16. Munich, 1980.

Laurent, M.-H. *Le bienheureux Innocent V (Pierre de Tarentaise) et son temps.* Vatican City, 1947.

Le Goff, J. "A Coronation Program for the Age of Saint Louis: The Ordo of 1250." In *Coronations. Medieval and Early Modern Monarchic Ritual*, 46–71. Berkeley, 1990.

——. "La perception de l'espace de la chrétienté par la curie Romaine et l'organisation d'un concile oecuménique en 1274." In *Histoire comparée de l'administration (IVe–XVIIIe siècles)*, 11–16. Munich, 1980.

——. "Saint Louis et les corps royaux." *Le temps de la réflexion* 3 (1982): 255–284.

Leclerc, J. " 'Pars corporis papae.' Le sacré collège dans l'ecclésiologie médiévale." In *L'homme devant Dieu. Mélanges offerts au Père Henri de Lubac*, vol. 2, 183–198. Paris, 1964.

Leclercq, J. *Recueil d'études sur Saint Bernard.* 3 vols. Rome, 1962–1969.

Lindberg, C. "Lines of Influence in Thirteenth-Century Optics: Bacon, Witelo and Pecham." *Speculum* 46 (1971): 66–83.

Lindner, D. "Die sogenannte Erbheiligkeit des Papstes in der Kanonistik des Mittelalters." *Zeitschrift der Savigny-Stiftung für Rechtsgeschichte*, Kanonistische Abteilung 53 (1967): 15–26.

Löwe, H. "Kaisertum und Abendland in ottonischer und frühsalischer Zeit." *Historische Zeitschrift* 196 (1963): 529–562.

Louis, P. "La génération spontanée chez Aristote." In *Actes du XIIe Congrès International d'histoire des sciences*, vol. 1, 291–305. Paris, 1970.

Lucchesi, G. *Per una Vita di S. Pier Damiani. Componenti cronologiche e topografiche.* 2 vols. Cesena, 1972.

Lulvès, J. "Die Machtbestrebungen des Kardinalats bis zur Aufstellung der ersten päpstlichen Wahlkapitulationen." *Quellen und Forschungen aus italienischen Archiven und Bibliotheken* 13 (1910): 73–102.

Maccarrone, M. "Die Cathedra Sancti Petri im Hochmittelalter." *Römische Quartalschrift* 75 (1980): 196–197 (repr. "La 'cathedra sancti Petri' nel Medio Evo: da simbolo a reliquia," in idem, *Romana Ecclesia Cathedra Petri*, vol. 2, 1249–1373. Rome, 1991).

————. "Il sepolcro di Bonifacio VIII nella Basilica Vaticana." In *Roma anno 1300*, 753–771.

————. "L'indulgenza del Giubileo del 1300 e la basilica di San Pietro." In *Roma anno 1300*, 731–752.

————. "La 'cathedra sancti Petri' nel Medio Evo: da simbolo a reliquia." In idem, *Romana Ecclesia Cathedra Petri*, vol. 2, 1249–1373.

————. *Romana Ecclesia Cathedra Petri.* 2 vols. Rome, 1991.

————. *Studi su Innocenzo III.* Padua, 1972.

————. " 'Ubi est papa, ibi est Roma.' " In *Aus Kirche und Reich. Studien zu Theologie, Politik und Recht im Mittelalter. Festschrift für Friedrich Kempf*, 371–382. Sigmaringen, 1983.

————. *Vicarius Christi. Storia del titolo papale.* Rome, 1952.

Maddalo, S. "Alcune considerazioni sulla topografia del complesso lateranense allo scadere del secolo XIII: il patriarchio nell'anno del Giubileo." In *Roma anno 1300*, 621–628.

————. "Bonifacio VIII e Jacopo Stefaneschi. Ipotesi di lettura dell'affresco della loggia lateranense." *Studi Romani* 31 (1983): 129–150.

Magri, D. *Hierolexicon.* Rome, 1677.

Maleczek, W. "Abstimmungsarten. Wie kommt man zu einem vernünftigen Wahlergebnis?" In *Wahlen und Wählen im Mittelalter*, 103 et seq. Sigmaringen, 1990.

————. "Das Kardinalskollegium unter Innocenz II. und Anaklet II." *Archivum Historiae Pontificiae* 19 (1981): 27–78.

————. *Papst und Kardinalskolleg von 1191 bis 1216.* Vienna, 1984.

Mann, H. K. *The Lives of the Popes in the Middle Ages.* vols. 15–17. London, 1929–1931.

Marini, G. *Degli archiatri pontificij.* 2 vols. Rome 1784.

McCready, W. D. "The Papal Sovereign in the Ecclesiology of Augustinus Triumphus." *Mediaeval Studies* 39 (1977): 177–205.

McGinn, B. "Angel Pope and Papal Antichrist." *Church History* 47 (1978): 155–173.

McVaugh, M. "The *Humidum Radicale* in Thirteenth-Century Medicine." *Traditio* 30 (1974): 259–283.

Melloni, A. *Innocenzo IV. La concezione e l'esperienza della cristianità come "regimen unius personae."* Genoa, 1990.

Meyer A. "Das päpstliche Spolienrecht im Spätmittelalter und die *licentie testandi.*" *Zeitschrift der Savigny-Stiftung für Rechtsgeschichte.* Kanonistische Abteilung 108 (1991): 399–405.

Miczka, G. *Das Bild der Kirche bei Johannes von Salisbury.* Bonn: 1970.

Miglio, M. " '*Vidi thiaram Pauli papae secundi.*'" *Bullettino dell'Istituto Storico Italiano per il Medio Evo e Archivio Muratoriano* 81 (1969): 273–296.

Mollat G. "*Miscellanea Avignonensia.* I. Notes sur trois fonctionnaires de la cour pontificale au début du XIVe siècle." *Mélanges d'archéologie et d'histoire* 44 (1927): 1–5.

Monferini, A. "Pietro di Oderisio e il rinnovamento tomistico." In *Monumenti del marmo. Scritti per i duecento anni dell'Accademia di Carrara,* 39–63. Rome, 1969.

Montini, U. R. *Le tombe dei papi.* Rome, 1957.

Moore, J. C. "Innocent's *De Miseria humane conditionis:* A '*Speculum Curiae*'?" *Catholic Historical Review* 67 (1981): 553–564.

Moroni, G. *Dizionario di erudizione storico-ecclesiastica.* 103 vols. Venice, 1849–1861.

Nardella, C. *Il fascino di Roma. Le "Meraviglie di Roma" di maestro Gregorio,* ser. La corte dei papi, 1. Rome, 1997.

Needham, J. "The Elixir Concept and Chemical Medicine in East and West." *Organon* 11 (1975): 167–192.

———. *Science and Civilization in China.* vol. 2. Cambridge, 1974; vol. 4, Cambridge, 1980.

Negelein, J. von. "Die volkstümliche Bedeutung der weissen Farbe." *Zeitschrift für Ethnologie* 33 (1901): 53 et seq.

Nibbyl, P. H. "Old Age, Fever, and the Lamp Metaphor." *Journal of the History of Medicine* 26 (1971): 351–368.

Nussdorfer, L. "The Vacant See: Ritual and Protest in Early Modern Rome." *Sixteenth Century Journal* 18 (1987): 173–189.

O'Malley, J. W. *Praise and Blame in Renaissance Rome. Rhetoric, Doctrine, and Reform in the Sacred Orators of the Papal Court, c. 1450–1521.* Durham, NC, 1979.

O'Neill, Y. "Innocent III and the Evolution of the Anatomy." *Medical History* 20 (1976): 429–431.

Oldoni, M. " '*A fantasia dicitur fantasma*' (Gerberto e la sua storia)." *Studi Medievali.* 3rd ser., 21 (1980): 493–622; 24 (1983): 167–245.

Oldoni, M. "Gerberto e la sua storia. *Studi Medievali,* 3rd ser., 18 (1977): 629–704.

Pacaut, M. *Alexandre III.* Paris, 1956.

Palumbo, P. F. *Lo scisma del MCXXX.* Rome, 1942.

Paravicini Bagliani, A. *Cardinali di Curia e "familiae" cardinalizie dal 1227 al 1254.* 2 vols. Padua, 1972.

———. "Die Polemik der Bettelorden um den Tod des Kardinals Peter von Collemezzo (1253)." In *Aus Kirche und Reich. Studien zu Theologie, Politik und Recht im Mittelalter: Festschrift für Friedrich Kempf,* 355–362. Sigmaringen, 1983.

———. *I testamenti dei cardinali del Duecento.* Rome, 1980.

———. *Il trono di Pietro: L'universalità del papato tra Alessandro III e Bonifacio VIII.* Rome, 1996.

———. *La cour des papes au XIIIe siècle.* Paris, 1995.

———. "La mobilità della Curia romana nel secolo XIII: Riflessi locali." In *Società e istituzioni dell'Italia comunale: l'esempio di Perugia (secoli XII–XIV),* 155–278. Perugia, 1988.

———. "La storiografia pontificia del secolo XIII: Prospettive di ricerca." *Römische historische Mitteilungen* 18 (1976): 52–53.

———. *La vita quotidiana alla corte dei papi nel Duecento.* Rome, 1996.

———. *Medicina e scienze della natura alla corte dei papi nel Duecento.* Spoleto, 1991.

———. "Un frammento del testamento del cardinale Stephanus Hungarus (d. 1270) nel codice C 95 dell'Archivio del Capitolo di San Pietro." *Rivista di storia della Chiesa in Italia* 25 (1971): 167–182.

Pastor, L. *Storia dei papi.* 16 vols. Rome, 1931–1934.

Pastoureau, M. "L'Eglise et la couleur, des origines à la Réforme." In *Actualité de l'histoire à l'Ecole des Chartes,* 202–230. Paris, 1989.

Pereira, M. *L'oro dei filosofi. Saggio sulle idee di un alchimista del Trecento.* Spoleto, 1992.

———. "Un tesoro inestimabile: elixir e 'prolongatio vitae' nell'alchimia del '300." *Micrologus. Natura, scienze e società medievali* 1 (1993): 161–187.

Petrini, P. *Memorie Prenestine disposte in forma di annali.* Rome, 1795.

Petrocchi, M. "L'ultimo destino perugino di Innocenzo III." *Bollettino della Deputazione di Storia Patria per l'Umbria* 64 (1967): 202–207.

Petrucci, E. "Il problema della vacanza papale e la costituzione *'Ubi periculum'* di Gregorio X." In *Atti del Convegno di studio per l'VIII Centenario del 1o Conclave (1268–1271),* 69–96. Viterbo, 1975.

Picard, J.-C. "Etude sur l'emplacement des tombes des papes du IIIe au Xe siècle." *Mélanges d'archéologie et d'histoire* 81 (1969): 725–782.

Pits, J. *Relationum historicarum de rebus Anglicis liber primus.* Paris, 1619.

Pogatscher, H. "Von Schlangenhörnern und Schlangenzungen vornehmlich im 14. Jahrhunderte (Mit Urkunden und Akten aus dem Vaticanischen Archive)." *Römische Quartalschrift* 12 (1898): 162–215.

Pouchelle, M.-C. *Corps et chirurgie à l'apogée du Moyen-Age.* Paris, 1983.

Rangoni, T. *De vita hominis ultra CXX annos protrahenda.* Venice, 1550, 1553, 1560.

Rentschler, M. "Griechische Kultur und Byzanz im Urteil westlicher Autoren des 11. Jahrhunderts." *Saeculum* 31 (1980): 112–156.

Riché, P. *Gerbert d'Aurillac, le pape de l'an mil.* Paris, 1987.

Rigon, A. "Orientamenti religiosi e pratica testamentaria a Padova nei secoli XII–XIV (prime ricerche)." In *Nolens intestatus decedere. Il testamento come fonte della storia religiosa e sociale,* 41–63. Perugia, 1985.

Rocca, A. *De sacrosancto Christi corpore Romanis pontificibus iter conficientibus praeferendo commentarius.* In idem, *Thesaurus pontificiarum sacrarumque antiquitatum,* vol. 1, 37–73. Rome, 1745.

———. *Enarratio de universo ritu summi pontificis Sacrosanctam Eucharistiam in Missa solemniter sumentis.* Ed. Rocaberti. *Bibliotheca* IV, 1–19.

———. *Thesaurus pontificiarum sacrarumque antiquitatum.* 2 vols. Rome, 1745.

Roma anno 1300. Rome, 1983.

Roma nel Duecento. L'arte nella città dei papi da Innocenzo III a Bonifacio VIII. Turin, 1991.

Romanini, A. M. "Gli occhi di Isacco. Classicismo e curiosità scientifica tra Arnolfo di Cambio e Giotto." *Arte medievale.* 2nd ser., 2 (1988): 1–56.

———. "Ipotesi ricostruttive per i monumenti sepolcrali di Arnolfo di Cambio." In *Skulptur und Grabmal,* 107–128.

———. "Nuovi dati sulla statua bronzea di San Pietro in Vaticano.'" *Arte medievale.* 2nd ser., 4, no. 2 (1990): 1–49.

Rudloff, E. von. *Über das Konservieren von Leichen im Mittelalter. Ein Beitrag zur Geschichte der Anatomie und des Bestattungswesens.* Freiburg im Breisgau, 1921.

Rusch, B. *Die Behörden und Hofbeamten der päpstlichen Kurie des 13. Jahrhunderts.* Königsberg, 1936.

Ryan J. J. *Saint Peter Damiani and His Canonical Sources.* Toronto, 1956.

Sägmüller, J.-B. *Die Thätigkeit und Stellung der Cardinäle bis Papst Bonifaz VIII. historisch-canonistisch untersucht und dargestellt.* Freiburg im Breisgau, 1896.

Salmon, P. *Mitra und Stab. Die Pontifikalinsignien im römischen Ritus.* Mainz, 1960.

Salomon, R. *Opicinus de Canistris. Weltbild und Bekenntnisse eines Avignonesisschen Klerikers des 14. Jahrhunderts.* 2 vols. London, 1936.

Santi, F. "Il cadavere e Bonifacio VIII, tra Stefano Tempier e Avicenna. Intorno ad un saggio di Elizabeth Brown." *Studi Medievali,* 3rd ser., 28 (1987): 861–878.

Sarnelli, P. *Lettere Ecclesiastiche.* Venice, 1716.

Schimmelpfennig, B. "Die Bedeutung Roms im päpstlichen Zeremoniell." In *Rom im hohen Mittelalter. Studien zu den Romvorstellungen und zur Rompolitik vom 10. bis zum 12. Jahrhundert,* 47–61. Sigmaringen, 1992.

————. "Die Krönung des Papstes im Mittelalter dargestellt am Beispiel der Krönung Pius' II. (3. 9. 1458)." *Quellen und Forschungen aus italienischen Archiven und Bibliotheken* 54 (1974): 192–270.

————. *Die Zeremonienbücher der römischen Kurie im Mittelalter.* Tübingen, 1973.

————. "Ein bisher unbekannter Text zur Wahl, Konsekration und Krönung des Papstes im 12. Jahrhundert." *Archivum Historiae Pontificiae* 6 (1968): 43–70.

————. "Ein Fragment zur Wahl, Konsekration und Krönung des Papstes im 12. Jahrhundert." *Archivum Historiae Pontificiae* 8 (1970): 323–331.

————. "Papal Coronations in Avignon." In *Coronations: Medieval and Early Modern Monarchic Ritual,* 179–196. Berkeley, 1990.

————. "Papst- und Bischofswahlen seit dem 12. Jahrhundert." In *Wahlen und Wählen im Mittelalter,* 173–196. Sigmaringen, 1990.

Schipperges, H. *Die Assimilation der arabischen Medizin durch das lateinische Mittellalter.* Wiesbaden, 1964.

————. "Makrobiotik bei Petrus Hispanus." *Sudhoffs Archiv* 44 (1960): 129–155.

Schmale, F.-J. *Quellen zur Geschichte Kaiser Heinrichs IV.* Darmstadt, 1968.

————. *Studien zum Schisma des Jahres 1130.* Köln, 1961.

Schmarsow, A. *Raphael und Pinturicchio in Siena.* Stuttgart, 1880.

Schmidinger, H. "Das Papstbild in der Geschichtsschreibung des späteren Mittelalters." *Römische Historische Mitteilungen* 1 (1956–1957): 106–129.

Schmidt, C. *Studien zu den Pseudo-Clementinen.* Leipzig, 1929.

Schmidt, G. "Typen und Bildmotive des spätmittelalterlichen Monumentalgrabes." In *Skulptur und Grabmal,* 13–82.

Schmidt, T. *Alexander II. (1061–1073) und die römische Reformgruppe seiner Zeit.* Stuttgart, 1977.

————. "Papst Bonifaz VIII. und die Idolatrie." *Quellen und Forschungen aus italienischen Archiven und Bibliotheken* 66 (1986): 75–107.

Schmitt, C. B., and D. Knox. *Pseudo-Aristoteles Latinus. A Guide to Latin Works Falsefy Attributed to Aristotle Before 1500.* London, 1985.

Scholz, R. *Die Publizistik zur Zeit Philipps des Schönen und Bonifaz VIII.* Stuttgart, 1903.

Schramm, P. E. "Die Krönung in Deutschland bis zum Beginn des Salischen Hauses (1028)." *Zeitschrift der Savigny-Stiftung für Rechtsgeschichte.* Kanonistische Abteilung 55 (1935): 184–332.

———. *Herrschaftszeichen und Staatssymbolik.* 3 vols. Stuttgart, 1954–1956.

———. *Kaiser, Könige und Päpste.* 5 vols. Stuttgart, 1968–1971.

———. *Kaiser, Rom und Renovatio.* Leipzig and Berlin, 1929; 3rd ed. Darmstadt, 1962.

———. *Sphaira, Globus, Reichsapfel.* Stuttgart, 1958.

The "Secret of Secrets." Sources and Influences. London, 1982.

Servatius, C. *Paschalis II.* Stuttgart, 1979.

Sheehan, M. N. *The Will in Mediaeval England.* Toronto, 1963.

Signorelli, G. *Viterbo nella storia della Chiesa.* 2 vols. Viterbo, 1940.

Simi Varanelli, E. "Dal Maestro d'Isacco a Giotto. Contributo alla storia della 'perspectiva communis' medievale." *Arte medievale,* 2nd ser., 3 (1989): 115–142.

Siraisi, N. G. *Avicenna in Renaissance Italy. The 'Canon' and Medical Teaching in Italian Universities after 1500.* Princeton, 1987.

Skulptur und Grabmal des Spätmittelalters in Rom und Italien. Vienna, 1990.

Sommer, C. *Die Anklage der Idolatrie gegen Papst Bonifaz VIII. und seine Porträtstatuen.* Diss. phil., Freiburg im Breisgau, 1920.

Sot, M. "Mépris du monde et résistance des corps aux XIe et XIIe siècle." *Médiévales* 8 (1985): 6–17.

Southern, R. W. *Robert Grosseteste. The Growth of an English Mind in Medieval Europe.* Oxford, 1986.

Spinelli, L. *La vacanza della Sede apostolica dalle origini al concilio Tridentino.* Milan, 1955.

Steinmann, E. "Die Zerstörung der Grabdenkmäler der Päpste von Avignon." *Monatshefte für Kunstwissenschaft* 11 (1918): 145–171.

Stickler, A. M. " 'Imperator vicarius papae.' Die Lehren der französisch-deutschen Dekretistenschule des 12. und beginnenden 13. Jahrhunderts über die Beziehungen zwischen Papst und Kaiser." *Mitteilungen des Instituts für Oesterreichische Geschichtsforschung* 62 (1954): 165–212.

Strnad, A. A. "Giacomo Grimaldis Bericht über die Öffnung des Grabes Papst Bonifaz' VIII. (1605)." *Römische Quartalschrift* 61 (1966): 145–202.

Stroll, M. *Symbols as Power. The Papacy following the Investiture Contest.* Leiden, 1991.

———. *The Jewish Pope. Ideology and Politics in the Papal Schism of 1130.* Leiden, 1987.

Struve, T. *Die Entwicklung der organologischen Staatsauffassung des Mitte-lalters.* Stuttgart, 1978, 34–35.

Tangl, M. "Die *Vita Bennonis* und das Regalien- und Spolienrecht." *Neues Archiv der Gesellschaft für ältere Geschichtskunde* 33 (1907–1908): 77–94.

Tea, E. "Witelo prospettico del XIII secolo." *L'Arte* 30 (1927): 14–27.

Tenenti, A. *Il senso della morte e l'amore della vita nel Rinascimento.* Turin, 1957.

Théry, G. *Autour du décret de 1210: I. David de Dinant. Etude sur son panthéisme matérialiste.* Kain, 1925.

Thorndike, L. *A History of Magic and Experimental Science.* 8 vols. New York, 1923–1958.

———. *Michael Scot.* London, 1965.

Thorndike, L., and P. Kibre. *A Catalogue of Incipits of Mediaeval Scientif Writings in Latin.* London, 1963.

Tierney, B. *Foundations of the Conciliar Theory. The Contribution of the Medieval Canonists from Gratian to the Great Schism.* Cambridge, 1955.

———. *Origins of Papal Infallibility 1150–1350.* Leiden, 1972. 2nd ed. 1988.

Tillmann, H. *Papst Innozenz III.* Bonn, 1954.

Toubert, P. *Les structures du Latium médiéval. Le Latium méridional et la Sabine du IXe siècle à la fin du XIIe siècle.* 2 vols. Rome, 1973.

Träger, J. *Der reitende Papst. Ein Beitrag zur Ikonographie des Papsttums.* Munich and Zurich, 1970.

Treitinger, O. *Die oströmische Kaiser- und Reichsidee nach ihrer Gestaltung im höfischen Zeremoniell.* Jena, 1938; repr. Bad Homburg, 1969.

Turner, V. W. *The Ritual Process. Structure and Antistructure.* London, 1969.

Ullmann, W. *The Growth of Papal Government in the Middle Ages.* 3rd ed. Cambridge, 1970.

Valois, N. *La France et le Grand-Schisme.* 4 vols. Paris, 1896–1902.

Van Dijk, S. J. P. "The Urban and Papal Rites in Seventh and Eighth-Century Rome." *Sacris Erudiri* 12 (1961): 411–487.

Van Dijk, S. J. P., and J. H. Walker. *The Origins of the Modern Roman Liturgy.* London, 1959.

Vanel, C. *Histoire des conclaves depuis Clement V jusqu'à present.* Paris, 1689.

Vauchez, A. *La sainteté en Occident aux derniers siècles du Moyen Age.* Rome, 1981.

Versnel, H. S. "Destruction, 'Devotio' and Despair in a Situation of Anomy: the Mourning for Germanicus in Triple Perspective." In *Perennitas: Studi in onore di Angelo Brelich,* 541–618. Rome, 1980.

Voci, A. M. *Nord o Sud? Note per la storia del medioevale palatium aposto-licum apud Sanctum Petrum e delle sue cappelle.* Vatican City, 1992.

Vogel, P. *Nikolaus von Calvi und seine Lebensbeschreibung des Papstes Innozenz IV.* Munich, 1939.

Vregille, B. de. *Hugues de Salins, archevêque de Besançon, 1031–1066.* 3 vols. Lille-Besançon, 1983.

Wasner, F. "De consecratione, inthronisatione, coronatione summi pontificis." *Apollinaris* 2, no. 8 (1935): 249–281.

———. "Literarische Zeugen für eine Federkrone der Päpste im Mittelalter." *Ephemerides Liturgicae* 60 (1960): 409–427.

Watt, J. A. "The Constitutional Law of the College of Cardinals from Hostiensis to Johannes Andreae." *Mediaeval Studies* 33 (1971): 127–157.

———. "The Term 'Plenitudo Potestatis' by Hostiensis." In *Proceedings of the Second International Congress of Medieval Canon Law,* 161–187. Vatican City, 1965.

Wattenbach, W. *Das Schriftwesen im Mittelalter.* 4th ed. Graz, 1958.

Weiss, R. "Jacopo Angeli de Scarperia (c. 1360–1410–11)." In *Medioevo e Rinascimento. Studi in onore di Bruno Nardi,* 803–827. Florence, 1955.

Welborn, M. C. "The Errors of the Doctors According to Friar Roger Bacon of the Minor Order." *Isis* 18 (1932): 52–53.

Wickersheimer, E. *Dictionnaire biographique des médecins en France au Moyen Age.* 2 vols. Paris, 1936.

Wilks, M. J. " 'Papa est nomen iurisdictionis.' Augustinus Triumphus and the Papal Vicariate of Christ." *Journal of Theological Studies,* n.s., 8 (1957): 71–91.

———. *The Problem of Sovereignty in the Later Middle Ages.* Cambridge, 1963.

Williams, S. J. "The Early Circulation of the Pseudo-Aristotelian 'Secret of Secrets' in the West." *Micrologus. Natura, scienze e società medievali* 2 (1994): 127–144.

Winslow, C.-E. A. *The Conquest of Epidemic Disease. A Chapter in the History of Ideas.* Madison, 1980.

Zarncke, F. *Der Priester Johannes,* vol. 1. In Abhandlungen der phil.-hist. Classe der königlich Sächsischen Gesellschaft der Wissenschaften, vol. 8. Leizpig, 1879.

Zerbi, P. *Papato, impero e 'respublica christiana' dal 1187 al 1198.* Milan, 1980.

Zoepffel, R. *Die Papstwahlen und die mit ihnen im nächsten Zusammenhange stehenden Ceremonien in ihrer Entwicklung vom 11. bis zum 14. Jahrhundert.* Göttingen, 1871.

INDEX